D1000354

9-42

# THE CLUB AND CORAL MUSHROOMS (CLAVARIAS) OF THE UNITED STATES AND CANADA

BY

WILLIAM CHAMBERS COKER, 1872-1953

KENAN PROFESSOR OF BOTANY, UNIVERSITY OF NORTH CAROLINA

WITH NINETY-TWO PLATES

DOVER PUBLICATIONS INC., NEW YORK

Published in Canada by General Publishing Company, Ltd., 30 Lesmill Road, Don Mills, Toronto, Ontario.

Published in the United Kingdom by Constable and Company, Ltd., 10 Orange Street, London WC 2.

This Dover edition, first published in 1974, is an unabridged republication of the work originally published by The University of North Carolina Press in 1923 under the title *The Clavarias of the United States and Canada*.

*International Standard Book Number: 0-486-23101-1*
*Library of Congress Catalog Card Number: 74-82202*

Manufactured in the United States of America
Dover Publications, Inc.
180 Varick Street
New York, N.Y. 10014

# INTRODUCTION

In preparing this study of American Clavarias my work has been greatly facilitated by generous coöperation from many sources. In American herbaria, Dr. W. A. Murrill at the N. Y. Botanical Garden, Dr. H. D. House at the N. Y. State Museum, Drs. Farlow and Thaxter at the Agassiz Museum, and Mrs. Flora W. Patterson at the U. S. Dept of Agriculture have allowed the free use of their material and supplemented my collections by many gifts. In Europe I have been particularly befriended by Dr. Lars Romell of Stockholm, who has recently acquired the very valuable herbarium of the Abbé Bresadola and has not only allowed me its free use but has also furnished much Swedish material. Dr. H. O. Juel of Upsala has done the unusual favor of sending me for study all the Clavarias at present contained in the herbarium of Elias Fries. At Leyden Miss Catherine Cool, Curator in the Ryks Museum, placed the Persoon Herbarium at my disposal and assisted me to a better understanding of Oudemans's species. In London Miss Wakefield at Kew Herbarium has shown unfailing kindness for a number of years and has given me valuable material of European and American origin.

My collections have been accumulated through a number of years with the help of many correspondents. Mr. S. H. Burnham has sent much material from New York, both fresh and dried. Miss Ann Hibbard from Vermont and Mr. H. C. Beardslee from Asheville have furnished valuable collections and notes. Outside of this state I have collected living material from Hudson Falls (Vaughns), Lake George, and Bronx Park, N. Y.; Redding, Conn.; and Hartsville, S. C. Most of our North Carolina material has come, of course, from Chapel Hill, a region very rich in fungi of all kinds, and other members of the Botanical Department staff have been of great assistance in collecting. During the past August (1922) the author with Mr. H. R. Totten, Miss Alma Holland, and Mr. J. N. Couch spent two weeks in Blowing Rock and the neighboring mountains getting together a valuable lot of fungi, many of them Clavarias. These are the ones referred to as collected by "Coker and party." About one-fourth of the material (with notes) prepared on this trip was unfortunately lost on the return, being mistaken for something valuable by a misguided thief.

In preparing the plates of microscopic detail I have been assisted by Miss Holland and Mr. Couch. Miss Holland has made many of the drawings and done all of the ink work. Mr. Couch has made sections and done much of the drawing. The photographs have, with a few exceptions, been made by me, and a good many of them have been developed and printed by Mr. Totten. The plates in color have been painted by the following:

Miss Mary E. Eaton—pl. 1, figs. 5 and 6; pl. 9, figs. 2-4; pl. 19, figs. 3 and 4; pl. 23; pl. 28, figs. 1 and 4; pls. 39 and 63.

Miss Dorothy Coker—pl. 19, fig. 2; pl. 28, fig. 5; pl. 50, fig. 3.

Miss Gladys Coker—pl. 9, fig. 1; pl. 50, fig. 1.

Miss H. C. v. d. Pavord Smits—pl. 50, fig. 2.

Miss Cornelia S. Love—pl. 1, figs. 2, 3, 4, and 8; pl. 28, figs. 3 and 6.

Miss Alma Holland—pl. 28, fig. 2.

Miss Ann Hibbard—pl. 1, fig. 7; pl. 19, fig. 1.

Mrs. Edith Branson Smith—pl. 1, fig. 1.

All of the paintings and photographs except that of *C. Murrilli* were made from the living plants.

Recently there has appeared Burt's important paper on the North American Species of *Clavaria* (see p. 14). As the present study was in proof at the time, I have made but sparing reference to his work, and only when there is divergence of opinion. The second volume of Buller's Researches on Fungi has also just reached me. In this several pages are devoted to spore formation and discharge in the Clavarias. The only important observation recorded by him concerns spore discharge in *C. formosa,* which was found to resemble closely that of other Hymenomycetes. He says (p. 185):

"Shortly before a spore was to be discharged, a drop began to be excreted at the spore-hilum. As soon as this drop had grown for about five seconds and had attained a diameter equal to about three-quarters or the whole of the diameter of the spore, the spore was discharged. The spore and drop were shot away from the sterigma together, the spore doubtless with the drop clinging to it as in other Hymenomycetes. The four spores of each basidium were discharged successively in the course of a few minutes."

Buller makes the mistake of saying that the basidia of *Clavariae* have four sterigmata and four spores. There are numerous exceptions to this. He expresses doubt as to the presence of a hymenium on the top of the club in *C. pistillaris*. We have found that the hymenium does in fact completely cover the top (see also Harper, Mycologia **5**: 263. 1913).

I have made few references to Rafinesque's unrecognizable species. The curious may find them in Burt's monograph.

The genus *Clavaria* as at present constituted is so large and polymorphic as to be impossible of definition except in the most general terms and then only vaguely and without sharp distinctions from its relatives. The family *Clavariaceae* as represented with us is usually divided into six genera, *Lachnocladium, Pterula, Clavaria, Pistillaria, Typhula* and *Physalacria*.* Of these, *Pistillaria* and *Typhula* cannot be satisfactorily separated from each other, and can with difficulty be distinguished from certain small Clavarias. In several slender Clavarias the stems are sharply distinct from the clubs, thus leading to *Typhula,* while such species as *C. mucida,* and *C. vernalis* lead directly to *Pistillaria.* The presence of a sclerotium at the base is sufficient to separate some species of *Typhula* and *Pistillaria* from *Clavaria,* but a sclerotium is absent in other species. The genus *Lachnocladium* was established to include those species of tough structure and with tomentose surface, but as now constituted it is in complete confusion with *Clavaria* (see p. 194).

I am not attempting to treat other genera of *Clavariaceae,* but am including the only species of *Lachnocladium* I find in Chapel Hill and also the two largest American species of *Typhula,* one of which is commonly referred to *Clavaria.*

---

*I exclude *Sparassis*, which is now known to belong to the *Thelephoraceae.* See Journ. Elisha Mitchell Sci. Soc. **36**: 193. 1921. *Physalacria* has also been excluded recently (see p. 8). The genus *Acurtis* was established by Fries to contain Schweinitz's *C. gigantea.* I have examined the authentic specimen in the Curtis Herbarium and agree with Burt that it is an aborted agaric.

In addition to the genera above mentioned and those discussed under the genus *Clavaria,* there have been several others proposed. Patouillard in his Essai taxonomique Hymen., p. 44, 1900, has got these together in convenient form and adequately defined them. For convenience I give below his descriptions of the genera now accepted by him, but not treated by me, and not yet fully accepted by mycologists.

*Ceratella* (Quél.) Pat.   Hymen. Eur., p. 157. 1887.   (Used as a sub-genus or group name by Quélet in Enchiridion, p. 222. 1886) :

"Waxy or tough, filiform, simple or branched, sessile or stipitate, ending in a point.   Hymenium surrounding the middle part of the plant, lacking at the base and at the top.   Flesh formed of parallel, not very numerous hyphae, septate, often encrusted with calcium.   Basidia as in *Pistillaria*; cystidia pointed, projecting, delicate, small; spores hyaline, smooth.   Small species, reviving when moistened, growing in colonies on vegetable débris.   Examples are *C. aculeata, C. Queletii, C. Helenae, C. macrospora, C. acuminata."* [All as *Pistillaria* in Sacc. Syll. **6**: 758, and **11**: 142. If this genus is accepted difficulties will arise with other species now included in *Clavaria.*  For example, *C. vernalis* has a conspicuous sterile tip, which is usually covered with crystals in the dry state.   Other well known species of *Clavaria,* as *C. aurantio-cinnabarina, C. filipes,* and sometimes *C. helveola,* have sterile tips which in drying shrink less and take a different color, appearing like little caps set on the ends of the clubs].

*Pistillina* Quél.   Compt. Rend. Assoc. Fr., 1880, p. 671.   1881. (*Sphaerula* Pat.   Tab. Fung., fasc. 1, p. 27. 1883).

"Receptacle quite small, erect or hanging, slightly tough, formed from a cylindrical stem, glabrous or tomentose, enlarged at the top into a convex disk covered by the hymenium and sometimes edged with hairs.   Flesh filamentous as in *Pistillaria.*   Basidia with 2-4 sterigmata.   Spores hyaline, ovoid, smooth."
Here belong *P. hyalina, P. brunneola, P. capitata.* [All as *Pistillaria* in Sacc. Syll. **6**: 759.   This genus seems to me to belong very doubtfully in the *Clavariaceae,* but probably to be related to *Cyphella* in the *Thelephoraceae*].

*Hirsutella* Pat. Revue Mycol. **14**: 69. 1892. (=*Matruchotia* Boulanger, Revue Gén. Bot. **5**: 401. 1893).*

"Receptacle filiform, erect, fleshy, waxy or tough, simple or branched. Flesh filamentous, rather compact, composed of a small number of hyphae, parallel and septate. Hymenium separated into solitary parts, scattered over all the parts of the receptacle; basidia 1-2-4-spored, generally with elongated sterigmata; cystidia none; spores hyaline, ovoid, smooth. Small species, growing on dead organic matter.

"This genus includes five or six European and two American species. *Hirsutella entomophila* Pat. with one-spored basidia rises from a hypochnoid layer which surrounds the bodies of dead Coleopteras at the Equator; *H. setosa* Pk. (*Pterula*), which grows in the United States on old polypores, is a tough species with 2-spored basidia and extremely elongated sterigmata, sometimes septate or branched (abnormally); *H. gracilis* (Desm.) is more delicate and grows on rotten weeds around Paris; *H. varians* (Boul.) has been observed in laboratory cultures.

"*Hirsutella,* very distinct in its discontinuous hymenium, is the lowest form of the *Clavaria* type; it has a marked tendency to take the hypochnoid arrangement and resembles certain hyphomycetes in its forms with irregular sterigmata."

*Baumanniella* P. Hennings. Engler's Bot. Jahrb. **23**: 543. 1897. Exactly like *Physalacria,* except that the spores are brown.

"Only one species is known, *B. Togoensis* P. Henn. from tropical Africa, which has one-spored basidia and rather gelatinous receptacle."

## CLAVARIACEAE

Plants erect, simple and slender or club-shaped, or more or less forked or branched in an antler-like or coral-like or dendroid manner, or (in *Pterula*) composed of very many hair-like branches from a simple base; size varying from simple little slender hairs or rods to large, heavy, much branched masses; texture soft, fleshy and brittle or waxy, or toughish and pliable; hymenium covering most of the plant, usually all except a more or less well defined part of the base or stem, which may fade imperceptibly into the upper part or be more or less sharply delimited by a change in size or color. In some species of *Clavaria* there are sterile lines or areas here and there on the plant, particularly in the forks,

---

* According to Speare the original species of *Hirsutella* is really a Hyphomycete (see Petch in Trans. Brit. Myc. Soc. **9**: 93. 1923).

which are distinctly velvety or plush-like, and such sterile places may occur in both the brittle and pliable species. Spores white or yellowish or brownish, smooth or rough to spiny. Subiculum none, the mycelium penetrating the substratum; obvious rhizomorphs present in some species.

### KEY TO THE GENERA RECOGNIZED

Plants club-shaped or cylindrical or much branched in a coral-like or broom-like manner, branches or clubs not so delicate as to be hairlike on drying; texture fleshy and brittle or pliable, never very tough or leathery; neither hymenium nor growing tips tomentose.............................*Clavaria* (p. 8)

Plants small to large, branched, hymenium tomentose, or, if smooth, the tips of the growing branches strongly tomentose; texture pliable, very tough; spores white or brown, smooth or rough..............*Lachnocladium* (p. 194)

Plants much branched from a delicate base, the branches very slender, hairlike on drying..........................................................*Pterula* (p. 202)

Plants very small, simple, club-shaped and less than 2 cm. high, the short stalk relatively stout; a sclerotium present in some species
*Pistillaria* (not treated)

Plants simple or sparsely branched, small, slender, the clubs cylindrical or narrowly fusiform; the cylindrical stem smaller and (with a few exceptions) sharply distinct; a sclerotium often present
*Typhula* (p. 200)

Plants small, with a slender stalk supporting an irregular, swollen bladder, the under side of which is covered with the hymenium.............*Physalacria**

## Clavaria

Upright, simple, or slightly to repeatedly branched, the hymenium glabrous and extending over all the plant (amphigenous) except the stem when that is discrete, a variable area at the base when the stem is not discrete, and also excepting in many cases certain sterile and often plush-like areas in the angles of the branches which may extend rather extensively in some species

---

*In a recent paper Krieger, for apparently good reasons, removes this genus from the *Clavariaceae* and places it in a primitive position in the *Agaricaceae* (Bull. Maryland Acad. Sci. **3**: 7. 1923). He finds the cap (club) of *P. inflata* to be two-sided (dorsi-ventral) with the upper side sterile and of a different color and texture, and he considers the folds on the lower surface as more or less gill-like. Krieger changes the generic name to *Eoagaricus,* but the rules of nomenclature do not permit such a change. Two North American species of *Physalacria* have been described: *P. inflata* (Schw.) Peck (Bull. T. B. C. **9**: 2, figs. 1-5. 1882), a plant about 1.3-2.7 cm. high; and *P. Langloisii* E. & E. (Journ. Myc. **4**: 73. 1888), a minute plant only a fraction of a millimeter high. We have the former in Chapel Hill (No. 7034).

into lines or areas among the branches. Texture fleshy and brittle or waxy, or often toughish and flexible, but not truly leathery or hard. Spores white or yellowish to brown, smooth or rough to asperulate. Basidia 2-4-spored, clavate. Cystidia absent in nearly all species, but well developed in *C. pyxidata.* Hymenium usually simple, but in a number of species doubled or even quadrupled by the laying down of new layers over the old, as in many polypores. Saprophitic, or in a few species parasitically associated with algae.

The Clavarias vary greatly in form and size from very small simple clubs or rods to large coral-like masses weighing several pounds. Most of the larger and a number of the smaller ones grow on the ground, but many species grow on rotting leaves or on wood. The stem, if present, is not sharply marked off as a rule from the spore-bearing part of the plant, but is usually sterile, as is shown under a lens by the appearance of its surface, which is different from the more waxy hymenium above. In a few species, however, the stem is distinctly indicated by a different color or an abrupt reduction in size or by both.

Most of the species are tender and may be used for food if large enough, but they vary decidedly in palatability, and some are apparently unwholesome. Those that we have found to be very good and that have the best reputation for food are *C. botrytis, C. flava,* and their kin. Only one (*C. dichotoma*) has been reported as causing sickness (Leuba, Champ. Comest., p. 77). It is probably a form of *C. cinerea* (*C. cristata*). It is to be noted, however, that Quélet seems to consider many Clavarias as unwholesome (Aperçu Qualités Utiles ou Nuisibles des Champ., p. 12. 1884. Abstract from Mém. Soc. Sci. phys. et nat. Bordeaux, 3rd ser., **2**). McIlvaine (Am. Fungi, p. 513) has tested many of the Clavarias and does not find any of them dangerous. Of *C. cinerea* he speaks most highly, while some European authors regard it as unwholesome. Among edible mushrooms of New York Peck includes *C. botrytis, C. flava,* and *C. cristata* to represent the genus (Rept. N. Y. St. Mus. **48**: 307. 1895. 2nd ed., p. 209, pl. 39. 1897). He remarks that no poisonous species are known. Later (Mem. N. Y. St. Mus. **3**, No. 4: 178, pl. 66. 1900) he illustrates *C. pistillaris* among edible species and regards it as a luxury, as does also McIlvaine.

The genus comprises such a varied assortment of species as to be easily divided into a number of groups of a validity at least equal to accepted genera of agarics and other families of fungi. To distinguish sharply such groups is, however, no easier than in most cases of such splitting; and we are inclined to choose here a course that we should like to see much more generally followed, which is to let the old genera alone until it becomes a greater inconvenience to retain them than to subdivide them. It is quite right to indicate the natural groups of species under a genus either under the title of groups or sub-genera; but there is no good end accomplished by establishing genera that are harder to define than are the species that compose them.

We have attempted below to arrange the species in natural groups so far as is possible with our present knowledge of their structure.

1. Plants small, isolated (not cespitose); simple or slightly branched; of flexible or brittle texture; spores smooth and white. Growing on the ground or in moss or on rotten wood covered with algae. Related to *Typhula* and *Pistillaria*. Here belong *C. filipes, C. gracillima, C. subfalcata, C. fuscata, C. acuta, C. argillacea, C. mucida, C. luteo-ochracea, C. biformis, C. vernalis, C. Macouni.* This is in part the group *Holocoryne* of Fries, to which some have been added and some withdrawn. In its frequently cespitose habit *C. argillacea* connects this group with the following.

2. Plants typically (?) cespitose or in small clusters (individuals may be isolated), simple, subcylindrical to clavate or fusiform; spores white or (in one species) pale yellow, smooth or (in one species) asperulate. Growing on the ground: *C. helveola, C. rosea, C. fumosa, C. purpurea, C. nigrita, C. vermiculata, C. citriceps, C. appalachiensis, C. fusiformis, C. pulchra, C. aurantiocinnabarina, C. asperulospora, C. inaequalis.* This is in greater part the group *Syncoryne* of Fries.

3. Plants of small to medium size, single or a few in a cluster, simple or branched from a single slender stem or from several slender stems united at the ground; pliable, not brittle; spores of moderate size, spherical to suboval, smooth, white; basidia 4-spored. Growing on the ground: *C. muscoides, C. cineroides.*

4. Plants of small to medium size; single, simple or much branched, not brittle; white, gray, pallid, smoky, dull purplish, etc.

(never yellow on the hymenium); spores white, subspherical, smooth, rather large; basidia 2-spored: *C. cristata* (with *C. rugosa, C. cinerea,* etc.), *C. amethystinoides, C. ornatipes.* This group makes up the genus *Clavulina* of Schroeter (Krypt. Fl. v. Schlesien **3**: 442. 1888) and it is a good genus according to all ordinary standards, and includes the most easily defined group of Clavarias.

5. Plants large or moderately small clubs with soft, spongy, white flesh which is solid, or in age hollow. Spores large, smooth, white: *C. pistillaris, C. ligula.* This group leads to *Craterellus.*

6. Plants long, slender, simple clubs; pliable and with a large hollow surrounded by a thin layer of flesh; spores white, smooth, large. Growing on leaves and twigs or on wood: *C. fistulosa* and *C. contorta.* This group is of peculiar structure and its relationships are not obvious. It is probably nearest the preceding group.

7. Plants small, branched from several crowded stems, not very slender; flesh very fragile and brittle; spores minute, white, smooth. Growing on ground in woods: *C. amethystina.* This group contains a single, isolated species, the relationships of which are quite obscure.

8. Plants small or (in a few species rather large), not cespitose, pliable and toughish, branched from a distinct stalk, slender throughout, spores minute, white, asperulate or angular, or (in two cases) smooth. Growing on the ground, or (in two cases) on wood or trash: *C. rufipes, C. crocea, C. vestitipes, C. pulchella, C. Kunzei, C. arborea, C. asterella, C. subcaespitosa, C. lentofragilis, C. angulispora, C. pyxidata.* This group and the next lead to *Lachnocladium.*

9. Plants rather small to large, much branched, pliable; spores smooth or nearly so. Growing on wood or beds of leaves and twigs. This group may be divided into three sections: (a) Small plants on leaves and with narrow, smooth, nearly white spores: *C. byssiseda, C. Patouillardii*; (b) Small plants on leaves, with small, nearly smooth, yellow to ochraceous spores: *C. gracilis, C. subdecurrens*; (c) Larger plants on wood or leaves, with more plump, faintly rough, buffy to ochraceous spores: *C. stricta, C. apiculata, C. suecica, C. acris, C. pinicola.*

10. Plants small to large; nearly always much branched and usually from a bulky base; brittle or pliable. Spores yellow or ochraceous, usually warted or asperulate but in some cases smooth,

rarely very small. Growing on earth or in humus. This large group contains a varied assortment of species which are so intricately related that it is difficult to arrange them in any well-defined series or in natural clans that would contain more than a few species. The few species with large, smooth spores form an obvious clan. They are further distinguished by the soft, not brittle flesh and pale color. These are *C. Strasseri, C. obtusissima,* and *C. secunda.* Another natural assembly is that composed of *C. botrytis, C. subbotrytis, C. sanguinea, C. flava,* and *C. divaricata.* Their chief characteristics are the crisp, rigid, brittle flesh, densely branched habit, and the pale and only faintly roughened spores.

It is this group 10 that composes in great part the genus *Clavariella* Karsten as amended by Schoeter in Krypt. Fl. v. Schlesien **3** : 447, 1888, and with further amendment by the addition of *C. flava, C. botrytis,* and their kin, which from Fries's day to very recently most authors have erroneously classified as white-spored. Karsten also made the error of including here *C. pistillaris, C. ligula, C. fistulosa* and *C. paradoxa* which are white-spored; but Schroeter corrected this error. Schroeter confines the genus *Clavaria* to all the white-spored species not included in his genus *Clavulina,* which, as above stated, comprised the *cristata* group. In redefining Karsten's genus *Clavariella,* Schroeter made the mistake of saying that the spores were smooth. In fact, in most species of *Clavaria,* the spores, if distinctly colored, are rough.

11. Plants large to small, isolated, or in small clusters, branched, stem not bulky, texture fleshy, but not very brittle; color strong, ochraceous, cinnamon or brown, tending to green or purple in some cases; spores dark, ochraceous or brown, pip-shaped, spiny or warted. Growing on rotting leaves or humus: *C. grandis, C. cyanocephala, C. longicaulis, C. Broomei, C. Murrilli, C. decurrens, C. abietina, C. myceliosa.* This is a well marked group and is represented from the arctic to the tropic regions.

The genus *Ramaria* of Holmskjold (Beata Ruris, p. XVII) included all branched Clavarias and if not too strictly interpreted it did no great violence to natural relationships. It was, however, not recognized by Persoon and has not been accepted since except as a sub-genus or group. Holmskjold confined *Clavaria* to the simple, club-shaped species and did not further subdivide the Clavarias. Persoon, in his Mycologia Europaea (1: 160. 1822), recognized only the genus *Clavaria* and divided the species into four groups: (a) branched or coral-like; (b) clubs elongated, thickened, obsoletely branched; (c) simple, the club not divided; (d) *Typhulae*: firm, furnished with a rather distinct and elongated stem. [This included species now referred to *Typhula* and *Pistillaria*].

In arranging the species of *Clavaria,* Fries introduced the subheadings that have been generally used since. They are (a) *Ramaria,* branched species, which are subdivided into white-spored and ochre-spored, placing *C. flava* and *C. botrytis* in the white-spored group in error; (b) *Syncoryne,* simple, but bases fasciculate, sub-connate, cespitose; (c) *Holocoryne,* simple, clavate, bases discrete.

Aside from extreme differences in size, texture, method of branching and color, the spores of the Clavarias furnish by far the most reliable characters in classification. Fortunately they show a wide range in size, shape, surface and color and they often establish a species with certainty that would otherwise be obscurely defined. The size of the basidia is roughly adjusted to that of the spores and, except for the number and length of the sterigmata, which is often of use, they help but little if the spores are known. In our study of the hymenium we have come across the important fact, heretofore unknown, that in some species there is a renewal of the hymenium by periodic growth so that a younger hymenium is superimposed as a new layer over the old one, resulting in two or more layers of basidia, as in many polypores. This is well shown in *C. grandis* (pl. 90, fig. 1), *C. stricta, C. apiculata, C. abietina* and its relatives, *C. decurrens, C. subdecurrens* (pl. 89, fig. 1), etc. Most species with this habit are otherwise remarkable in having in the multiple hymenium vast numbers of included spores which were retained and overgrown instead of being shed. These spores are often arranged in rows, thus clearly indicating the number of hymenial layers laid down. This is particularly true of the first three species mentioned; in the others the spores are usually more evenly scattered, showing more irregular proliferation. The structure of the flesh is not in any way remarkable among fungi, and while the size and arrangement of the component threads vary decidedly and are often similar in related groups, they are rarely of much use in separating related species. The threads may be slender and densely packed or large and loosely packed, regular or irregular, with or without clamp connections.

## LITERATURE

The literature has been referred to throughout this work under the species, but for convenience we will add here the longer American lists and the more recent monographs.

Burt.　The North American Species of *Clavaria,* with Illustrations of the Type Specimens.　Ann. Mo. Bot. Gard. **9**: 1, pls. 1-11.　1922.

Cotton and Wakefield.　Revision of the British *Clavariae.*　Trans. Brit. Myc. Soc. **6**: 164.　1919.

Kauffman.　Fungi of North Elba.　Bull. N. Y. St. Mus. **179**: 80.　1915.

Massee.　British Fungi, p. 433, pl. 34 and pl. 38, fig. 6.　1911.

Moffat.　The Higher Fungi of the Chicago Region.　Bull. Chicago Acad. Sci. **7**: 141.　1909.

Morgan.　Journ. Cin. Soc. Nat. Hist. **11**: 86.　1888.

Peck.　Rept. N. Y. St. Mus. **24**: 81, 104.　1872.

Rea.　British Basidiomycetes, p. 705.　1922.

Schweinitz.　Synopsis fungorum Carolinae superioris.　Schr. Nat. Ges. Leipzig **1**: 20, pls. 1 and 2.　1822.

Schweinitz.　Synopsis fungorum in America boreali media degentium. Trans. Amer. Phil. Soc. II, **4**: 141.　1832.

### Key to the Species of Clavaria

Plants simple, or at times forked or lobed or slightly branched, single or crowded into groups (cespitose)................................................................ 1

Plants with a slender stem, but usually more or less branched above, the branches comparatively few and not much smaller (at times thicker) than the stem; spores (except in *C. Murrilli,* where they are long and spiny) subspherical, smooth, rather large (individual plants in this section vary to simple or only flattened or antlered above) ........ 7

Plants as above, but usually more branched and spores smaller.............. 9

Plants much branched from several to numerous slender stems that arise together at the base; color pale gray......................*C. cineroides* (p. 78)

Plants as above, but color salmon with yellow tips, in age ochraceous (see also *C. formosa*)................................................*C. conjunctipes* (p. 131)

Plants branched and more bulky, branches usually numerous and the stem
 not slender or very distinct......................................................................11
1. Long, threadlike and pliable; occurring in large colonies among leaves
               *Typhula* (p. 200)
1. Elongated and pliable, but not threadlike and often thickened upward,
 with a large hollow and very thin flesh; spores about 8-18μ long
               *C. fistulosa* (p. 87)
1. Club-shaped, usually much thickened upwards, simple or lobed, color
 usually reddish tan or fleshy brown but varying to chocolate or (in
 youth) rosy; flesh pure white, soft and spongy, thick, often hollowed in age; spores ovate-elliptic or long-elliptic, about 9-18μ long.. 2
1. Texture and habit varied, if hollow then the flesh thick in comparison;
 spores, if elongated, smaller (except in *C. argillacea*)..................... 3
2. Large and thick, growing in deciduous or mixed woods, spores ovate-
 elliptic, about 7-11μ long....................................*C. pistillaris* (p. 83)
2. Smaller, growing in needles or twigs of conifers; spores long-elliptic,
 about 11-19μ long....................................................*C. ligula* (p. 86)
3. Growing on decorticated, rotting logs that are covered with green algae;
 very small........................................................*C. mucida* (p. 30)
3. Growing on rotten logs or pure humus; stem yellow and distinct from
 the club; spores subspherical, about 5 x 6μ
            *C. appalachiensis* (p. 53)
3. Growing as a parasite on live mosses.....................*Eocronartium**
3. Growing on earth or humus or as a saprophyte in moss................ 4
4. Odor of garlic (onion), at least when crushed; spores 4.4-6 x 8-10μ
              *C. fuscata* (p. 23)
4. No odor of garlic............................................................... 5
5. About 2-5.5 cm. high, white or pale yellow, stem distinct from the club;
 spores 4.5-6 x 8-10.5μ..................................*C. subfalcata* (p. 21)
5. Like *C. subfalcata* except for the narrower spores, which are 3.6-4 x
 7.4-10μ......................................................*C. gracillima* (p. 23)
5. Like *C. subfalcata* but smaller and the spores about 4-6μ long on an
 average..........................................................*C. filipes* (p. 20)
5. Resembling *C. filipes,* but 3-7 cm. tall, pure white, and spores 6-9 x 7-10μ
              *C. acuta* (p. 25)
5. Dull white to cream color, thickened and rugose to lobed above; spores
 subspherical, smooth, large.................................*C. rugosa* (p. 68)
5. Deep orange-red, cespitose or single; spores subspherical, about 5 x 6μ
         *C. aurantio-cinnabarina* (p. 60)
5. Rosy or pink, cespitose or single; simple or flattened or toothed above;
 spores rod-elliptic, 3.5 x 6.6-7.5μ.........................*C. rosea* (p. 40)
5. Blackish brown (amber to dusky sepia), single or cespitose; spores
 ovate-elliptic, 2.7-3.2 x 5.5-6.3μ.........................*C. nigrita* (p. 43)

---

* Such plants have been considered as species of *Clavaria* until recently when Atkinson has shown them to belong to the *Auriculariaceae* (Journ. Mycol. **8**: 106. 1902). For
a full study of this species (*Eocronartium muscicola*) see Fitzpatrick. Phytopathology
**8**: 197. 1918, and Amer. Journ. of Bot. **5**: 397. 1918. According to Fitzpatrick there
is only one species, which has appeared under a good many names.

5. Wood-brown, 4-7 cm. high; spores globose, echinulate
C. asperulospora (p. 63)

5. Dingy yellow or pale cinereous; spores minute, 3-3.7 x 4.4-5.2$\mu$
C. Macouni (p. 34)

5. White, or the tips yellowish, very brittle, densely clustered to single; spores pip-shaped to ovoid, variable in size and form, about 2.5-3.5 x 4-6.5$\mu$............................................................C. vermiculata (p. 45)

5. Grayish or smoky flesh color, tips soon blackish; spores not very difrent from the above...............................................C. fumosa (p. 50)

5. Purplish or isabelline; very hollow; spores long, about 2.5-4 x 7-10$\mu$
C. purpurea (p. 51)

5. Plant some shade of yellow or orange or greenish yellow or pale buff
   Spores warted, subglobose..................................C. inaequalis (p. 63)
   Spores smooth ...................................................................... 6

6. Egg yellow, long-clavate or cylindric, not pointed, stuffed or hollow; spores oblong-ovoid with a large eccentric mucro, about 4-6 x 6-7$\mu$
C. pulchra (p. 58)

6. Yellow, hollow (unless flattened), thickest near the middle, pointed, the tips soon darker and shrunken; spores spherical, about 5-7$\mu$ thick
C. fusiformis (p. 54)

6. Buffy yellow, cylindrical, 1.5-5 cm. high, brittle; in small clusters or single; flesh yellowish; spores commonly 2-3 x 6-8$\mu$
C. helveola (p. 37)

6. As above, but stouter, the stem more distinct and the spores larger, about 5-6 x 10-11$\mu$.................................................C. argillacea (p. 28)

6. Pale yellowish, small, 0.6-1.3 cm. high, single, usually forked or antlered above, toughish, the base covered with scurf or hairs; odor fetid; spores minute, oval, 2.2-3.5 x 3.5-4.5$\mu$...... } C. luteo-ochracea (p. 32) / C. biformis (p. 34)

6. Color of plant and size of spores as in C. luteo-ochracea, but not forked above, base not scurfy-hairy and no bad odor........C. citriceps (p. 49)

6. Yellow, very small, simple, gregarious, about 8.5-12.5 mm. high, thickened above; spores rod-elliptic, about 2-3 x 6-11$\mu$
C. vernalis (p. 35)

7. Stem long, dark brown, the lower half or third hispid with stiff, straight, brown hairs................................................C. ornatipes (p. 67)

7. Stem long, pale flesh color, loosely covered with long, flexuose, whitish hairs.......................................................................C. Murrilli (p. 190)

7. Stem not hispid or with long fibers (the stem may be short-tomentose or velvety or scurfy, particularly at the base) ................................ 8

8. Plant a pale, livid flesh color, up to about 4.5 cm. high; thickened upward; taste slight...................................C. amethystinoides (p. 65)

8. Plant dull yellow, clear yellow, or ochraceous yellow; single or clustered, slender throughout; taste rank and bitter
C. muscoides (p. 80)

8. Plant varying from dull pallid or creamy white to grayish flesh color or grayish lavender, the lower part sometimes blackish (from a para-

site), or yellowish; thickened or expanded upward with or without branches, the tips simple or crested.  These are simple forms of
*C. cristata* (p. 68)

8.  Plants 1-2 cm. high, with a distinct brownish stem and pale club which is once or twice forked or antlered................................*C. rufipes* (p. 106)

9.  Growing on wood, the branches terminating in expanded cups, from the margins of which other branches spring; color yellow to tan or brownish; taste usually acrid; spores smooth, 2.2 x 4μ
*C. pyxidata* (p. 92)

9.  Not growing on wood and the branches not expanded into cups..........10

10. Pure white, or at times pale pinkish upward, pliable; odor of old ham; spores nodulated, 5-7.5μ long...............................*C. angulispora* (p. 103)

10. Pure white, pliable, small, odorless;  spores very small, minutely asperulate, 2.5-3.5 x 3.5-4.5μ...............................*C. Kunzei* (p. 95)

10. White or nearly so, larger and more fragile than *C. Kunzei* and spores 3.4-4 x 4-5.2μ and more distinctly asperulate
*C. subcaespitosa* (p. 101)

10. Form and spores of *C. Kunzei,* but color white to alutaceous, and terminal branches rose pink, at least when young
*C. arborea* (p. 105)

10. Pure white or pale brown or cream, except for rufescent stem or stem base; small; spores smooth, about 2.8-3 x 4-5.5μ......*C. rufipes* (p. 106)

10. White, the stalk gray; spores oval to subglobose, asperulate, 4-6μ thick...............................*C. lentofragilis* (p. 102)

10. Ochraceous, flexible; spores oboval, 2.5-3 x 4-5μ, asperulate
*C. asterella* (p. 105)

10. A beautiful clear violet color when fresh; spores ovate-elliptic, smooth, 3.3-4 x 3.7-6.6μ...............................*C. amethystina* (p. 90)

10. Rich chrome orange or golden yellow throughout, very small and delicate; spores subspherical, obscurely asperulate, 2.5-2.7 x 3-3.3μ
*C. crocea* (p. 107)

10. Like *C. crocea,* in form and spores, but stem white and branches lavender...............................*C. pulchella* (p. 109)

10. Like *C. crocea* in color, but up to 2.5 cm. high, and stem scurfy and paler; spores minutely asperulate, 3-3.7 x 3.5-4.5μ
*C. vestitipes* (p. 110)

11. Growing on wood (trunks, stumps or fallen branches and twigs) or on bark at base of trees................................................................ 12

11. Growing on decaying needles of coniferous trees (or rarely on very rotten coniferous wood); size small to medium......................14

11. Growing on the ground and in rotting leaves or humus in deciduous or mixed woods......................................................18

12. Branches usually expanded above into a series of saucers from the margins of which new branches arise; taste usually peppery; spores minute, 2.2 x 4μ...............................*C. pyxidata* (p. 92)

12. Branches not ending in expanded saucers, and taste not peppery; spores larger........................................................................................................13
13. On wood of deciduous trees; spores 3.8-4.4 x 7.5-9µ....*C. stricta* (p. 162)
13. On wood of coniferous trees or on bark at their bases; spores 3.7-5.5 x 7.4-10µ.............................................................................*C. apiculata* (p. 157)
    *C. pinicola* (p. 161)
13. As above but taste acrid and spores about 6-7.4µ long
    *C. acris* (p. 162)
13. On twigs and small branches of deciduous trees or from leaves mixed with them; spores smooth, 2.9-4.2 x 10-15µ........*C. byssiseda* (p. 152)
14. Plant rather small, brownish, with a slender stem which extends into the leaves as a whitish root covered with long woolly hairs
    *C. Murrilli* (p. 190)
14. Not as above........................................................................................................15
15. Tips lavender, other parts creamy ochraceous....*C. subdecurrens* (p. 172)
15. Tips not lavender........................................................................................16
16. Whitish when young, then delicate flesh color, the base pale ochraceous; spores light yellowish ochraceous, smooth or nearly so, 3-3.3 x 4.8-6µ; odor distinct, a medicinal fragrance........................*C. gracilis* (p. 169)
16. Flesh color, in age tan or pale cinnamon; odorless, taste bitter when fresh and when dry; flesh when dry very soft and chalky friable; spores light buffy ochraceous, minutely rough, 2.5-3.7 x 7.4-8µ
    *C. suecica* (p. 168)
16. Yellowish cinnamon or creamy ochraceous; spores ochraceous............17
17. Growing among rotting pine needles; not showing green stains; spores distinctly short-spinulose, 3.4-4 x 6.3-10µ
    *C. abietina,* form (p. 182)
17. Growing among hemlock or spruce (and fir?) needles; spores minutely warted, 3-3.7 x 5-8.5µ.
    Showing green stains at least in age
    *C. abietina,* typical form (p. 179)
    Not showing green stains............*C. abietina, flaccida* form (p. 184)
17. Growing on redwood needles in the Pacific states; small and delicate; spores minutely papillate, 2-2.2 x 3.5-4µ.............*C. myceliosa* (p. 178)
18. Flesh (at least below) gelatinous and translucent; taste of tobacco
    *C. gelatinosa* (p. 137)
18. Stem pale or clear lilac; body smoky gray or smoky cinnamon when mature; spores cinnamon-buff.................................*C. fennica* (p. 135)
18. Tips of the branches rosy red, at least when young, and strongly contrasting with the pale body; spores light buffy yellow
    *C. botrytis* (p. 111)
18. Tips wine color (pale rosy vinaceous) after early youth, then darker vinaceous and finally dull brick-brown; body light tan when fresh, the stout stem often stained vinaceous rose; spores striated, rod-elliptic, about 3.3-4 x 11-13µ.................................*C. rufescens* (p. 139)

18. Like *C. rufescens* in form, texture and color of body, but tips do not become wine-color nor does the base stain rosy purple when bruised; spores much smaller, 3-4 x 6.6-8µ.................................*C. verna* (p. 141)

18. Shape and texture as in *C. rufescens* and base staining wine color when bruised, but color a faint lavender-pink in body and odor strong of cocoa butter.................................................*C. cacao* (p. 151)

18. Tips pale lavender-pink when young; then pinkish cinnamon; stem distinct; cinnamon-brown; flesh when dry very friable and chalky
*C. subspinulosa* (p. 133)

18. Tips yellowish until maturity, body creamy flesh color or a clearer pink; flesh not very crisp or brittle, distinctly pinkish until maturity; when dry very friable and chalky; spores usually distinctly rough, about 4-6 x 8.5-12µ.................................*C. formosa* (p. 127)

18. Colors and texture when fresh about as in *C. formosa* (tips clear light yellow, body saffron), but flesh not chalky when dry, bases very slender and crowded, and spores smooth and much smaller (4-4.8 x 5.5-8.3µ).................................*C. conjunctipes* (p. 131)

18. As in *C. conjunctipes,* but odor fragrant-oily and bases less slender and crowded.................................*C. c.* var. *odora* (p. 132)

18. Tips white when young; body, and tips also later, a clear yellow; flesh very crisp and brittle.................................*C. flava* (p. 120)

18. Ochraceous buff to orange-buff with tint of cream above, flesh-orange below; spores about as in *C. botrytis*.........*C. flava* var. *aurea* (p. 124)

18. Clear pale yellow upward, pale fleshy cream in body, base white; spores rough, 4-4.5 x 10-11µ.................................*C. flava* var. *subtilis* (p. 125)

18. Deep flesh color or coral pink all over to near maturity, the tips concolorous or, when young, paler with tint of cream; flesh crisp and brittle as in *C. botrytis*
*C. subbotrytis* and var. *intermedia* (pp. 116, 117)

18. Light egg-yellow or creamy pink, all parts when bruised staining deep blood-red or brownish red.................................*C. sanguinea* (p. 118)

18. Entire plant whitish, becoming cream colored
*C. xanthosperma* (p. 141)

18. Fleshy yellow, tips divaricating; spores nearly smooth, 9-12.5µ long
*C. divaricata* (p. 126)

18. Pale creamy tan; flesh soft, not brittle, stem plump and distinct, odor rather rancid like old ham.................................*C. secunda* (p. 150)

18. Rich buffy orange all over, the base not staining vinaceous or brown
*C. aurea* (p. 142)

18. Rich buffy orange or brownish tan with tint of pink or light ochraceous yellow; stem indistinct, the pointed base easily staining brown or vinaceous brown; spores 3.7-5.3 x 7.5-13µ
*C. aurea* var. *australis* (p. 144)

18. Plants about 1.5-3 cm. high; color dull creamy white then olivaceous yellow; flesh turning dull pink at once when cut; spores pip-shaped, warted, 2.5-3 x 5-6.5µ.................................*C. decurrens* (p. 174)

18. Plants 4-10 cm. high; buffy yellow, then isabella color; flesh turning pink as above; spores also the same

18. Color pale leather-tan, the base darker; small; flesh not pink when cut; spores smooth, 2.2 x 7.4-7.7µ............................C. Patouillardii (p. 156)

18. Pale drab except for the olive green tips; spores rough, 4 x 10-12µ

18. Color pale cream to creamy tan; base stout, not changing when bruised; flesh soft, moderately brittle, odor mildly rancid on fading; spores long, smooth (rough in a form), 3-4.4 x 9-14.5µ

18. As above, but spores 14-18µ long.............................C. Strasseri (p. 149)

18. Color deep brown or rusty brown, at least after maturity; stem distinct; spores strongly warted or spiny, deep colored.........................................**19**

19. Plant stout, usually large, deep brown with the tips whitish; spores antique brown, set with long, sharp spines, about 6.3-7 x 11-13µ

19. Base slender and ending in a long, whitish, woolly root which runs among the leaves...........................................................C. Murrilli (p. 190)

19. Base without a rhizomorph or woolly root; spores reddish ochraceous, distinctly papillate, 4.4-6 x 12.5-18.4µ......................C. Broomei (p. 186)

19. As above, but at times with a smooth, pinkish rhizomorph and spores with larger, blunt papillae, 4.8-5.3 x 8-11µ.........C. longicaulis (p. 187)

19. Like C. longicaulis, but said to be intensely caerulean (blue or green?) above, and spores larger and with still larger papillae, 6-7.5 x 9-15µ

**Clavaria filipes** B. & Rav.  Grevillea 2: 17.  1873.

PLATES 1 AND 81

Always single and simple, gregarious, 1.3-2.4 cm. tall, stem as long as or longer than the club from which it is distinct in smaller size, more translucent color and much tougher texture; club terete, nearly cylindrical, brittle but not very fragile, about 1-1.4 mm. thick, bluntly pointed, pale whitish cream or greenish cream, the tips concolorous in youth then yellowish then reddish; stalk slender, flexible, glabrous except above, where it is pruinose, quite tough, pale creamy flesh color, the base often distinctly surrounded by a little boot or spreading pad of white mycelium; tasteless and odorless.  In drying the plants become dark cartilaginous in color and appearance, and frequently the tips can be seen to be less shrunken, taking the shape of a little cap.

Spores (of No. 2806) white, elliptic, with a small eccentric mucro, smooth but often granular with the appearance of being punctate, when quite fresh only a few with an oil drop, 3.7-4.4 x 5.2-7.5µ, most about 4 x 6µ.  Basidia 4-spored, 4.8-5.5 x

$22\mu$. Hymenium about $35\mu$ thick, densely set with large and small crystals; threads of flesh variable in diameter, up to $9\mu$ thick, closely packed, parallel in longitudinal section, clamp connections present.

On comparison of the type of *C. filipes* at Kew, we have no doubt our plants are the same. There are three plants preserved in good condition, all with long, slender stalks very distinct from the club and the little mycelial boot is obvious; spores few but apparently similar, $3.7\text{-}4.2 \times 5.5\text{-}7.4\mu$. The original description (adapted) is: Pale rufous; stem filiform, distinct, fistulose, about one inch long, springing from a white mycelium; club long, cylindric, curved, about as long as the stem. On the ground, South Carolina, Ravenel, No. 1488. [The words "pale rufous" almost certainly refer to the dried plants.]

The types of *C. tenuipes* B. & Br. at Kew are unlike our plants and are certainly a different species (see Cotton and Wakefield in Trans. Brit. Myc. Soc. **6**: 186. 1919).

From solitary plants of *C. fragilis* and *C. helveola* the present species is distinguished by the longer, tougher, and more distinct stem, the different spores, and the usually different color.

Illustration: Burt. Ann. Mo. Bot. Gard **9**: pl. 9, fig. 83. 1922.

North Carolina: Chapel Hill. No. 2804. On bare soil under *Spirea,* July 29, 1917. No. 2806. On damp soil covered with algæ and moss protonema, under hardwoods, July 30, 1917.
South Carolina: Ravenel. (Kew Herb., type).
Alabama: Pieters. (Kew Herb., as *C. falcata*).

## Clavaria subfalcata Atk. Ann. Myc. **6**: 58. 1908.

### PLATES 2, 81, AND 91

Single or sparingly gregarious, simple, slender, 2.5-5.7 cm. high, the stalk distinct, 0.8-2.8 cm. long, 1-1.5 mm. thick, terete, glabrous except for the faintly fibrous base, pale yellow to pale lemon yellow, varying in some of the younger or more delicate to translucent white. Club cylindric, often curved, 0.7-2.6 mm. thick, terete or compressed, not rugose, pale creamy white in youth, becoming slightly more yellowish, some with a faint wine tint above, drying dull ochraceous or buff; tips rounded, concolorous. Flesh tender, fibrous, rather brittle, slivering but not snapping at an angle of 45°, concolorous, stuffed and often hollowed by grubs; taste and odor none.

Spores (of No. 5630) pure white, smooth, oval to oblong-elliptic, with a large oil drop and a small eccentric mucro, 4.5-6 x 8-10.5μ.   Basidia 4-spored, 6.8-7.5μ thick.

This is certainly *C. subfalcata* in spite of the fact that Atkinson does not mention any color except white.   We find it not at all rare at Blowing Rock in exactly the same kinds of places in which Atkinson found his plants.   (He also found it on sphagnum on Grandfather Mountain.)   In obviously related groups on the same bank one finds colorless plants (usually the youngest specimens) mingled with the colored ones.   We have studied an authentic specimen of *C. subfalcata* (No. 10689 from Blowing Rock, N. C., mentioned in the original description, now in the Bresadola Herbarium) and find spores identical with No. 5630. There are also two other collections of this plant in the Bresadola Herbarium from Atkinson, one (No. 14108) under the unpublished name of *C. albella* (spores "7-9 x 5-6μ"), the other (No. 13460) with spores 5-5.5 x 8-9.3μ.   The original description of *Clavaria subfalcata* is as follows:

"Plants small, entirely white when fresh, yellowish when dry, rarely white, very slender, 1-3 cm. high, 1 mm. stout; clavula dull white; stipe distinct and transparent, with white mycelium spreading over substratum.   Basidia 4-spored.   Spores oval-sub-elliptical, thin-walled, granular, smooth, 7-10 x 5-7μ, in age with a large oil drop.   Near *Clavaria affinis* but spores not punctate."

The present species is obviously very near *C. gracillima* (which see).   Their nearest relative is *C. fuscata* which can hardly be distinguished except by the odor of garlic and the two-spored basidia.   *Clavaria sphagnicola* Boud. (Bull. Soc. Myc. Fr. **33**: 12, pl. 4, fig. 3. 1917) is very near and perhaps identical with the present species, but is described as having the stalk not distinct and the color as shown is a brighter yellow.   *Clavaria argillacea* differs distinctly in being larger and much stouter upward, in the thicker and shorter stem, and in the more crowded habit.

Illustration:   Burt.  Ann. Mo. Bot. Gard. **9**: pl. 9, fig. 80.  1922.

North Carolina: Blowing Rock.   Coker, No. 5573.   In *Cladonia* and mosses on a roadside bank, August 19, 1922.   Spores 4.4-6.6 x 7.8-11μ.   No. 5630.   Same site as above, August 20, 1922.   No. 5869.   On bank by roadside, August 27, 1922.   (Above colls. in U. N. C. Herb.).   Also found by Atkinson.   (Cornell Herb. and Bresadola Herb., types).
Grandfather Mountain.   Atkinson.   (Cornell Herb.).

New York:  Ithaca, etc.  (Cornell Herb.).

Long Island.  Cold Spring Harbor, October 27, 1912.  Harper.  (N. Y. Bot. Gard. Herb., as *C. vermiculata*).  "Nearly white, solitary, obtuse, 4.5 cm. high."  We find the spores to be smooth, elliptic, about 5 x 10.5$\mu$.

**Clavaria gracillima** Pk.  Rept. N. Y. St. Mus. **28**: 53, pl. 1, fig. 9.  1876.  (Not *C. gracillima* Wakker.  De Ziekten van het Suikerriet op Java, p. 195.  1898.)

### PLATE 91

Peck's description follows:

"Simple, very slender, smooth, about 1' high, rather tough; club acute or acuminate, pale yellow, a little thicker than the long slender distinct bright yellow shining stem.

"In this species, as in *C. argillacea*, the hymenium is quite distinct from the stem."

The types at Albany look exactly like *C. subfalcata* in general appearance, size, etc., but we find the spores to be distinctly narrower and of somewhat different shape from the latter.  They are smooth, subelliptic to pip-shaped, with somewhat curved apical mucro, 3.6-4 x 7.4-10$\mu$.  The basidia are club-shaped, 4-spored, about 6 x 30$\mu$.  While this difference does not seem great, it has proved consistent in all collections of *C. subfalcata* examined, and we therefore hesitate to combine them.  It would probably be best to consider the difference only varietal.

Illustration:  Burt.  Ann. Mo. Bot. Gard. **9**: pl. 9, fig. 87.  1922.

New York:  Northville.  Among moss in a pasture.  (Albany Herb., type).

**Clavaria fuscata** Oud.  Arch. Néerl. **2**: 35, pl. 1, fig. 1.  1867.  *C. foetida* Atk.  Ann. Myc. **6**: 56.  1908.

### PLATE 81

Plant 1.5-2.1 cm. high (up to 6 cm. in *C. foetida*), the colorless, translucent stalk as long as or longer than the opaque white or pale yellow, blunt club, with which it contrasts strongly but into which it fades gradually.  Stalk about 0.9 mm. thick; club 1.4 mm. thick, larger and more yellowish upward.  Base of stem smooth but springing from a more or less obvious mycelial film.  Texture of club brittle, snapping clean at 45°, stem not brittle, bending on itself without breaking. Odor strong of garlic, taste mildly similar. The odor of the undisturbed plant is noticeable only when close to the nose, but if put in water or crushed a little it may be detected a foot or more away. When young and very fresh the plants are white, but the club very soon begins to turn a dull creamy yellow, which is the color of the dried plants (the stalk remaining colorless until dry).

Spores (of No. 3459) smooth, oval-elliptic, with a large oil drop, 4.4-6 x 8-10μ. Basidia (of No. 3485) about 6.6-7.5μ thick, 2-spored.

We have, fortunately, been able to see authentic specimens from the type locality (Amsterdam, in a conservatory box containing *Philodendron*), collected by Oudemans himself and now in the Fries Herbarium. They are the size of Atkinson's *C. foetida,* and it seems now obvious that the two species are the same, though one would not be sure of it from the descriptions. The data as to spores and basidia of *C. fuscata* seem never to have been published. We find them to agree closely with Atkinson's figures (spores of *C. fuscata* subspherical to short-elliptic, smooth, 5.5-7.4 x 7-8.5μ; basidia 2-spored, 5-6μ thick). Oudemans does not mention any distinct odor, but Miss Catherine Cool of the Ryks Museum, Leyden, has given us notes on the fresh condition and a painting which supply important details. She says: "The specimens here figured were collected by me in November, 1918. When fresh the fungus is of a pure white color; collected they turn, especially on the top, to a brownish color. When undisturbed they have no odor, but when collected the odor of onion is very strong." Miss Cool's plants were taken from the same conservatory box as the original collection, and she says they have appeared there every month in recent years. This data leaves no distinction of any consequence between this and the American plant.

After writing the above we received from Miss Cool fresh plants collected by her on the roots of *Cyathea* in the Botanical Gardens at Leyden, November 11, 1922. To our surprise the plants arrived in living condition, undecayed, and their strong odor of garlic was still very noticeable. The clubs had faded a little and were not brittle; when quite fresh they may have been more fragile. Miss Cool has no notes on this point. The stems of these slightly faded plants were nearly white, not sharply distinct from the dull cream colored clubs.   For a later and fuller description of *C. fuscata* by Oudemans, see Rév. Champignons **1**: 439. 1892.

Our Chapel Hill plants are a small form of the species. Otherwise they agree well with the European and New York plants.

The type of *C. foetida* in Ithaca consists of one good plant and a few fragments.   A note accompanying it says "odor of skunk cabbage."   The plant is long and slender and largest in the middle.   We could find no spores.   Atkinson's description follows:

"Plants white, yellow when dry, stipe not distinct, gradually tapering below, 4-6 cm. high, 1.5-2 mm. stout.   Odor of garlic. Basidia 2-spored.   Spores oboval, granular, then with a large oil drop, 6-9 x 5-7μ."

Illustration:   Burt.   Ann. Mo. Bot. Gard. **9**: pl. 9, fig. 81 (as *C. foetida*). 1922.

North Carolina: Chapel Hill.   No. 3459.   On sandy soil with humus at Meeting of the Waters, August 16, 1919.   No. 3475.   In damp, sandy humus, deciduous woods, August 22, 1919.   Spores 4.8-6.6 x 7.5-9.8μ. No. 3485.   Same spot as No. 3475, August 23, 1919.

New York:. Ithaca.   Ferguson.   (Cornell Herb., as type of *C. foetida*, No. 7740).

**Clavaria acuta** Sow.   Engl. Fungi, pl. 333. 1803.
?*Clavaria falcata* Pers.   Comm., p. 81 (213). 1797.

PLATES 81 AND 92

This classical product of conservatory tubs has rarely been collected in America.   We have found it in some quantity in a large tub in the main conservatory range in the New York Botanical Garden.   The plants ran considerably smaller than usually reported, but were otherwise typical.   They were growing in the same tub with *C. luteo-ochracea,* which see for comparison.   Our plants may be described as follows:

Single or approximated in small clumps, 1-2 cm. high, narrowly clavate or cylindrical, terete, about 1-1.3 mm. thick above, tapering downward, the stalk about 0.5-1 cm. long and very translucent; club blunt or a little pointed; milk-white throughout; texture brittle, snapping clean on bending; solid.   Taste slight, a little mouldy; odor none.

Spores white, smooth, subspherical with one side usually flattened, and with a distinct apical mucro, 6.5-8.5 x 7.5-10μ. Basidia 4-spored, considerably enlarged at the end, 7-9 x 25-30μ.

The plant reaches a considerably larger size than shown in our collection. Cotton says (Trans. Brit. Myc. Soc. **3**: 31. 1908) "3-7 cm. high, slender, 2-3 mm. thick." Cotton says further:

"The frequent occurrence of *C. acuta* in greenhouses has been noted by several writers. Schroeter, for instance, states (Kryptogamen Flora von Schlesien, vol. iii: p. 444) that in Breslau Botanical Gardens it regularly occurs in certain large pots, producing crops which continue for several weeks. At Kew the plant behaves in a similar manner. Presumably, the mycelium is introduced with the turfy-loam employed in potting. It is quite possible that the plant described by Persoon (1797) as *C. falcata* (a name kept up in Continental works) is the same species as *C. acuta*. Persoon's description is, however, hardly sufficient to justify the adoption of his name."

We have found but one plant in American herbaria that seems to be what is referred to this species or to *C. falcata* by European botanists. It is a collection under the name of *C. falcata* by Schweinitz from Salem, N. C., now in the Curtis Herbarium at Cambridge. There are two plants on clay soil, 1.5-2 cm. high, the stalks apparently distinct and a little darker than the clubs, about 5-6 mm. long; clubs tapering towards the stalk, one pointed, one sub-acute at tip, rugose-wrinkled, ochraceous, about 1 mm. thick. The spores are subspherical, 7-8μ in diameter and exactly like the spores of our *C. acuta* and of the European *C. acuta* from Cotton (Wales). The latter are, according to our measurements, 6.5-8μ thick. Another collection in the Curtis Herbarium under the same name from Alabama (Pieters) appears to be different, and is probably not *C. falcata*. Plants in the Cornell Herbarium labelled *C. acuta* (No. 9659) look like *C. vermiculata* and from the full notes attached are almost certainly that species.

In the Curtis Herbarium are also three collections labelled *C. acuta*—Society Hill, S. C. (Curtis), Santee Canal, S. C. (Ravenel), and Massachusetts (Sprague). All are very small clubs growing on earth. No spores could be found on any of them and it is more than likely that none of them is *C. acuta*.

As understood by Patouillard, *C. falcata* seems to differ from the English idea of *C. acuta* in the two-spored basidium and the less distinct stem.   He says of the former (Tab. Fung., p. 116) : "Quite simple, entirely white and smooth, club cylindrical, obtuse at tip, glabrous; basidia two-spored, spores white, spherical; stalk colorless, pellucid.   Height 4-5 cm.   On earth in woods, autumn." His figure 258 shows 4 plants, basidia and spores, the latter perfectly spherical, the basidia with two sterigmata.   Size of spores not given, but they are shown about the same diameter as the thickness of those of *C. pistillaris* on the same page.   The stalks of the plants are not shown as clearly distinct from the clubs.   According to Fries *C. acuta* has a distinct stalk while *C. falcata* does not.   *Clavaria falcata* var. *citrinopes* Quélet differs only in the yellow stem (Patouillard, Tab. Fung., p. 21, fig. 41).

From the description it may easily be that *C. pampeana* Speg. (Fungi Argentini IV.   Anal. Soc. Cientif., Argentina, **12** : 18 [of separate].   1881) is *C. acuta*.   The large, subspherical spores are in close agreement (6-7 x 7-11μ.).

Juel (cited under *C. cristata*) has studied a plant he calls *C. falcata*.   It was unique among the Clavarias he studied in having usually 7, often 6, or rarely 8 sterigmata and spores to a basidium.   The spindles in the basidium are long and narrow and nearly longitudinal; the spores long, smooth and uninucleate (pl. 2, figs. 36-41).   The spores look more like those of our *C. subfalcata* than of any other species of similar shape.

Illustrations:  ?Micheli.   Nov. Plant. Gen., pl. 87, fig. 5. 1729 (referred to
    *C. falcata* by Persoon).
  ?Patouillard.   Tab. Fung., fig. 258 (as *C. falcata*). 1884; fig. 41 (as *C. falcata* var. *citrinopes*). 1883.
  Sowerby.   Engl. Fungi **3** : pl. 333. 1801.

North Carolina :  Salem.   Schweinitz. (Curtis Herb., as *C. falcata*).   "Non rara locis muscosis."

New York :  New York Botanical Garden.   Coker, No. 3189a.   On earth in a tub, September 21, 1918.

**Clavaria argillacea** Pers.   Comm., p. 74 (206).  1797.
  ?*C. flavipes* Pers.   Neues Mag. Bot. **1**: 117.  1794.
  *C. ericetorum* Pers.   Obs. Myc. **2**: 60.  1799.
  *C. pallescens* Pk.   Bull. N. Y. St. Mus. **131**: 34.  1909.
  *C. obtusata* Boud.   Bull. Soc. Myc. Fr. **33**: 12, pl. 4, fig. 2.
    1917.

PLATE 81

We have not yet seen this in the fresh state and have found
it only twice in American collections (as *C. pallescens* Pk.)*.   It
is apparently a rare species, and seems nearest *C. helveola,* but is
easily distinguished from that (and from *C. luteo-alba*) by the
more distinct stem, thicker and more clavate form, and larger
spores.   *Clavaria ericetorum* is represented in Persoon's herbarium by two lots of single and cespitose plants.   The thickened
clubs have slender, distinct stalks, and the appearance is as usual
in European herbaria.   We were not able to find any spores on
them.   *Clavaria argillacea* is not represented, but there is little
doubt that they are the same.   In the Kew Herbarium plants labelled *C. argillacea* from Brandenburg (Sydow, Mycotheca germanica, No. 453) agree fully with the English plants described
below.   The spores are smooth, oblong-elliptic, 5-7 x 9-12$\mu$; basidia 4-spored, about 6.8$\mu$ thick; hymenium about 55$\mu$ thick.
Threads of flesh up to 18$\mu$ thick in center of the plant, becoming
much smaller just under the hymenium.   A collection from
France (Boudier) in Bresadola's herbarium also seems the same;
spores 4.5-5.5 x 9-11$\mu$.   We have examined plants kindly sent us
by Dr. Cotton and compared them with Peck's type of *C. pallescens* and find them to agree.   In the dried state they are quite
unlike *C. helveola.*   The following description is from Cotton and
Wakefield (Trans. Brit. Myc. Soc. **6**: 191. 1919):

"Plants simple, gregarious, 2-5 cm. high, pale greenish-yellow,
fragile; smell none, taste like tallow.   Clubs cylindrical or flattened, with one or more grooves, surface often minutely channelled, apex blunt.   Stem distinct, yellowish.   Internal structure

---

* In the Underwood collection in the New York Botanical Garden are several plants
pressed on a card and labelled *C. argillacea*. No locality is given and they may be
European.  They look like the European plants of that name and have about the same
spores, 4-5 x 7.4-8.5$\mu$.

almost pseudo-parenchymatous in transverse section, even when old; cells regular, 10-14μ in diameter, with small narrow filaments (4-5μ in diameter) between; segments 50-70μ long towards the margin, but up to 200-300μ in the center. Basidia conspicuous, about 70μ long, contents granular, sterigmata 4. Spores smooth, hyaline, cylindric to elliptic with a minute lateral basal apiculus, 10-11 x 5-6μ (or sometimes 10-14 x 6-7μ), contents granular.

"Habitat. In heathy places. Not uncommon."

Peck describes *C. pallescens* as follows (adapted) :

Club simple, loosely cespitose or sometimes gregarious, about 1 inch tall, clavate, obtuse, generally terete, soft, fragile, stuffed or hollow, pale buff fading to whitish, more persistent lemon-yellow within; stem distinct, short, glabrous, 2-4 mm. long, pale yellow; spores white, oblong or ellipsoid, 6.3-7 x 8.9-12.7μ. [We find them to be rod-elliptic with a small eccentric mucro, 4.2-5.4 x 9.3-12.2μ]. Dry gravelly soil near clumps of lambkill, *Kalmia angustifolia* L., South Acton, Mass., October.

Peck adds that the species is allied to *C. ligula,* but in this he seems to be wrong. A cespitose habit is not mentioned by Cotton and Wakefield, but among the examples sent us by the latter are several close groups of three or four. The obtuse, club-shaped form is a marked character of the species. In the dried state the plants are spatulate and taper downward from a broad tip.

Patouillard's idea of the species seems to agree very well with the above, except that his fig. 587 shows the spores as pip-shaped. He describes the plant (Tab. Fung., p. 34) as fascicled, obtuse, attenuated at the base, cylindrical, pale clay color. Spores ovoid, 8 x 5μ; basidia 4-spored. He recognizes as distinct both *C. ericetorum* and *C. flavipes.* For the former he shows compressed, twisted plants forked at tip, two touching at base, about 12.5 cm. high; spores 10 x 5μ (fig. 585). For the latter he shows (fig. 586) simple clubs, scattered or fascicled, cylindrical or flattened, attenuated to a "citron yellow stalk." Spores ovoid or subglobose (no dimensions given); basidia 4-spored. The stalk does not appear distinct.

*Clavaria obtusata* as represented in the herbarium of the University of Paris (Savigné, November, 1913) is to all appearances

the present species.   The spores are oblong-elliptic, 4-5.5 x 8-10μ.
The only important difference appearing from the description is
that the stalk is said to be indistinct from the club.

    *Clavaria Daulnoyae* Quél. (Asso. Française Avanc. Sci., 1891,
p. 470 (p. 7 of separate), pl. 3, fig. 36) should be compared with *C.
argillacea,* as no differences of importance appear from the description or figure.   For a comparison with *C. subfalcata* see that
species.

    The present species has been reported from America by sev-
eral authors, as Schweinitz, Berkeley, and Peck, but their records
are all quite doubtful.   In the Curtis Herbarium a collection by
Schweinitz from Salem, N. C., labelled *C. argillacea* has spores
which are minute, 2.3 x 3.7μ, and cannot be correctly determined.
Also one from him in the Kew Herbarium so labelled is not this
but probably *C. helveola* or *C. vermiculata.*   Another collection so
called by Peck from the Catskills at Albany are not this but poor
specimens of *C. ornatipes.*

Illustrations: Boudier.   Icon. Myc. **1**: pl. 175.   In color.   Photographic
    copy by Burt in Ann. Mo. Bot. Gard. **9**: pl. 9, fig. 85. 1922.
    Britzelmayr.   Hymen. Südb., Clavariei, fig. 32.
    Burt.   Ann. Mo. Bot. Gard. **9**: pl. 8, fig. 71 (as *C. pallescens*). 1922.
    Cooke.   Brit. Fung., pl. 689 (as *C. argillacea* var. *flavipes*).
    Flora Danica **11**: pl. 1852, fig. 2; pl. 1966, fig. 1 (as *C. flavipes*).
    Gillet.   Champ. Fr. **5**: pl. 99 (105).   Good.
    Patouillard.   As cited above.
    Peck.   As cited above.
    Persoon.   Comm., pl. 1, fig. 4 (as *C. flavipes*).
    Swanton.   Fungi and How to Know Them, pl. 29, fig. 1. 1909.

Massachusetts: South Acton.   Davis.   (Albany Herb., as type of *C. pal-
    lescens*).   "One season's collection developed a strong smell of sul-
    phuric ether."
    Boston.   Davis.   Growing in *Polytrichum* moss.   (Albany Herb.).


**Clavaria mucida** Pers.   Comm., p. 55 (187). 1797.   (Not *C.
    mucida* of Fl. Danica, pl. 1305, fig. 1, which is *Calocera fur-
    cata*).

PLATES 3 AND 81

    Clubs slender, simple, or at times forked into 2 to 6 candelabra-
like branches, or with a few small branches at any point, usually

about 4-9 mm. high, rarely up to 1.5 cm., nearly white when young, then pale cream, the rather sharp apex soon becoming brick-red to almost black; delicate, but tough, and bending on themselves without breaking, solid, rather abruptly narrowed below to a stalk which is not distinctly marked off and is a third or a fourth the total length.    Taste slightly woody; odor none.

Spores (of No. 3579) pure white, smooth, elliptic with a more or less pointed mucro end, 1.8-2.3 x 5.2-7.4μ.    Basidia 4-spored, 3.7-4.4μ thick; hymenium about 12μ thick, extending all over the tip; threads of flesh 2.8-4.8μ thick, with septa far apart, clamp connections present.

The plants have the remarkable habit of always growing in association with the alga *Chlorococcus,* which forms a continuous deep green coat on the log beneath them.    They are never found except with the alga, and the species is in a fair way to become a lichen, or is already a primitive lichen.    In the Botanical Gazette (**37**: 62, figs. 16 and 17. 1904) we have published a note with drawings, calling attention to the resemblance of this species to a lichen in habit.    Persoon in his original description and later Schweinitz note the constant association with a crust of green powder and Fries refers to its growth with *Chlorococcus* (Epicrisis, p. 580).    In his Danish Fungi in Herbarium of E. Rostrup, p. 368, 1913 (Copenhagen), J. Lind says of *C. mucida,* "Surely no *Clavaria* species, rather any lichen."    In America it seems to grow only on *Nyssa.*    It is recorded from Louisiana to Canada, in Europe and New Zealand.    The European *C. mucida* from Stockholm (Romell) has spores distinctly thicker and somewhat shorter than ours, and it might, therefore, be best to make the American form a variety.

This peculiar species is rare but widely distributed.    We have found it several times at Chapel Hill, growing singly in very populous colonies on soggy, decorticated black gum logs in shady, cool places near streams.    We have calculated that there were about 23,000 plants on the log from which No. 3579 was taken.

*Clavaria mucida* var. *Curtisii* Berk.( Grevillea **2**: 17. 1873) is probably not different.    The original description is (translated) : "Club-shaped, short, luteous, tip fuscous; stem white, arising from small, circular, white mycelium.    No. 974 is once forked and narrow.    On wet-rotting stumps." It was described from South Carolina (Ravenel, No. 974).

Illustrations: Atkinson.    Stud. Am. Fungi, fig. 193.
 Coker.   As cited above.
 Hard.   Mushrooms, fig. 398. 1908.
 Persoon.   Comm., pl. 2, fig. 3. 1797.   Photographic copy by Burt in Ann. Mo. Bot. Gard. 9: pl. 9, fig. 77. 1922.

North Carolina: Chapel Hill.   No. 38a.   On a decorticated wet log, October 8, 1908.   No. 3579.   On a soggy, decorticated, gum log, November 2, 1919.   No. 3886.   On a blackgum log in Strowd's lowgrounds, December 13, 1919.
 Wilmington.   (Curtis Herb.).
 Salem.   (Schweinitz Herb. and Curtis Herb.).

South Carolina: Hartsville.   Coker, No. 5841.   On deciduous log in swamp, August 31, 1922.   (U. N. C. Herb.).
 Society Hill.   (Curtis Herb.).

New Jersey: Newfield.   Ellis.   (N. Y. Bot. Gard. Herb., N. Am. Fungi, No. 332).

Pennsylvania: Lehigh Valley.   Herbst.   (Schweinitz Herb.).

New York: Lake Placid.   Mrs. Britton.   (N. Y. Bot. Gard. Herb.).

Massachusetts: Pittsfield.   Pierson.   (N .Y. Bot. Gard. Herb. and U. N. C. Herb.).

Ohio: Rendville.   Kellerman.   (N. Y. Bot. Gard. Herb.).

Indiana: Fern, Putnam Co.   Underwood.   (N. Y. Bot. Gard. Herb.).

Canada: Macoun.   (Albany Herb.).

**Clavaria luteo-ochracea** Cavara.   Fungi Long. Exs., No. 64. 1892.

PLATES 1 AND 91

Plants single, gregarious, 0.6-1.3 cm. tall (up to 2.5 cm. in Burnham, No. 39), gradually tapering downward, openly forked above once or twice like antlers, and flattened there, or more rarely simple clubs; surface above glabrous, at base more or less distinctly scurfy-hairy (up to ⅓ way up), the basal hairs at times longer than the diameter of the plant; color pale creamy to pale citric yellow, some pale lemon yellow below.   Texture toughish-fleshy, only cracking when bent on self; odor distinct and bad, a little like a stink horn, taste none.   Stem not discrete from the hymenium.   The dried plants are blackish upward, reddish cartilaginous downward, tough, not brittle.

Spores (of No. 16a) minute, smooth, oval or nearly pip-shaped, hyaline, 2.2-3 x 3.5-4.4μ.   Basidia (of B. No. 39) 4μ thick with 4 delicate sterigmata; hymenium 30-35μ thick; threads of flesh 3.7μ thick, parallel in center, slightly irregular just under the hymenium, clamp connections present.

This is easily different from any well known American species.   It is separated from *C. citriceps* by smaller spores of different shape, bad odor, hairs at the stem base and (in our plants) by the more habitually forked tips.   The plant in texture, habit, and form reminds one most of *C. amethystinoides* (Hartsville, No. 42) which easily differs in much darker color and much larger size and spores.   We have found this plant but twice, but Mr. Burnham has sent us a gathering which seems to be the same. The species may be of tropical origin.   It is not closely related to *C. acuta,* which is also found in conservatory tubs.

The original distribution of the species is well represented in the New York Botanical Garden, and we have carefully compared our plants with it.   The dried plants are exactly alike except that the types are not branched in the lot shown.   The peculiar tawny setae at the base are quite obvious and furnish an easy means of separating the species from its relatives.   The spores are of characteristic shape and the same as in our plants, 3-3.5 x 4-4.8μ.   Accompanying the distributed plants are printed notes, the descriptive part of which is as follows (translated):

"Gregarious, fragile, yellowish; club cylindrical, simple, rarely bifurcate or spatulate, compressed or striate, glabrous, 2-5 cm. high, stalk brownish-ochraceous; basidia densely crowded, 30 x 5-6μ, 4 sterigmata; spores globose to ellipsoid, base obliquely acuminate, smooth, uniguttulate, 4-5 x 3-4μ."

In his discussion Cavara says that the spores are peculiar in that some are at first smooth, then slightly warted, but this can hardly mean anything more than collapse, for they are well shown to be smooth (pl. 91, fig. 4) on the plants distributed.

*Clavaria Cyatheae* Henn. (in Sacc. Syll. **9**: 250. 1891) as described would not positively exclude this species except for the spores which are said to be ferruginous (dimensions not given). Branching is not mentioned.

North Carolina: Chapel Hill. No. 2674. Low damp woods by branch, July 14, 1917. Spores 2.5-3.4 x 3.7-4.5μ.

New York: New York Botanical Garden. Coker, No. 16a. On earth in a tub, in the main conservatory range, September 21, 1918. (U. N. C. Herb.). Associated with *C. acuta* which was easily different in clearer, white, translucent stem, simple clubs (in this case), much greater brittleness, lack of odor, and different spores.

  Vaughns. Burnham, No. 39. On earth in woods. (U. N. C. Herb.). Spores oblong-elliptic, smooth, hyaline, 2.2 x 3.5μ. The plants are exactly like No. 16a in the dry state except a little taller, and the spores are the same.

## Clavaria biformis Atk. Ann. Myc. 6: 56. 1908.

### PLATE 91

The type of *C. biformis* at Ithaca shows little, single, sparingly branched or simple plants with smooth, subspherical spores about 2.2-3.5 x 3.5-4μ. The co-type (No. 10699, Blowing Rock, N. C.) is the same thing, with spores 2.8-3.6 x 3.5-4μ. The species is probably a form of *C. luteo-ochracea,* but we are retaining it at present.

Atkinson's description follows:

"Plants dull white to sordid yellow, in age tips usually darker, cylindrical, base only slightly more slender, 1-4 cm. high, 0.5-1.5 mm. stout, usually simple, or one or two times dichotomously branched. Basidia 20-25 x 4-5μ, 4-spored. Spores oboval, white, smooth, granular or with an oil drop, 3-4 x 2.5-3μ."

Illustration: Burt. Ann. Mo. Bot. Gard. 9: pl. 9, fig. 79. 1922.

North Carolina: Blowing Rock. Atkinson, No. 10699. (Cornell Herb. and U. N. C. Herb.).

New York: Ithaca. On leaf mold in woods, August 8, 1902. Atkinson. (Cornell Herb., No. 13432. Type).

## Clavaria Macouni Pk. Rept. N. Y. St. Mus. 47: 150 (24 of Bot. ed.). 1894.

### PLATES 91 AND 92

This seems to be a good species. In the dry state the type plants are very small, simple, dull brown, flattened and channelled by collapse. Microscopic examination shows the hymenium about 40μ thick; basidia 4-spored, 5-5.5μ thick; spores smooth, often punctate internally, subelliptic to pip-shaped, 2.8-3.4 x 4.8-6.2μ. From Cotton's description his *C. Crosslandii* seems to be this species, but we have not been able to see the type (Trans. Brit. Myc. Soc. **6**: 187. 1919). From the description *C. affinis* Pat. and Doassans may be this or perhaps small isolated specimens of *C. vermiculata* (Tab. Fung., p. 205, fig. 470. 1886). The original description of *C. Macouni* follows:

"Clubs single or clustered, 6 to 10 lines high, obtuse or sub-acute, dingy greenish yellow or pale cinereous; spores minute, elliptical, 5μ long, 3μ broad."

Illustration:   Burt.  Ann. Mo. Bot. Gard. **9**: pl. 8, fig. 69.  1922.

Canada:   Among mosses under cedar trees.  Macoun.  (Albany Herb., type).

**Clavaria vernalis** Schw.   Schr. Nat. Ges. Leipzig **1**: 112.  1822.
    ?*C. paludicola* Libert.   Pl. Crypt. Arduennae, No. 322.  1837.
    *C. clavata* Pk.   Bull. Buf. Soc. Nat. Sci. **1**: 62. 1873.

PLATES 82 AND 92

Plants single, gregarious in extensive colonies, simple (one plant seen with four little prongs), 7-12 mm. high; clubs clavate to nearly cylindric, the usually thickened tip rounded or abruptly pointed, 1-2 mm. thick; tapering downward to the short (2-2.5 mm. long), poorly defined, terete and glabrous stalk, which is slightly incrassated at the base; color of club watery ochraceous to dull orange above, fading downward to the whitish and sub-translucent stalk. Flesh of the same color as the surface, watery, pliable and toughish, cracking but not snapping when bent double; solid; taste slightly moldy; odor none.

Spores (of No. 6071) white, smooth, narrowly elliptic and somewhat curved, 2-3 x 8-11μ. Basidia 4-spored, clavate, 3.7-4.8 x 18-25μ. Hymenium without cystidia or other peculiar cells, absent over the central region of the tip which in some individuals may be distinguished even when fresh by a little groove which surrounds it. Threads of flesh about 2.3-4μ thick, clamp connections present.

Our plants are like *C. vernalis* in all essentials, as habitat, season, gregarious but scattered habit, size and color, sterile tip, and shape of spores. It is true that the spores of No. 6071 average longer than in other collections, but it is probable that the difference would be reduced if good spore prints of the others were measured. As in the case of *C. mucida,* this species is intimately associated with algae and may with good reason be considered a lichen. Our Chapel Hill plants grow on ground covered with several sorts of blue-green algae, the most common being *Gleocapsa,* with which are mixed in good quantity an *Oscillatoria* and the protonema of the moss *Pogonatum.* Our figures (pl. 92, figs. 5-7) show the algae with the *Clavaria* mycelium in close contact, in one case with finger-like processes wefting the algal cell as in many lichens.

We have examined a northern collection of *C. vernalis* (Reliquiae Farlowianae, No. 311) and find that in it also the tips are quite sterile, as shown in longitudinal section. See the genus *Ceratella* (p. 6). In the Schweinitz Herbarium is a pill box of mossy earth labelled *C. vernalis,* but on examination with a lens we could find no trace of a *Clavaria.* Note that while Schweinitz says "on bare earth" his specimen shows the same mossy soil of other collections. Peck's type plants of *C. clavata* from Sand Lake, N. Y., are in good condition. The little thick clubs, which arise from densely mossy soil, are dull ochraceous in the dry state with broad tips which are often whitened with abundant crystals. We could find no spores on them, but in another good collection from Lake Pleasant spores were plentiful and we find them to be smooth, rod-elliptic, 2.6 x 6-6.5µ. Basidia 5.5µ thick. In his description of *C. clavata,* Peck mentioned the green, confervoid stratum from which the plants arise; and, as shown by his labels, he later considered his species the same as *C. vernalis.*

A collection from Newfield, N. J., at the New York Botanical Garden (Ellis) looks the same, and we find spores about the same, 2 x 5µ. The following notes accompany the specimen: "Spores oblong, smooth; base of the stem white where not covered with the green confervoid growth which overspreads the bare damp soil from which the plants arise . . . with *Drosera rotundifolia.* Club-shaped above, about ½ in. high, yellow (rather pale yellow) above." The word confervoid is used here probably in a rather loose sense. On examining the earth we find numerous *Chlorococcus*-like cells and apparently a little moss protenema. These were the plants distributed by Ellis (N. Am. Fungi, No. 613) as *C. clavata* Pk.

At Kew is represented *C. paludicola* Libert (No. 322) which in the dried state is so like *C. vernalis* as easily to pass for it. Unfortunately, however, our slide shows no spores that can be determined with certainty. The little plants are less than a cm. high, dark, the upper part thick and rugose, some of them tipped with a paler, unshrunken cap. The description on the label is (translation): "Sparse, small, somewhat compressed, rugose, thickened upward, yellow, drying orange."

Illustration: Peck. Rept. N. Y. St. Mus. **25**: pl. 1, fig. 9 (as *C. clavata*). 1873.

North Carolina: Chapel Hill. No. 6071. With algae and moss protonema on a clay bank near Forest Theatre, March 24 and 27, 1923.
　Wilmington. No. 5962. On bank of branch on golf links, December 28, 1921. Spores narrow, bent-elliptic and pointed at mucro end, 2 x 8-9.7$\mu$. Threads of flesh 2.8-11$\mu$ thick.

New Jersey: Newfield. Ellis. (N. Y. Bot. Gard. Herb., as *C. clavata*).

New York: Sand Lake. Peck. (Albany Herb., as *C. clavata*).
　North Elba. Peck. (Albany Herb.).
　Lake Pleasant. Peck. (Albany Herb.).

Massachusetts: Sharon. Piguet. (U. N. C. Herb. from Farlow Herb.).

**Clavaria helveola** Pers. Comm., p. 69 (201). 1797.
　　*C. helveola* Pers. Myc. Europ. **1**: 180. 1822.
　　*C. citrina* Quélet. Bull. Soc. Bot. de France **23**: 330, pl. 3, fig. 14. 1876. (Not. *C. citrina* Rafinesque).
　　?*C. luteo-alba* Rea. Trans. Brit. Myc. Soc. **2**: 66, pl. 3, fig. B. 1904.

PLATES 1, 4, AND 81

Plants cespitose in small groups (rarely over 12 in a group) or often single ones in the same colony, simple or a little forked or knobbed, or sometimes with an antler-like branch, length 1.5-5 cm., thickness 1-2.5 mm., nearly equal except for the short constricted stem which is more or less distinct; club usually bent and wavy and at times grooved and compressed, the tip blunt, often shrinking to a point and becoming ochraceous, then reddish or nearly black; color light buffy yellow with or without a faint greenish tint and often with a tint of flesh color (apricot), ochra-

ceous when bruised or wilting, the stem a clearer and more translucent color and not rarely tinted with green and marked with in-
herent green fibrils.   Flesh solid, or with a small irregular hollow, color of surface except for a lighter center, fragile and brittle, but not quite so much so as in *C. fragilis,* and usually not snapping with so clean a break, the center more loosely fibrous than
the surface; taste woody musty and at times a good deal like tallow, not strong; odor none.

Spores (of No. 2755) white, smooth, elliptic, slightly bent,
2.2-3 x 7-8.2μ, most about 2.3 x 7.5μ.   Basidia (of No. 4368)
4.8-6.6μ thick with 2-4 sterigmata; buried in the hymenium so that
the tips of the sterigmata just reach the outer surface of the hymenium, which is about 45μ thick.   Threads of the context shaped
in cross section like parenchyma cells.

This is the plant that has usually been referred to *C. inaequalis*
in American herbaria, but we must now apply that name to another
species.   From Persoon's description it would seem highly probable
that our plants are his *C. helveola,* the yellow color, fuscous tips in
age, closely set but not connate bases, etc., all agreeing perfectly;
but we have not been able to prove this from the type plants in his
herbarium.   There are two sheets under this name and one of
the variety *dispar.*   The former look like ours, but we have found
no good *Clavaria* spores on them (mold spores are present).   The
so-called variety looks much like *C. muscoides* and the spores are
about right for that species.

A pale form is found that is puzzling and might easily be referred to *C. fragilis* unless care is used.   Such a form is represented by collections No. 2788 and No. 2818 which were pale
creamy flesh color (very pale apricot).

The species is, like *C. vermiculata,* gregarious on mossy lawns,
etc., as well as in woods, and has the same shape and habit as that
species, from which it may be distinguished by the taste, color,
less rugose club and by the larger spores.   We have little doubt
that *C. luteo-alba* of England is a form of the present species.
Plants kindly sent us by Dr. Cotton are just like ours in the dry
state and have identical spores, smooth, ovate, with one distinct
oil drop, 3.5 x 5-7μ.   It is also to be observed that in several of
our collections not otherwise distinct a taste of tallow was noticed.
The original description of *C. luteo-alba* calls for the tips to be con-

stantly whitish, but later observations by Cotton show that this is not always the case (Trans. Brit. Myc. Soc. **3**: 30. 1908. Also **6**: 191. 1919). It is significant that *C. helveola* is not recognized in England by Cotton and Wakefield. Cotton refers to a plant he has met with which he thought to be the one often labelled *C. helveola* in herbaria, or by some writers incorrectly taken to be *C. inaequalis* (Trans. Brit. Myc. Soc. **2**: 165. 1908), but he later refers his plant to *C. luteo-alba* (Trans. Brit. Myc. Soc. **3**: 30. 1908). It seems hardly possible that a species not at all rare in both the northern and southern states should be unrepresented in England. Maire reports *C. luteo-alba* from France and gives his own description (Bull. Soc. Bot. Fr. **26**: 196. 1910).

*Clavaria incarnata* Weinm. may be the same as the flesh-colored form of this (our No. 2788) as a collection so determined from T. M. Fries (Sweden) in the Curtis Herbarium has similar spores, about 3.5 x 6μ. The species is, however, said to be purplish within. It is not represented in the Fries Herbarium at Upsala. There is also a collection under this name in the Curtis Herbarium from New Jersey (Ellis) that has the same appearance, but we could not get good spores from it. *Clavaria rosea* is equally doubtful, but see notes under that species. We have a good collection of a plant from Upsala sent us by Romell, determined (probably by von Post) as *C. purpurea*, but which in the dry state is like *C. helveola*. The spores are like those of our plants, 3.7-4 x 6.5-7.5μ. There seems to be no reasonable doubt that *C. citrina* Q. is also the same. The greenish base and the pip-shaped spores of about the same length, while they agree with this, exclude all other species that are at all near. From the description *C. Schroeteri* P. Henn. (Verh. Bot. Ver. Prov. Brandenburg **37**: 26. 1895), which is the same as *C. compressa* Schroeter, strongly suggests an antlered form of *C. helveola*. *Clavaria Daigremontiana* Boud. (Bull. Soc. Myc. Fr. **33**: 10, pl. 1, fig. 4. 1917) is like *C. helveola* in size, shape and color but is sulcate with numerous furrows and has spores 3-3.5 x 5-6μ.

Illustrations: Boudier. Icon. Myc. **1**: pl. 175.
  Cotton. Trans. Brit. Myc. Soc. **3**: pl. 11, fig. C. (Spores, as *C. luteo-alba*). 1909.
  Rea. As cited above.
  Quélet. As cited above (as *C. citrina*).

North Carolina: Chapel Hill. No. 2285. Woods near Howell's branch, June 28, 1916. Stuffed when young, hollow in age, the simple blunt tips abruptly brick color; spores 2.9-3.3 x 6-6.7μ. No. 2433. In short grass and moss in Dr. Mangum's lawn, July 27, 1916. Spores with a small eccentric mucro, the distal end often narrowed, 2.5-3.6 x 5.6-7μ. No. 2654. Low damp woods, July 12, 1917. Color rather light egg-yellow. Spores 3.7-4 x 5.5-6.7μ. No. 2755. In mossy grass, July 24, 1917. No. 2770. Same spot as No. 2433, July 23, 1917. Spores 2.5-3.7 x 6.2-8μ. No. 2774. Same place as No. 2433, July 26, 1917. No. 2788. Under spireas, bare earth, July 27, 1917. Just like the typical *C. helveola* except in color, which is pale creamy flesh color (very pale apricot) when quite fresh with the tips soon ochraceous and then reddish. Spores 2.5-3.3 x 4.8-5.9μ. This form may be what is called *C. incarnata* Weinm. Nos. 2793 and 2805. In same place as No. 2433, July 28, and 29, 1917. No. 2818. Same spot as No. 2788, August 1, 1917. Color as in No. 2788. Spores as in usual form, 2.3-3 x 6-7μ. No. 4368. Damp ravine near iron spring, frondose woods, July 4, 1920. As usual in color, etc.; taste rather rank and somewhat like tallow; spores (print) 3.7-4 x 7.5-8.2μ.

Blowing Rock. Coker and party, No. 5571. (U. N. C. Herb.). Orange form. Spores 3-3.7 x 5-7μ.

South Carolina: Hartsville. Coker, No. 18. September, 1916. (U. N. C. Herb.). Taste rather musky, not pleasant, odor none. Spores white, smooth, 2.5-3 x 6.6-7μ.

New York: Hudson Falls. Burnham, No. 6. (U. N. C. Herb.). Among moss on ground, July 23, 1917. Buffy yellow with a faint tint of flesh color, brittle; flesh colored like the surface, taste of tallow. Spores elliptic to pip-shaped, 3.7-4 x 6.3-7.4μ.

**Clavaria rosea** Dalm. in Swartz. Acta Holm., p. 157. 1811.

?*C. rubella* Pers. Comm., p. 81 (213) 1797. (Not *C. rubella* Schaeff.)

*C. Swartzii* Dalm. Svensk Botanik, pl. 558. 1818.

PLATE 81

Plants cespitose or single, about 1.5-3 cm. high and varying from slender to stouter (1-2.5 mm. thick in dried state) and from quite simple to flattened and toothed at the end like a cock's comb; color when fresh "a beautiful pink" (Burnham), when dry a dull reddish ochraceous; spores hyaline, smooth, rod-elliptic, 3.5 x 6.6-7.5μ. Basidia 7μ thick with 4 short, delicate sterigmata. Hyphae 11μ thick, without clamp connections.

*Clavaria rosea* is at present in an unsatisfactory state. Plants so labelled in herbaria are not alike, and the species is not represented in the Fries Herbarium. The only simple pink or rosy plants which we have seen from America are those from Colorado distributed by Clements as *C. rosea* and a collection from Vaughns, N. Y., sent us by Burnham. It is from the last that we have drawn up the above rather inadequate description.

It will be noticed that these spores cannot be distinguished from those of *C. helveola,* and except for color no other difference can be made out. Clement's plants are small, cespitose, clavate and have spores just like the above, smooth, long-elliptic, clear, 2.5-3.4 x 5-8μ. Our pale flesh colored plant (No. 2788) that we are considering a form of *C. helveola* is intermediate and has the same spores. Plants received from Romell (Sweden) determined as *C. rosea* are accompanied by colored drawings which are clear pink to reddish pink. The spores of one collection (Helsingland) are noted as 5-7.5 x 2.5-3μ, in agreement with the American collection. At the Kew Herbarium there is no authentic material of *C. rosea.* A collection by Crossland from Hebden Bridge, determined as *C. rosea*, also has spores like the American plants. It is obvious, however, that the plant interpreted as *C. rosea* by Cotton and Wakefield (l.c., p. 188) is different from those above mentioned, and with their interpretation plants so named in the Bresadola Herbarium seem to agree. Bresadola's plants are from Nice (Barla, coll. 1889). The spores are not like those of *C. helveola,* but are distinctly more plump, 4-5.5 x 6-8.5μ. These measurements agree with those given by Cotton and Wakefield. In the Persoon Herbarium there are three plants that in the dry state look like *C. fragilis.* The spores are like those of *C. rosea* from Bresadola, large and plump, 4-6 x 5-8μ. Persoon (Myc. Europ., p. 185) refers to Fries's statement that the apex in drying becomes yellowish (Obs. Myc. 2 : 290. 1818). Of *C. rubella,* Persoon says, "dilute to watery red, 2-4 plants together, but not cespitose or fascicled." There is no plant under this name in his herbarium. If *C. rosea* is to be accepted as a good species, we think it best to accept at present the interpretation of Romell, whose plants are from the same country as those of Dalman and Fries.

For convenience we give below Cotton and Wakefield's interpretation of the species:

"Plants simple, solitary or in groups of 3-7, 2-4 cm. high, fragile, bright rose-pink; taste and smell none. Clubs slender, cylindrical or compressed, equal or tapering upwards, smooth, solid, 2-5 mm. thick, apex blunt or pointed. Stem fairly distinct, paler, sometimes yellowish. Flesh whitish, deep rose beneath the hymenium. Internal structure of frequently septate, irregular hyphae, 7-12μ. in diameter, semi-parenchymatous in transverse section; crystals sometimes present. Basidia conspicuous, 35-40 x 7-10μ, granular or guttulate, sterigmata 4, erect. Spores copious, smooth, hyaline, ovoid or broadly elliptical, 7-10 x 5-6μ. Amongst grass, moss, etc. Rare. . . . Easily distinguished from other British species by the bright, rose-pink colour."

See under *C. helveola* for remarks on *C. incarnata* which may be the same as *C. rosea.*

It is not known which of the above interpretations is represented by the illustrations by Krombholz and Winter given below.

On account of the confusion involved in the publication of *C. rosea* and *C. Swartzii,* it is well to explain that Swartz first used the name *C. rosea* in Acta Holm. (see above) as a manuscript name of Dalman's for a species which the latter intended to describe. Swartz says (translation): "Herr Dalman who has seen the greater part of these species growing in Westergotland has also communicated to me information about a new species which he has found, which he intends to describe under the name of *C. rosea*; it is shorter with entirely white foot. Clubs bent but not twisted, rose and yellow color at top." Later Dalman (J. W., not Olaus, as given by Lindau and Sydow) published as *C. Swartzii* a plate in Svensk Botanik (see above). This was evidently the publication referred to by Swartz. Still later Fries (Obs. Myc. **2**: 290, pl. 5, fig. 2. 1818) described the plant more fully and accepted Dalman's name *C. rosea* as published in Swartz's work. He did not, however, refer here to *C. Swartzii* as a synonym, but did so in his later work.

Illustrations: Dalman, as cited above (as *C. Swartzii*). Shows a rosy pink plant with tips yellowish in withering.
Fries. Obs. Myc. **2**: pl. 5, fig. 2. 1818.
Krombholz. Abbild. u. Beschr., pl. 53, fig. 21. 1841.
Winter. Rabenhorst's Krypt. Fl. **1**: 294, fig. 2. 1884.

New York: Vaughns. Burnham, No. 44. Beside a buried maple stick, woods, July 25, 1916. (U. N. C. Herb.).

Colorado: Clements. (N. Y. Bot. Gard. Herb.).

## Clavaria nigrita Pers. Comm., p. 79 (211). 1797.

### Plates 1 and 82

Single or cespitose in small groups (usually 1-7), the stems not fused above ground, but scarcely touching or nearly touching at base, about 2-7 cm. high and 1-2.5 mm. thick, simple and almost cylindrical or tapering towards the top, with the tips bluntly pointed or not rarely the tip knobbed or a little flattened-expanded or (rarely) with one or two short, antler-like prongs near the end, and sometimes flattened and contorted like a ram's horn throughout, the base slightly contracted into a short stalk which is concolorous and not sharply defined above (the hymenium descending unevenly), but which is made conspicuous below by a white, scurfy tomentum which usually covers about half of the stem and fades upward into a mere pruinosity; except when young and still growing the surface is closely and conspicuously *rugose-wrinkled* from the tip to the base or near it; color when quite young about Saccardo's umber, then darkening to a deep dusky sepia with the tips soon blackening, the base white with tomentum; flesh soft and elastic, usually breaking only in part even when bent on itself, colored like the surface and translucent-watery when quite fresh and damp, becoming lighter and more fibrous-looking later; odorless and quite tasteless, made up of closely packed hyphae about 6.3-9.4$\mu$ thick, their cells much longer than thick.

Spores ovate-elliptic, an eccentric mucro on the larger end, smooth, white, 2.7-3.2 x 5.5-6.3$\mu$. Basidia 4-spored, about 9$\mu$ broad at end, sterigmata about 7$\mu$ long.

Growing in mossy shaded lawns in wet weather in summer.

This remarkable species was found associated with *C. helveola, C. fragilis, Hygrophorus Peckianus, H. conicus, H. chlorophanous,* etc. It is quickly distinguished from any other *Clavaria* by its dark color, elastic texture and close, longitudinal wrinkles. It is very hard to find, being almost invisible against the earth and humus. When dried it becomes quite black, the tomentum of the base becoming tawny.

In the dried state our plants agree well with plants from Ithaca (see below) that Bresadola considered C. *nigrita,* and the spores are the same. We find the spores to be smooth, ovate, 2.2-3 x 4.5-6.6$\mu$. However, Bresadola's description does not agree very well (Fungi Trident. **1**: 62, pl. 67, fig. 4). He describes it as brittle, hollow, flattened, with a central channel and with a fari-nose odor. No mention is made, moreover, of the remarkable, close-set ridges that distinguish our plants. However, the orig-inal description would not exclude our plant. It is described as cespitose, black, long-clavate, 1.9 cm. long, 4 mm. thick, flexuose, subcompressed, apex attenuated, at times erect, at times reflexed, substance fragile, hollow inside, when dry superficially subcorru-gated. This is very like ours except for being hollow and fragile. There is in the Schweinitz Herbarium a collection from Bethlehem labelled *C. nigrita* Pers. Its spores are few and uncertain and mixed with others, but some seem about like those of our plant. The little dried up plants do not help much. There is also a fragmentary collection from Schweinitz at the Kew Herbarium. *Clavaria striata* Pers. is excluded by its much lighter color and constantly hollow club which is only sparsely striated; and *C. lum-bricoides* Wiggers (Primitiae Florae Holsaticae, p. 107. 1780)* differs in light color (sordid white, then grayish ash, then lead color) and hollow club (which is not said to be ridged). The latter may be what we are calling *C. fumosa.*

*Clavaria cinereo-atra* Rick (Broteria **5**: 12. 1906) resembles the present species in its simple, rugose, blackish cinereous clubs, but is quite different in its large subglobose spores, 15$\mu$ in diame-ter. *Clavaria Greleti* Boud. (Bull. Soc. Myc. Fr. **33**: 13, pl. 4. 1917) is of the same size and color as *C. nigrita,* but has sub-spherical spores 7-8$\mu$ thick, and is not said to be sulcate.

Illustration: Bresadola. Fungi Trid. **1**: pl. 67, fig. 4. 1884.

North Carolina: Chapel Hill. No. 2794. Many plants in scattered colonies in moss and thin grass under elms and crepe myrtle in Dr. Mangum's lawn, July 28, 1917.

New York: Ithaca. Atkinson. (Bresadola Herb.). "Sp. hyaline, sub-stramineous, 5-6 x 3$\mu$." In the dry state this looks like ours and has the same spores.

---

* This name does not appear in Saccardo. The book is extremely rare and was published at Kiel, Germany, as a doctor's dissertation. Dr. Barnhart has a copy.

**Clavaria vermiculata** Micheli.    Nova Plant. Gen., p. 209, pl. 87,
    fig. 12. 1729.    (Also Scopoli in Fl. Carn. **2**: 483. 1772.)
  *C. cylindrica* Bull.    Herb. Fr., p. 212, pl. 463, fig. 1. 1789.
  *C. fragilis* Holmsk.    Beata Ruris **1**: 7, pls. 2 and 3. 1790.
  *C. gracilis* Sow.    Engl. Fungi, pl. 232. 1797.
  *C. eburnea* Pers.    Syn. Met. Fung., p. 603. 1801.
  ?*C. canaliculata* Fr.    Obs. Myc. **2**: 294. 1818.    (Not *C. can-
    aliculata* Ehrenb.).
  *C. vermicularis* Fr.    Syst. Myc. **1**: 484. 1821.
  *C. alba* Pers.    Myc. Europ. **1**: 175. 1822.    (Not *C. alba* Pers.
    ibid., p. 161).
  *C. pistilliforma* Pers.    Myc. Europ. **1**: 183. 1822.
  ?*C. corynoides* Pk.    Rept. N. Y. St. Mus. **31**: 39. 1879.
  *C. nivea* Quél.    Asso. Française, p. 3, pl. 3, fig. 11. 1901.
    (22nd. supplement to Champ. Jura, etc.).

PLATES 5, 6, AND 82

Plants gregarious in clusters of two or three to a dozen, or, in
the typical *vermiculata* form, to many; often a good many single
individuals scattered among the clusters; bases when clustered
fused or only approximate, depending on the density of the clusters; 1-6 cm. high (usually about 3-4.5 cm.), rarely reaching a
height of 9 cm. in stout forms in woods (as Burnham, No. 11);
1.5-2.5 mm. thick at thickest point which is at or above the middle,
or when flattened sometimes as much as 4.7 mm. wide, tapering
slightly downward and more rapidly at the base which is decidedly
smaller, and which when looked down on from above is distinctly
marked off from the hymenium by its much more watery and
translucent appearance; not conspicuously mycelioid at the foot,
the apex blunt; usually simple but not rarely with the apex
grooved or knobbed or with an antler-like branch at any point
(very rarely with several flattened branches); typically curved
at base, the club straight or wavy and often channeled or with
longitudinal wrinkles (not closely and regularly furrowed as in
*C. nigrita* and *C. appalachiensis*); color pure watery white when
young and fresh, but nearly always becoming tinted with light
citron yellow at the tip and often with pale creamy flesh color below; in drying all parts become buff color.    Flesh very delicate
and brittle, snapping with a clean break at less than 45° of bending, solid or rarely hollow; almost tasteless, odor none.    Hyphae

in cross section like parenchymatous cells in shape.    After drying
the plant will revive its shape if dropped in water (thus differing
from *C. fumosa*).

Spores (of No. 2751) variable, even in the same plant, white,
smooth, ovate-pip-shaped, 2.6-3.6 x 4.4-6μ.    Basidia (of C. & B.
No. 130) 5.9-6.6μ thick; hymenium 40μ thick; hyphae about 7.4μ
thick, parallel, closely packed, no clamp connections.

Persoon has described two plants as *C. alba,* both in Mycologia
Europaea.    The first (p. 161) is the large, branched plant, considered the same as *C. coralloides* by Fries and Saccardo.    The
other (p. 175) is represented in Persoon's herbarium by six single
plants or cespitose clusters.    They are small, slender and quite
simple and resemble the *fragilis* form of *C. vermiculata.*  We find
that the spores also agree with this species (smooth, oval,
3.5-3.8 x 4-5μ), and we are therefore considering it the same.

The types of *C. eburnea* in Persoon's herbarium look like *C.
fragilis* and have the same spores, oval, smooth, 3.5 x 4.5-6μ.
There is a sheet of *C. vermiculata* in Persoon's herbarium.    The
plants resemble ours closely.    *Clavaria canaliculata* Fr. may be a
form of this species, but Quélet's illustration (Champ. du Jura et
des Vosges, pl. 21, fig. 1) does not look like it.

Cotton is in our opinion quite right in reducing *C. fragilis* to
*C. vermiculata* (*C. vermicularis* Fr.) (Trans. Brit. Myc. Soc.
**3**: 32. 1907).    He refers to the fact that Schroeter had combined
the two in 1885 (Krypt. Flora Schlesien, p. 445), though he
adopted the name *C. fragilis* instead of the earlier one.    After
studying many collections from different states both fresh and
dried, we can find no satisfactory distinctions.    Single or sparsely
grouped plants are often found among dense clumps of the typical
*vermiculata* form and this form also shows often the yellowish tip
in both the densely crowded and single plants.    The spores while
variable in length are essentially similar in all forms and their
length cannot be correlated with other qualities of the plant.
*Clavaria corynoides* is represented in Albany by the type collection.
There are several slender little clubs that look just like small,
scattered plants of the *fragilis* form.    Spores few but those found
are similar, nearly pip-shaped, 3 x 5-6μ.    This may be *C. helveola,*
but the white stem would seem to agree better with *C. vermiculata.*

Peck has a collection from Sand Lake, N. Y., labelled *C. fragilis* var. *solida,* but he does not seem to have published this name.    No difference appears in the dried plants.    A collection in the Curtis Herbarium from E. P. Fries, Upsala, (as *C. fragilis*), is like ours and has similar spores.    Quélet distinguishes between *C. vermiculata* and *C. fragilis,* the former being entirely white, the latter a little yellowish at the apex and smaller.    He does not refer to the solitary habit at times.    There seems to be nothing to distinguish Quélet's *C. nivea* from the yellowish tipped form of this except the slightly longer spores.    Rosenvinge finds that in *C. vermicularis* the cells of the flesh may contain one to four nuclei, and that the mature spores have regularly two nuclei (Ann. Sci. Nat. Bot. Series 7, **3**: 75, pl. 1, figs. 1-3. 1886).    He finds that the spore of *C. fragilis* has but one nucleus (no figures) and thinks that in these cases as in others the number of nuclei in the spore is of systematic importance.    One cannot be sure what plants he determines as *C. vermicularis* and *C. fragilis.*    Juel (cited under *C. cristata*), on the contrary, finds the spore of what he calls *C. fragilis* to have two nuclei (pl. 3, figs. 87-90), resulting from a division in the maturing spore.    He further finds the basidia 4-spored, the basidia and hymenium much as in *C. muscoides* and *C. subtilis.*    The latter author has sent us (as *C. fragilis*) a collection from Upsala which is like ours; spores smooth, oval, 3-3.7 x 3.8-5.4μ.

Illustrations: Barla.   Champ. Nice, pl. 41, figs. 14-16. 1859.
  Bolton.   Hist. Fung. Halifax, pl. 111, fig. 1 (as *C. gracilis*).   1789.
  Britzelmayr.   Hymen. Südb., Clavariei, figs. 58 (as *C. fragilis*) and 56 (as *C. vermicularis*).
  Buller.   Researches on Fungi 2: fig. 62. 1922.   Photograph by Miss E. M. Wakefield.
  Bulliard.   Herb. France, pl. 463, fig. 1 (as *C. cylindrica*).   1789.
  Clements.   Minnesota Mushrooms, fig. 76 (as *C. juncea*).
  Flora Danica, pl. 1783, fig. 2; pl. 1966, fig. 2 (as *C. vermiculata*) ; and pl. 775, fig. 2.
  Hard.   Mushrooms, fig. 395 (as *C. vermicularis*).   1908.
  Holmskjold.   Beata Ruris **1**: pls. 2 and (yellow form) 3 (both as *C. fragilis*). 1790.   Photographed in part by Burt in Ann. Mo. Bot. Gard. **9**: pl. 9, fig. 74. 1922.
  Gillet.   Champ. France **5**: pl. 103 (109) (as *C. fragilis,* both white and yellow forms).   1874-78.

Greville.   Scott. Crypt. Fl. **1**: pl. 37 (as *C. fragilis*).   Yellow, more than doubtful, possibly *C. fusiformis*. 1823.

Michael.   Führer f. Pilzfreunde, Vol. 3, No. 26. 1905.

Micheli.   Nov. Pl. Gen., pl. 87, fig. 12. 1729.

Patouillard.   Tab. Analyt. Fung., fig. 468. 1886.

Quélet.   Champ. Jura Vosg. **1**: pl. 21, fig. 3. 1872.

Sowerby.   Engl. Fungi, pl. 90 (upper figures). 1797; pl. 232 (as *C. gracilis*). 1799.

Swanton.   Fungi and How to Know Them, pl. 29, fig. 6. 1909.

North Carolina: Chapel Hill.   No. 1786.   In leaves in woods, September 14, 1915.   Spores 2.5-2.8 x 4-5$\mu$.   No. 2335.   Mouldy earth on margin of drain under bushes, July 1, 1916.   Spores 2.5-3 x 4.5-6$\mu$.   Basidia 5-5.5$\mu$ thick, four-spored.   Plants simple, very slender, scattered, 2-4 cm. high, 1.5-2 mm. thick near the yellowish top, tapering downward and much smaller at the base, but no sharply defined stalk.   This form is exactly like Peck's *C. corynoides*.   No. 2434.   In short grass and moss in Dr. Mangum's lawn, July 27, 1916.   Spores 2.2-2.6 x 5.6-6.7$\mu$.   No. 2751.   In mossy grass in a yard, July 22, 1917.   Spores 2.6-3.6 x 4.4-6$\mu$.   No. 2759.   In mossy grass in Dr. Mangum's yard (same spot as No. 2434), July 23, 1917.   Spores 2.2-2.9 x 4-6.6$\mu$.   No. 2773.   Mossy grass in lawns, July 26, 1917.   Spores ovate, 2-2.6 x 4.4-5.2$\mu$.   No. 2787.   Same spot as No. 2434, July 27, 1917.   One of these plants was remarkably expanded and branched, looking just like a caribou antler with five prongs and 2.7 cm. wide.   This plant was very pale creamy flesh below and white above, but most of the plants of this collection were white or very pale cream with tips a clear light yellow.   No. 2782.   Same spot as No. 2335, July 27, 1917.

Flat Rock.   Memminger. Mss. (as *C. fragilis*).

Pink Bed Valley.   Murrill and House. (U. N. C. Herb.).

Alabama:   Auburn.   Earl and Baker, No. 55. (N. Y. Bot. Gard. Herb.).

Tennessee:   Burbank.   Thaxter. (Thaxter Herb.).

New Jersey:   Newfield.   Ellis and Everhart.   No. Am. Fungi,. No. 2027. (Kew Herb.).

New York:   West Park. (N. Y. Bot. Gard. Herb.).   "Pure white."

Vaughns.   Burnham.   Nos. 11 and 82.   C. & B. No. 130. (U. N. C. Herb.).

N. Y. Bot. Gard.   Earle.   On earth in woods. (U. N. C. Herb.).   Spores ovate-elliptic, 2.5-2.9 x 4.4-5$\mu$.

Connecticut:   Redding.   No. 28.   In moss under maples, September 6, 1919.   Spores smooth, oblong, 2.3-3.3 x 4.3-5.5$\mu$, shaped like those of *C. fragilis* of Chapel Hill.   No. 4932.   August 2, 1919.   Spores smooth, elliptic to pip-shaped, 2.8 x 4.5-5.5$\mu$. (U. N. C. Herb.).

California:   Mt. Tamalpais.   Eastwood. (N. Y. Bot. Gard. Herb.).   "Pure white like spaghetti."   Spores elliptic, about 3 x 5$\mu$.

## Clavaria citriceps Atk.    Ann. Myc. **6**: 56. 1908.

PLATES 1 AND 82

Plants gregarious, single or cespitose in twos or threes, 3-4 cm. high, slender; club 1.5-2 mm. thick, tapering below into a more slender stalk about 1 cm. long and not sharply distinct; stalk subtranslucent or opaque. Club opaque, bluntly rounded at tip when just grown, but immediately beginning to wither at tip and becoming acute. Color milk-white, with a pale yellow tint toward the tip when young, the withered tip soon a deeper watery yellow. The withering and accompanying change of color proceeding downward until the entire club is involved. Texture quite brittle when very fresh, soon much less brittle in incipient withering; solid or partly hollow. Taste and odor none.

Spores (of No. 3428) minute, smooth, subspherical, 3-3.5 x 4-4.5µ, smaller and more spherical than in *C. vermiculata*. Basidia 4-spored, 3µ thick.

The dried plants of the type at Ithaca are similar in appearance to ours. They are simple, moderately stout, single or 2-4 cespitose. The spores are very few, but those found are the same. They are smaller than the spores of *C. helveola* and average shorter than those of *C. vermiculata;* the shape is, moreover, distinctly more spherical than in either of the others. The species is very near *C. vermiculata* and may be only a variety of it. The latter is often yellowish at the tip, but the present species is yellowish over a larger extent of the club, and the spores are differently shaped and average smaller. For a comparison with *C. luteo-ochracea,* see that species. From the description *C. Michelii* Rea (Trans. Brit. Myc. Soc. **2**: 39. 1903) may not be different from the present species.

Atkinson's description of *C. citriceps* follows:

"Plants subclavate, 1.5 cm. high, 2-3 mm. stout, citron yellow, white below, deeper yellow when dry. Spores oval, white, smooth, with an oil drop, 4-5 x 3µ."

Illustration: Burt. Ann. Mo. Bot. Gard. **9**: pl. 10, fig. 90. 1922.

New York: Ithaca. On ground in woods. C. O. Smith. (Cornell Herb., No. 13461).

Connecticut: Redding. Coker, No. 3428. In moss under maple, August 23, 1919.

**Clavaria fumosa** Pers.   Obs. Myc. **1**: 31.  1796.

PLATES 7 AND 82

Plants densely cespitose and fused at the very base, about 4-10 cm. long and 1.7-5 mm. thick, tapering at the base, sometimes compressed and furrowed, and rarely branched or antlered, no distinctly marked stem, color pale creamy or smoky flesh, the base nearly white and the blunt or rather pointed apex soon becoming brownish and shrunken; texture very tender and moderately brittle, usually snapping with a clean break when bent at about 45°, at times more brittle and snapping very easily, inside solid or in large plants often a little hollowed by the separation of the fibers, and sometimes decidedly hollow in age; no distinct central cylinder.   Practically tasteless and odorless.   In drying the plants become a soaked brownish ochraceous, beginning at the tip, and develop a large hollow which is surrounded by scarcely more than a shell.

Spores white, elliptic, smooth, 3-4 x 4.8-7.5µ.  Basidia 4-spored, 5.5-9µ thick; hymenium about 37µ thick; threads of flesh very densely packed.

This species is closely related to *C. vermiculata* and resembles it in habit and texture.   It may be distinguished by the average larger size, the smoky tint, the tips becoming blackish in withering and by the plant not regaining its shape when placed in water after drying.   This last is a very convenient test for distinguishing the two species without notes on the fresh state.   The spores are very much alike, but those of *C. fumosa* average somewhat longer.   They are slightly smaller than European specimens of *C. fumosa* from Italy (Bresadola) and Germany that we have examined, but the shape is the same.   The German plants (Sydow, Mycotheca germanica, No. 454, Kew Herb.) have spores 3.4-4 x 5.5-8µ (rarely 10µ).   Plants from America (Lloyd) in Bresadola's herbarium are exactly like ours.   According to Fries (Hymen. Europ., p. 675), *C. striata* Pers. (Comm., p. 78) is probably the same as *C. fumosa*.

Illustrations: Britzelmayr.  Hymen. Südb., Clavariei, figs. 34 and 76. Krombholz.  Abbild., pl. 53, fig. 18.  1841.

North Carolina: Chapel Hill.  No. 708.  On ground in woods, June 20, 1913.  The plants only 2.5-3 cm. high.  No. 924.  On ground in woods,

October 16, 1913. No. 1396. On bare earth in woods, October 21, 1914. Plants 1.5-3.5 cm. high. Spores 2.5-3.4 x 5.1-6.8μ. No. 2402. On ground in woods, July 20, 1916. No. 2669. In damp mixed woods, July 14, 1917. No. 2732. Mixed woods, July 21, 1917. No. 2815. Low mixed woods, July 30, 1917. A very light lot, almost white in lower third. No. 3478. Damp ground, August 22, 1919. Spores elliptic, 4 x 5-7.5μ.

Asheville. Miss Burlingham. We cannot find spores on this collection, but the dried plants seem identical with ours.

Pink Bed Valley. Miss Burlingham. (U. N. C. Herb.). Spores 3-3.3 x 5-6μ.

Blowing Rock. Coker and party, No. 5765. On earth in mixed woods, August 24, 1922. (U. N. C. Herb.). Spores 3-3.5 x 5.6-7.4μ.

New York: Vaughns. Coker and Burnham, No. 112. (U. N. C. Herb.). Ithaca. (Albany Herb.).

Connecticut: Redding. Coker. (U. N. C. Herb.). Color pale smoky flesh, tips fading black; spores ovate to pip-shaped, about 3 x 4.8-7μ.

## Clavaria purpurea Müll. Fl. Dan., pl. 837, fig. 2. 1780. (Not C. purpurea Schaeff.)

C. nebulosa Pk. Bull. Torr. Bot. Club 25: 326. 1898.

### PLATES 8 AND 82

Gregarious and densely cespitose in clumps up to 20 individuals, a few single, 2.5-6.5 cm. high, usually crooked and twisted, flattened and channelled, 2-6 mm. broad the flat way, dull brown with a tint of smoky purple (about avellaneous to fawn or wood-brown), nearly cylindrical or narrowly fusiform, rather abruptly pointed, ending below in a short, terete, ill-defined stem which is white from a plush-like tomentum below; apex of club quickly becoming black and withering flabby; surface dull, in many places glaucous. Flesh white, or when soaked nearly the surface color, solid but easily becoming hollow by the separation of the fibers, fragile, dry, tender, and flaky, snapping at 45°; taste none; odor distinctly musty, about like a gourd. Threads of flesh near the hymenium 7.5-11μ thick, in center of club 15-19μ thick, regularly parallel and composed of cells about 55-95μ long, with occasional clamp connections and usually constricted and rounded at the joints.

Spores (of No. 4860) smooth, white, elliptic, 3.7-4.5 x 8.5-12μ. Basidia very inconspicuous, clavate, about 30μ long and 7μ thick with 4 short sterigmata.

Our reference of this plant to *C. purpurea* follows a comparison with European collections. A careful microscopic study of a plant from Romell, Sweden, determined as *C. purpurea,* shows a close agreement with our No. 4860; basidia about 6.6μ thick, 4-spored, the spores smooth, long, 3.7-4.8 x 8-11μ.; threads of flesh up to 10μ thick near center; color when dry blackish above or nearly all over with the surface of a peculiar plush-like character which under the lens looks like sponge. Dried plants of No. 4860 have the same surface, a condition which appears only after drying. In this species the dried plants are always badly collapsed. The Swedish plants, like ours, grew in coniferous woods, and this seems to be true for the species wherever found. At Kew are two collections of *C. purpurea* that are exactly like those from Romell. They are Rabenhorst-Winter, Fungi Europaei, No. 2930 from Finland in pine woods (Karsten) and F. F. Karsten Exs. No. 438. Others so named are very doubtfully the same, and Cotton and Wakefield's description of *C. purpurea* may be based on another species, as they give the spores broader and shorter than in any example we have seen.

American representatives of this species are rarely seen in herbaria. In Albany is a collection from New Brunswick determined as *C. purpurea* that agrees with the above. The plants are lightly cespitose (3-4 together) or single, 1-3 mm. thick, 5-8 cm. high, tapering at both ends, acute, very hollow and often compressed, then up to 5 mm. wide in center, base white, slightly scurfy or nearly smooth. Color in dry state smoky brown, tending to become brown at the tips or at any point. Spores 3.8-4.5 x 8.5-13μ, rarely up to 15.5μ.

Peck's *C. nebulosa* is this species. We have examined the type and find the spores to be smooth, oblong-elliptic, with small eccentric mucro, 3.6-4 x 7.4-11μ. Basidia 5.5-6.5μ thick, 4-spored; hymenium about 45μ thick, without crystals; threads of flesh parallel in longitudinal section, up to 15μ thick in center, smaller just under the hymenium, constricted at the joints, no clamp connections seen.

Illustration: Burt. Ann. Mo. Bot. Gard. **9**: pl. 8, fig. 72 (as *C. nebulosa*). 1922.

North Carolina: Camp Bragg. J. S. Holmes. (U. N. C. Herb.). No. 4860. On coarse sandy soil in pine forest in opening made by a dead pine, April 14, 1921.

Colorado: Dark Canyon. Clements. (N. Y. Bot. Gard. Herb.). Spores 3 x 8-9μ. These are labelled *C. purpurea,* but they are doubtfully that species. A photograph accompanying the plants looks exactly like *C. fumosa* and the spores are scarcely larger than the upper limit in that species.

Newfoundland: Sandy Point. Waghorne. (Albany Herb., as type of *C. nebulosa*; also plants from the type locality in N. Y. Bot. Gard. Herb.).

New Brunswick: Miss Horne. (Albany Herb.).

Utah: Uinta Mtns., alt. 10,000 ft. Watson. (N. Y. Bot. Gard. Herb.). Spores about 3.5-4 x 8.5-9μ.

## Clavaria appalachiensis n. sp.

### PLATES 10 AND 91

Plants simple, single or rarely cespitose in groups of 2-4, gregarious in small numbers; height 3-9 cm., the stem very distinct and sharply defined, 1-4 cm. long, terete, smooth and shining, lemon yellow except for the whitened and subtomentose base. Club 2-6 cm. long, 1.5-5 mm. thick, straight or bent, equal, terete or less often compressed, delicately but very distinctly and regularly ridged and furrowed longitudinally (as in *C. nigrita*); color varying from pale fleshy yellow to light cream or creamy yellow, the rounded tips concolorous, then fading brownish. Flesh of club concolorous, very tender and brittle, snapping clean at an angle of 45°, solid but usually soon hollowed by grubs; stem tough and pliable, not breaking when bent on self, with a cartilaginous rind and softer center. Taste and odor none.

Spores (of No. 5650, type) white, smooth, subspherical, 4.8-6.5 x 5.5-7.2μ, with a large oil drop and a distinct mucro. Basidia 4-spored or (a few) 2-spored, 7.3-8.5μ thick. Threads of flesh parallel, about 4.8μ thick under the hymenium, larger towards the center, where they are about 14μ thick on an average.

We have found the species only in frondose woods on very rotten deciduous logs (probably chestnut) or on pure leaf mold and at an elevation of about 4000 feet. Known at present only from North Carolina and Pennsylvania. It is a well marked plant and easily distinguished by its shining yellow, sharply defined stem; solid, delicately channelled, pale and brittle club, lack of taste and odor and rather large, smooth, subspherical spores. From *C. fusiformis*, which is apparently nearest and has the same spores, it is separated by most of the characters just mentioned as well as by the typically single habit. Usually only one to four are found in one place and the individuals are separated by several inches. The only other simple plant with about the right spores is *C. pellucidula* Britz. (Hymen. Südb., p. 290, fig. 38). Whether it is the same or not cannot be gathered from the incomplete description, but the bases are flexuose and the clubs thickened upward and no distinct stem is mentioned. *Clavaria luteo-ochracea* differs in darker and less distinct stems, smaller spores and basidia and different appearance in the dried state. (See specimens in the N. Y. Bot. Gard. Herb.). *Clavaria Daigremontiana* Boud. with longitudinally ridged clubs is easily different (see note under *C. helveola*).

North Carolina: Blowing Rock. Coker, No. 5650. On rotten deciduous log, August 21, 1922. (Type.) No. 5788. On very rotten portion of a log, August 25, 1922. Spores 4.2-5.5 x 5-6.6$\mu$. No. 5830. In leaf mold and on very rotten wood, August 26, 1922. No. 5861. In humus and on rotting wood, August 27, 1922. Hymenium about 80$\mu$ thick. (All in U. N. C. Herb.).

Pennsylvania: Buck Hill Falls, August, 1920. "Growing singly in light woods; yellowish white." Mrs. Delafield. (U. N. C. and N. Y. Bot. Gard. Herb.). Spores 4.8-6 x 6-7.4$\mu$. Basidia 7.4-8$\mu$ thick, 4-spored, or (not rarely) 2-spored. The dried plants are like the type.

**Clavaria fusiformis** Sowerby.   Engl. Fungi, pl. 234.   1799.
   *C. fasciculata* Villars.   Hist. Plant. Dauph. **3**: 1052. 1789.
   *C. platyclada* Pk.   Bull. Torr. Bot. Club **23**: 419. 1896.
   *C. compressa* Schw.   Trans. Am. Phil. Soc. II, **4**: 182.   1832.
      (Not *C. compressa* Berk. or *C. compressa* Schroeter).
   *C. ceranoides* Pers.   Syn. Met. Fung., p. 594.   1801.

Plates 11, 12, and 82

Plants simple, usually densely fascicled, about 3-7 cm. long or rarely up to 18 cm. long (as in a collection from Sand Lake, N. Y., at Albany), cavernously hollow unless flattened and then often not hollow, cylindrical or more often flattened and grooved on the sides, at times broadest near the tip and narrowly spatulate, again more tapering, abruptly or gradually pointed, 2-12 mm. wide above the middle, tapering downward to a slender, paler base about 1.5-2 mm. thick, which is not sharply defined from the club. Not rarely the plants are much contorted and fantastically curved, resembling at times a ram's horn. Color a deep primrose yellow, or duller brownish yellow, the tip or the whole becoming water-soaked and brownish in age, the very base light yellow and somewhat incrassated. Color unchanged or darker in drying. Texture moderately brittle, cracking at a bend of 45° but not snapping clean. Taste bitter and farinaceous, disagreeable (lost on drying) or varying to quite mild.

Spores (of No. 1362) light yellow (fading to cream color in the herbarium) or in some collections white, subspherical with a small mucro, 5.1-6.7$\mu$ in diameter. Basidia club-shaped, about 7.5$\mu$ thick, mostly 4-spored, but usually also some 2-spored in the same plant, the sterigmata about as long as the diameter of the spores.

The species is widely distributed, occurring on humus or mossy soil in woods. It is easily distinguished by its rather large size, bright color, vaguely defined stem, typically cespitose habit, and rather large, spherical spores. Not rarely there are single plants among the clustered groups. This species with *C. platyclada* Pk. comprises a very puzzling group of forms. The type collection of the latter is well preserved in Albany and we have studied it carefully. In the dried state the plant cannot be distinguished from many collections usually referred to *C. fusiformis* either in appearance or microscopic detail. The plants are not hollow but neither are many flattened plants of *C. fusiformis*. In the type of *C. platyclada* the spores are smooth, spherical, 4.4-6.6$\mu$ thick; basidia 5.5-6.6$\mu$ thick, mostly 4-spored, but a good many 2-spored; hymenium about 90$\mu$ thick, light olivaceous under the microscope.

While at Blowing Rock in August, 1922, we studied the group carefully in the fresh condition, hoping to distinguish two species. We first found that the taste varied from quite bitter to quite mild in different collections; next it was found that some lots cast a pure white spore print while with others brought in the same day the spore print was distinctly creamy yellow. Flattened members of any lot were usually not hollow, while terete members were.

Our early hopes that we had found distinctive characters were soon broken down by entire lack of any correlation of characters. In No. 5790 the taste was not bitter, the spores were creamy yellow, and the clubs were hollow; in No. 5507 the spores were pure white in a good print, the taste was not bitter and the clubs were hollow; in No. 5586 the taste was rankly bitter, the spores were pure white, and some plants (not flattened) were hollow; in No. 5679 the taste was mild, the spores were white, and the clubs were hollow. In two collections from the identical spot and evidently from the same mycelium taken at Hartsville, S. C., one in 1916, the other in 1917, the first (No. 12) was quite bitter, the second (No. 26) was scarcely bitter but distinctly farinaceous. The spores in both were yellowish. It then appears that if there are two species they can at present be separated only by the color of the fresh spores in good prints, and as the European form of *C. fusiformis* is said to have the spores yellow when fresh (Cotton and Wakefield, p. 184) it may still be that *C. platyclada* is a slightly different plant (form or variety) distinguished by its white spores and perhaps by other slight differences that have so far escaped us. *Clavaria compressa* Schw. is almost certainly this. A collection under that name in the Schweinitz Herbarium has spores subspherical, smooth, 4.8-6 x 6-7μ. In the Curtis Herbarium is also a fragment from the Schweinitz Herbarium, so named, which is about 2.5-3 mm. broad, flat and channelled, with spores 5.5 x 6.7μ; the basidia 2-4 spored. Persoon (Myc. Europ., p. 178) referred to *C. fusiformis* the plant which he first described (Comm., p. 73) as *C. fasciculata,* but later gave the latter as a synonym of *C. inaequalis.* However, his interpretation of *C. inaequalis* could hardly have been the one now accepted. The description of *C. fasciculata* Villars while short is good and leaves little doubt that it is the same as the present species. The only plant of that name in Persoon's herbarium is labelled *C. fasciculata* DC.,* sent by Mangeat. It looks just like *C. fusiformis* and has the same spores, which are subspherical with a sharp mucro, 5-6 x 6-7.5μ (counting mucro).

---

* DeCandolle described *C. fasciculata* in Syn. Plant. Flora Gall., p. 19, 1806. without giving any authority, and this may have given rise to a misunderstanding in regard to the author of the species.

In the Schweinitz Herbarium a collection of this is labelled *C. inaequalis* Fr., with spores as above described, 5.5-6.5μ in diameter.

Peck reports *C. austera* Britz. (Rept. **54**: 155. 1901) and says: "Ground in woods. Lake Placid. Sept. Miss N. L. Marshall. A small tufted species allied to *C. inaequalis,* from which it may be distinguished by the greenish tint of the clubs." We have examined this collection and find the spores exactly like those of *C. fusiformis,* 5.5-6μ thick. The real *C. austera* can hardly be this as they are shown by Britzelmayr as *single* olive green clubs. We think Miss Marshall's collection is a somewhat greenish form of *C. fusiformis. Clavaria coliformis* Boud. (Bull. Soc. Myc. Fr. **33**: 11, pl. 3, fig. 2. 1917) may be an abnormal form of this.

Illustrations: Burt. Ann. Mo. Bot. Gard. **9**: pl. 8, fig. 67 (as *C. compressa*) ; fig. 68 (as *C. platyclada*). 1922.

Britzelmayr. Hymen. Südb., Clavariei, fig. 26.

Cooke. Handb. Brit. Fung., p. 335. 1871.

Dumée. Nouvel Atlas Champ., pocket edition, pl. 56. 1911.

Gillet. Champ. Fr. **5**: pl. 104 (110). 1874-78.

Hard. Mushrooms, fig. 397. 1908.

Hussey. Ills. Brit. Fung. **1**: pl. 18. 1847.

McIlvaine. Am. Fung., pl. 138, fig. 1. 1900.

Patouillard. Tab. Fung., fig. 565. 1887.

Price. Illustrations of Fungi, pl. 14, fig. 93. 1865.

Sowerby. As cited above and also pl. 235 (as *C. rugosa*). Pl. 234 is photographed in Ann. Mo. Bot. Gard. **9**: pl. 8, fig. 66. 1922.

North Carolina: Chapel Hill. No. 1362. On mouldy earth in road, October 16, 1914.

Pink Bed Valley. Murrill and House, No. 368. July 1908. Also Burlingham, 1907. (N. Y. Bot. Gard. Herb.).

Blowing Rock. Atkinson. (Cornell Herb.). Also Coker. Nos. 5507, 5586, 5679, 5790. (U. N. C. Herb.).

South Carolina: Hartsville. Coker, No. 12. In low, mossy, flat woods under maples and long leaf pine, September 9, 1916. Taste very bitter, also farinaceous. Spores yellowish, 5-6μ thick. No. 26. On same spot as above, June 4, 1917. Taste farinaceous but scarcely bitter. Spores as in No. 12. No. 64. Again on same spot, June 15, 1918.

Ravenel, No. 1080. (Kew Herb.).

Pennsylvania: Bethlehem. (Schw. Herb. and Curtis Herb.). Spores 5 x 6.5μ.

Pocono Lake Preserve. Vogler. (U. N. C. Herb.).

Buck Hill Falls. Mrs. Delafield. (N. Y. Bot. Gard. Herb.).

New York: Ithaca. Atkinson. (Cornell Herb.).
  Numerous other places in New York are represented by collections at
  Albany and in the N. Y. Bot. Gard. Herb.
Massachusetts: Sprague. (Curtis Herb. and Kew Herb., as *C. tetragona*.)
  Spores smooth, 4-4.5 x 4.5-5.2µ.
  Farlow. (Kew Herb.).
Vermont: Stratton. Spores spherical, 5.5-7.5µ.
  Newfane. Miss Hibbard. (U. N. C. Herb.).
New Hampshire: Chocorua. Farlow. (U. N. C. Herb. from Farlow Herb.,
  as *C. inaequalis*). Spores smooth, subspherical, 5-6.5µ thick. Basidia
  4.5-6µ thick, usually 4-spored (rarely 2).
Maine: Davis. (Albany Herb., as *C. platyclada*).

**Clavaria pulchra** Pk. Rept. N. Y. St. Mus. **28**: 53, pl. 1, fig.
    10. 1876.
  *C. angustata* Pers. (Sense of Schw.). Comm., p. 72 (204),
    pl. 1, fig. 3. 1797.
  *C. persimilis* Cotton. Trans. Brit. Myc. Soc. **3**: 182. 1909.

PLATES 1, 6, 13, AND 82

Plants gregarious, mostly cespitose in clusters of several to
about twenty, often single or in twos and threes, not densely fascicled or fused at base in large groups as in *C. fusiformis* or *C.
fumosa*, but several individuals may be so fused; 1.5-7.4 cm.
high, 1.2-6 mm. thick near the top, long club-shaped or nearly
cylindrical, at times compressed and grooved, tapering downward,
the stem not distinct from the club, except for decidedly lighter
color usually, the base incrassated or not so; apex bluntly rounded,
not apiculate; surface smooth, egg-yellow, the base and at times
the apex lighter, or the apex may be darker. Flesh toughish,
elastic, cracking but not snapping at 45°, stuffed or varying to im-
perfectly or distinctly hollow at maturity; taste sweetish and pleasant, odor none.

Spores (of No. 1717) white, oblong-ovoid with a prominent
mucro on one side near the large end, usually with a distinct oil
drop, 4.6 x 6-7µ. Basidia (in dried plants) about 5-7µ thick, 4-
spored, smaller than in *C. fusiformis*.

On bare earth or decaying leaves in deciduous or mixed woods.
  The type of *C. pulchra* agrees in all respects with our plants so
far as can be seen in the dried state, and the spores are of the
same characteristic shape, 4.4 x 6.7µ. Our plants (No. 1717) have

been compared with specimens of *C. persimilis* from Wales (Dr. Cotton), and seem clearly the same, the spores also having the characteristic shape, but running a little shorter than in Chapel Hill plants. The British plants are described by Cotton as having the internal structure composed of loosely packed, longitudinally-running filaments 3-6µ in diameter. Our collections vary from stuffed to hollow.

This species is nearest *C. fusiformis,* which normally differs in larger size, fasciculate habit, strong taste and different spores. Separate plants of the latter, which are often found among colonies of cespitose ones, are distinguished from *C. pulchra* by their company, their spores, and their bitter or farinaceous taste. From *C. helveola, C. pulchra* is easily distinguished by the deeper color, and the very different spores. At the New York Botanical Garden is a collection of this from Bresadola labelled in error *C. similis* Boud. and Pat. The spores are smooth, 4.5 x 6-6.8µ, shaped as in *C. pulchra. Clavaria similis* Boud. and Pat. has strongly warted spores. In the Bresadola Herbarium plants from Ithaca, N. Y., (C. O. Smith) determined by Bresadola as *C. platyclada* Pk. are *C. pulchra,* as shown by appearance and spores. The type of *C. angustata* no longer exists, but a good collection in the Curtis Herbarium from the Schweinitz Herbarium so labelled has spores like the present species, sub-oval, 5-6.3 x 6.3-7µ. From the description and figure the real *C. angustata* may be *C. inaequalis.*

Illustrations : Burt. Ann. Mo. Bot. Gard. **9** : pl. 10, fig. 93. 1922.
 Peck. As cited above.

North Carolina : Chapel Hill. No. 1717. In sandy soil in deep woods, September 9, 1915. Clubs hollow. No. 3149. Near same spot as No. 1717, August 9, 1918. In some of the groups the stems were distinctly lighter than the club for at least a cm. Others showed less difference. Spores 4.5-5 x 6-6.7µ, with large oblique apiculus. No. 3767. Mixed woods by Battle's Branch, November 18, 1919. No. 5877. Low, mixed woods, September 30, 1922. Spores typical.
 Blowing Rock. Coker and party. (U. N. C. Herb.). Some of these plants were very large for this species, but the spores are typical.

Alabama : Atkinson. (Cornell Herb.).

New York : Catskill Mts. Gereshoy. (U. N. C. Herb.). Spores as usual, about 4.5 x 6.3µ.

Chappaqua.  (N. Y. Bot. Gard. Herb., as *C. vermicularis*).  Spores 5.5 x
    6.5-7μ.
Frostburg.  (Albany Herb.).  Spores typical, 4.8 x 6.6μ.
Forge.  Peck.  (Albany Herb.).
Sandlake.  Peck.  (Albany Herb.).  Spores typical.
Tripoli.  Burnham, No. 83.  (U. N. C. Herb.).
Ithaca.  C. O. Smith.  (Bresadola Herb., as *C. platyclada*).
Connecticut:  Redding.  Coker.  4 collections, September 6, 1919.  (U. N.
    C. Herb.).  Spores as usual, 4-4.8 x 5-7.5μ.
Vermont:  Newfane.  Miss Hibbard.  (U. N. C. Herb.).
Maine:  Sebec Lake.  Murrill.  (N. Y. Bot. Gard. Herb.).

## Clavaria aurantio-cinnabarina Schw.  Trans. Am. Phil. Soc. II, 4: 183.  1832.

### PLATES 1 AND 82

Plants loosely clustered, some single, 1.5-4 cm. high, simple,
the tips blunt or rather pointed, and sometimes a little flattened
or knobbed, 1.2-2.6 mm. thick, nearly equal, at times channeled,
usually crooked, base without a distinct stem or color; entire plant
a deep orange-red (orange-chrome of Ridgway); flesh moderately
brittle, not snapping with a clean break and only after a bend of
45° or more, color of surface when very fresh, but soon the surface becomes lighter by fading to buffy orange, leaving the flesh a
deeper color, solid, quite mild and almost tasteless, but with a distinct though not very strong fetid-aromatic odor, a little like a
wharf or sewer but not so bad (noted by all of four persons who
tested it).  The base may be faintly paler than the club, but where
the hymenium ends can scarcely be distinguished even with a lens.
In drying the plants become a lighter orange-buff.  The tips when
dry are sharply different from the clubs, being very smooth, not
wrinkled, not shrunken and therefore larger and of a deeper
ochraceous red color.  A section shows them to be sterile over the
upper half.  They look in the larger plants like distinct caps.
This contrasting tip in the dried state is also found in *C. vernalis*,
*C. filipes* (No. 2804) and to a less noticeable extent in *C. helveola*.
    Spores (of No. 2801) apparently yellowish (from a thin print
on a slide), but perhaps white, smooth, subspherical, with an eccentric mucro of moderate size, most of the space occupied by the
cheesy or oily matter, the vacuoles eccentric as in *C. fusiformis*,

4.8-5.5 x 5.5-6.3μ.    Basidia 5.5-7.4μ thick, 4-spored (rarely 2-spored) ; hymenium 100-130μ thick, set with many small crystals; hyphae 4.4-5.5μ thick, clamp connections few.

Easily distinguished from others of the same shape and habit by the deep rich orange-red color, solid flesh and subspherical, smooth spores.

There is a good collection of this from Schweinitz (Bethlehem, Pa.) in the Curtis Herbarium.   The plants look like ours and have the same smooth, unshrunken tips like caps and the same spores, 5.1-6.5 x 6.5-7.4μ.    There is also at Kew a collection from Schweinitz of similar appearance.   American plants determined as *Clavaria miniata* Berk. (Hooker's Lon. Journ. Bot. **2**: 516 (416 in error). 1843) are almost certainly the present species, as indicated both by appearance and spores (see below).   The type of *C. miniata* at Kew Herbarium from Africa has about the same appearance, and the spores, while not abundant enough to be convincing, are apparently smooth, subspherical, 5.5-7.4μ thick.   In Bresadola's herbarium is a specimen of *C. aurantia* Cooke (Grev. **16**: 33. 1887) from Victoria (No. 50, probably a part of type), which has exactly the appearance of the present species in the dried state and is probably a close relative.   The spores are slightly different, being a little more elongated, 4.5-5 x 7-7.4μ.    *Clavaria straminea* Cotton (Trans. Brit. Myc. Soc. **3**: 265, 1910 and **3**: pl. 11, 1909, which is incorrectly labelled *C. persimilis*) has almost identical spores, but is described as straw colored with a cinnamon yellow stem that is darker than the hymenium and as being odorless.   It is hardly probable that our plant is the same as *C. cardinalis* Boud. et Pat. (Jour. de Bot. **2**: 341, pl. 8, fig. 2.   1888. Also Icon. Myc. **1**: pl. 174) which has the same color, size and spores.   There is a collection of it at Albany sent by Patouillard which we have examined.   They do not seem just the same as ours, the tips not being set off in the dry plant by non-shrinking and the color is not quite the same.   Moreover, they grew on the trunk of a fern, *Todea barbara,* brought to Paris from Australia, while the American species grows on earth.   The spores are subspherical, 5.5μ in diameter, and are like those of our plant.   Another authentic plant of *C. cardinalis* from Patouillard at Kew is

like the one at Albany. The spores are smooth, subspherical,
5 x 6μ. *Clavaria rosacea* Henn. (Fungi Madagaskar, p. 19, pl. 2,
fig. 5) seems indistinguishable from the last except in color, which
is given as rosy. Compare also *C. laeta* B. & Br. (Journ. Linn.
Soc. **14**: 76. 1875 [1873]). The plant Lloyd reports from Florida
as *C. laeta* is probably the same as ours (Letter 63, p. 9). From
the description it seems probable that *C. helicoides* Pat. and Dem.
(Bull. Soc. Myc. Fr. **26**: 44. 1910) is the present species, but we
have seen no specimen.

Illustration: Burt. Ann. Mo. Bot. Gard. **9**: pl. 8, fig. 65. 1922.

North Carolina: Chapel Hill. No. 2801. On earth with humus, low
    damp woods near Judge's Spring, July 28, 1917. No. 2816. Same spot
    as No. 2801, July 30, 1917. No. 5230. In swampy, deciduous woods,
    June 24, 1922. Base of stem slightly enlarged and whitened with my-
    celium. Spores 4-4.8 x 4.8-6μ.

South Carolina: Santee Canal. Ravenel. (Curtis Herb. 992 (101). Little
    reddish, slender clubs 5-12 mm. high, so nearly covered with the glue as
    not to yield spores. As *C. miniata*). This is probably the collection
    reported by Berkeley in Grevillea **2**: 17. 1873.

Alabama: Auburn. Wet clay mixed with rotting leaves, December 3, 1899.
    Mrs. F. S. Earle. "Simple, bright orange-yellow, basidia with two
    sterigmata." The dried plants in this collection are very slender; an-
    other collection (November, 1900) is stouter. Both have the same color,
    yellowish buff, and the same spores and peculiar tips. Spores sub-
    spherical, smooth, 4-5 x 5-6μ. Basidia two-four-spored, about 7μ thick.
    Also another collection on damp ground. July 13, 1897. F. S. Earle.
    Spores 4.8-5.5μ. "Scattered over considerable area in small tufts, simple
    or branched sparingly from base, dark reddish orange, tips slender and
    soon drying, becoming darker when dry." (Three above in U. N. C.
    Herb.).

Pennsylvania: Bethlehem. Schweinitz. (Curtis Herb.).
    McIlvaine. (Albany Herb., as *C. aurantio-cinnabarina*.). It may be cor-
    rectly determined, but looks more like *C. fusiformis*.

New York: Cold Spring Harbor. Dodge and Seaver. (N. Y. Bot. Gard.
    Herb., as *C. rosea*). Spores 4.8-7μ in diameter.

    Burnt Hills. Peck. (Albany Herb., as *C. miniata*). These little plants
    are cespitose, simple, short, thick, sharp-pointed above and also con-
    tracted below; in dried state buffy yellow or dull ochraceous. Spores
    smooth, globose, with a small mucro, about 5μ in diameter.

## Clavaria asperulospora Atk.    Ann. Myc. **6**: 55.   1908.

PLATE 81

This seems to be a good species with spores unlike any other *Clavaria* of similar form.   The dried plants are quite simple, much shrunken, apparently not hollow, nearly black, the very base paler.   A part of the type from Bresadola's herbarium shows the spores to be spherical, asperulate, with a distinct, pointed mucro, 4.8-6.2μ thick (omitting mucro).

Atkinson's description follows:

"Plants clustered, wood-brown, 4-7 cm. high, 2-3 mm. stout, cylindrical, blunt, tapering below.   Basidia abruptly clavate, 30 x 10-12μ, 4-spored.   Spores globose, white, echinulate, pedicellate, 6-7μ."

Illustration:   Burt.   Ann. Mo. Bot. Gard. **9**: pl. 10, fig. 99.   1922.

New York:   Ithaca.   Whetzel.   (Cornell Herb., type).

## Clavaria inaequalis Müller.    Fl. Danica, pl. 836., fig. 1.   1780.
  ?*C. polymorpha rufa*.   Fl. Danica, pl. 775, fig. 1.   1778.
  ?*C. rufa* Pers.   Comm., p. 71 (203).   1797.
   *C. echinospora* Boud. & Pat.   Journ. de Bot. **2**: 341.   1888.
      (Not *C. echinospora* Berk. & Br. or *C. echinospora* P. Henn. Monsunia **1**: 141.   1899).
   *C. similis* Boud. & Pat.   Journ. de Bot. **2**: 446, pl. 8, fig. 1. 1888.   (Not *C. similis* Pk.).
   *C. dissipabilis* Britz.   Hymen. Südb., p. 289, Clav. fig. 28. 1885.
  ?*C. bifurca* Bull.   Herb. Fr., p. 207, pl. 264.   1785.

PLATES 50 AND 81

This species has been badly confused, but is now easily recognized through the work of Cotton, who has cleared up the difficulties (Trans. Brit. Myc. Soc. **2**: 163.   1908).   It has been often reported in America, but most if not all such reports (except Burt's recent one from Massachusetts and Vermont) were based on some other interpretations of the species than the one here accepted.    We have not yet met with this in the living state nor have we seen a native specimen in any American herbarium, though many are under this name.    Most of such are *C. helveola*. The following is Cotton's description in Massee's British Fungi and Lichens, p. 434.*

"Hymenophore simple or rarely with 1-2 short branches, cylindrical or compressed, tip blunt or pointed, deep yellow to rich orange, flesh white, 1-2½ in. high (spores colourless, sub-globose, sharply warted, 5-6μ diam.).

"Often confused with *C. fusiformis,* from which it differs by its deeper colour, not growing in dense tufts, and globose, warted spores.    Among grass in woods, parks, lawns, etc.    Common."

*Clavaria echinospora,*** which seems certainly to be the same, was separated from *C. inaequalis* principally on the strongly warted spores.    Cotton also thinks *C. rufa* the same (Trans. Brit. Myc. Soc. **3**: 33.   1909).    *Clavaria geoglossoides* Boud. and Pat. (Bull. Soc. Myc. Fr. **8**: 42, pl. 6, fig. 1.   1892) may be the same, but we think there is an error in their interpretation of the spores, which are described as smooth then sparsely warted, and some are drawn smooth, while others are warted like those of *C. inaequalis*. The assumption would then be that the smooth ones are immature. A plant in the herbarium of the University of Paris (Rouen, Boudier) labelled *C. similis* var. *geoglossoides* is evidently the same as this.    The name was apparently provisional and never published.    We have a collection of *C. inaequalis* from Epping Forest, England (Cotton).    Spores about 4.5-5.5μ in diameter.

*Clavaria inaequalis* is listed by Curtis as common in damp woods but it is almost certain that his plant was not the one defined above.

Fries considers *C. bifurca* a synonym of *C. inaequalis*.    In Persoon's herbarium plants labelled *C. bifurca* may be this, but we could find no good spores.    We have examined plants of *C. similis* from Leyden (Miss Cool) and from Westphalia in Bresadola's herbarium and find the spores as described, about 5-7μ thick and strongly warted.

---

* For a fuller description, see Trans. Brit. Myc. Soc. **6**: 189. 1919.
   ** The name *C. similis* was substituted by the authors on finding the first published name preoccupied.

Illustrations: Boudier and Patouillard.   Journ. de Bot. 2: pl. 8, figs. 1a
    and 1b (as *C. echinospora*). 1888.
Boudier and Patouillard.   Journ. de Bot. 2: pl. 8, fig. 1 (as *C. similis*).
    1888.
Britzelmayr.   As cited above.
Cotton.   Trans. Brit. Myc. Soc. 3: pl. 11, fig. B. (spores).   1909.
Müller.   As cited above.   Photographed in part by Burt in Ann. Mo. Bot.
    Gard. 9: pl. 9, fig. 89. 1922.
Sowerby.   Engl. Fungi, pl. 253 (lower figs.).   1800.

Reported by Burt from Massachusetts and Vermont (l.c., p. 56).

## Clavaria amethystinoides Pk.   Bull. Torr. Bot. Club 34: 102. 1907.

### Plates 9, 14, 82, and 83

Plants single, gregarious, never cespitose (rarely two together), up to 6.3 cm. tall, distinctly stalked, compressed and
channelled, at times quite simple, but usually cusped or antlered
or palmately branched or variously lobed, much in the fashion of
the *Krombholzii* or *rugosa* form of *C. cristata,* or at times even
more branched like *C. muscoides;* the tips blunt or pointed and
blackening in age; club when simple tapering downward from the
broadened end, 3-6 mm. thick; when branched up to 3.6 cm. broad;
the distinct stalk 0.6-3.5 cm. long, the sterile part (or true stalk)
up to 2.6 cm. long to the descending hymenium, about 0.7-2.2 mm.
thick, nearly glabrous except for the velvety tomentose base, the
stem and usually the club somewhat crooked; color of hymenium
a pale livid flesh color (about fleshy tan or pale drab) at times approaching fawn (in the type said to be very pale lilac), the stem
a little darker and more watery-looking; flesh solid and color of
surface in all parts, soft and rather waxy-brittle in the club, tough
and pliable in the stem; taste slight, mildly flattish alkaline, odor
none.

Spores (of Hartsville, No. 42) pure white, plentiful, smooth,
almost filled with a slightly eroded sphere, subspherical, 5.9-7.5
x 7.5-8.5μ.   Basidia (of No. 4532) 7-9.7 x 22μ, with two sterigmata.   Hymenial layer 37-130μ thick, proliferating irregularly
and containing embedded spores.   Hyphae of flesh loosely packed,
about 9μ in diameter with many septa and a few clamp connections.

The stem may be distinguished from the hymenium with the
naked eye by a slight or decided difference in color, and under a
lens by different surface texture.   The plant has the spores and

other microscopic detail of *C. cristata* and is most like the rugose form of that species, but it differs in the more consistently discrete stem and different color.   However, as some forms of *C. rugosa* have very distinct stems, it may be that the present species is also nothing more than a form of the polymorphic *C. cristata*. Similar plants were collected by Curtis years ago at Society Hill, S. C., and determined as *C. fuliginea*.   In regard to this collection, Curtis says (in Curtis-Berkeley Ms. at Kew Gardens, copy at N. Y. Bot. Gard.) : "Base of stem pale brown.   Branches white clay color, solid, brittle, turgid, becoming hollow, tipped with brown.  July.  Shade of trees."

We have carefully compared the type of *C. amethystinoides* with our plants and find them closely similar.   The microscopic detail in both cases is that of all other species of the *C. cristata* group, and we are entering this detail under the collections cited below.   We have found the thickness of the hymenium to be of no importance in classification in this group, as it increases with the age of the plant.

*Clavaria Barlae* Bres. is near this species, but the color of the dried plants is brighter and the spores are smaller, "4-5 x 5-6$\mu$." (compared in the Bresadola Herb.).

Near this species seems also *C. gigantula* Britz. which is very similar in shape and with a distinct stalk, but that is paler and larger and has larger spores, 9-10 x 10-12$\mu$.   (Bot. Centralblatt **71**: 95. 1897 and *Clavaria* fig. 98).   *Clavaria ligata* Britz. (Hymen. Südb. **5**: 290, fig. 37) seems also related and is possibly the same.

Illustration: Burt.  Ann. Mo. Bot. Gard. **9**: pl. 8, fig. 63.  1922.

North Carolina: Chapel Hill.  No. 4532.  In damp sphagnum bog among moss, July 26, 1920.  Characters exactly iike No. 42 except running larger and more branched; a few quite simple.  In a few cases part of the hymenium was darker, approaching fawn.  Spores spherical, 7.4-9$\mu$ in diameter.  No. 4565.  By pond opposite cemetery, pine woods, damp soil, July 27, 1920.  Hymenium 37$\mu$ thick in young plants and up to 110$\mu$ thick in old ones.  No. 5296.  On damp, mossy bank under beech, July 6, 1922. A very large form, up to 10 cm. high. Spores 6-8 x 7.4-10$\mu$.

Blowing Rock.  Coker and party, No. 5626.  In black leaf mold at Glen Mary Falls, August 20, 1922.  (U. N. C. Herb.).

South Carolina: Hartsville.  No. 42.  In loose sandy soil or with thin moss and liverworts under *Pinus taeda* with undergrowth of sweet gum, etc.,

August 7, 1917. No. 63. In black humus under *Cyrilla* and red maple, damp, flat woods in Ellis's pasture, June 15, 1918.

Society Hill. Curtis, No. 1265. (Curtis Herb. and Kew Herb., as *C. fuliginea?*).

Massachusetts: Stow. Davis. (N. Y. Bot. Gard. Herb. Part of type). Spores 5.5-7.4 x 7.4-8.5μ. Hymenium about 110-130μ thick; basidia about 5.8μ thick. Threads of flesh much intertwined, up to 7.4μ thick.

## Clavaria ornatipes Pk. Bull. N. Y. St. Mus. **122**: 18, 160. 1908.
*Lachnocladium ornatipes* (Pk.) Burt. Ann. Mo. Bot. Gard. **9**: 65, pl. 11, fig. 102. 1922.

### PLATES 9, 15, AND 83

Single and scattered, sparsely gregarious, 2.5-9 cm. tall; stem long, slender, distinct, dark brown, hispid on the lower third or half; fertile part smooth or often rugose, usually thicker, simple (rarely) or divided into two or several upright, often palmate branches; color, excepting the stem, grayish, fleshy brown; tips blackish in fading; texture fleshy and semi-brittle as in *C. cristata*, and taste the same as in that species.

Spores white, smooth, subspherical, 8.5-9.3 x 9.3-10.5μ. Basidia 7.4-10μ thick, about 30μ long, 2-spored; hymenium about 100μ thick; hyphae very variable and irregular, with many septa, no clamp connections. Just under the hymenium the threads are replaced by large swollen cells.

This unique and inconspicuous species is not rarely found if one knows how to look for it. In the south it is known only from the mountains. It occurs in low, swampy woods, usually among mosses, and is nearest *C. amethystinoides*. Peck first reported this as *C. trichopus* Pers. ( Rept. N. Y. St. Mus. **24**: 82. 1872), but later with good reason considered it as distinct. Persoon's description and figure of *C. trichopus* would certainly exclude the present plant, which is far from white at all stages. The stiff, red-brown hairs which clothe the lower third (¼-½) of the plant make the species easy to recognize, and sharply distinguish it from all others. Overholts reports it from State College, Pennsylvania (Mycologia **12**: 135. 1920).

Illustration: Burt.  As cited above.

North Carolina: Blowing Rock.  Coker and party, No. 5620.  In deep
woods mold near Glen Mary Falls, August 20, 1922.  Typical.  Spores
7.4-8.2 x 8.5-9.5μ.  No. 5671.  In moss and humus on Cone estate,
August 22, 1922.  Up to 8.8 cm. high.  Also several other collections
in similar locations.  (All in U. N. C. Herb.).

Virginia: Mountain Lake.  Murrill.  Abundant on a wet clay bank, July
1909.  (U. N. C. Herb.).  Spores 8-8.5 x 9.3-10.5μ.

New York: Sand Lake.  Peck.  Wet places among sphagnum in woods.
(Albany Herb.  Type).

Ithaca.  Atkinson.  (Bresadola Herb., Stockholm).

Catskills.  Peck.  (Albany Herb., as *C. argillacea*).  Spores subspherical,
about 7.5-9.3μ thick.

Connecticut: Redding.  Coker, No. 29.  At base of a hemlock and in moss
on rock by brook, September 7, 1919.

Massachusetts: Stow.  In a swamp at base of a maple in woods composed
mostly of deciduous trees, a conifer here and there.  Simon Davis.
(Albany Herb. and U. N. C. Herb.).  Mr. Davis says: "Attracted my
attention because of its two colors.  The branches being of a dull leaden
gray, while the stem was fuscous and adorned with erect, sharp-pointed
spines."

**Clavaria cristata** (Holmsk.) Pers.  Syn. Met. Fung., p. 591.
1801.

*C. coralloides* L. (in part).  Fl. Suecica, 2nd. ed., p. 457. 1755.

*C. albida* Schaeff.  Fung. Bavar., p. 116, pl. 170. 1763.

*C. laciniata* Schaeff.  Fung. Bavar., p. 122, pl. 291. 1770.

*C. cinerea* Bull.  Herb. Fr., p. 204, pl. 354. 1787.

*C. rugosa* Bull.  Herb. Fr., p. 206, pl. 448, fig. 2. 1789.  (Not
*C. rugosa* in sense of Sowerby, Engl. Fungi, pl. 235.)

*C. elegans* Bolton.  Hist. Fung. Halifax, p. 115, pl. 115. 1789.

*C. amethystea* Bull.  Herb. Fr., p. 200, pl. 496, fig. 2. 1790.

*Ramaria cristata* Holmsk.  Beata Ruris **1**: 92, pl. 23. 1790.
(p. 97, Persoon's ed.  1797).

*C. fimbriata* Pers.  N. Mag. Bot. (Romer's), p. 117. 1794.

*C. trichopus* Pers.  Comm., p. 50 (182), pl. 4, fig. 3. 1797.

*C. fallax* Pers.  Comm., p. 48 (180). 1797.

*C. palmata* Pers.  Comm., p. 45 (177). 1797.  (Not *C. palmata* Scop.)

*C. grisea* Pers.  Comm., p. 44 (176). 1797.

*C. grossa* Pers.  Comm., p. 50 (182). 1797.

*C. macropus* Pers.    (Sense of Fries and Bresadola).    Comm.,
    p. 51 (183), pl. 1, fig. 2.  1797.

*C. fuliginea* Pers.    Myc. Europ. **1**: 166. 1822.

*C. alba* Pers.    Myc. Europ. **1**: 161. 1822.

*C. cristata* var. *curta* Junghuhn.    Linnaea **5**: 407, pl. 7, fig.
    2b. 1830.

*C. cristata* var. *flexuosa* Junghuhn.    Linnaea **5**: 407, pl. 7,
    fig. 2a. 1830.

*C. afflata* Lagg.    (Sense of Bresadola).    Flora **19** (1): 231.
    1836.

*C. Krombholzii* Fr.    Epicr., p. 572. 1838.

*C. lilacina* Fr.    Hymen. Europ., p. 667.   1874.   (Not *C. li-
    lacina* Jungh. in Lév. Champ. exot., p. 216. 1844).

?*C. dichotoma* Godey in Gillet.    Hymen. Fr., p. 766.  1874.

*C. Schaefferi* Sacc.    Syll. Fung. **6**: 693. 1888.

*C. sphaerospora* E. & E.    Journ. Mycol. **4**: 62. 1888.

*C. sublilacina* Karst.    Finlands Basidsvampar, p. 375. 1889.

*C. Herveyi* Pk.    Rept. N. Y. St. Mus. **45**: 84. 1892.  *Rugosa*
    form.

*C. Favreae* (Quél.) Sacc. & Trav.    Syll. Fung. **19**: 321. 1910.
    (As *Ramaria* in Assn. Fr. Avanc. Sci. **22**: 489, pl. 3, fig. 13.
    1893.

*C. cinerea* var. *gracilis*.    Rea.    Trans. Brit. Myc. Soc. **6**: 62.
    1917.

*C. mutans* Burt.    Ann. Mo. Bot. Gard. **9**: 31, pl. 6, fig. 41.
    1922.

*C. histrix* E. & E. (herbarium name).*

---

* So far as can be ascertained from rather poor figures and very inadequate
descriptions we take the following "species" of Britzelmayr to be forms of *C. cristata*:
*C. gregalis* Britz.  Hymen. Südb. **8**: 286.
*C. arctata* Britz.  Hymen. Südb. **8**: 286.
*C. crassa* Britz.  Hymen. Südb. **8**: 286.  Purplish form.
*C. macrospora* Britz.  Hymen. Südb. **8**: 287.
*C. unistirpis* Britz.  Hymen. Südb. **8**: 287.
*C. pseudoflava* Britz.  Hymen. Südb. **7** (10): 14, fig. 62 (Clav.)
*C. subfastigiata* Britz.  Hymen. Südb. **7** (10): 14, figs. 43, 64 and 78 (Clav.).
*C. clavaeformis* Britz.  Hymen. Südb. **7** (10): 14, fig. 67 (Clav.).
*C. rugosa* form *fuliginea*. Hymen. Südb. **7**: (10): 14, fig. 68 (Clav.).  Blackened
    by parasite.
*C. extans* Britz.  Hymen. Südb. **8**: 10, fig. 12 (Clav.).  Referred previously by
    Britzelmayr to *C. Kunzei.*
*C. obtusiuscula* Britz.  Hymen. Südb. **17** (Bot. Centralb. **71**: 95. 1897).  Separate,
    p. 19.
*C. gigantula* Britz.  Hymen. Südb. **17** (Bot. Centralb. **71**: 95. 1897).  Separate.
    p. 19.

PLATES 9, 16-19, AND 83

Remarkably variable in both form and color. The typical form is whitish or pallid, slender, narrow, about 2-3 mm. thick below and 3-6 cm. high, long-stalked with a few or several branches which are rather abruptly crested at the ends with small, pointed, more or less crowded branchlets; sometimes there is a single slender stalk with a dense crest at the tip, or there may be several stalks attached near the base and these may branch near the middle. Other forms besides the typical are also included in the following notes. At times none of the branches is crested or some may be crested and others not; also the stem may be very short and the branches numerous and forming a contorted tuft or the stem may be much flattened and expanded upwards, with a few irregular flat branches, or with no branches but rugose-wrinkled or knobbed. The tip is sometimes flattened and expanded like an antler, and in less complex forms the plants are apt to be somewhat enlarged and flattened upwards. Color white at base and usually light grayish flesh color elsewhere except the tips which are creamy white when young, then becoming colored more like the branches and easily blackening after maturity. The color varies from dull or creamy white to lavender-gray (or with a tint of this color with tan) or smoky lavender, pale to deep mouse gray, ash color, drab, or dull yellow with all admixtures of these colors; surface even below, more or less channelled and wrinkled upwards. Flesh dry, toughish, not brittle, bending on itself without a complete break, creamy white, softer inside, and usually with one or two small uneven cavities in center from the separation of the fibers; odor almost none, taste mild, not very pleasant, somewhat bitterish musty, at times a little like that of *Agaricus campestris*.

Spores (of No. 2221) when fresh pure white, smooth, regular, subspherical to short-elliptic, 5.2-7.4 x 7-9.2$\mu$; after standing for some time they become yellowish and often irregular by collapsing. Basidia two-spored in all forms, the long stout sterigmata usually curved inward. Hymenium of No. 4561 thick (110-165$\mu$) and with many spores irregularly embedded through most of its area, indicating a great increase in thickness by irregular proliferation. In No. 4899 the hymenium is much thinner (50-60$\mu$) and there are few or no more embedded spores than would naturally be dragged in by the knife.

Common in deciduous or coniferous woods on earth or humus, often in thin grass in groves or lawns and rarely on very rotten trunks of deciduous or coniferous wood; probably the most widely distributed and commonest of Clavarias. Plants under dense hemlock cannot be distinguished from those in open deciduous groves except for a somewhat ranker taste. "Edible and of the best quality."—McIlvaine.

Not rarely this species is attacked on the stem by a blackish parasite, giving the lower part a very dark color. This condition is Persoon's *C. fallax* (as β under *C. cristata*) which he describes as attacked by such a parasite. He says (Syn. Met. Fung., p. 592): "The sickly condition of the fungus is caused by a certain *Sphaeria,* living on it as a parasite, which on first sight makes it resemble a *Xylaria.*" The parasite is now known as *Scoletotrichum Clavariarum.* Another striking form is smoky purplish above with the stem rather abruptly buffy brown, as shown in pl. 9, fig. 4. This might well be called form *bicolor.*

The great variability of this plant has led to many names and much confusion. The large, smooth, subspherical spores, pliable texture, and blackening tips are the surest guides. Persoon notes the polymorphic character of *C. cristata* and says "white to brownish subcinereous," but he includes *C. cinerea* as distinct. Sowerby (pl. 378) also notes this variability, saying: "It is equally variable in form and color, but mostly white."

In the Persoon Herbarium *C. cristata* is represented by eight sheets of the species and several so-called varieties. Some have the form of *C. cinerea,* some are rugose above and with long slender stalks, one called var. *decurtata* is a common form, while others are typical with cristate tips. Almost all variations are represented except the simplest *rugosa* form. *Clavaria fimbriata* is represented by two good plants which are obviously *C. cristata,* and *C. rugosa* is shown by several good collections and is like ours. The spores are smooth, subspherical, 6.5-9.5 x 7.5-11μ. In the same herbarium are three good plants of *C. fuliginea* which are evidently a color form of *C. cristata,* having the same habit, size, and spores, as well as crested tips (spores oval, smooth, sometimes tapering toward the mucro end, 6-7.4 x 7.4-9.5μ). *Clavaria grisea* is well represented in Persoon's herbarium by two sheets, which show that it is *C. cinerea,* as Cotton has asserted. The spores are smooth, subspherical, 5.5-6.5 x 7.4-9μ. The observation by Persoon that the spores are brown-red is an error (Cotton. Trans.

Brit. Myc. Soc. **3**: 184. 1909). As Persoon himself considers *C. grisea* and *C. cinerea* as synonyms of *C. fuliginea* (Myc. Europ., p. 166) we are safe in disposing of it here. *Clavaria fuliginea* as determined in the Schweinitz Herbarium is *C. cinerea,* with spores 6.5 x 7.5µ. In the Curtis Herbarium plants so labelled are *C. amethystinoides.* Fries considers *C. trichopus* a synonym of *C. cristata,* and plants in Bresadola's herbarium (Cavelante) so determined are a form of *C. cristata* with spores subspherical, 5.5-7.4 x 6-8µ; basidia 5.5-6.2µ thick with two sterigmata. *Clavaria albida* in Bresadola's herbarium is also *C. cristata,* with spores oval to subspherical, 6-7.5 x 7.5-9µ. We have received also two collections from Romell (Sweden) labelled *C. albida* which are the same. The white form often swollen upward, such as ours from Redding, Conn., is the one that is at times referred to *C. coralloides* by European botanists, as Romell. The *C. coralloides* of Persoon's herbarium is a large branched plant that might pass for a highly developed form of *C. Krombholzii* except for the spores, which are so different as to exclude it. They are subelliptic, slightly rough, 4-4.8 x 10.5-13µ. That Fries's idea of *C. macropus* Pers. is the *Krombholzii* form of *C. cristata* is shown by a good collection by him (Upsala) at Kew (spores smooth, oval, 6.6-7 x 8-8.5µ). This is also the disposition of the species by Bresadola. In his herbarium is a plant so named which is easily seen to be a small form of *C. rugosa,* with spores "8-9 x 7.5-8.5µ." The species is not represented in Persoon's herbarium, and so must remain doubtful. If the *C. dichotoma* Godey distributed by Roumeguère as No. 3115 of his Fungi Gallici exsiccati is authentic, the name is a synonym of *C. cristata.* An example at Kew is like the latter in appearance and has the same spores, 5-6.5 x 6.3-7.4µ. However, Bourdot and Maire (Bull. Soc. Myc. Fr. **36**: 72. 1920) give the spores as smaller, 3.5-4 x 4.5-5µ. Otherwise their description does not exclude a form of *C. cristata.* Saccardo proposed the name *C. Schaefferi* to represent *C. lilacina* Fr. and *C. purpurea* Schaeff. He gives the spores of the plant he had in mind as 8-10 x 6-8µ, which show it to be the purplish form of *C. cristata.* Schaeffer's plate looks so much like what we are calling *C. amethystina* that it would be so referred with confidence except for the large spores figured on the same plate. *Clavaria coliformis* Boud. (Bull. Soc. Myc. Fr. **33**: 11, pl. 3, fig. 2. 1917) is probably the *rugosa* form of this species.   The spores are given as 7μ thick, spherical.

Spores of *C. histrix* from West Virginia, at the New York Botanical Garden, are 5.2-6 x 7-8.4μ and those of our No. 2221 are the same.   At the New York Botanical Garden is also the type of *C. sphaerospora* E. & E.   They look like simple or sparingly branched forms of *C. cristata* and have the same spores, 6-7.4 x 7-8μ.   The type plants of *C. Herveyi* show it to be the *rugosa* form of this species.   Plants from Bresadola at the New York Botanical Garden determined by him as *C. grossa* Pers. look just like small *C. cinerea* and have spores subspherical, 6-8 x 7-9μ (Bres.).   In the Curtis Herbarium are a good many collections labelled *C. cristata*.   Most of them are true, as one from the Schweinitz Herbarium (spores 6.6 x 7.5μ) and one from E. P. Fries, Upsala (spores 7.3 x 8μ) ; some look like *C. stricta* and one from Peck seems to be *C. byssiseda,* and a Rhode Island collection (Olney) is perhaps C. *Kunzei*.   In the same herbarium a collection from Bordeaux, France, labelled *C. grisea* is the *cinerea* form of *C. cristata,* with large subspherical spores.   Two other collections from Europe labelled *C. cinerea* are like our plants. There is none from Fries under *C. cinerea*.   From the description *C. comosa* Pat. (Bull. Soc. Myc. Fr. **22**: 196. 1906) may be Rea's var. *gracilis* of *C. cinerea*.

Many students prefer to divide this group into several species, but we have been unable to find any differences either in gross character or in microscopic detail of sufficient importance or consistency to enable us to distinguish species within the group.   Romell, too, writes (April 16, 1920) that he does not see any distinct limit between *C. cristata, C. cinerea,* and *C. rugosa*.   Maire and Juel have studied nuclear division in the basidia of this group.   The former found that in *C. rugosa* the spindle was more or less parallel with the long axis of the basidium and that the spores were uninucleate (Bull. Soc. Myc. Fr. **18**: 85, pl. 2, figs. 15-20. 1902). He says that *C. grisea* is similar to *C. rugosa* in all essential characters.   Juel studied *C. cinerea* and *C. cristata* and found them like Maire's two species and like each other (Nova Acta Reg. Soc. Sci. Upsaliensis, sér. 4, **4**: 1. 1916).   In *C. cinerea* he finds (pl. 2, figs. 28-32) eight nuclei in the basidium and one passes into each of the two spores.   The six other nuclei remain in good condition in the protoplasm of the basidium, but there is no evidence of further spore production. Of *C. cristata* (pl. 2, figs. 33-35) he says that "in microscopic structure it stands very near to *C. cinerea.*" See also Patouillard in Tab. Fung., p. 67, fig. 154.

We have studied carefully numerous specimens of these forms and find that they can be divided into two rather indistinct groups, based on a slight difference in the size of the spores and a tendency to become yellow in the dried state in one group and gray or brown in the other. There are, however, many exceptions, and the gap is bridged by numerous intermediate forms. The difference seems to be regional rather than specific, the northern plants more frequently tending to the *rugosa* form and often with slightly larger spores. Typical results of spore measurements in the two groups are given in tabular form below.

*Rugosa-Krombholzii* forms:

Redding, Conn., No. 25................................Spores 7-9.3 x 8-11μ.
Chocorua, N. H. (Farlow)..............................Spores 7-9.3 x 8.5-10.5μ.
Vaughns, N. Y. (Burnham, No. 38)....................Spores 7-8 x 7.6-9.5μ.
West Fort Ann, N. Y. (Burnham, No. 28)...........Spores 7-9.3 x 8.5-10.5μ.
Sand Lake, N. Y. (Peck)..............................Spores 6.8-9 x 8.2-10.5μ.
Monands, N. Y. (Peck)................................Spores 7-8.7 x 8-10μ.
Pink Bed Valley, N. C. (Murrill & House, No. 375) Spores 7.4-8.8 x 8.5-10μ.
West Albany, N. Y. (Peck)...........................Spores 7.4-9.3 x 8-11μ.
Chocorua, N. H. (Farlow, No. 374)..................Spores 7-8.5 x 7.5-9.6μ.
Vaughns, N. Y. (Burnham, No. 29)...................Spores 7-9.3 x 8-11μ.
Hudson Falls, N. Y. (Burnham, No. 49).............Spores 7.4-9.5 x 8.5-11μ.
Blowing Rock, N. C., No. 5572.......................Spores 7-8.5 x 8-10.2μ.
Blowing Rock, No. 5616..............................Spores 7.4-9.5 x 9-10.5μ.
Blowing Rock, No. 5676..............................Spores 7.5-8.5 x 8-10.5μ.
France (Patouillard).................................Spores 7.5-9.2 x 9-11μ.
Redding, Conn. (Coker)..............................Spores 7.4-9.3 x 8.5-10.5μ.
Ludlow, Vt. (Miss Hibbard, No. 3)..................Spores 7-8.5 x 8-10.5μ.
Chocorua, N. H. (Farlow, No. 310a)................Spores 7.6-9.3 x 8-11μ.
Chocorua, N. H. (Farlow, No. 310b)................Spores 7.4-9.3 x 8.2-11μ.

*Cristata-cinerea* forms:

Chapel Hill, No. 2246................................Spores 6-8 x 7.4-9μ.
No. 2251...............................................Spores 6.5-7 x 7-8.5μ.
No. 2221...............................................Spores 5.5-7.4 x 7.4-9.2μ.
No. 2387...............................................Spores 5.5-7.5 x 7.4-10.5μ.
No. 2417...............................................Spores 6-7.5 x 7.4-9.5μ.
No. 2636...............................................Spores 5.5-7 x 7-8.6μ.
No. 2660...............................................Spores 5.5-7.4 x 7-9μ.
No. 2694...............................................Spores 6-7.5 x 7.4-9μ.
No. 2702...............................................Spores 6-7.5 x 7.5-9.3μ.

No. 2733.................................................................................................Spores 6.3-7.6 x 7-9μ.
No. 2809.................................................................................................Spores 5.5-7.3 x 7-8.5μ.
No. 3091.................................................................................................Spores 5.5-7.5 x 7.5-9.3μ.
No. 3108.................................................................................................Spores 5.6-7.2 x 6.7-9μ.
No. 3394.................................................................................................Spores 6-7.6 x 7-9.3μ.
No. 4566.................................................................................................Spores 5.5-7.4 x 7-8.5μ.
No. 4899.................................................................................................Spores 6-7.4 x 7.5-9.3μ.
Lake George, N. Y. (Coker, No. 8)....................................Spores 5.5-7.5 x 7.4-8.5μ.
Vaughns, N. Y. (Burnham, No. 26)....................................Spores 5.5-7 x 7-8.6μ.
West Fort Ann, N. Y. (Burnham, No. 35)..................Spores 6-8 x 7.5-9.5μ.
West Fort Ann, N. Y. (Burnham, No. 46)..........Spores 6.5-7.5 x 7.5-9.3μ.
Newfane, Vt. (Miss Hibbard, No. 10)....................Spores 6.5-7.6 x 7.6-9.3μ.
Pocono Lake Preserve, Pa. (Vogler)....................Spores 6-7.5 x 7.5-9.3μ.
Vaughns, N. Y. (Burnham, No. 110)....................Spores 6-7.6 x 7.4-8.6μ.
New Providence, Bahamas (No. 215)....................Spores 5.5-7 x 6.6-7.4μ.
Falls Church, Va. (Murrill)........................................Spores 6-7.4 x 7-8.5μ.

From the above it will be seen that the spores of the *cristata-cinerea* forms run smaller on the average than those of the *Kromb-holzii-rugosa* group, but we give below some exceptions to this.

*Rugosa-Krombholzii* forms:
Chapel Hill, No. 3573.................................................Spores 6.5-7.2 x 7-8.6μ
Chapel Hill, No. 5148.................................................Spores 6.5-7.5 x 7.5-9.7μ.
Lake Winnesquam, N. H. (Miss Hibbard)..................Spores 6.6-8 x 8-9.3μ.
Delmar, N. Y. (Peck)..............................................Spores 6-7.8 x 7.4-8.8μ.
Newfane, Vt. (Miss Hibbard, No. 4)....................Spores 6.8-7.7 x 7.4-9.3μ.

*Cristata-cinerea* forms:
Newfane, Vt. (Miss Hibbard, No. 11)....................Spores 7-8.5 x 8-10.5μ.
Washington Co., N. Y. (Burnham, No. 1)..........Spores 7-8.4 x 7.4-10.5μ
West Fort Ann, N. Y. (Burnham, No. 3)..........Spores 6.3-8.5 x 7.4-9.5μ.
Vaughns, N. Y. (Burnham, No. 27)....................Spores 6.6-8.5 x 8.5-11μ.

Illustrations: Badham. Esculent Fungi Engl., pl. 5, fig. 5 (as *C. cinerea*),
    fig. 6 (as *C. rugosa*) ; pl. 15, fig. 4 (as *C. rugosa*), fig. 5 (as *C. cinerea*).
    1847.

Berkeley. Outlines Brit. Fung., pl. 18, fig. 3 (as *C. rugosa*), fig. 4 (as *C.
    umbrina*). 1860.

Bolton. Hist. Fung. Halifax, pl. 115. 1789.

Britzelmayr. Hymen. Südb., Clavariei, figs. 3-4 (as *C. lilacina*), fig. 5 (as
    *C. gregalis*), figs. 6, 66 (as *C. arctata*), fig. 7 (as *C. cristata*), fig. 8 (as
    *C. rugosa*), fig. 9 (as *C. macrospora*), fig. 10 (as *C. unistirpis*), fig. 11
    (as *C. Krombholzii*), fig. 12 (as *C. Kunzei*, later called *C. extans*), fig.
    39 (as *C. grossa*), fig. 40 (as *C. amethystina*), fig. 47 (as *C. cinerea*),
    fig. 48 (as *C. coralloides*), fig. 63 (as *C. Schaefferi*), fig. 67 (as *C.
    clavaeformis*), fig. 68 (as *C. rugosa* form *fuliginea*). 1879-97.

Bulliard. As cited above.

Burt. Ann. Mo. Bot. Gard. **9**: pl. 7, fig. 59 (as *C. Herveyi*) ; pl. 9, fig. 82
    (as *C. sphaerospora*). 1922.

Cooke. A Plain and Easy Account of Brit. Fung., 1st. ed., pl. 17, fig. 1 (as *C. cinerea*), fig. 3 (as *C. rugosa*) ; 3rd ed., pl. 10, fig. 2 (as *C. cinerea*) ; pl. 7, fig. 3.

Cordier. Champ. Fr., pl. 46, fig. 2 (as *C. cinerea*), fig. 3 (as *C. amethystina*). 1874.

Dufour. Atlas Champ., pl. 68, fig. 149 (as *C. cinerea*). 1891.

Fries. Sverig. Atlas Svamp., pl. 92, figs. 1-3 (as *C. cristata*), figs. 4-5 (as *C. coralloides*). 1860-66.

Gibson. Edible Toadstools and Mushrooms, pl. 31 (as *C. umbrina* and *C. rugosa*). 1895.

Gillet. Champ. Fr. **5**: pl. 108. (114) (as *C. rugosa* and *C. Krombholzii*).

Greville. Scott. Crypt. Fl. **2**: pl. 64 (purplish *cinerea* form). 1824.

Hard. Mushrooms, fig. 393. 1908.

Holmskjold. Beata Ruris **1**: pl. 23 (as *Ramaria cristata*), pl. 20 (as *R. ornithopodioides*). 1790.

Krombholz. Abbild. u. Beschr., pl. 5, figs. 14-15 (as *C. cristata*) ; pl. 53, figs. 9-10 (as *C. grisea*), figs. 11-12 (as *C. palmata*), fig. 13 (as *C. cristata*), figs. 14-17 (as *C. Kunzei*) ; pl. 54, figs. 13-17 (as *C. rugosa*), figs. 18-20 (as *C. grossa*). 1831-1846.

Lanzi. Funghi Mang., pl. 13, fig. 4 (as *C. amethystina*). 1902.

Leuba. Champ. Comest., pl. 43, fig. 6 (as *C. cinerea*). Figure 5 is called the same but is more than doubtful. 1890.

Lloyd. Myc. Notes No. 65: pl. 178, figs. 1935 and 1936 (as *C. laciniata*). 1920.

Michael. Führer f. Pilzfreunde. Vol. 2, No. 26, (as *C. coralloides*), No. 28 (as *C. cristata*). 1901; Vol. 3, No. 30 (as *C. grisea*). 1905.

Maire. As above cited (*C. rugosa*).

Nees von Esenbeck. Systema, pl. 16, fig. 151   1817.

Patouillard. Tab. Analyt. Fung., fig. 154 (as *C. cinerea*), fig. 381 (as *C. rugosa*), figs. 37 and 261 (as *C. cristata* and var. *minor*). 1883-1886.

Peck. Rept. N. Y. St. Mus. **48**: pl. 39, figs. 8-12 (as *C. cristata*). 1894.

Persoon. Comm., pl. 2, fig. 4 (as *C. fallax* var *cristata*) ; pl. 4, fig. 3 (as *C. trichopus*). 1797.

Quélet. Champ. Jura Vosg. **1**: pl. 20, fig. 5 (as *C. rugosa*). Also in Asso. Française **16**: pl. 21, fig. 12 (as *C. fimbriata*). 1887.

Rea. Trans. Brit. Myc. Soc. **6**: pl. 2, fig. 4 (as *C. cinerca* var. *gracilis*). 1917.

Rolland. Atlas Champ., pl. 103, No. 230; No. 232 (as *C. cinerea*) ; No. 233 (as *C. rugosa*). 1910.

Schaeffer. Fung. Bavar., pl. 170 (as *C. albida*). 1763; and pl. 291 (as *C. laciniata*). 1770.

Sicard. Hist. Nat. Champ., pl. 62, fig. 320 (as *C. cinerea*), figs. 314 and 330 (as *C. cristata*). 1883.

Swanton. Fungi, pl. 29, fig. 7 (as *C. rugosa*), fig. 9 (purplish form of *C. cinerea*). 1909.

Taylor. Food Products I, Frontispiece, fig. 8 (as *C. cinerea*). fig. 9 (as *C. rugosa*). 1894.

North Carolina: Chapel Hill. No. 2221. Swamp of New Hope Creek, June 24, 1916. No. 2251. Mossy grass under oaks, June 25, 1916. No. 2384. Mossy soil, June 28, 1916. No. 2387. On ground in low place in woods, July 18, 1916. No. 2417. In low woods near branch, July 22, 1916. Large plants, 8 cm. tall and 4 cm. wide. No. 2591. Rocky hillside, mixed woods, July 5, 1917. No. 2627. Upland woods, July 10, 1917. Spores 5.5-7.4 x 6.6-8$\mu$. No. 2636. Under cedars at "The Rocks," July 11, 1917. No. 2647. Low damp woods, July 11, 1917. Basidia 5-7.4$\mu$ thick. No. 2660. Mixed upland woods, July 12, 1917. No. 2686. Low damp woods, July 16, 1917. Pure white form; tips very little crested. No. 2694. Low damp woods near base of Laurel Hill, July 17, 1917. No. 2702. Mixed woods by branch, July 17, 1917. This is a form that might pass for *C. rugosa*. No. 2733. Mixed upland woods, July 21, 1917. No. 2746. On earth in woods, July 20, 1917. Form *C. rugosa*. Spores 5.5-7 x 7-8$\mu$. No. 2809. In thin grass in lawns, July 29, 1917. Color varying from light creamy gray to deep mouse-gray or smoky lavender. This connects with *C. rugosa, C. cristata,* and *C. cinerea.* No. 3293. On Dr. Pratt's lawn, June 1, 1919. No. 3573. Mixed woods, October 31, 1919. Plants pure white. No. 4561. Damp soil, woody elevation, July 27, 1920. *Cinerea* form. Threads of flesh closely packed, 4-7$\mu$ thick; hymenial layer 66$\mu$ thick; basidia 6.2-7$\mu$ thick. No. 4566. Mixed woods but mostly pines, July 27, 1920. A paler, smaller form, approaching the typical *C. cristata,* but with a smoky tint. No. 4899. Mixed woods, October 6, 1921. Lavender form.

Dillingham. Elevation of 3400 feet. J. S. Holmes. (U. N. C. Herb.).

Louisiana: St. Martinsville. Langlois. (N. Y. Bot. Gard. Herb.).

West Virginia: Fayette Co. Nuttall. (N. Y. Bot. Gard. Herb.).

District of Columbia: Takoma Park. Williams. (N. Y. Bot. Gard. Herb.).

New Jersey: Newfield. Ellis. (N. Y. Bot. Gard. Herb.). Spores ovate, about 6.5 x 8$\mu$.

Pennsylvania: Pocono Lake Preserve. Vogler. (U. N. C. Herb.). Gregarious, much branched from a distinct, short base; when young rather light drab, the tips quite pale, turning smoky drab after maturity; tips toothed as a rule, but some decidedly crested, easily blackening.

New York: Vaughns. Burnham, No. 110. Aug. 1, 1919. Plants flesh colored to white. (U. N. C. Herb.).

New York Botanical Gardens. Murrill. (N. Y. Bot. Gard. Herb.).

Lake Placid. Murrill. (N. Y. Bot. Gard. Herb.).

Connecticut: Redding. Coker. Sept. 7, 1919. (U. N. C. Herb.).

Vermont: Newfane. Miss Hibbard. (U. N. C. Herb.).

Ludlow. Miss Hibbard. (U. N. C. Herb.).

New Hampshire: White Mountains. Ellis. (N. Y. Bot. Gard. Herb.).
 Chocorua. Farlow. (U. N. C. Herb. from Farlow Herb., as *C. rugosa*).

California: Pasadena. McClatchie, No. 204. (N. Y. Bot. Gard. Herb., as
 *C. cinerea*).

Canada: Ottawa. Macoun. (N. Y. Bot. Gard. Herb.). Spores as in
 Chapel Hill plants.
 London. Dearness. (N. Y. Bot. Gard. Herb., as *C. cinerea*, E. & E. Fungi
 Columbiana, No. 1215).

Newfoundland: Waghorne. (N. Y. Bot. Gard. Herb.). Spores about
 $7 \times 8.7\mu$.

Bahama Islands: New Providence. (N. Y. Bot. Gard. Herb., No. 215).

Porto Rico: Johnston. (N. Y. Bot. Gard. Herb.). Dark form. Spores
 smooth, subspherical, $7 \times 9\mu$.

## Clavaria cineroides Atk. Ann. Myc. **7**: 367. 1909.

### PLATES 20 AND 83

This species was described from Chapel Hill plants collected
by us, and the following is the original description by Atkinson:
 "Plants very much branched from base, 7 cm. high, 5-6 cm.
broad, trunk absent. Plants uniformly gray when fresh. Base
of branches whitish in drying, upper portion of plant becoming
pale ochre or buff. Branches dichotomous, slightly clavate, numerous. Axils acute or rounded. Tips usually bidentate, teeth
rounded. Plants somewhat tough. Basidia slender, 4-spored,
$40\text{-}45 \times 7\mu$. [We make them $5.5\text{-}6.2\mu$ thick when measured in
water from the dried state; hymenium about $75\mu$ thick, packed
with small crystals.] Spores globose, smooth, white, pedicellate,
with large oil drop, $4\text{-}6\mu$. The plant resembles *Clavaria cinerea* in
color when fresh but the spores are much smaller, the branches
more slender. In size and shape the spores resemble those of
*Clavaria fusiformis* but the plant is very different from that
species."

 This species has not been reported except from Chapel Hill, but
we have recently found it in the mountains and we find several
American collections and one European that appear the same. Of
the American lots one was in Peck's herbarium (Vaughns, Burnham collection) mixed with *C. Kunzei*; two others were sent us
by Burnham for determination. The lot from Vaughns has just
the shape of the type, with long slender branches which divide
two or three times with open axils, the primary branches scurfy

and fused together into the ground and one or two centimeters above it. One collection from Tripoli is shorter and stouter, with thicker tips, but otherwise like the others. The Chapel Hill plants were pale gray when fresh, and it is probable, since they have been mistaken for *C. Kunzei,* that they may vary to almost white. The species is nearest *C. muscoides,* which is very similar in spores and other microscopic characters, but which is easily separated by different color and usually smaller size. Our plants are entirely different from *C. cinerea* and are larger and stouter than *C. Kunzei* and with quite distinct spores. The European plants were sent us by Romell (Carlberg's Park, Stockholm), who was much interested in them and could not place them in any European species. He makes a note that "as to shape not unlike *Cl. fastigiata* but color white. Spores globose, 7μ." We find the spores smooth, spherical with a distinct mucro and large oil drop, 6-7μ thick. All collections show the base to be scurfy as in *C. muscoides,* the tips of the branches (when dry) abruptly sub-translucent and cartilaginous-looking.

Illustration: Burt. Ann. Mo. Bot. Gard. **9**: pl. 8, fig. 61. 1922.

North Carolina: Chapel Hill. No. 100. On ground among pine needles, mixed woods on hillside by Fern Walk, October 2, 1908. Type (Cornell Herb., No. 22640 and U. N. C. Herb.).

Linville Falls. Coker and party, No. 5751. (U. N. C. Herb.).

New York: Tripoli. Burnham, Nos. 32 and 99. (U. N. C. Herb.). Spores (of No. 99) smooth, spherical, 5-6.2μ thick; basidia 6.2-7.7μ thick, 4-spored; hymenium 35-50μ thick, with no crystals; hyphae 3.7μ thick, roughly parallel, closely packed.

Vaughns. Burnham. (Albany Herb. and U. N. C. Herb.). Spores subspherical, smooth, 5-6μ.

Ithaca. Atkinson. (Cornell Herb., as *C. dealbata* Berk.). Spores subglobose with strong mucro, 4.4-5.5μ thick.

Chappaqua. Mrs. Murrill. (N. Y. Bot. Gard. Herb., No. 542). Spores spherical, 4-5.5μ thick.

**Clavaria muscoides** L.    Flora Suecica, 2nd ed., p. 457. 1755.
  *C. fastigiata* L.    Flora Suecica, 2nd. ed., p. 457. 1755.
  *C. corniculata* Schaeff.    Fung. Bavar., pl. 173. 1763.
  *C. pratensis* Pers.    Comm., p. 52 (183). 1797.
  *C. furcata* Pers.    Comm., p. 52. 1797.
  *C. vitellina* Pers.    Myc. Europ. **1**: 170. 1822.
  *C. similis* Pk.    Rept. N. Y. St. Mus. **43**: 24 (70). 1890.    (Not
      *C. similis* Boud. & Pat.).
  *C. Peckii* Sacc.    Syll. Fung. **9**: 249. 1891.    (Not *C. Peckii*
      Sacc. & D. Sacc.).
  *C. helveola* var. *dispar* Pers.    Myc. Europ. **1**: 181. 1822.
  *C. fellea* Pk.    Rept. N. Y. St. Mus. **51**: 292. 1898.
  *C. muscoides* var. *obtusata* Britz.    Hymen. Südb., Clavariei,
      fig. 45. 1879-97.
  *C. muscoides* var. *obtusa* Pk.    Rept. N. Y. St. Mus. **47**: 151
      (25 in Bot. ed.). 1894.
  *C. straminea* Cotton.    Trans. Brit. Myc. Soc. **3**: 265, pl. 11,
      fig. D. 1909-10.

PLATES 9, 21, AND 83

Plants small, 2-5 cm. high, slender, quite variable in form, from simple and single to clustered and fused at base and several times branched above, terete or channelled, stem distinct, usually long, branches none or a few knobs to several or many (usually a few near the top), the angles open; tips bluntish; color varying from rather pale dull yellow to deep clear yellow or ochraceous yellow, shading downward to darker brown, the base white-scurfy and more or less rooting and, when clustered, fused below; in drying unchanging or becoming a light leather color.  Flesh moderately brittle, breaking at 45°, taste rank, farinaceous and bitter.

Spores (of one of our collections from Lake George, N. Y.) white, smooth, spherical, with an abrupt mucro, 5-7.5μ.  Basidia about 7-10μ thick, with 4 curved sterigmata which are about 7.5μ long; among the basidia are also found delicate hyphae with tips a little swollen.

Not rare in deciduous woods or pastures in humus or moss from the mountains of this state northward, and we have found it once in Chapel Hill.  Schweinitz and Curtis also record it from North Carolina.  We have seen no collections from the southern states except our own. The basidia in American plants are certainly 4-spored and so are the British, according to Cotton and Wakefield (Trans. Brit. Myc. Soc. **6**: 181. 1919). Patouillard's figure shows but two sterigmata (l. c., fig. 564).

Fries considered *C. corniculata* the same as *C. muscoides,* and plants in the Persoon Herbarium (collected by Persoon) under the former name have all the appearance of the latter; another collection from Chaillet is different  The types of *C. pratensis* in the herbarium of Persoon are *C. muscoides,* with spores subspherical, 4.5 x 4.8-5.5μ. In the Persoon Herbarium is one lot of *C. vitellina* (type). They are small, crowded, nearly simple, cartilaginous-looking plants with spores like *C. muscoides,* 4-5.5μ thick. *Clavaria fastigiata* is only a more open and spreading form with blunter tips. *Clavaria fellea* and *C. similis* Pk. (*C. Peckii* Sacc.) are also the same, the plants looking exactly alike in the dried state and the descriptions agreeing well. Spores of the types have been examined and agree with *C. muscoides. Clavaria muscoides* var. *obtusa* Pk. is a form with tips thicker than usual. The scurfy base, abruptly translucent tips (when dry) and stalks fused from the ground are just like *C. muscoides* and the spores are identical. Moreover, there are just such forms in other herbaria and all gradations occur between this and other smaller, more yellow forms.

No differences of any importance between *C. straminea* and *C. muscoides* appear from Cotton's description of the former. Simple plants of the latter are not at all rare (pl. 9, fig. 3) and could hardly be better described than by Cotton's diagnosis for *C. straminea.* An authentic collection from Cotton (Haslemen, October 15, 1913) studied by us confirms the identity of the two species. From the description and figures *C. tenella* Boud. ( Bull. Soc. Myc. Fr. **33**: 11, pl. 4, fig. 1. 1917) strongly suggests this species, and as there are no discrepancies we suspect their identity. Near this species seems also *C. umbrinella* Sacc. (=*C. umbrina* Berk. See Sylloge **6**: 695. 1888), which differs in color and more branched habit. A bit of the type from Kew Herbarium has spores smooth, nearly pip-shaped, 4-5 x 5-6μ; basidia about 6.2μ thick, with 4 long sterigmata; hymenium about 40μ thick (pl. 92, figs. 9 and 10).

Juel (cited under *C. cristata*) finds that two transverse nuclear divisions occur in the tips of the basidia, that the young spore contains a visible nucleus, but that as a rule in the ripe spore *none can be seen;* basidium 4-spored (pl. 3, figs. 75-80). He has sent us good plants of this species which are like ours, with spores 4.5-6μ thick.

Illustrations: Bernard.   Champ. Rochelle, pl. 42, fig. 3.   1882.

Britzelmayr.   Hymen. Südb., Clavariei, figs. 44 and (as var. *obtusata*) 45.

Bulliard.   Herb. Fr., pl. 358, figs. D, E.   1787; pl. 496 (as *C. coralloides*) 1790.

Burt.   Ann. Mo. Bot. Gard. **9**: pl. 7, fig. 56 (as *C. Peckii*); fig. 57 (as *C. m.* var. *obtusa*); fig. 58 (as *C. fellea*).   1922.

Cooke.   Brit. Fungi, pl. 696.

Cotton.   As cited above.

Dufour.   Atl. Champ., pl. 69, No. 153 (as *C. fastigiata*).   1891.

Flora Danica, pl. 775, fig. 3.   1778; pl. 836, fig. 2 (as *C. muscoides* var.). 1780.

Gillet.   Champ. Fr. **5**: pl. 106 (112).

Holmskjold.   Beata Ruris **1**: pl. 21 (as *Ramaria muscoides*) and pl. **22** (as *R. fastigiata*).   1790.

Lanzi.   Funghi Mang., pl. 13, fig. 3.   1902.

Michael.   Führer f. Pilzfreunde, Vol. 3, No. 29 (as *C. fastigiata*).   1905.

Patouillard.   Tab. Fung. **2**: fig. 564.   1887.

Persoon.   Comm., pl. 4, fig. 5 (as *C. pratensis*).   1797.

Schaeffer.   Fung. Bavar., pl. 173 (as *C. corniculata*).   1763.   Photographed in part by Burt in Ann. Mo. Bot. Gard. **9**: pl. 7, fig. 55.   1922.

Swanton.   Fungi, pl. 29, fig. 2 (as *C. fastigiata*).   1909.

North Carolina:   Chapel Hill.   No. 7131.   By branch below athletic field, September 20, 1923.   Spores 4.8-6.2μ thick.

Blowing Rock.   Coker and party, No. 5807.   (U. N. C. Herb.).   Spores 4.4-5.3μ thick.

District of Columbia: Washington.   Braendle.   (U. N. C. Herb.).

Pennsylvania:   Buck Hill Falls.   Mrs. Delafield.   (N. Y. Bot. Gard. Herb.).

New York:   Vaughns.   Burnham, No. 41.   August, 1912.   Spores spherical, about 5.5μ thick.   B. No. 42.   September 15, 1912.   B. No. 45. "Yellowish when fresh."   B. No. 66.   August 13, 1915.   C. & B. No. 116. In maple woods, September 2, 1917.   Clustered and fused below, rarely single.   B. No. 118. October 19, 1919.   Spores 4-6μ in diameter. (All in U. N. C. Herb.).

Lake George.   Coker, No. 7.   (U. N. C. Herb.).   Spores spherical, smooth, white, 5-6.5μ thick.

Jamesville.   Underwood.   (U. N. C. Herb.).

Bronx. Murrill and Volkert. (N. Y. Bot. Gard. Herb.). This is the largest specimen we have seen, and is very much branched; dried plant 5 cm. broad. Spores subspherical, smooth, 4-5 x 5-5.5$\mu$.

Catskill Mts. Gereshoy. (U. N. C. Herb.).

Connecticut: Belleville. Macoun. (U. N. C. Herb.).
West Goshen. Underwood. (N. Y. Bot. Gard. Herb. and U. N. C. Herb.).
Redding. Coker. (U. N. C. Herb.).

New Hampshire: Meredith. Miss Hibbard, No. 8. (U. N. C. Herb.).

## Clavaria pistillaris L. Flora Suecica, 2nd. ed., p. 456. 1775.

*Craterellus pistillaris* Fr. Epicr., p. 534. 1838.
*Craterellus unicolor* Berk. & Rav. Grevillea **1**: 148. 1873.
*Craterellus corrugis* Pk. Bull. Torr. Bot. Club **26**: 69. 1899.
*Clavaria truncata* Lovejoy. Bot. Gaz. **50**: 385. 1910.

### PLATES 22, 23, AND 83

Plants very variable in form and size, up to 20 cm. long, typically long-pestle-shaped, the thick tip as a rule rugose-channelled, the center often flattened or even depressed and at times perforated into a central hollow after maturity; tapering downward to a small encrusted base which when growing among loose leaves and twigs may penetrate them for some distance; not rooted when growing on earth; commonly single, again growing in clusters with connate bases, as shown by the form represented in plate 23, where the tips were in several cases flattened and forked like an antler and the young plants sharply pointed and rosy; color at maturity ochraceous or leather color or discolored to darker (at times chocolate, McIlvaine). Flesh white, tender, soft, dryish, often collapsing irregularly in age so as to form a hollow; taste pleasant but mildly bitter-peppery; odor none.

Spores (No. 27 of Redding, Conn.) variable in size, pure white, smooth, elliptic, with mucro end often curved, 3.7-4.5 x 7.4-10$\mu$; in a typical New York plant from the Albany Herbarium they were 5.5-7 x 10-11.5$\mu$. Basidia 6.8-7.7$\mu$ thick; hymenium about 65$\mu$ thick, covering the top as well as the sides of the plant; hyphae of context about 4.8$\mu$ thick, with clamp connections.

Edible and very good. Not rare in the northern states, less common in the south except in the mountains. At Chapel Hill we have never found very large plants, but that is not surprising as we are near the coastward limit of the species in the southern states. Most of our plants represent *Craterellus unicolor* (and with this Burt agrees), but some are larger, and after studying fresh plants both here and in the north we see no reason to consider the southern form distinct. Peck's *Craterellus corrugis* has spores no longer than *C. unicolor* and a collection from Redding, Conn., (pl. 23) has spores even smaller.

This species with *C. ligula,* represents apparently an approach toward *Craterellus* and there has been confusion in its treatment, some authors treating forms of *C. pistillaris* as *Craterellus* species, for example *C. unicolor* which Burt retains in *Craterellus*. Burt follows Fries in accepting both *Craterellus pistillaris* Fr. and *Clavaria pistillaris* L. (Ann. Mo. Bot. Gard. **1**: 340, pl. 16, figs. 11-13; pl. 17, fig. 14. 1914). In our opinion they are the same thing if Schaeffer's plate 169 which is referred to by both Fries and Burt is accepted as representing *Craterellus pistillaris*. Schaeffer's plate 290 (as *Clavaria gemmata*) cited by Fries as *Craterellus pistillaris,* may represent a different plant, as the spores are shown by Schaeffer as spherical. However, if the spores are spherical it is not the plant that Fries and Burt have in mind. See Harper's good photo of *Craterellus pistillaris* in Mycologia **5**: pl. 95. 1913. He says he agrees with Atkinson that the plant he shows should be considered a "variety" of *Clavaria pistillaris*. Atkinson says "form," not variety, and is in this correct, we think. None of the rather numerous named varieties of this species seems to be anything more than growth forms. The *C. pistillaris* of Persoon's herbarium is like ours. Those labelled var. *minor* are somewhat larger than our smallest specimens. *Clavaria mira* Pat. (Bull. Soc. Myc. Fr. **23**: 71. 1907) should be compared with this species. *Craterellus taxophilus* Thom (Bot. Gaz. **37**: 215, figs. 1-8. 1904), a small plant with small spherical spores, approaches the shape of *C. pistillaris* and has been transferred to *Clavaria* by Lloyd (Myc. Notes No. 64: 1008, fig. 1856. 1920). Burt retains it in *Craterellus*. In all forms of *C. pistillaris* we have seen the hymenium is continuous over the top. Where the apex is caved in and the surface layer fissured, the hymenium extends to the very edge of the fissure. There is therefore no analogy in this respect to *Craterellus*.

Jüel (cited under *C. cristata*) studied microscopically both *Craterellus pistillaris* and *Clavaria pistillaris* (as he calls them) and decides that they are so similar that the former is only a variety of the latter (pl. 2, figs. 42-48 for *Craterellus* and pl. 2, figs. 49-52 for *Clavaria*).   In both the basidia are 4-spored, the spores uninucleate, the basidia with 4 or not rarely 8 nuclei.

Illustrations: The species has been very often illustrated, and some of the least good or most inaccessible figures are here omitted.   (See also Burt and Harper as cited above) :

Atkinson.   Stud. Am. Fungi, fig. 192.   1900.

Buller.   Researches on Fungi 2: fig. 61.   1922.

Bulliard.   Herb. Fr., pl. 244.   1785.

Corda.   Icon. Fung. 5: pl. 10, fig. 76.   1842.   Basidia and spores; basidia 4-spored.

Flora Danica, pl. 1255.   1799.

Gillet.   Champ. Fr. 5: pl. 107 (113).

Hard.   Mushrooms, fig. 396.   1908.

Holmskjold.   Beata Ruris 1: pls. 4 and 5.   1790.

Krombholz.   Abbild. u. Beschr., pl. 54, figs. 1-11.   1841.

Lanzi.   Funghi Mang., pl. 12, fig. 2.   1897.

Lorinser.   Die Schwämme, pl. 2, fig. 6.   1876.

Lloyd.   Myc. Notes No. **64**: pl. 158, fig. 1755 (as *C. unicolor* and *C. truncata*).   1920.

McIlvaine.   Am. Fungi, pl. 138, figs. 2 and 3.   1900.

Migula in Thomé.   Krypt.-Fl. Deutsch. **3**, 2, 1 : pl. 24.   1912.

Moffat.   Chicago Acad. Sci. Bull. **7**: pl. 22, fig. 2.   1909.

Patouillard.   Tab. Fung., fig. 260.   1884.

Peck.   Mem. N. Y. St. Mus. **3**: pl. 66, figs. 15-17 (as var. *umbonata*).   1900.

Persoon.   Comm., pl. 3, figs. 8-9.   1797.

Quélet.   Champ. Jura Vosg. 1: pl. 21, fig. 2.   1872.

Rolland.   Atlas Champ., pl. 104, No. 235.   1910.

Schaeffer.   Fung. Bavar., pl. 169.   1763.

Sicard.   Hist. Nat. Champ., pl. 62, fig. 322.   1883.

Sowerby.   Engl. Fungi, pl. 277 (*C. herculanea*).   1800.

Venturi.   I miceti del agro Bresciano, pl. 36, figs. 1-3.   1845-1860.

Venturi.   Studi Micol., pl. 12, figs. 114-115.   1842.

North Carolina: Chapel Hill.   No. 1913.   On ground in woods, October 22, 1915.   Spores pure white, ovate to elliptic, smooth, 5.1-5.5 x 7.2-9$\mu$. No. 1994.   In mixed woods by stream, November 23, 1915.   No. 3793. Mixed woods by branch, November 23, 1919.   Spores 5-6 x 8.5-11.5$\mu$. No. 3885.   In loose sandy soil, December 13, 1919.   No. 4770.   In humus, January 16, 1921.   Spores 4-5 x 8-11$\mu$.

Hillsboro.   Curtis.   (Curtis Herb.).

Blowing Rock.   Coker and party, No. 5623.   (U. N. C. Herb.).

Linville Falls.   Coker and party, No. 5759.   (U. N. C. Herb.).

Pink Beds.   Miss Burlingham, No. 280.   (U. N. C. Herb.).

New York: Tripoli. Burnham, No. 15. (U. N. C. Herb.).
  Vaughns. Burnham, No. 68. Spores smooth, elliptic, 3.8-5.5 x 8-11.8$\mu$.
    B. No. 71. Spores large, 5.5-7 x 9.3-12.5$\mu$. C. and B. No. 139. In
    frondose woods, September 2, 1917. (All in U. N. C. Herb.).
Connecticut: Redding. Coker, No. 27. (U. N. C. Herb.).

**Clavaria ligula** Schaeff. Fung. Bavar., p. 116, pl. 171. 1763.
  *C. caespitosa* Wulfen in Jacq. Misc. **2**: 98, pl. 12, fig. 2. 1781.
  *C. pulvinata* Pers. Comm., p. 65. 1797.
  *C. luteola* Pers. Comm., p. 66. 1797.

PLATES 28 AND 84

Plants about 2-7 cm. high and 3-12 mm. thick above, simple,
single or at times two or three fused at base, long-claviform, thickened upward and there crumpled and channelled and often flattened; obtuse or less often pointed or even cuspidate; the bases
scurfy-villose nearly or quite up to the hymenium; color when
fresh (in plants we have seen) dull pink, soon fading to leather
color or with tints of fawn or buff added, the base white and expanding into the mycelium; not rooted. Flesh soft, white, pliable
when fresh, very brittle and friable when dry.

Spores (collection from Adirondacks, New York Botanical
Garden Herbarium) white, smooth, subelliptic, 4.5-5 x 15-18.5$\mu$.
Basidia 7-8.5$\mu$ thick, 4-spored; hymenium about 74$\mu$ thick, and
containing many brownish granules; hyphae of context about 4.4$\mu$
thick, much twisted, without clamp connections.

Always growing on coniferous leaves or trash and apparently
not rare in the northern states. Not yet reported from the south.

Juel (cited under *C. cristata*) finds two transverse nuclear
divisions near the basidium tip which is 4-spored, the spores elongated, smooth, uninucleate. Three or four chromosomes were observed in the spindles (pl. 3, figs. 70-74).

Illustrations: Clements. Minnesota Mushrooms, fig. 75. 1910.
  Dufour. Atlas Champ., pl. 69. 1891.
  Flora Danica, pl. 837, fig. 1. 1780.
  Krombholz. Abbild., pl. 54, fig. 12. 1841.
  Lanzi. Funghi Mang., pl. 12, fig. 1. 1897.
  Michael. Führer f. Pilzfreunde, Vol. 2, No. 21. 1901.

Migula in Thomé. Krypt.-Fl. Deutsch. **3**, 2, 1: pl. 24B, fig. 1. 1912. Color wrong.

Schaeffer. As cited above. Photographic copy by Burt in Ann. Mo. Bot. Gard. **9**: pl. 10, fig. 95. 1922.

Wulfen. As cited above.

Pennsylvania: Buck Hill Falls. In pine leaves, September 20, 1919. Mrs. J. R. Delafield. (N. Y. Bot. Gard. Herb. and U. N. C. Herb.).

New York: Tripoli. Burnham, No. 70. (U. N. C. Herb.).

Adirondacks. In pines, August, 1915. Murrill. (U. N. C. Herb.). Spores smooth, hyaline, 4.5-5 x 15-18.5$\mu$.

Westport. Peck. (Albany Herb.). Cespitose form.

Catskills. Gereshoy. (U. N. C. Herb.). Spores about 4.2 x 15$\mu$.

New Hampshire: White Mountains. Underwood. (U. N. C. Herb.).

Maine: Friendship. Morris. (Albany Herb. and U. N. C. Herb.).

Utah: San Juan County. Among coniferous trash, August 21, 1911. Garrett. (U. N. C. Herb.). Spores very large, 5.5-6 x 18.5-23$\mu$.

Canada: Quebec, Seven Islands. Robinson. (N. Y. Bot. Gard. Herb. and U. N. C. Herb.).

**Clavaria fistulosa** Holmsk. Annalen d. Botanik **17**: 64. 1796.

?*C. contorta* Holmsk. Beata Ruris **1**: 29. 1790.

*C. tuberosa* Sow. Engl. Fungi, pl. 199. 1799.

*C. Ardenia* Sow. Engl. Fungi, pl. 215. 1799.

*C. macrorhiza* Schwartz. Sv. Vet. Akad. Nya. Handl. **32**: 155, pl. 6, fig. 1. 1811.

?*C. brachiata* Fr. Hymen. Europ., p. 677. 1874.

?*C. alnea* Schulz. in Kalch. Icon. Hymen. Hung. **4**: pl. 35, fig. 7. 1877.

*C. pilipes* Müll. Flora Dan., pl. 1076, fig. 1.

PLATE 84

We have not met with this or any of the other species or forms in this well marked group in the living state, and draw the descriptions from dried plants and from notes of other collectors.

Plants simple, single, about 7-20 cm. long, slenderly clavate, with the tips acute in youth, but usually blunt later, and often inflated or flattened above, slender below; stem at base covered with dense more or less matted fibers which extend among the twigs and leaves; color varying from rather pale leather color through yellowish to reddish; entire plant very hollow; flesh thin and toughish.

Spores white, smooth, oblong to pip-shaped, size (in a plant from Ithaca, N. Y.) 5-7 x 10-14μ.; in a plant from Sweden (Romell) 5-6 x 12-14μ.; and in another from Saxony (Wagner) 5-5.5 x 12-14μ.

Growing on ground from rotting twigs and other detritus in coniferous (and deciduous?) woods in northern regions.   Not reported from the southern states but should be looked for in the balsam and spruce forests of our high mountains.

In the Curtis Herbarium are collections from Virginia, Massachusetts, and Maine, all of which seem true.   In the same herbarium is a collection received through Schweinitz from Massachusetts (Torrey), which is a *Mitrula* as shown by asci and spores. This is the collection on which Schweinitz based his report of *C. contorta* from Massachusetts, which is therefore an error (Trans. Am. Phil. Soc. II, **4**: 182).

Von Höhnel (Oesterr. Bot. Zeit. **54**: 425. 1904) regards *C. contorta* as a morbid form of this (an opinion shared by others), but for this he is criticised by Lind (Ann. Myc. **5**: 272. 1907), who says that they are quite distinct and that *C. fistulosa* is found on beech and *C. contorta* on alder and that the spores of the former are much smaller than those of the latter.   Harper, however, finds the spores of two typical plants of *C. contorta* practically the same as those of *C. fistulosa,* 6-9 x 14-18μ, and other characters the same also, the plants very hollow after the early stages.   Spores of a European plant of *C. contorta* from Bresadola at the New York Botanical Garden are said to be 7-9 x 14-20μ.   We find them to be 5.5-7.4 x 12-15μ.   Two other collections in his herbarium have spores in one case 6.5-8 x 15-18μ, in the other about 8 x 18.5μ.   Another collection from America on dead birch (Ithaca, Atkinson), labelled *C. Ardenia,* has spores 6-7.4 x 13-16μ. From the looks of things in Bresadola's herbarium it would seem certain that *C. contorta, C. brachiata,* and *C. alnea* are the same, and also that *C. fistulosa, C. Ardenia,* and *C. macrorhiza* are the same, but that the two groups are possibly different.

The usual description of *C. contorta* is as follows: "Simple, erumpent, stuffed, spongy-fleshy, soft to the touch, somewhat twisted, rugose, obtuse, pruinose, watery-yellow. On dead branches of alder, hazel, etc., 2.5-3 cm. high, 6-9 mm. thick."

The spore measurements given by different authors for *C. contorta* are so different as to indicate errors in determining it. *Clavaria molaris* Berk. (Grevillea **7**: 5. 1878) was originally described as allied to *C. contorta,* but no type exists, and the color, size and habit of growth suggest *Corticium pezizoideum.* The typical *C. fistulosa* certainly grows on coniferous twigs, whether on deciduous twigs also, we do not know. See Harper for a good discussion with photographs of all the forms and species of this group (Mycologia **10**: 53. 1918). *Clavaria Ardenia* is the form with inflated end, while *C. macrorhiza* is the form with a long, root-like extension among the leaves. Harper has found all these forms at Neebish, Michigan.

Illustrations: Boudier. Bull. Soc. Myc. Fr. **33**: pl. 1, fig. 5 (as *C. contorta*). 1917.

Flora Danica, pl. 1852, fig. 1.

Harper. Mycologia **10**: pl. 3 (as *C. Ardenia*) ; pl. 4, fig. A (as *C. fistulosa*), fig. B. (as *C. macrorhiza*), fig. C. (as *C. contorta*). 1918.

Holmskjold. Beata Ruris **1**: pl. 6 (as *C. fistulosa*) and pl. 12 (as *C. contorta*). 1790. Photographed in part by Burt in Ann. Mo. Bot. Gard. **9**: pl. 10, figs. 96, 97. 1922.

Kalchbrenner. Ic. Hymen. Hung., pl. 35, fig. 7. 1874.

Krombholz. Abbild., pl. 5, fig. 19. 1831.

Michael. Führer f. Pilzfreunde, Vol. 2, No. 22 (as *C. Ardenia*). 1901.

Migula in Thomé. Krypt.-Fl. Deutsch. **3**, 2, 1: pl. 24B, fig. 2 (as *C. Ardenia*). 1912.

Sowerby. Engl. Fungi, pl. 215. 1799.

New York: Bassadoga. Peck and Clinton. (Albany Herb.).

Catskill Mountains. Peck and Clinton. (Albany Herb.).

Ithaca. Atkinson. (Cornell Herb., as *C. Ardenia*).

Maine: Cumberland. Blake. (N. Y. Bot. Gard. Herb.). "Solitary on ground in woods."

Canada: Avon, Ontario. Dearness. (N. Y. Bot. Gard. Herb.). "On ground in coniferous swamps."

**Clavaria amethystina** (Batt.) Pers.    Comm., p. 46. 1797.    (Not
     *C. amethystea* Bull.).
     *Coralloides amethystina* Batt.    Fung. Agr. Arim. Hist., p. 22,
     pl. 1, fig. c. 1759.
     ?*C. purpurea* Schaeff.    Fung. Bavar., p. 117, pl. 172. 1763.
     (Not *C. purpurea* Müll.).
     *C. lavendula* Pk.    Bull. N. Y. St. Mus. **139**: 47. 1910.

Plates 24, 25, 28, and 84

Plants small, densely cespitose and more or less connate at
base; height 1.5-7.5 cm., usually simple to near the top and there
branching dichotomously or irregularly into two or several short
branches, which usually divide again at their tips into a few
sharp teeth; color when quite fresh a beautiful deep clear violet,
which is darkest upwards and very light and tinted with buff at
base.    Flesh very brittle and tender, solid, pellucid, violet; taste
mild, odor none.

Spores white, smooth, ovate-elliptic, pointed at one end,
3.3-4 x 3.7-6.6µ.

This attractive little plant is not common, but we find it every
year on the ground in deciduous woods.    No other *Clavaria* is
quite so fragile, the branches snapping with a clean break at the
slightest pressure.    In drying the color fades rapidly to buffy or
grayish tints and the texture becomes more pliable.    It has not
been reported before from this state, and is scantily represented
in herbaria.    There has been much confusion both in this country
and in Europe in regard to it, due largely to Bulliard's plate 496
which as *C. amethystea* represents an entirely different plant, a
form of *C. cristata,* which is also Fries's *C. lilacina.*    As a result
both species appear in herbaria under either name or as *C. purpurea.*    Spore measurements given by Saccardo and a good many
others are wrong.

The descriptions by Persoon and Fries leave little doubt of
what plant they had in mind as *C. amethystina.*    Fries refers to
Schaeffer's plate as good and to Bulliard's as hardly good (Epicr.,
p. 571), and later (Bull. Soc. Bot. Fr. **24**: 79. 1877) says that
there is no doubt that *C. lilacina* and *C. amethystina* are different
and that Bulliard's figures may be the former.    Our plants are

exactly like Schaeffer's plate 172 (*C. purpurea*) in shape, the only difficulty being the large spores as figured. We can at least safely say that our plant is the same as *Ramaria amethystina* as understood by Holmskjold (Beata Ruris, p. 110, pl. 28). His figures are excellent, and he speaks of the flesh as pellucid, a clear distinction between this and *C. cristata*. The reference to Holmskjold is the only one given by Persoon in Syn. Met. Fung, p. 590. For *C. Schaefferi* see under *C. cristata*. *Clavaria lavendula* Pk. is the same, as shown by the type, which has similar appearance and spores (about 3 x 6μ). A few other collections in Peck's herbarium labelled *C. amethystina* are also the same.

Illustrations: Battarra. As cited above. Photographic copy by Burt in Ann. Mo. Bot. Gard. **9**: pl. 8, fig. 62. 1922.
Berkeley. Outlines Brit. Fungi., pl. 18, fig. 2. 1860.
Cooke. Plain and Easy British Fungi, 2nd ed., pl. 17, fig. 2.
Gibson. Edible Toadstools and Mushrooms, pl. 31. 1895.
Hard. Mushrooms, fig. 387. 1908.
Holmskjold. Beata Ruris **1**: pl. 28 (as *Ramaria amethystina*). 1790.
Lanzi. Funghi Mang., pl. 13, figs. 4a, b, c. (b is good; the others are probably *C. cinerea* forms). 1897.
McIlvaine. Am. Fung., pl. 139, fig. 1. 1900.
Roques. Atlas Champ., pl. 1, fig. 2. 1864. Good.
Schaeffer. As cited above.
Venturi. Studi Micol., pl. 12, fig. 113. 1842.

North Carolina: Chapel Hill. No. 2282. Damp soil in path, June 28, 1916. No. 2622. By path in low mixed woods, July 9, 1917. Spores 3.3-3.7 x 5.5-6.7μ. No. 3423. By road west of cemetery, August 6, 1919. No. 3463. In deciduous woods, August 16, 1919. Plants very deep purple. No. 4363. On damp ground in deciduous woods, July, 1920. Very large for this species. Spores ovate to pip-shaped, 3.5-4.4 x 5.4-6.5μ.

South Carolina: Aiken. Ravenel. (Curtis Herb.). Two collections.

Alabama: Auburn. Earle. (N. Y. Bot. Gard. Herb.; no name). Spores about 3.5 x 6μ.

New York: Several localities. Peck. (Albany Herb., as *C. lavendula* and *C. amethystina*).
Onondago Valley. Underwood. (N. Y. Bot. Gard. Herb.).

Massachusetts: Stow. Davis. (Albany Herb., as type of *C. lavendula*). Spores about 3 x 7.2μ.

**Clavaria pyxidata** Pers.   Comm., p. 47 (179). 1797.
>   *C. coronata* Schw.   Trans. Am. Phil. Soc. II, **4**: 182. 1832.
>   ?*C. chondroides* Berk.   London Journ. Bot. **1**: 140, pl. 6, fig. 3. 1842.
>   *C. Petersii* B. & C.   Grevillea **2**: 7. 1873.
>   *C. javanica* Sacc. & Syd.   Syll. Fung. **14**: 238. 1890. (*C. coronata* Zipp. in Lév. Ann. Sci. Nat., 3rd. Ser., **2**: 215. 1844.)

PLATES 26, 27, AND 84

Plants up to 12 cm. high, often small, springing in clumps from an amorphous base which may enter the wood or may form a resupinate mass on the surface of the wood, these masses varying in extent from 1 to several cm.; main stem slender, 1.5-2.5 mm. thick, densely coated at base (if it is at all protected) with a dense, rather long, whitish or brownish pink pubescence, which also covers the entire resupinate mass when present; stems round or flattened and channelled, enlarging upward and dividing simultaneously like an umbel into several branches which spread out rather strongly and then turn up again; primary branches expanding suddenly at their tips into little cups from the margins of which spring the branchlets of the third degree; these may again end in cups with similar branches which finally terminate in smaller cups with little teeth on the rims.   Color of all parts when young and fresh a rather light clear yellow, about baryta yellow of Ridgway (or varying to a soaked straw-color), which in age or on drying or bruising becomes a dull ochraceous, beginning at the tips.   Sometimes certain parts become pallid pinkish before becoming ochraceous.   Flesh quite pliable and not at all brittle, tough and very peppery to the taste, as a rule, but varying to nearly mild (rarely).

Spores (of No. 1875) pure white, smooth, ovate to pip-shaped, about 2.3 x 4μ.   Basidia (of No. 3593) 4-spored, 3.7-4.4μ thick, very inconspicuous; hymenium about 26μ thick, set with a few small crystals and with many cystidia of two kinds: one kind is fusiform, pointed, hyaline, and almost empty; the other is cylindrical with rounded tips and dense contents, resembling somewhat a gleocystidium.   Both kinds project several microns beyond the basidia.   Hyphae parallel, 3.7μ thick just under the hymenium, up to 12μ thick and much intertwined in center.   Clamp connections present.

This is one of the most widely distributed of all species of plants. It is easily recognized by the cup-shaped expansions at the end of the branches and by the peppery taste and small, white spores. Young plants often lack the cups and if halted may reach maturity without their formation. In such cases the peppery taste which persists in drying will usually prevent confusion. Such small forms without cups are *C. Petersii,* as shown by good collections (the types and co-types) from Pieters at Kew and in the Curtis Herbarium. One of the Curtis plants was examined for spores which proved to be like those of *C. pyxidata,* smooth, minute, 2.5-3 x 4-4.5μ. The very characteristic brown hairs at the base are rarely mentioned, but if looked for are a decisive character. When the plant springs from very dense, smooth wood the tomentum is scarcely visible, but between bark and in crevices it is very conspicuous. One collection of *C. pyxidata* in the Bresadola Herbarium (Fungi Schemnitzienses) shows well the characteristic tomentose base. The types of *C. Petersii* (at Kew) show the tomentose base only slightly. Ravenel's Fungi Car. Exs. Fasc. 5, No. 33 (as *C. Petersii*), shows fine examples with good cups and brown tomentum at the base.

That this is *C. coronata* Schw. is almost certain. The latter is represented in his herbarium by a plant not in good condition, but not different apparently and with exactly the same spores, which are about 2-2.4 x 3.5-4μ. In Persoon's herbarium plants labelled *C. coronata* are well shown to be typical *C. pyxidata.* Bresadola also regards *C. coronata* and *C. pyxidata* as the same, as shown by a note in his herbarium.

*Clavaria chondroides* from Surinam (type at Kew) looks exactly like *C. pyxidata* (dark reddish cartilaginous) except that there are no cups. The absence of cups, however, is not important as the plants are small and the branches are clustered. As spores could not be found, the identity is not certainly established. Plants on the same sheet from Ceylon (no name) are typical *C. pyxidata.* *Clavaria javanica* Sacc. (*C. coronata* Zipp.) is not different. Authentic plants from Léveillé (Java) at Kew are like *C. pyxidata* in the dried state, and the spores are the same, 3-3.5 x 3.8-4.2μ. *Clavaria candelabra* Massee (Kew Bull. Miscell. Information Nos. **153-154**: 172. 1899) seems closely related to *C.*

*pyxidata* and may be the same, but has distinct, slender stalks with white mycelium at the base and somewhat larger spores. The type of *C. colensoi* Berk. (in Hooker, Flora Novae-Zelandiae **2**: 186. 1855) is in the dried state exactly like *C. pyxidata,* with cupped tips, cartilaginous color, etc., and furthermore has brown hairs at base, according to the description. However, a slide fails to show the spores of *C. pyxidata,* but does show a much larger, dark, smooth, ovate spore, 5-6.5 x 7-8.5µ.

Illustrations: Buller. Researches on Fungi 2: fig. 63. 1922.

Burt. Ann. Mo. Bot. Gard. **9**: pl. 6, fig. 48 (as *C. Petersii*) ; pl. 7, fig. 49 (as *C. coronata*). 1922.

Flora Danica, pl. 1304, fig. 1. 1806.

Hard. Mushrooms, fig. 389; also fig. 394 (as *C. coronata*). 1908.

Persoon. Comm., pl. 1, fig. 1. 1797. Photographed in part by Burt in Ann. Mo. Bot. Gard. **9**: pl. 6, fig. 47. 1922.

North Carolina: Chapel Hill. No. 359. On a very rotten log, October 11, 1911. Spores about 2.5 x 4.2µ. No. 1611. On rotting wood, July 15, 1915. Spores short-elliptic, about 2.2 x 4µ. No. 1875. On a rotting log of a deciduous tree, September 24, 1915. No. 3103. On a deciduous stump, May, 1918. Taste very peppery. No. 3593. On leaves, mixed woods, November 4, 1919. Taste very peppery; color pallid tan, brownish below. Spores pure white.

Blowing Rock. Coker and party, No. 5687. (U. N. C. Herb.). Spores typical.

South Carolina: Santee. Ravenel. (Curtis Herb., Cornell Herb., Kew Herb.).

Alabama: Pieters. (Curtis Herb., as *C. Petersii*).

Louisiana: Langlois. (Path. and Myc. Herb., Washington, as *C. Berkeleyi*).

Pennsylvania: Ohiopyle. Murrill. (N. Y. Bot. Gard. Herb.).

New York: Vaughns. Burnham. (U. N. C. Herb.). "Acrid when fresh." Also another collection. (U. N. C. Herb.). "Taste not very peppery."

Clyde. Cook. (N. Y. Bot. Gard. Herb.).

Connecticut: Redding. Seen by the author.

Massachusetts: Stockbridge. Murrill and Thompson. (N. Y. Bot. Gard. Herb.).

New Hampshire: Chocorua. Farlow. (U. N. C. Herb. from Farlow Herb.).

Indiana: Fern. Underwood. (N. Y. Bot. Gard. Herb.).

Michigan: Hicks. (N. Y. Bot. Gard. Herb.).

Missouri: Demetrio. (N. Y. Bot. Gard. Herb.).

Cuba: Wright. (Kew Herb.).

**Clavaria Kunzei** Fr.    Syst. Myc. **1**: 474. 1821.

?*C. subtilis* Pers.    Comm., p. 51 (183), pl. 1, fig. 2. 1797.

*C. chionea* Pers.    Myc. Europ. **1**: 167. 1822.

*C. subcorticalis* Schw.    Trans. Am. Phil. Soc. II, **4**: 182. 1832.

?*Lachnocladium subsimile* B. & C.    Grevillea **1**: 161. 1873.

*C. velutina* E. & E.    N. Am. Fungi, Ser. 2, No. 2024. 1888.

*C. asperula* Atk.    Ann. Myc. **6**: 54. 1908.

?*C. asperulans* Atk.    Ann. Myc. **6**: 55. 1908.

PLATES 29 AND 84

Branching from the ground into clustered and often fused stalks of variable length. Individual tufts delicate, slender throughout, about 2-6 cm. tall, and 1.5 cm. broad, usually; at times up to 9 cm. high and 6 cm. broad; branching quickly or tardily into several branches which curve outward at base, making broad, more or less lunate angles, then upright again, and branching about twice more into two or three branchlets, which terminate in rather abruptly pointed prong-like tips; main stems and usually the lower parts of the main branches often decidedly rough pubescent, with sterile, scurfy-velvety lines and areas extending higher up the plant in most cases, but often this pubescence is practically absent; entire plant pure milk white, but in drying the plant turns a tan or buff brown, the upper parts usually becoming reddish translucent like cartilage, or less often a deep opaque brown; flesh white, toughish, not brittle, but soft and flexible; cells of flesh closely packed, parallel, somewhat sinuous, about 4-5$\mu$ thick; taste and odor none. Sometimes the main and secondary divisions broaden before branching and rather resemble the horns of an elk. There is much variation in the extent of the sterile areas, some of the plants showing them over most of the middle region, others having very few of them. All parts are typically slender, but there is great variation in this respect, at times the branches and stems are so numerous and delicate as to almost resemble a *Typhula* when dried; again they are few and much coarser.

Spores white, spherical, minutely asperulate (under oil immersion) or some apparently smooth, 2.5-3.5 x 3.5-4.5$\mu$. Hymenium (of No. 4683) 55-65$\mu$ thick, apparently 2-layered; basidia about 4-6$\mu$ thick, 4-spored.

Gregarious on soil, rotting bark, or moss in moist deciduous woods, rarely in coniferous woods. Miss Hibbard, as well as

Burnham and Allen, notes that the plant turns pinkish at base when rubbed or on exposure. We have not noted this. The color may soon become less pure white, sordid, or yellowish as fading or drying begins.

This is a well marked species distinguished by small size, white color, delicate habit, usually scurfy-tomentose stem and areas, tenacious substance, and very small, subspherical spores. Aside from its near relatives, *C. subcaespitosa* and *C. angulispora,* which see for comparison, the species is superficially most like *C. gracilis* from which it differs in the white color, tomentose areas, lack of odor, shorter spores, preference for deciduous woods and absence of stringy mycelium.

*Clavaria Kunzei* has been variously interpreted by European authors, and has been badly confused. The difficulties were indicated when Krombholz figured a plant as *C. Kunzei* (Abbild., pl. 53, figs. 14-17. 1841) which Fries denied as that species and referred to as illustrating a new species which he called *C. Krombholzii* (Epicr., p. 572. 1838). It is evident that Krombholz's plates (pl. 53, figs. 15 and 16; pl. 54, figs. 18-20) were issued before the text (1841) or that Fries had seen the drawings before they were published. Krombholz refers in the text (heft 7, p. 20) to Fries's new name *C. Krombholzii* as a synonym of *C. Kunzei,* but from the former's good figures we have little doubt that his species is a coarse, non-cristate form of *C. cristata,* as represented by our Nos. 2702 and 2746.

Quélet describes *C. Kunzei* (Champ. du Jura, etc., pt. 3, p. 16, pl. 2, fig. 11. 1875) as sub-hyaline, snow white (citrine on drying), inodorous; spores oblong, white, etc. The figure looks like our plant, but judging from the figure and description of the spores, they are quite different (no dimensions given). Britzelmayr (Hymen., p. 287, Clavariei, fig. 12) describes and figures a very different plant from Quélet's with spores subspherical, 9-12 x 8$\mu$ (apparently a form of *C. cristata*). In another place (Hymen., pt. 10, p. 179) he gives the spores as colorless with a yellowish nucleus, 9-10 x 8$\mu$. Saccardo's note "spores globose, 9-12 x 8$\mu$, hyaline," was probably taken from Britzelmayr, and is incorrect. That Schweinitz followed Krombholz in his conception of *C. Kunzei* is shown by a collection in his herbarium which is *C.*

*Krombholzii* Fr. with spherical spores about 6μ in diameter.   A collection at Albany from Finland by Karsten shows that Karsten's idea of the species is entirely different.   The plant is on pine bark and does not look at all like ours (no spores could be found).

Cotton has recently referred an English species to *C. Kunzei,* and has, it seems to us, interpreted the species correctly (Trans. Brit. Myc. Soc. **3**: 180. 1909).   He does not associate it with our American names, but a plant from Chelsea, England, sent us by him is like ours and has similar spores, about 3μ thick and minutely warted.   Fries's original description and Cotton's description also agree well with our plant.

Our species is certainly *C. chionea,* as shown by the well preserved type specimens in Persoon's herbarium.   They are just like our plants and have spores minutely rough, subspherical, 3.7μ in diameter.   One of the typical plants sent from Persoon may now be found at Kew.   Fries himself later asserted the identity of his and Persoon's plant.   The type of *C. subtilis* is not represented in the Persoon Herbarium and its identity is very doubtful. A plant labelled *C. subtilis* in the Bresadola collection at the New York Botanical Garden (Sontagberg, Strasser) is exactly like our Maine plant in appearance and spores.   The tips are translucent and tend to split up into fibers in both this and ours.   Another from him (Trentino) labelled *C. gracilis* is not our *C. gracilis* but the above, with the same appearance and spores (4 x 4.8μ, minutely warted), and this is true of several collections labelled *C. gracilis* in the Bresadola Herbarium at Stockholm.   The interpretation by Bourdot and Galzin of *C. subtilis* differs from that of Bresadola.   They give the spores as "finely rugose, 5-6 x 7-8μ." (Bull. Soc. Myc. Fr. **26**: 216. 1910).   We have received several collections of *C. Kunzei* from Romell: one (Stockholm, Sept. 4, 1898) labelled with a question has spores subspherical, minutely rough, 3.4-3.8 x 3.8-4.8μ; another (Aug. 8, 1912), spores about 3 x 3.7μ; and a third (Sept., 1915) labelled *C. gracilis* has spores subspherical, about 4μ thick.   For another collection of *C. Kunzei* see so-called *C. flaccida* in the Fries Herbarium.

In the Schweinitz Herbarium is part of a plant of his *C. subcorticalis* in good condition which proves his species to be *C.*

*Kunzei.* The spores of the specimen are subspherical, asperulate, about 3µ in diameter. We have examined plants of *C. asperula* in the Cornell Herbarium from Ithaca and from North Carolina, and find them identical in appearance and spores with our Chapel Hill plants. There is also an authentic specimen from Ithaca in the Farlow Herbarium. We have not been able to find the type of *C. asperulans* at Ithaca, but from the description it is probably the same as *C. asperula*. *Clavaria velutina* is shown by the type from Newfield, N. J., to be this species, with spores minutely warted, subspherical, about 2.5-3.2µ thick. A letter from Dr. Farlow to Ellis at the New York Botanical Garden shows that he had compared specimens of *C. velutina* from Ellis with *L. subsimile* in the Curtis Herbarium and thought them the same. In Bresadola's herbarium a collection from Atkinson of typical *C. Kunzei* is labelled "*C. velutina* E. & E.=*L. semivestitum* B. & C.", but we find the spores of the latter species quite different. *Clavaria dealbata* Berk. (Hooker's Journ. Bot. **8**: 275. 1856. *Lachnocladium dealbatum* (Berk.) Cooke. Grevillea **20**: 10. 1901) is very near this species. The spores of the type at Kew (Spruce, No. 159) are almost identically like those of the present species, spherical, minutely asperulate, 3-3.4µ thick (pl. 91, fig. 10); but the dried plants look more like *C. angulispora*. From the types at Kew and in the Curtis Herbarium *C. pallida* B. & C. (Journ. Linn. Soc. **10**: 338 [1868] 1869) does not seem separable from *C. dealbata*. The spores are the same in both the Kew and Curtis specimens, minutely warted, spherical, about 3-3.7µ thick.

It is apparently this species that Oudemans had in mind in reporting *C. subtilis* (Kruidk. Arch., 3rd ser., **2**: 674. 1902). He says: "Species growing on the ground, small, simple or branched (once or twice forked) at the stem, branches slender, white or pale gray, reaching about the same level. Spores colorless, 2 x 3.5µ in diameter. Height of our examples 1-2 cm.; thickness, 0.5-1.5 mm. On earth in shady places."

Our microscopic study of sections of a number of specimens that we are referring to *C. Kunzei,* while agreeing rather closely in the size and appearance of the plant as well as in the size and form of the spores and basidia, and size and arrangement of context threads, show on the other hand certain differences that may or may not indicate varietal, or possibly specific distinction. We have not been able to correlate these differences and they are moreover of doubtful systematic value. We give below three examples illustrating some of this variation:

No. 40.  Vaughns, N. Y.
Spores obscurely asperulate, 2.8 x 3.2$\mu$.
Basidia about 4-4.4$\mu$ thick.
Hymenium 25-35$\mu$ thick, densely packed with large and small crystals which are insoluble in KOH.
Threads of flesh 2-6$\mu$ (average about 4$\mu$) thick, parallel in longitudinal section, closely packed; no clamp connections seen.

No. 59a.  Vaughns, N. Y.   (Part of the collection in Albany).
Spores minutely but obviously asperulate, 2.7-3.5 x 3-4$\mu$.
Basidia 3.7-6.6$\mu$ thick (usually about 4$\mu$), 4-spored.
Hymenium about 100$\mu$ thick; a few crystals present.
Threads of flesh 4-7.5$\mu$ thick (most about 5$\mu$ thick), parallel in longitudinal section; clamp connections present.

No. 63a.  Long Island, N. Y.
Spores smooth or nearly so, 3 x 4$\mu$.
Basidia 4.8-6.2$\mu$ thick, 4-spored, fusiform.
Hymenium 30-37$\mu$ thick.
Threads of flesh 3-4.8$\mu$ thick, parallel in longitudinal section; no clamp connections seen.

Juel (cited under *C. cristata*) finds in *C. subtilis* (determined by Dr. R. E. Fries) the basidia and hymenium much as in *C. muscoides,* basidia 4-spored, spores uninucleate (pl. 3, figs. 81-83).

Illustrations: Britzelmayr.  Hymen. Südb., Clavariei, fig. 13 (as *C. subtilis*).  (Fig. 69, so labelled, cannot be the same).
Burt.  Ann. Mo. Bot. Gard. **6**: 272, fig. 11 (as *L. subsimile*).  1919; **9**: pl. 6, fig. 44 (as *C. asperula*) ; fig. 45 (as *C. asperulans*) ; pl. 11, fig. 103 (as *C. subcorticalis*).  1922.
Persoon.  Comm., pl. 1, fig. 2 (as *C. subtilis*).  1797.
Rea.  Trans. Brit. Myc. Soc. **6**: pl. 2, fig. 5 (as *C. chionea*).  1917.
North Carolina: Chapel Hill.  No. 1704.  In tufts in colonies, wet soil in woods, September 8, 1915.
Asheville.  Beardslee.  (U. N. C. Herb.).  Spores exactly like those of Chapel Hill plants, asperulate, 3.5$\mu$ in diameter.
Blue Ridge Mountains.  Atkinson.  (Cornell Herb., as *C. asperula*).
Pink Bed Valley.  Murrill and House.  (U. N. C. Herb.).  Spores minutely asperulate, subspherical, 3.4 x 4$\mu$.

Salem.   Schweinitz.   (Curtis Herb., as *C. subtilis*).   Spores, minute, rough, 3 x 4.5µ.   Other collections so labelled there are not this.

Blowing Rock.   Coker and party.   (U. N. C. Herb.).

Dillingham.   Elevation 3600 feet.   J. S. Holmes, No. 4683.   (U. N. C. Herb.).   Very slender, nearly simple collection, once forked or with a few prongs; channelled and ridged, the axils flattened.   Spores minutely rough, 3.5-4µ thick.

South Carolina:   Ravenel.   (Kew Herb., as *C. subtilis*).   The plants are like ours.   Spores typical, 3.4-3.8 x 4-4.5µ.

District of Columbia:   Washington.   Braendle.   (Albany Herb.).

New Jersey:   Newfield.   Ellis.   (N. Y. Bot. Gard. Herb., as type of *C. velutina*).

Pennsylvania:   Buck Hill Falls.   Mrs. Delafield.   (N. Y. Bot. Gard. Herb.).

New York:   Vaughns.   Burnham.   No. 22.   "White when fresh; handsome."   Spores about 2.6 x 3.5µ.   No. 36.   Spores rough, 3µ thick.   No. 37.   Spores 3.5-3.9 x 4-5.2µ, minutely warted.   No. 40.   September 22, 1912.   See microscopic data above.   No. 64.   "Pure white when fresh."   Spores smooth or nearly so, 3 x 3.5µ.   No. 111.   "Snow white. No odor or taste when fresh unless very slightly farinaceous."   (All in U. N. C. Herb.).   Also collection (Albany Herb., our No. 59a) with which was mixed *C. cineroides*.   See microscopic data above.

Forge.   Peck.   (U. N. C. Herb.).   Spores minutely rough, 2.2-3.5 x 3-4µ.

Sand Lake.   Peck.   (Albany Herb.).   Spores rough (?), 2.5 x 3.3µ.

Monengo Creek.   (Schw. Herb., as *C. subcorticalis*).

Croghan.   Peck.   (U. N. C. Herb.).   Spores rough, 2.5 x 3.5µ.

Adirondack Mountains.   Murrill.   (N. Y. Bot. Gard. Herb.).   Spores nearly smooth, 2.5 x 3µ.

Long Island.   Dodge and Seaver.   (U. N. C. Herb., No. 63a).   See microscopic data above.

Massachusetts:   Newtonville.   Allen.   (Albany Herb.).   "Pure white, turning pink at base when touched."   Spores as usual, nearly smooth.

Vermont:   Newfane.   Miss Hibbard, No. 7.   (U. N. C. Herb.) .   "Pure white when growing, but turns pink when picked."   Spores smooth or nearly so, 2.2-3 x 3.5-4µ.

New Hampshire:   Chocorua.   Farlow.   (U. N. C. Herb. from Farlow Herb., as *C. corniculata*).   Spores spherical, 3-4µ thick.

Maine:   Calais.   L. F. MacNichol.   (U. N. C. Herb.).   "Among moss and hemlock or spruce leaves, September, 1916."   Spores nearly smooth, 2.6-3 x 3-3.5µ.

Bar Harbor.   Miss White.   (N. Y. Bot. Gard. Herb., No. 150).

Michigan:   Mrs. J. A. Cahn.   (Cornell Herb., as *C. velutina*).

Ohio:   Waynesville.   Morgan.   (Kew Herb., as *C. subtilis*).   Spores as usual, about 4µ in diameter.

Canada: Ottawa. Macoun. (Albany Herb., as *Lachnocladium semives-titum*). Spores minutely asperulate, 3.5-4.5µ thick.

Jamaica. Morce's Gap. On ground in woods, 5000 ft. elevation. Murrill. (N. Y. Bot. Gard. Herb. and U. N. C. Herb.).

## Clavaria subcaespitosa Pk.    Bull. N. Y. St. Mus. **167**: 39. 1913.

### PLATE 84

We have not seen this except in the dry state, but have examined the type at Albany, two other collections from the type locality sent us and the N. Y. Botanical Garden by Miss Hibbard, and also two collections sent by her from Newfane, Vermont. The types are as large as any of the other specimens, brittle, tan to cream color, the base rooting and branching at or below the ground, less than a cm. thick, a little scurfy tomentose below but not so much so as *C. Kunzei,* which seems to be a near relative. The spores are small, but distinctly larger than in the latter (3.4-4 x 4-5.2µ) and are shaped much as in *C. pulchra,* the minute, warty spines much more numerous than in *C. Kunzei.* According to Miss Hibbard the spores are white. Other differences from *C. Kunzei* are larger size and greater fragility.

We believe that this is the same as *C. lentofragilis* Atk., the spores being the same and the descriptions agreeing in all important respects. However, we have not been able to compare an authentic specimen of the latter side by side with this, so are retaining both for the present. It is also possible that this is *C. elongata* Britz. His entire description is, "Entirely white; spores 3-4µ, very rough, with fine and short spines." His figure 50 is like our plants.

In size, form and color in the dry state *C. cineroides* is similar, but that has very different spores. Peck's description of *C. subcaespitosa* is as follows:

"Forming dense tufts 7.5-12.5 cm. tall, fragile, white or whitish, the stems united at the base, three to five times dichotomously divided, the terminal branchlets obtuse or subacute, both stems and branches solid, soft, becoming thinner and flattened or angular in drying, flesh white, taste mild; spores broadly ellipsoid or subglobose, 4-5 x 3-4µ. Ground. Ellis. Mass. September."

Miss Hibbard has kindly sent us her notes on the fresh condition of the plants collected in 1920, which are as follows:

"When growing the color is pure white, almost translucent, fragile, tips when young cuspidate, when older the rounded tips prolong and become pitchfork shape. Dichotomous forking. As the moisture dries out the color becomes a pale cream white and looks more opaque. On some the bruises have turned a pale brownish lavender, or lavender-brown, a tint combining both colors, and as one glances across the tips in certain lights there is a hint of the same color. Does not bruise easily. I make the taste to be tardily and slightly acrid but not peppery.

"The stem of all specimens are not subcaespitose but show a very shallow trunk with the first branches creased to the base when not divided. Tomentose at base. Base sometimes stained brown by the earth."

Illustration:    Burt. Ann. Mo. Bot. Gard. **9**: pl. 6, fig. 39. 1922.

Massachusetts: Ellis. Miss Hibbard. (Albany Herb., type). Also specimens (U. N. C. and N. Y. Bot. Gard. Herb.) from the type locality.

Vermont: Newfane. Miss Hibbard. (U. N. C. Herb.). Spores subspherical, broader at mucro end, distinctly short-spinulose, 3.5-4.2 x 4-6μ.

## Clavaria lentofragilis Atk.    Ann. Myc. **6**: 57. 1908.

### PLATE 84

This is known only from the type, which we have examined at Ithaca. It is a large plant with a distinct stalk and a vast number of slender tips. It has the general appearance of *C. stricta*. Atkinson's description follows:

"Plants 15 cm. high, tufts 12 cm. broad; trunks 2-4 cm. long by 2-3 cm. thick, dividing into several short branches which are repeatedly dichotomously branched, axils slightly rounded; tips short, conic. Trunk gray, branches white, tips soft and fragile. Spores white, oval to subglobose, asperulate, 4-6μ in diameter. Taste and odor not marked."

Illustration: Burt. Ann. Mo. Bot. Gard. **9**: pl. 7, fig. 54. 1922.

New York: Long Island. On very rotten wood in sphagnum swamp. Atkinson. (Cornell Herb., type, No. 20242).

**Clavaria angulispora** Pat.    Bull. Soc. Myc. Fr. **4** : 41, pl. 13, fig.
    4. 1888.
*C. nodulosperma* Atk.    Ann. Myc. **7** : 368. 1909.
*Lachnocladium dubiosum* Bres. in Rick, Pilze Bras.    Broteria
    **5** : 13, pl. 6, fig. 3. 1906.    (No description, for which see
    Ann. Myc. **18** : 50. 1920).

PLATES 30 AND 84

This beautiful species which is usually pure white is known in
North America only from North Carolina and was described by
Professor Atkinson as a new species from plants collected by us.
It seems almost certain, however, that it had been published twice
before from South America.    Atkinson's description is as follows:

"Plants stalked, very much branched, 3-4 cm. high, branching,
2-3 cm. broad.    Stems slender, about 3 mm. in diameter.    Primary branching dichotomous or subpalmate.    The branches
branching in a similar way, more or less flexuous and often
slightly flattened.    Axils acute or rounded.    Plants entirely
white, flour-white, soft, flexible, not brittle.    Spores white, angular to tuberculate like the spores of some species of *Inocybe,*
3-3.5 x 5-7μ.    C. U. Herb., No. 22641, on ground, mixed woods by
Fern Walk near Sparrow's Pond, Chapel Hill, N. C., W. C.
Coker, October 2, 1908."

The plant is abundant in humus or rotting wood in deciduous
woods near branches in Chapel Hill during summer and fall and
since the above description was written we have made numerous
other collections, some of which were much larger plants than the
first.    Our description follows:

Plants 3-11 cm. high, and 2-8 cm. broad.    Stalks long and
slender and extended below into an obvious, thready, white mycelium; main branches often much flattened upward in an antler-
like fashion, terminating in numerous, short, flattened, pointed
branchlets; entire plant pure chalky white as a rule, but occasionally varying to pale pink especially upward, tough and quite pliable
to rather rigid and moderately brittle; taste pleasant and mild;
odor distinctly of old ham.

Spores (of No. 2404) pure white, angular-tuberculate, 3-3.8 x 4.6-7.4µ.  Basidia 6-7µ thick, 4-spored; hymenium (of No. 4433) 40-60µ thick; threads of flesh 2-3µ thick, parallel, clamp connections present.

In drying the plant does not become ochraceous or brownish, but remains white or nearly so.   The photograph shows the habit of branching better than words.   Small plants of this species are similar in size, shape and color to C. Kunzei, but are easily distinguished from it by absence of tomentum on the stalks, smell of old ham, and larger, nodular spores.

There is no reasonable doubt that this is C. angulispora Pat., described from Venezuela on earth in woods, which agrees in every important respect except that he gives the basidia as 2-spored. The spore drawings show the same surface as ours and the shape may be easily matched in our collections.

Lachnocladium dubiosum is certainly this species.   The appearance of the type in Bresadola's herbarium is identical, and the spores also agree.

Illustration: Burt.  Ann. Mo. Bot. Gard. **9**: pl. 6, fig. 46 (as C. nodulosperma, in error nodulospora).  1922.

North Carolina: Chapel Hill.  No. 844.  On ground in mixed woods, September 26, 1913.  Spores 2.7-3.3 x 4.6-5.2µ.  No. 1169.  By path in oak leaves.  Spores elliptic, nodular-roughened, 2.5-3.4 x 4.2-5.1µ.  A fine lot of plants.  No. 1281.  Under pines near branch, September 29, 1914.  Spores 3.4-5.1 x 4.2-5.9µ.  No. 1846.  In damp woods, Fern Banks, September 19, 1915.  No. 2404.  On wooded bluff near Meeting of Waters, July 20, 1916.  No. 3339.  Mossy cool bank by creek, June 12, 1919.  Spores 2.9-3.7 x 4.8-5.5µ.  No. 3355.  By branch near Meeting of the Waters, deciduous woods, June 14, 1919.  Typical plants, but one distinctly light pink nearly all over, two others with very pale tint of pink.  Spores as usual.  No. 3466.  Oak woods by spring, damp ground, August 18, 1919.  No. 3442.  Damp ground by Strowd's spring, August 16, 1919.  No. 4433.  Deciduous woods by Battle's Branch, July 17, 1920.  A very much branched, short-stalked collection, 7 cm. broad and 6 cm. high.  No. 4393.  Woods near Meeting of the Waters, July 13, 1920.  One of these plants had a very odd form, the distinct stem flaring out suddenly into a kind of plate, the margin breaking up into a fringe of short branches, and a few little branches sticking up from the surface of the plate.  Plate with fringe 2.5 cm. broad. (Many other collections from similar places).

Winston-Salem.  Schallert.  In moist woods, September 10, 1922.  Spores as usual.

**Clavaria arborea** Atk.    Ann. Myc. **6**: 56. 1908.

The following is the original description:

"Plants very much branched dichotomously, curved and sometimes deformed, white to alutaceous, terminal branches rose-pink, or yellowish brown probably when old. Basidia 4-spored. Spores obovate, asperulate, white, 3-4 x 2-3μ."

We have examined the type and also another collection in Ithaca from the same place. The former consists of one plant and pieces. It is repeatedly but not abundantly branched and rather tall and narrow. No spores could be found on it. The second collection is smaller and only slightly branched, the branches spreading.

As the spores and basidia do not differ much in the description from those of *C. Kunzei* and *C. subcaespitosa* it may be a color form of one of them.

Illustration: Burt. Ann. Mo. Bot. Gard. **9**: pl. 6, fig. 38. 1922.

New York: Varna. On ground in woods. Whetzel. (Cornell Herb., type, No. 13647).

**Clavaria asterella** Atk.    Ann. Myc. **6**: 55. 1908.

PLATE 84

This is known only from Mt. Mitchell. The type consists of one tall, narrow plant with very numerous tips; the spores as described. Atkinson's description is as follows:

"Plants ochraceous, 5-7 cm. high. Trunk short, primary branches open, bases divaricate, axils rounded, upper branches fastigiate. Plants soft, flexible. Spores small, white, oboval, inequilateral in side view, with an oil drop, 4-5 x 2.5-3μ, with a few scattered short spines."

Illustration: Burt. Ann. Mo. Bot. Gard. **9**: pl. 7, fig. 52. 1922.

North Carolina: Mt. Mitchell. On leaf mold, September, 1901. Atkinson. (Cornell Herb., type, No. 11914).

**Clavaria rufipes** Atk.    Ann. Myc. **6**: 57. 1908.

PLATE 91

Plants isolated, sparsely gregarious, arising from a distinct mycelial pad; slender and delicate, 1-2 cm. high, nearly filiform when dry; stem usually distinct from the club, 6-8 mm. long, pale brown, enlarging into the creamy and very pale brownish flattened club which expands above and divides in most cases into a few crooked horns or thickish flattened lobes which may divide again; surface glabrous; texture pliable, but not tough, easily broken. The dry plants have brown stems and dull ochraceous hymenium.

Spores pip-shaped to ovate, smooth, hyaline under the microscope, a distinct oil drop, 3-3.7 x 3.9-5.5µ. Basidia about 4µ thick, 2-4-spored, the sterigmata often quite long, up to 10µ; hymenium about 25µ thick.

The types of *C. rufipes* are like our plants and have identical spores, smooth, pip-shaped to oval, 2.8-3 x 4.5-5.5µ. The fertile parts of our plants have a little color, but are so pale as to make only a slight discrepancy in color as described for the type. The species seems related to *C. delicata* Fr., of which we have examined two lots from Fries, one at Kew and one in the Curtis Herbarium. They recall our plants in appearance and have spores exactly the same (in the Curtis specimens) or nearly the same (a little longer in the Kew specimens). In the former they are 2.6-2.9 x 4.4-5µ; in the latter 2.5-3 x 5-6µ (pl. 91, fig. 9). The branches are, however, more filiform and much longer, and are not flattened, and Fries describes his species as villose below and as white. *Clavaria delicata* is not known to occur in America. Atkinson's description follows:

"Plants entirely white, base of stem tinged rufous, about 2 cm. high, branched like *Clavaria muscoides,* tips blunt and slightly enlarged. Basidia 4-spored. Spores oboval, granular, then with an oil drop, smooth, 4-6 x 2.5-3µ."

Illustration: Burt. Ann. Mo. Bot. Gard. **9**: pl. 6, fig. 43. 1922.

North Carolina: Blowing Rock. Coker and party, No. 5501. On bits of wood, twigs and leaves under *Rhododendron,* August 17, 1922. (U. N. C. Herb.).

New York: Ithaca. On ground in woods, October 10, 1902. Whetzel. (Cornell Herb., No. 14037. Type).

**Clavaria crocea** Pers. Comm., p. 57 (189). 1797.

PLATES 28 AND 84

Growing separately or in clusters of 2-4, with the stems approximate but not fused. Plants very delicate, 1-1.5 cm. high, 6-8 mm. broad, stalk distinct, about ¼ to ½ the entire height, minutely furfuraceous, branched in an open way 3 or 4 times, the angles lunate, tips acute, the branches terete; color throughout a rich chrome-orange or in one form golden yellow; texture tender, but quite elastic and not brittle; flesh color of surface; taste and odor none. In drying the color becomes more intense—a deep red-orange in the orange form, while in the yellow form it becomes dull ochraceous.

Spores (of No. 21, print) white, subspherical, obscurely asperulate, 2.5-2.7 x 3-3.3μ. Basidia (of No. 4660) about 3μ thick, 4-spored; hymenium about 20μ thick; threads of flesh 2.5-5.5μ thick, clamp connections present.

The above description, except for mention of a yellow form, is drawn from our collection from Redding, Conn. (No. 21), which may be considered the typical form. The plants were growing in a fine colony covering an area of less than a square foot and the individuals were remarkably regular in size, color and form.

We do not think there can be any doubt that our plants are correctly referred to this species, which is unsurpassed for delicacy and beauty, and is one of the rarest of Clavarias. Persoon's description is in perfect agreement and his colored figure is of the same shape and size although of slightly different color (distinctly more reddish). Except the next there is no other earth-growing American species of such extreme delicacy. *Clavaria crocea* has been reported only a very few times since Persoon's day. Berkeley includes it as British in his Outlines (p. 280), but Cotton and Wakefield place it among excluded species. The plants at Kew on which Berkeley based his record are very delicate, long-stemmed, branched above, about 1 cm. tall, ochraceous in dry state. It may be correctly determined, but we could find no spores. Schweinitz reports it as very rare at Bethlehem (Syn. Fung., p. 181), and there is a good plant so labelled in his herbarium. Britzelmayr's figure of what he calls *C. crocea* is something quite different from Persoon's plant (Hymen. Südb., Clavariei, fig. 24).

The spore measurements given by Saccardo are taken from Brit-zelmayr and are thus incorrect.    The only illustration of the true *C. crocea* is Persoon's in Icon. Descr. Fung., pl. 9, fig. 6. 1798. The illustration by Pabst under this name (Crypt.-Flora, etc., **2**: pl. 21. 1875) is too large and coarse to represent this species.

From small branched forms of *C. muscoides* this species dif-fers in much greater delicacy, richer color, absence of taste and different spores.    The form of *C. crocea* that we have found at Chapel Hill and Blowing Rock is exactly like the Connecticut plants except for the golden yellow color (a change to green when bruised was noted in No. 4660), and it is very likely that this last form is the *C. tetragona* of Schweinitz (Schr. Nat. Ges. Leipzig **1**: 112. 1822) of which no type or authentic specimen is known to exist.    We have not noticed an angular tendency in the species, but that compressed or angled forms may occur is not at all improbable, and this is indeed suggested by the fact that Atkinson referred to *C. tetragona* an Ithaca plant (No. 23376) which is the same as our *C. crocea,* with spores minutely asperu-late, 3 x 4µ.    The description of *C. sulphurascens* Schw. (Trans. Amer. Phil. Soc. II, **4**: 182. 1832) strongly suggests *C. crocea,* but the color is not just right.    No type or authentic specimen is known.

*Clavaria pulchella* Boud. (*C. exigua* Pk., etc.) cannot be dis-tinguished from this species except by the color, and it is possible that it is only a color form of *C. crocea.*    There is also possibly a white form of this species.    In the Bresadola Herbarium is a col-lection of *C. crocea* collected by O. Jaap under alders which, from the determination, is presumably of a yellowish or saffron color and has spores 2.2-2.5 x 3-3.5µ.    With these were growing plants which were pure white, but otherwise of exactly the same appear-ance.    We find the spores to be subspherical, obscurely rough, 2-3 x 2.5-3.7µ.    Bresadola has referred these to *C. subtilis,* with which they agree except for very small size and somewhat smaller spores.    The two species are evidently related, as is also *C. vestitipes.*

North Carolina: Chapel Hill.   No. 4660.   Mixed woods in hog pasture, September 28, 1920.   Small specimens, agreeing with the Connecticut plant in all particulars except depth of color and change to green when crushed; 3-5 mm. high, several times forked, orange yellow, somewhat paler toward base, tips pointed. Flesh color of surface, green when crushed, tender but not very brittle, splintering when bent at 45°. Spores about 2.6μ thick. No. 4805. In humus under rotting oak limb, January 20, 1921. Base attached by a little mat of mycelium. Branches of very unequal length. Spores subspherical, 2.2-2.8 x 3-3.6μ. No. 4843. In woods mold under rotting oak log, March 14, 1921. Spores subspherical, with one distinct oil drop, 3.4-3.7μ in diameter.

Blowing Rock. Coker and party, No. 5599. In deep mold, mixed woods, August 20, 1922. Golden yellow. Spores smooth or obscurely rough, 1.8-2.5 x 3-3.7μ. Also two other collections. (U. N. C. Herb.).

Pennsylvania: Bethlehem. Schweinitz. (Schw. Herb.).

New York: Ithaca. Atkinson. (Cornell Herb., No. 23376, as *C. tetragona*, and U. N. C. Herb.).

Connecticut: Redding. Coker, No. 21. In black woods mold at foot of a dead chestnut tree, "The Glen," September 7, 1919. (U. N. C. Herb.).

**Clavaria pulchella** Boud.   Bull. Soc. Myc. Fr. **3**: 146, pl. 13, fig. 2. 1887.

   *C. tenuissima* Sacc.   Michelia **1**: 436. 1878. (Not *C. tenuissima* Lév. Ann. Sci. Nat., 3rd Ser., **5**: 156. 1846).

   *C. Bizzozeriana* Sacc.   Syll. **6**: 693. 1888.

   *C. exigua* Pk.   Rept. N. Y. St. Mus. **54**: 155. 1901.

   *C. conchyliata* Allen.   Trans. Brit. Myc. Soc. **3**: 92. 1908.

PLATE 84

We have not seen this in the living state and adapt the following from Peck's description of *C. exigua*:

Very small; stem slender, dichotomously or somewhat irregularly branching, white, branches delicate lavender color or the lower white toward the base, tips subacute, axils rounded; spores minute, globose, 2-2.5μ broad. Among fallen leaves in woods. Floodwood. September. The whole plant is scarcely more than six lines high. The coloring of the upper part is very delicate and beautiful.

We have examined the type of *C. exigua* and find the plants to be minute, delicate, branched, almost hair-like, with a few minute hyaline spores (many large brown spores of a mold intermixed). The plants are springing from fallen leaves of deciduous woods.

There is no doubt that it is the same as the species entered above as synonyms, of which *C. pulchella* has precedence. As Cotton and Wakefield give certain structural details not mentioned by others, we quote the following from them (as *C. Bizzozeriana*):

"Plants branched, very small, not more than 1 cm. in height, solitary or in groups, at first violet, becoming discoloured with age. Stem reddish-yellow, pubescent below, with rooting base. Branching irregular, dichotomous, the axils of the branches patent; branches very slender, 0.5 mm. thick, erect, apices blunt. Flesh white. Internal structure filamentous, filaments 3-4μ in diameter. Basidia 15-18 x 3-4μ; sterigmata 2-4. Spores hyaline, smooth, globose or subglobose, 2.4-3.5μ in diameter, 1-guttulate."

A bit of the co-type of *C. tenuissima* at Kew Herbarium is exactly like *C. exigua* in the dried state and has the same spores, 2.5-3.6μ thick. *Clavaria conchyliata* is not represented at Kew, but Cotton and Wakefield consider it a synonym of *C. Bizzozeriana,* and the description agrees well. In the Bresadola Herbarium at Stockholm are plants from Nice (Barla, coll.) determined by Bresadola as *C. pulchella.* They are also like *C. exigua* with the same spores, which are subspherical, very minutely rough, 2.2-3μ thick. Bresadola's notes gives the spores as "4 x 2.5-3; basidia 25 x 5-6μ."

In every way except color this species seems to agree perfectly with *C. crocea,* and we have but little doubt that it is simply a color form of that species. Saccardo gives the spores of *C. crocea* as 2-3 x 6-7μ, taking the figures from Britzelmayr apparently. The latter, in our opinion, had an entire misconception of the species.

Illustration: Burt. Ann. Mo. Bot. Gard. 9: pl. 8, fig. 64 (as *C. exigua*). 1922.

New York: Floodwood. Peck. (Albany Herb., as type of *C. exigua*).

**Clavaria vestitipes** Pk.    Bull. N. Y. St. Mus. **116**: 34. 1907.
  *C. bicolor* Pk.    Bull. N. Y. St. Mus. **54**: 954. 1902.    (Not *C. bicolor* Massee or *C. bicolor* Rafinesque).
  *C. Peckii* Sacc. & D. Sacc.    Syll. **17**: 196. 1905.    (Not *C. Peckii* Sacc.    Syll. **9**: 249. 1891).
  *Lachnocladium vestitipes* (Pk.) Burt.    Ann. Mo. Bot. Gard. **9**: 67, pl. 11, fig. 104. 1922.    (In error as *L. vestipes*).

Plate 84

This species is known only from the type and the following is adapted from the original description of *C. bicolor*:

Small, 1.7-2.5 cm. high, gregarious; stem slender, 1-2 mm. thick, straight or flexuous, solid, tomentose, pale yellow, divided above into two or more short, orange colored compressed branches which are themselves once or twice dichotomously divided, tips acute, concolorous.

Under pine trees.    Bolton.    September.

The rather tough tomentose stem indicates an affinity to the genus *Lachnocladium.*

We have examined the type, which is well preserved at Albany, and find the spores to be subspherical to ovate, minutely asperulate, 3-3.7 x 3.5-4.5µ; basidia 4-spored, 4.4-5.5µ thick; hymenium about 20µ thick.    The species is apparently very near *C. crocea,* but, as now known, differs in larger size, more tomentose stem and slightly larger spores.    As the species name *bicolor* was antedated, it was changed to *Peckii* by Saccardo, but as this was also antedated (Syll. **9**: 249. 1891, see under *C. muscoides*), it was changed again to *vestitipes* by Peck.

Illustration:  Burt.   As cited above.

New York:  Bolton.   Peck.   (Albany Herb., as type of *C. bicolor*).

**Clavaria botrytis** Pers.    Comm., p. 41 (174). 1797.
>?*C. acroporphyrea* Schaeff.    Fung. Bavar., pl. 176. 1763.
>?*C. plebeja* Wulfen in Jacq. Misc. **2**: 101, pl. 13. 1781.
>*C. purpurascens* Paulet in Paulet & Lév.    Icon. Champ., p. 113, pl. 194, fig. 6. 1855.
>*C. botrytoides* Pk.    Bull. N. Y. St. Mus. **94**: 21 and 49, pl. 93, figs. 5-7. 1905.
>*C. conjuncta* Pk.    Bull. N. Y. St. Mus. **105**: 16 and 42, pl. 102. 1906.

PLATES 31, 32, AND 85

Plants usually about 7-11 cm. tall and 3-6 cm. wide, but often larger and reaching 15 x 15 cm., branching at the ground from a short white base which is pointed below and rooting, but not deeply; branches usually rugose, upright or the marginal ones broadly spreading, rather crowded, much branched near the top and finally terminating in a usually crowded mass of delicate and

pointed to very blunt and thick cusps; angles open and spreading;
color white at base, pallid cream on the main branches, the upper
parts with a slight tint of flesh, with the tips rather abruptly a
clear rose-pink in youth, but usually fading completely before maturity (in some cases the entire plant at maturity is very pale, almost white).    Flesh delicate and very brittle, but firm and turgid
(crisp), colored like the surface in all color forms; taste mild and
pleasant, krauty, somewhat like green peanuts or pea hulls, at
times faintly bitterish; odor similar.    There are often very small
aborted branchlets at the base, and these nearly always retain the
pink tip-color, even when it has quite faded elsewhere.    In age
the color becomes a deeper tan or brownish tan and the tips if
bruised or fading slowly turn a deep, dull brick-brown.    Whitish
forms with tips quite faded cannot easily be distinguished from
pale forms of C. flava.

Spores elliptic, light buff-yellow, minutely rough to almost
smooth, usually about 3.8-4.2 x 7.5-10μ.    Basidia (of B. No. 72)
8μ thick, very irregular, 4-spored; hymenium about 30μ thick;
threads of flesh roughly parallel, no clamp connections seen.

An abundant species and one of the most esteemed as an esculent.    It is more cauliflower-like than most others, the crowded
tips, particularly in youth, presenting a series of abrupt terraces.
There is great variation in the stoutness of the tips, which are
sometimes delicate, sometimes very thick and blunt.

The rose-tipped plant here described is one of several closely
related and variable color forms that might with some reason be
considered as one species.    We have thought it best to separate the
pink-bodied form, after much hesitation, as a species, because of
its much deeper-colored spores that average longer.    All these
forms or nearly related species have the following characters:
Flesh turgid, brittle and with a krauty taste and odor; branches
usually rugose, arising at the ground from a short, tapering, white
root; tips abruptly of a different color in youth, concolorous in
age; the flesh colored like the surface.

This species has been much confused with C. rufescens, both
in this country and in Europe, as is shown by the ambiguous
descriptions and antagonistic spore measurements.    In 1873 Peck
referred a plant with pinkish red tips to C. rufescens (Rept. N. Y.

St. Mus. **25**: 83), this being probably *C. botrytis,* but later he gave a new name, *C. botrytoides* (above cited), to a plant with short, roughish spores (the real *C. botrytis*) and referred the species with long, smooth spores (*C. rufescens*) to *C. botrytis* (Rept. N. Y. St. Mus. **48**: 309. 1894. The colored figures, pl. 39, figs. 5-7, are doubtful.) Many of Peck's plants in the Albany Herbarium labelled *C. botrytis* are really *C. rufescens.* The latter species can be easily distinguished by the tips being a light wine color (pinkish purple), not at all the deep, clear, rosy pink of this; and also by the less brittle texture, bitterish taste and quite different spores.

That we have referred the correct plant to *C. botrytis* does not seem doubtful if we accept the interpretation of *C. rufescens* as expressed by Fries, Krombholz, Britzelmayr, Rolland, and others. Schaeffer's plate 288, on which *C. rufescens* is based, shows a plant with more dull red tips than the clearer pink-red tips of his plate 176 (upper fig.), on which Persoon based his *C. botrytis.* In Persoon's herbarium there is nothing authentic under this name. There is one plant and a fragment labelled *C. botrytis* with a question. They are not typical looking, but the spores are about like those of our plants, 4-5.5 x 8-10µ, and are certainly not those of *C. rufescens* (*C. botrytis* of Maire and others). Bresadola seems to have confused this species and *C. rufescens,* in some cases certainly reversing them, as shown by both the appearance of the plants and the spores. For example, one plant examined in his herbarium, labelled *C. botrytis,* has spores longitudinally striate, 4-5.5 x 11-16µ, which agrees with our *C. rufescens.* Britzelmayr's figure of *C. rufescens* (Clavariei, fig. 16) shows a yellowish plant with dull brown tips ("reddish to brownish-red," he says), and Krombholz's fine and unmistakable colored figures (pl. 53, figs. 1-3) of *C. botrytis,* to which Fries refers, should establish the species definitely. *Clavaria acroporphyrea* Schaeff. may be this, but the tips are shown and described as purplish and it may be *C. rufescens.*

British authors, as Stevenson (British Fungi) and Cotton and Wakefield, do not recognize *C. rufescens,* and have evidently included it under *C. botrytis.* The *C. botrytis* of the latter authors (Trans. Brit. Myc. Soc. **6**: 172. 1919) is quite a different plant from ours if the spores be considered the distinguishing character.    Their description may be a composite, but the spores they give are like those of our *C. rufescens* both in size and in the characteristic longitudinal striations.   In the Kew Herbarium is a good collection from Epping Forest (Berkeley, 1879) now in the *botrytis* fascicle with spores given as "15 x 6μ, reticulated" by Cotton.    This seems to be the *C. botrytis* of Cotton and Wakefield. Miss Wakefield examined our slide of the spores of the plant and said they answer to their *C. botrytis*.    Maire's interpretation of *C. botrytis* is certainly our *C. rufescens*.    He mentions the characteristic markings of the spores and the peculiar spotted appearance of the mature plant due to the gnawing of grubs (Bull. Soc. Myc. Fr. **27**: 449. 1911).   He thinks his plant probably the same as *C. sculpta* Beck (Verh. KK. Zool.-bot. Ges. Wien, **34**: 603, pl. 15, fig. 1. 1889).   Burt (l. c., p. 7) has followed the interpretation of Cotton and Wakefield.

*Clavaria conjuncta* seems certainly this (or *C. flava* with tip color wrongly shown), the dried plants having the same characteristic appearance and the spores being alike, rough, 3.5-4.4 x 8-10μ in the type.   It is probable that *C. plebeja* is this species, but the tips are shown as pinkish purple.

Illustrations: Atkinson.   Stud. Am. Fungi, pl. 70 (as *C. formosa*) and fig. 191.   1900.

Badham.   Esculent Fung. Engl., pl. 16, fig. 2 (as *C. coralloides*.)   1847.

Barla.   Champ. Nice, pl. 40, figs. 1-3.   1859.

Bresadola.   Funghi Mang., pl. 101.   1899.

Britzelmayr.   Hymen. Südb., Clavariei, fig. 2.

Burt.   Ann. Mo. Bot. Gard. **9**: pl. 1, fig. 2 (as *C. botrytoides*) ; fig. 3 (as *C. conjuncta*).   1922.

Corda.   Icon. Fung. **5**: pl. 10, fig. 75.   1842.   (Basidia and spores).

Cordier.   Champ. Fr., pl. 47, fig. 2.   1874.

Fries.   Sverig. Atl. Svamp., pl. 35. 1861.   Fine.   Photographic copy by Burt in Ann. Mo. Bot. Gard. **9**: pl. 1, fig. 1.   1922.

Gillet.   Champ. Fr. **5**: pl. 101 (107).   1874-78.

Hard.   Mushrooms, fig. 392 (as *C. formosa*) and fig. 386.   1908.

Harzer.   Abbild. Pilze, pl. 67.   1842-45.

Jacquin.   As cited above.   Deformed.

Krombholz.   Abbild., pl. 53, figs. 1-3.   1841.   Fine.

Lanzi.   Funghi Mang., pl. 14, fig. 1.   1902.   Fine.

Lenz.   Pilze, pl. 17, fig. 66.   1890.   (7th ed.).

Leuba.   Champ. Comest., pl. 40.   1890.

Lorinser.   Die Schwämme, pl. 3, fig. 1.   1876.

Michael.   Führer f. Pilzfreunde, Vol. 1, No. 24.   1898.

Migula in Thomé.   Krypt.-Fl. Deutsch. **3, 2,** 1: pl. 24D, fig. 2.   1912.
The spores (fig. 3) are wrong.

Paulet.   As cited above.   Good.

Peck.   Bull. N. Y. St. Mus. **105**: pl. 102 (as *C. conjuncta*).   1906; **48**:
pl. 39, figs. 5-7 (doubtful; tip color right, but body more like *C. rufescens*).   1894; **94**: pl. 93, figs. 5-7 (as *C. botrytoides*).   1905.

Price.   Illustrations of Fungi, pl. 11, fig. 76.   1865.

Richon & Roze.   Atl. Champ., pl. 67, figs. 1-3.   1887.

Rolland.   Atlas Champ., pl. 103, No. 231.   1910.   Good.

Sowerby.   Engl. Fungi, pl. 278 (as *C. coralloides*).   1803.

Venturi.   Studi Micol., pl. 12, fig. 111.

Vittadini.   Descr. Funghi Mang., pl. 29, fig. 1.   1835.

Viviani.   Funghi Ital., pl. 54, figs. 1-3.   1834.

North Carolina: Chapel Hill.   No. 343.   Woods back of South Building,
September 16, 1910.   No. 344.   Mixed woods, September 15, 1910.
Spores minutely rough, 3.7-4.4 x 7.4-9.4μ.   No. 661.   By path from
east gate of campus, October 29, 1912.   Spores nearly smooth, 3.8-4.4 x
7.4-9.3μ.   No. 2395.   In oak woods, July 18, 1916.   No. 2596.   On
rocky hillside, mixed woods, July 5, 1917.   Not very brittle.   Spores
minutely rough, 3.8-4 x 7.7-9.3μ.   No. 2628.   Upland woods, July 10,
1917.   Taste scarcely bitter.   Spores 3.3-4 x 7.5-10.3μ.   No. 2854.   Mixed
woods south of campus, October 2, 1917.   No. 2863.   Mixed woods,
October. 4, 1917.   Spores 3.3-3.7 x 7.3-8.2μ.   No. 2899.   Mixed woods
October 8, 1917.   Typical.   Spores nearly smooth, 3.5-4 x 6.6-9.5μ.

Salem.   (Schweinitz Herb.).

Hillsboro.   Curtis.   (Curtis Herb.).

South Carolina: Aiken.   Ravenel.   (N. Y. Bot. Gard. Herb. and Kew
Herb.).

Pennsylvania: Bethlehem.   (Schweinitz Herb.).

New York: Bolton Landing.   (Albany Herb., as type of *C. conjuncta*).
Spores rough, 3.5-4.4 x 8.1-9.3μ.

Port Jefferson.   (Albany Herb., as type of *C. botrytoides*).   Spores rough,
4.5 x 8.5-11.5μ.

Alcove.   Shear.   (N. Y. Bot. Gard. Herb.).

Long Island.   Bauer.   (N. Y. Bot. Gard. Herb.).   Also collections from
Sandlake, Gansevoort, and other places.   (Albany Herb.).

Minnesota: Clements.   (N. Y. Bot. Gard. Herb., as *C. formosa*).

California: Trappers' Lake.   (N. Y. Bot. Gard. Herb.).

## Clavaria subbotrytis n. sp.

### PLATES 28, 33, AND 85

Plant 7.5-10 cm. high, 5.5-9 cm. broad, branches numerous, upright, close; tips not terraced, short, bluntly rounded; color coral pink all over when young, fading to creamy ochraceous except in the upper part at full maturity (the stem base remaining pinkish or white).    Flesh concolorous and remaining pink longer than the surface, tender but hardly so brittle as in *C. botrytis;* odor and taste slightly krauty.    Stem short but clean and smooth, glabrous and without aborted twigs, tapering to a clean point below.

Spores (of No. 4679) nearly smooth, elliptic, *cinnamon-ochraceous,* with a distinct tint of rose in the denser parts of a print, 3-3.7 x 7.4-9$\mu$.    Basidia (of No. 3297) 6.5-9.5$\mu$ thick, irregular, 4-spored; hymenium 55-65$\mu$ thick; threads of flesh variable in diameter.    No clamp connections seen.

Distinguished from *C. botrytis* by the deeply colored spores, the clean, smooth, sharply pointed stem, pink color all over until near maturity (the upper part remaining pink until well after maturity), absence of sharply contrasting red tips in youth, and by the quite different appearance in the dry state.    Distinguished from *C. conjunctipes* var. *odora* by slight odor, narrower and rougher spores, much more solid and brittle flesh, the threads of which are narrower; much deeper flesh color with tips soon concolorous; base not so slender and plants not so compound towards base.    From *C. formosa,* which has yellow tips in youth, it differs in greater brittleness, deeper pink color, narrower and smoother spores of a more cinnamon color, and in the quite different texture when dry.    The imbedded part of the stem base may be either pink or white.    In No. 4679 it remained pink after the central region of the plant had turned ochraceous.    Wounds and bruises do not turn red or wine color.    When quite young the very tips were creamy in No. 2621, but soon lost this and became concolorous.    In No. 4679 this was not obvious as the plant was nearly mature when collected.

North Carolina: Chapel Hill.  No. 2621.  At base of a hickory tree, low damp woods, near Woodland Theatre, July 9, 1917.  Pink all over except for the very tips which are creamy in youth.  Spores very minutely rough, 3.3-3.7 x 7-9.3μ.   No. 3297.   In humus, deciduous woods, June 6, 1919.   Delicate pinkish salmon all over with tints of light ochraceous in maturing parts; tips scarcely creamy when young.   Flesh distinctly pink and with a tendency to sliver when broken.   Spores 3.3-3.7 x 7.7-9.3μ.   No. 4679.   Mixed woods by Battle's Branch, October 21, 1920.  (Type).

## Clavaria subbotrytis var. intermedia.

### PLATES 34 AND 85

Plants about 5-12 cm. high and 3.5-11 cm. broad; base usually rather massive and more or less set with little aborted twigs, contracted in the ground to a point, and at times branched at the ground; branches very numerous, more or less cauliflower-like, moderately rugose, the tips blunt and simple or cusped; deep flesh color or a clear coral pink or rarely salmon-yellow (No. 3055) all over except the white base, the tips concolorous or paler with tints of cream; when very young all parts lighter, the tips whitish or creamy; in age or on drying becoming light ochraceous.   Flesh flesh colored or clear coral, very brittle and firm, tender and almost tasteless and odorless (a faint krauty taste and odor); when dry rather soft and pliable, not chalky-friable or very fragile.

Spores (of No. 2847) cinnamon-ochraceous in a thick print (not yellowish ochraceous), elliptic, nearly smooth, 3.5-4.5 x 9.4-11μ; basidia 4-spored, about 7.5μ thick; threads of the flesh (in middle region) densely packed, slender, 5.5-6.3μ thick.

This plant is intermediate between *C. botrytis* and *C. subbotrytis* as is shown by the body and base of the one and the plant-color and deeply tinted spores of the other.   The spores average longer than in *C. subbotrytis* and a little longer than in *C. botrytis* and *C. flava*.   We are treating the plant as a variety of *C. subbotrytis* because of the deep spore color which is just the same in both.

North Carolina: Chapel Hill.   No. 781.   In woods south of athletic field, two plants, September 17, 1913.   Flesh white at base, flesh colored above, moderately brittle, not chalky when dry.   Spores smooth, 3.3-3.7 x 8.3-9.5μ.   No. 2824.   Rocky hillside, deciduous woods, September 11, 1917.   Tips abruptly pale lemon-yellow to whitish.   Spores 3.7-4.2 x 9-10.5μ.   No. 2825.   Rocky hillside, deciduous woods, September 11, 1917.   Just like No. 2824 except that most of the plant was strongly rugose, a conspicuous feature, and the tips were only slightly lighter than the flesh colored upper third—middle region pallid cream.   Flesh color of surface.   Spores 3.5-4 x 8.5-10.6μ.   No. 2847.   Upland frondose woods, October 1, 1917. (Type).   No. 2853.   Under pine and dogwood south of campus, October 2, 1917.   Spores minutely rough, 3.8-4 x 8.5-11$\mu$.   No. 3055.   Deciduous woods in Strowd's lowgrounds, May 23, 1918.   Color white below, salmon yellow above.   Spores slightly rough 3.7-5 x 8.5-11$\mu$.   No. 4316.   In cool, low, deciduous woods, May 31, 1920.   Spores rather light ochraceous with faint tint of salmon, 2.8-3.7 x 7-9.3$\mu$.

New York: Lake George.  Coker, No. 112.  (U. N. C. Herb.).  Oak and maple woods.  Prospect Mountain trail, September 3, 1917.  Pink throughout except the cinnamon-pink base; rugose.  Flesh also strongly pink.  Spores exactly as in No. 2847, 3.8-4 x 9.7-11$\mu$, but too few for color to be seen.

## Clavaria sanguinea Pers.   Obs. Myc. 2: 61, pl. 3, fig. 5. 1799.

### PLATES 35 AND 85

Plant about 6-8.5 cm. high and 4.3-7.5 cm. broad, arising from a single or divided stem about 1.5-2 cm. long above ground and 1-1.8 cm. thick, which is typically pinched in at the ground and extended into a smaller, tapering, pointed root, or the root may be so short as to be but a point on the stem; main branches 2-5, upright with narrow angles or more or less flared, branching tardily or rather soon into upright, crowded branchlets which re-branch immediately into numerous, closely crowded, upright terminals, forming a remarkably plane surface exactly as in a cauliflower, which end in several blunt cusps; color when young pallid white below, light egg-yellow above, the tips deepest, at times with a tint of pink added to the yellow or the yellow pale and the creamy pink predominating; towards maturity becoming paler above, but at all ages becoming stained when bruised with deep blood-red or brownish red or brick-brown, and in age the whole plant assuming this color in great part, only here and there the pallid remaining in areas or strips.   Flesh colored like the sur-face, but not changing to red except superficially, mild (faintly acid-woody), odorless or with a faint anise odor on standing a while in the laboratory.   Threads of the flesh about 7.4$\mu$ thick, get-ting smaller near hymenium, no clamp connections seen.

Spores (of No. 2656) rather light yellow-ochraceous, smooth, elliptic with a large eccentric mucro, 3-3.8 x 7.5-8.5$\mu$, most about 3.7 x 7.8$\mu$.   Basidia (of No. 4394) long-clavate, 4-spored, 7$\mu$ thick.

A distinct and well marked species, that it seems to us should be referred to *C. sanguinea* of Persoon.   His figure, which is in color, looks much more like our plant than like any other, and the description fits unusually well. Fries treats *C. sanguinea* as another name for *C. spinulosa,* but Persoon notes the close relationship to *C. botrytis* (also obvious in our plants) which is very unlike *C. spinulosa.* Persoon says: "Stem subsucculent, red, branches elongated, branchlets multifid, minute, yellowish. Rare in forests. The figure referred to shows only a part of this fungus, for the natural size is larger by half. The stem is moderately thick, filled with a reddish juice, divided into many elongated branches, which turn yellow toward the apex. The branchlets, on the contrary, are very slender, short, slightly bent, leather color."

Recognized by the pointed base and the red or brick-brown color when rubbed or in age. The base even in youth is nearly always streaked with these stains. All the plants we have found so far have been reclining and one-sided. Easily distinguished from *C. rufescens* by smaller size, different base, cauliflower-like tips and different spores; from *C. formosa* by the simple terete stem without grooves, by the dark stains, by cauliflower-like terminals, and by the different spores. The short, crowded, closely packed terminals and rather long parallel secondaries and tertiaries give the upper half of the plant exactly the appearance of a cauliflower head, more so than in any other species. The tips are nearly always more yellow than pink except in youngest plants, and are never more than very pale creamy flesh-pink. It is in this tip color sharply different from *C. botrytis* and *C. botrytoides,* not to mention the red stains and other differences.

Maire regards *C. sanguinea* as the same as *C. flava,* at least in part. His plant has red stains but the spores are 4-5 x 9-12μ. (Bull. Soc. Myc. Fr. **27**: 450. 1911).

North Carolina: Chapel Hill. No. 2629. Mixed woods near Battle's Branch, July 10, 1917. A single plant, 7 cm. high, 5 cm. broad; stem distinct, about 4 cm. long including the underground part, about half buried in the ground, branching rather thickly and ending in numerous small tips; color pallid creamy white all over except the tips which are tinted at first with pale yellow, but soon fade out, all parts turning a *deep rosy blood color* when bruised and the base soon stained with this color; texture not very brittle, rather rigid, taste mild, odor very little, but faintly like that of anise. Too young for spores. No. 2656. Damp

mixed woods, under pine tree, July 12, 1917.   No. 4394.   Woods near
Meeting of the Waters, July 13, 1920.   Spores creamy yellow, smooth,
3.7-4.4 x 6.2-8.2μ.

Massachusetts: Stockbridge.   Murrill and Thompson.   (N. Y. Bot. Gard.
Herb.).   October 3, 4, 1911.   "Straw-colored tips and branches, whiter
below, staining anywhere and especially below vinosus when bruised."
Spores elliptic, smooth or some apparently minutely rough, 3.5-4 x
7.8-9.6μ.   There is a photo accompanying this collection which looks like
our plants, and the spores are the same.

## Clavaria flava Schaeff.   Fung. Bavar., pl. 175. 1763.

?C. *lutea* Venturi.   I miceti del agro Bresciano, p. 36, pl. 41,
fig. 4. 1845-1860.

C. *flavobrunescens* Atk.   Ann. Myc. **7**: 367. 1909.

### PLATES 36, 37, 39, AND 85

Plants of moderate to good size, up to 11 cm. high and same
breadth, base as in C. *botrytis,* tapering, somewhat rooting;
branching at the ground into several rather slender, at times
broadly spreading, main branches, and in nearly all cases with
several or numerous small undeveloped peripheral ones at the base;
main branches soon rebranching several times in an irregular
manner to form a rather open mass, the ultimate tips usually delicate, but at times much thickened and blunt (as in No. 560),
more or less cusped; surface more or less rugose upwards; color
clear, not at all tan or ochraceous, varying from a clear pale cream
(in Nos. 1850 and 1855) to a light creamy yellow (maize-yellow
of Ridgway), or in the northern form to a deep, rich, clear prim-
uline or chrome yellow (Ridgw.) in youth, but becoming much
paler at and after maturity.   The color is about the same throughout in the pale form or paler downwards in the richer colored
forms, only the very base whitish at the ground and not turning
rose-wine when bruised, as in C. *aurea* var. *australis* and C. *rufescens*; tips concolorous when fresh, but usually turning a pale, clear,
soaked brown and then a darker brown when fading; if dried
quickly this change in color of the tips does not appear.   Flesh
very brittle, not white, but when quite fresh colored like the surface, or at least with a tint of cream (rarely almost colorless);
taste and odor very pleasant, distinctly krauty (faintly like green
peanuts).   When very young the entire plant is nearly white, the
tips pure white and without a trace of pink.

Spores (of No. 2855) about maize-yellow (Ridgw.), minutely
rough, elliptic, 3-4 x 7.4-10μ.

This plant is just like *C. botrytis* in form, texture, taste, and odor, but differs distinctly in color and does not reach the large size of the latter. Plants of *C. botrytis* with tips faded are a pallid, dull, fleshy cream, while the pink young tips of *C. botrytis* and the white tips of *C. flava* are an unfailing means of distinction.

From *C. aurea* var. *australis* and *C. rufescens* (No. 2845) this plant differs in smaller, more quickly branched base, different color, and in the very different spores. In fading some of the tips may become colored like those of *C. rufescens,* but the spores will easily distinguish them. From *C. formosa* which also has a multiple, pointed base, it differs in color, greater brittleness, and smaller, smoother spores.

*Clavaria flavobrunescens* is the same. The species was described by Atkinson from plants sent him by us from Chapel Hill.

In the interpretation of this species there has been great confusion. The plant taken for *C. flava* by Fries is doubtful, but is probably this. Krombholz's figure to which Fries refers is not good of our plant. Schaeffer's plate (on which the species is based) is much like our plant and not like our *C. aurea,* and the same may be said of Persoon's description. In Persoon's herbarium is a good plant of *C. flava* with spores 3.7-5 x 9-11µ. There are several European mycologists who have made it quite plain that they interpret the species as we do. Vittadini's figure of *C. flava* is excellent of our plant with the pointed base and right color and shape, and his figure of *C. lutea* (now accepted as a synonym of *C. flava*) is equally as good of ours. Richon and Roze also represent our plant well as *C. flava,* showing some of the tips as brownish, a point not mentioned or shown by others. Neither Gillet not Quélet illustrates *C. flava,* but the former's good description (Champ. France **1**: 764. 1878) makes it pretty plain that he has in mind our plant. He mentions the pale spores, fragile flesh and very agreeable taste. Quélet's description is inadequate, but does not exclude our plant. He refers to Barla's figure which might pass but is not good. Bresadola's figure is like ours in color but diverse in form and he describes *C. flava* as staining red on the stem and having longer spores. This would indicate a larger spored form of what we are considering *C. sanguinea.* Plants in his herbarium as *C. flava* look like ours in

the dried state, but have much longer spores. Maire considers
*C. sanguinea* the same as *C. flava* in sense of Fries and describes
it as having red stains with spores 4-5 x 9-12μ (Bull. Soc. Myc.
Fr. **27**: 450. 1911).

In England neither Berkeley nor his successors have recognized
*C. flava* and it may be our plant that they refer to *C. aurea*. Plants
from Europe at the N. Y. Bot. Garden labelled *C. flava* have been
examined. One from Karsten (Finland) has spores like ours,
3.8-4.5 x 7.8-10μ. One from de Thümen (Bohemia) has somewhat larger spores, 3.7-5 x 9-12μ. Both look like our plant in
the dry state, as does also the one from Saccardo. We have received a good collection of this from Juel (Upsala) with spores
like ours, minutely rough, 3.7-4.2 x 7.5-10μ. In the Curtis
Herbarium is a collection from South Carolina by Curtis and one
from the Schweinitz Herbarium. Both look like our plant and
have similar spores, in the former they are 3 x 7.5-8μ, and in the
latter, 3.8 x 7.5μ. Another plant in the Curtis Herbarium from
Society Hill, S. C., labelled *C. stricta* is also this (spores
3 x 7.5-8μ). In the Schweinitz Herbarium in Philadelphia plants
from Salem, N. C., and Bethlehem, Pa., are the same. Peck, Atkinson, McIlvaine, and Hard have also interpreted the species in
the same way. It would seem that the American representative
of *C. flava* is a form with somewhat smaller spores.

Juel (see citation under *C. cristata*) finds the basidia to be
4-spored with the nuclear spindles apical and transverse. He says
the species is very similar microscopically to what he considers *C.
aurea,* from which it differs only in the smaller, less warty and
paler spores. The spores of both are uninucleate.

Illustrations: Badham. Escul. Fung. Engl., pl. 16, fig. 1 (as *C. ame-
thystina*). 1847.
Barla. Champ. Nice, pl. 40, fig. 5. 1859.
Bresadola. Funghi Mang., pl. 100. 1899.
Britzelmayr. Hymen. Südb., Clavariei, fig. 1.
Bulliard. Herb. Fr., pl. 222 (as *C coralloides*). 1784. This is re-
ferred to by Fries as *C. aurea,* but looks little like it.
Cordier. Champ. Fr., pl. 46, fig. 1. 1874.
Dufour. Atlas Champ., pl. 69, fig. 151. 1891. Good.
Fries. Sver. Atl. Svamp., pl. 26. 1860-66.

Gibson.    Edible Toadstools and Mushrooms, pl. 31.    1895.    Also pl. 30 (as *C. formosa*) is probably *C. flava.*

Hard.    Mushrooms, fig. 385.    1908.

Holmskjold.    Beata Ruris 1: pl. 31 (as *Ramaria coralloides lutea*).    1790.

Juel.    Above cited.

Krombholz.    Abbild., pl. 53, fig. 8 (color not good); fig. 5 (as *C. botrytis* var. *alba*).    1831-46.    The nearly white form of this.

Lanzi.    Funghi Mang., pl. 14, fig. 2.    1902.    (Copied from Schaeffer and Cordier).

Laval.    Champ. d'après Nature, pl. 32.    1912.

Lenz.    Pilze, pl. 16, fig. 65.    1890 (7th ed.).    Good.

Leuba.    Champ. Comest., pl. 41.    1887-90.    This plate is labelled *C. aurea* but is not referred to under that species but under *C. flava,* which it is more like.

Lorinser.    Essb. Schwämme, pl. 2, fig. 7.    1876; (pl. 2, fig. 1, as *C. aurea* may also be *C. flava*).

Lönnegren.    Nord. Svampb., pl. 4, fig. 58.    1895.

Marshall.    Mushroom Book, pl. opposite p. 100.    1902.

Michael.    Führer f. Pilzfreunde, Vol. 1, No. 25 (as *C. flava*).    1898. Also Vol. 2, No. 25 (as *C. aurea*).    1901.    This is just like our *C. flava* and cannot be distinguished from his *C. flava* above.

Moffat.    Chicago Acad. Sci. Bull. **7**: pl. 23.    1909.

Murrill.    Edible and Poisonous Mushr. Chart, fig. 24.    1916.    Good.

Nees, Henry and Bail.    Syst. Pilze, pl. 27, figs. 1-3.    1858.    This differs slightly in the pinkish purple color of the very base.

Peck.    Rept. N. Y. St. Mus. **48**: pl. 39, figs. 1-4.    1894.    Not good.

Richon and Roze.    Atlas Champ., pl. 67, figs. 4-7.    1888.    Very good.

Schaeffer.    As cited above.    Photographic copy by Burt in Ann. Mo. Bot. Gard. **9**: pl. 4, fig. 19.    1922.

Venturi.    As cited above (doubtful).

Vittadini.    Descr. Funghi Mang., pl. 29, fig. 2.    1835.    Good.    His fig. 3 on same plate called *C. lutea* is also the same.    *C. lutea* Vent. is treated as a synonym of *C. flava* by Saccardo.

White.    Conn. Geol. and Nat. Hist. Surv. Bull. **3**: pl. 40.    1905.

North Carolina: Chapel Hill.    No. 560.    On ground in the woods, October 15, 1912.    Spores yellow, 3-4 x 7.8-10.3$\mu$.    No. 562.    Mixed woods back of campus, October 15, 1912.    Spores 3-4 x 7.5-9.8$\mu$.    No. 795. In damp woods in moss, September 19, 1913.    Spores smooth or a few minutely rough, 3-3.8 x 8-9.7$\mu$.    No. 2850.    Under pine and dogwood south of campus, October 2, 1917.    Spores 3.5-4.2 x 8-10$\mu$.    No. 2855. In mixed woods, October 2, 1917.    No. 2870.    Mixed woods, October 5, 1917.    Tips Naples yellow, main body pale creamy yellow with faint tint of flesh in shadows.    Spores 3-3.7 x 7.3-9$\mu$.    No. 2895.    Mixed woods, October 8, 1917.    Spores nearly or quite smooth, about 3.2 x 8.8$\mu$.    No. 2922.    Mixed woods south of athletic field, October 18, 1917.    Typical in every way except color very light cream, tips pallid white fading to pale brown then darker.    Spores nearly smooth, 3.7-4.1 x 7-9.4$\mu$.    No.

3150. In deciduous woods near stream, August 9, 1918. Small, up to 4 cm. high and 2-4 cm. broad; surface glabrous all over, color very pale yellow with tint of flesh, the tips most yellow when young, fading to pale flesh by maturity. No spores to be found (a curious fact, true for nearly all species of *Clavaria* collected this very hot week).

Salem. Schweinitz. (Schw. Herb.).

South Carolina: Society Hill. Curtis. (Curtis Herb.).

Pennsylvania: Bethlehem. Schweinitz. (Schw. Herb.).

New Jersey: Alpine. Boynton. (N. Y. Bot. Gard. Herb.). "Yellow, taste sweet, nutty."

New York: Vaughns. Burnham, No. 108. Under beech. (U. N. C. Herb.). Plant yellow. Spores typical, 4-4.5 x 8.5-9.3μ.

Bolton. Peck. (Albany Herb.). Spores rough, 4.5 x 9.9-11μ.

Albany and Lebanon Springs. Peck. (Albany Herb.). Spores nearly smooth, 4.5 x 11μ.

Connecticut: Redding. Coker, No. 26. September 6, 1919. Spores pale yellow, nearly or quite smooth, about 3.7 x 8.5μ.

## Clavaria flava var. aurea n. var.

### PLATES 38 AND 85

Plant not massive, about 9 cm. high and 4-5 cm. broad, stem distinct, clean and pointed below, quite glabrous, white at base; branches rather open, rugose, between orange-buff and ochraceous buff, with a tint of chrome upward when quite fresh, below more fleshy or salmon orange or apricot color; flesh only moderately brittle, colored like the surface; odor faintly rancid, taste mild, slightly krauty. Threads of flesh nearly parallel, about 7.4-10.8μ thick.

Spores (of No. 2851) buff-yellow, nearly smooth, elliptic, 3.1-3.7 x 6.6-9.3μ. Hymenium (of No. 2893) about 55μ thick; basidia 6.2-7.4μ thick with 4 long sterigmata.

This variety is distinguished by its rich color, less brittle flesh, clear, distinct, tapering stem, which comes to a point below and is not connected with mycelium except by a basal point, and by the somewhat smaller spores. It differs from *C. flava* var. *subtilis* (No. 2843) in smaller and smoother spores.

North Carolina: Chapel Hill. No. 2851. Under pine and dogwood south of campus, October 2, 1917. (Type). No. 2893. Mixed woods south of athletic field, October 8, 1917. A distinct plant; no other has so clean, slender and perfectly pointed a base. Base pure white, the yellow color deepening upward. Flesh not very brittle and thus differing distinctly from *C. flava* as well as in color and other ways. These had faded when found to a pinkish cinnamon upwards. Spores nearly smooth, 3.1-3.6 x 6.6-8μ.

New York: Lake George. Coker, Nos. 13 and 14. (U. N. C. Herb.). In oak and maple woods, Prospect Mountain trail, September 3, 1917. Color deep chrome yellow above, shading to a clearer yellow in middle and white at the pointed base; very delicate, divaricating; flesh yellow, tasteless and odorless. Spores nearly smooth, apparently yellowish, of No. 13, 3.3-3.8 x 7-9μ; of No. 14, 3.3-3.7 x 6.6-8.2μ.

## Clavaria flava var. subtilis n. var.

### PLATE 85

A clear rather pale yellow upward (near apricot yellow), pale fleshy cream elsewhere except the white, glabrous base, which tapers to a point; in most cases distinctly rugose upwards; odor very slight. When dry hard and not chalky or very fragile.

Spores (of No. 2843) elliptic, distinctly rough, but not so much so as in *C. formosa,* 4-4.5 x 10-11μ. Basidia 4-spored, about 9μ thick. Hymenium 55-70μ thick; basidia 7.4-8.9μ thick with 4 long, straight sterigmata. Hyphae of flesh about 7.5-11μ thick, nearly parallel, not densely packed.

Differs from *C. formosa* in the texture when dry, which is not chalky or very fragile, in absence of bitter taste when dry, in decidedly thicker and nearly parallel hyphae, and in more narrow and less rough spores. Differs from *C. flava* var. *aurea* (No. 2893) in thicker hymenium, thicker basidia and larger and rougher spores. Differs from *C. subbotrytis* (No. 2847) as follows: less brittle; much less flesh color and more yellow; base more slender; flesh nearly or quite white; taste mildly acid-bitter (*C. subbotrytis* is nearly tasteless). The flesh is dry and fibrous and softer than in the firmer, more brittle and less fibrous *C. botrytis, C. flava* and *C. subbotrytis.*

North Carolina: Chapel Hill. No. 2843. Upland frondose woods, October 1, 1917. (Type).

New York: Vaughns. Frondose woods, September 2, 1917. Coker and Burnham, No. 103. (U. N. C. Herb.). Color pale creamy flesh, the tips more yellow, base white; flesh color of the surface. Taste mild, odor none; base pointed, channelled. Spores yellowish ochraceous, 3.8-4.6 x 9.3-11.8μ, distinctly rough.

**Clavaria divaricata** Pk.    Bull. N. Y. St. Mus. **2**: 11. 1887.
(Not *C. divaricata* Karsten.   Symbolae Myc. Fenn. **32**: 10.
1893).

PLATES 40 AND 85

Plants about 5-7.5 cm. high and broad (up to 10 cm. high in the type), branched at the ground from a pointed base, with a rather open and spreading habit, tips minute, numerous, very sharp and tending to divaricate; color pale yellowish flesh below, shading upwards to fleshy yellow, the very tips abruptly very pale when young, but becoming concolorous at maturity.   Flesh very fragile and brittle, colored like the surface; taste pleasant and nutty; odor slight.

Spores ochraceous buff, minutely rough, 3.7-4.4 x 9.7-11.5μ. Basidia (of No. 3063) 6.2-9.3μ thick; hymenium 50-60μ thick; hyphae much intertwined just under the hymenium, clamp connections possibly present but difficult to make out.

The above description, except where noted, is drawn from our collection No. 15 from Lake George, New York.   The Chapel Hill collections listed are very similar and the spores alike, but the color of the plants is not identical.

We are referring these to *C. divaricata* which, on account of the form and certain other discrepancies (as the length of the spores), is being retained as a species although it is probably only a form of *C. flava*.   The type at Albany is a light, brittle plant with a strong tendency to be hollow when dry; the tips cartilaginous-looking, the remainder buffy ochraceous; spores slightly rough, 4-4.7 x 11.7-12.5μ.*

Illustration: Burt.  Ann. Mo. Bot. Gard. **9**: pl. 7, fig. 53.  1922.

North Carolina: Chapel Hill.   No. 1250.   By path in woods, September 23, 1914.   Plants short, thick, very coral-like, about 4.5 cm. high and 6-7 cm. wide, two or three short main branches from a common base; secondary branches short, spreading, numerous, ending in several small cusps; color a clear light yellow all over, nearly citron yellow.   Flesh white, rigid, but exceedingly brittle and fragile, taste nutty and pleasant, exactly as in *C. flava*.   No. 3037.   Woods in lowgrounds, pines and oaks predominating, May 18, 1918.   Spores 4-4.5 x 9-11μ.   No. 3063. Strowd's lowgrounds, deciduous woods, May 22, 1918.

---

* To this species Peck has referred a little plant on wood from Floodwood, N. Y. (Rept. N. Y. St. Mus. **54**: 171.  1901).   It is evident from the dried plant that this is entirely different, and is probably *C. byssiseda*.   No spores could be obtained from it.

New York: Lake George.   Coker, No. 15.   Prospect Trail, under chestnut
in clay loam, September 3, 1917.   (U. N. C. Herb.).
Sand Lake.   Peck.   (Albany Herb., type).

**Clavaria formosa** Pers.   Icon. et Descr. **1**: pl. 3, fig. 6. 1798.
*C. densa* Pk.   Rept. N. Y. St. Mus. **41**: 79. 1888.

PLATES 41, 42, AND 86

A medium sized to large (rarely small) plant up to 13 cm.
high by 11 cm. broad.   The main branches typically remain par-
tially free from each other all the way to the ground, being
separated at the surface by channels, and looking like several par-
tially fused plants which spring from the same spot.   Just at the
ground they are all suddenly pinched together into the little, inconspicuous rootlet from which they arise; branchlets upright,
ending often in minute cusps, axils rounded.   Surface smooth or
distinctly rugose in places; base white and glabrous, the main body
in youth usually a creamy flesh color but often a clearer pink
(about salmon-buff of Ridgway), the tips distinctly yellowish for
a variable distance, (often for about 5-10 mm., at times only abruptly at the apices); towards maturity the color fades to a creamy
tan then to light leather and finally a darker ochraceous tan or
leather color, the tips becoming concolorous.   Flesh distinctly pink
in youth, almost white after maturity, or often with a tinge of
flesh color even in age after the surface has changed color, delicate but only moderately brittle, not breaking with a clean snap
when bent at 45°, faintly and pleasantly sweetish-bitter.

Spores ochraceous, usually distinctly roughened, 4-5.3 x 8.3-
12.2μ, rarely shorter, the great majority about 4.5-5 x 9-11.3μ.
Occasionally there are nearly smooth spores among the rough ones
and rarely they are all nearly smooth.   Basidia (of No. 4636)
7.4-9.3μ thick, club-shaped and usually distinctly swollen at distal
end, with 2-4 sterigmata; hymenium 80-110μ thick; threads of
flesh very irregular and variable, 4.4-9.3μ thick, with many septa
and a few clamp connections; minute crystals present.

In the dried state this species and *C. subspinulosa,* which
seems nearest, are easily recognized by the soft and chalky-
friable flesh which is so brittle and fragile as scarcely to bear
transportation.   In herbaria they nearly always appear in a frag-

mented state.    In addition to this character *C. formosa* is recognized by its compound base appearing like several plants closely pressed or fused together, by the pinkish body and yellowish tips, by the slightly bitterish and not very brittle flesh, and by the thick, rough spores.    Forms of *C. subbotrytis* with pink body and yellowish tips are much more brittle when fresh and not friable when dry, and the taste and the spores are quite different.

In the herbarium of the University of Paris one good collection is correctly determined (Desmazières, No. 419) ; others from various places are different.    At Kew Gardens there are typical plants of our *C. formosa* determined as *C. aurea* by Cooke (Hereford, 1878).    The pointed base, chalky flesh and plump, warty spores distinctly marking them.    They are now in the *C. flava* fascicle, but are not referred to as *C. flava* by Cotton and Wakefield.    Our plants do not turn violet and then black when bruised, as is said by Cotton and Wakefield to be the case with the plant which they interpret as *C. formosa.*

In the Albany Herbarium this species is found under four different names,—*C. formosa, C. densa, C. compacta* (unpublished), and *C. formosa* var. *pallida* (unpublished).    The type of *C. densa* is nearly destroyed, but a plant from Round Lake, N. Y., labelled by Peck *C. densa* with a question is certainly this.    The spores of the type are rough, 4.5-5 x 8.2-9.5μ (our measurements).    The northern plants seem to have spores that average shorter.    The plant above mentioned labelled *C. compacta* has spores 4.5-4.8 x 7.5-8.2μ, rough.    We have one small plant from Chapel Hill (No. 2688) with chalky flesh and all the other ear-marks of this species in which the spores are quite short (4-5 x 7-7.8μ).

This species is exceptional among the larger Clavarias in that it may be determined with certainty from the type in Persoon's herbarium.    It is represented there by one good plant which has all the distinguishing characteristics in the dried state that are observable in our plants, including the chalky flesh and identical spores, which are 4-5 x 8-11μ.    As Persoon's description and his good illustration agree perfectly, there is no doubt that our plants are correctly interpreted.    Gillet's illustration shows clearly that his opinion is the same.    There is, however, much confusion to be noticed in various herbaria; for example, there is a plant from Bresadola at the New York Botanical Garden labelled *C. formosa* that is not that but *C. flava* or *C. botrytis* (spores nearly smooth, 3.7-4.4 x 7.4-8.5µ).   In his own herbarium Bresadola also has at least one collection of *C. flava* or *C. botrytis* determined as *C. formosa,* while one from America (Lloyd) so determined is like the type.   In the Curtis Herbarium is a plant from Society Hill, S. C., (unnamed) that is like ours here described.   The spores also agree and are 4.5-6.3 x 10-11.5µ.   In the same herbarium are plants named *C. formosa* from Salem (Schweinitz) and from Hillsboro (Curtis).   Both are *C. botrytis* as shown by appearance and spores.   At the Kew Herbarium a plant from Sulphur Springs, N. C., (Ravenel) labelled *C. aurea* is *C. formosa,* as are also a number of English collections labelled *C. aurea.*

Illustration: Burt.  Ann. Mo. Bot. Gard. **9**: pl. 2, fig. 9 (as *C. densa*). 1922.

Corda.  Icon. Fung. **3**: pl. 9, fig. 136.  1839.  (Basidia and spores).

Dufour.  Atl. Champ., pl. 69, No. 152.  1891.  (Larger volume, not pocket edition).  Very good, typical.

Gillet.  Champ. Fr. **5**: pl. 102 (108).  Good.

Gibson.  Edible Toadst., pl. 30.  1895.  (Doubtful, probably *C. flava*).

Hard.  Mushr., fig. 391 (as *C. spinulosa*).  1908.

Harzer.  Abbild. Pilze, pl. 7b, figs. 1-4 (as *C. flava*).  1842-45.

Krombholz.  Icon. Descr., pl. 54, figs. 21-22.  1841.

Lanzi.  Funghi Mang., pl. 12, fig. 4.  1902.

Leuba.  Champ. Comest., pl. 43, figs. 1-4 (as *C. dichotoma*).  1890.

Marshall.  Mushr. Book., pl. opposite p. 98 (doubtful).  1902.

McIlvaine.  Am. Fung., pl. 139, fig. 3 (doubtful).  1900.

Michael.  Führer f. Pilzfreunde, Vol. 2, No. 27.  1901.

Persoon.  Icon. Descr. Fung. **1**: pl. 3, fig. 6.  1798.

Richon and Roze.  Atl. Champ., pl. 66, figs. 1-2.

Rolland.  Bull. Soc. Myc. de France **9**: pl. 4, fig. 3.  1893.  Also in Atlas Champ., pl. 104, No. 234.  1910.  Good.

North Carolina: Chapel Hill.  No. 336.  Upland woods, September 22, 1908.  Spores 4.8-5 x 10.5-11µ, roughish.  No. 535.  On ground in Battle's Park, October 9, 1912.  Spores 4.5-5.2 x 9.6-11µ.  No. 543. Woods on side of hill in Battle's Park, October 10, 1912.  Spores elliptic, minutely but distinctly tuberculate, 4.5-5.3 x 9.3-11µ.  No. 784.  Battle's Park, September, 1913.  Spores 4.4-5.2 x 10.4-12.2µ.  No. 2439. Under a beech, mixed woods by creek, September 18, 1916.  Spores distinctly rough, 4-5 x 8.5-11.5µ.  No. 2634.  Upland woods, July 10, 1917.

Spores elliptic, with an eccentric mucro, slightly roughened, 4.8-5.5 x 9.7-11.5μ, most about 5.2 x 10.5μ. No. 2655. Mixed pine and oak woods near Meeting of the Waters, July 13, 1917. Spores 4-5 x 10-11μ. No. 2688. Under beech, upland woods, July 17, 1917. Spores slightly rough, 4-5 x 7-7.8μ. No. 2709. Mixed upland woods, July 19, 1917. Spores 4.5-5 x 10-11μ. No. 2826. Frondose woods, rocky hillside, September 11, 1917. Spores 4.8-5.2 x 9.3-11μ, most about 5 x 10.2μ. No. 2827. Rocky hillside, frondose woods, September 11, 1917. Spores 4.5-5.2 x 10-11μ. No. 2838. Frondose woods near Brockwell's spring, September 24, 1917. Spores 4.8-5.5 x 9.3-12.2μ. No. 2844. Upland woods, October 1, 1917. Spores distinctly rough even under low power, 4.4-5 x 10-11μ. No. 2849. Upland frondose woods, October 1, 1917. Spores 4-5 x 10-11.5μ. No. 2858. Frondose woods, October 1, 1917. Spores minutely rough, 4.4-4.8 x 10-11.8μ. No. 2878. Mixed woods, October 6, 1917. Spores 4.8-5.1 x 10-11μ. No. 2879. Frondose woods near Meeting of the Waters, October 6, 1917. Spores about 4.6 x 9-11μ. No. 2903. Mixed woods, south of athletic field, October 10, 1917. Spores nearly buff-yellow, roughened, 4.4-4.8 x 9.3-11μ. No. 3448. Pine and oak woods near Judge's Spring, August 16, 1919. Tips yellow, balance pinkish tan. No. 4636. Damp soil in frondose woods, August 16, 1920. (Many other collections from similar places).

Salem. (Schweinitz Herb.). Also Schallert, No. 15. (U. N. C. Herb.). Spores 5-6.5 x 9.5-11.5μ.

Pink Bed Valley. Murrill and House. (N. Y. Bot. Gard. Herb., No. 363). Spores rough, 4.6-5.5 x 9.5-11μ.

South Carolina: Society Hill. Curtis. (Curtis Herb., unnamed). Other collections from Society Hill, S. C., and Hillsboro, N. C., labelled *C. formosa* are not this species.

Virginia: Alta Vista. Among rotten bark and humus on ground in cool deep ravine, deciduous woods, July 15, 1918. Coker. (U. N. C. Herb.). Very small plants; color pale creamy flesh all over except the creamy yellow tips and white, distinct, pointed base; flesh not very brittle, no taste or odor of vegetable, but rather bitterish; base deeply inserted in mold; mycelium attached only at tip of base; spores 4.2-5.2 x 8.5-11.2μ.

Pennsylvania: Buck Hill Falls. Mrs. Delafield. (N. Y. Bot. Gard. Herb.).

New York: Fort Ann. Burnham, No. 73. (U. N. C. Herb.). Northeast of Tripoli, August 19, 1915. Spores rough, 4.4-5.2 x 8.2-10.5μ.

Vaughns. Burnham, No. 96. Mixed woods near Tripoli, September 7, 1917. Spores rough, 4.4-5 x 9-11μ. B. No. 116. Same place as No. 96, August 31, 1919. (Both in U. N. C. Herb.).

Sand Lake. Peck. (Albany Herb., as var. *pallida*). Spores rough, 4.4-5 x 8.5-9.7μ.

Lake George. Coker, No. 5. (U. N. C. Herb.). In chestnut leaves, September 3, 1917. Spores broadly elliptic, rough, ochraceous, 4.8-5.2 x 9.3-11μ.

Gansevoort and Adirondack Mountains. Peck. (Albany Herb.). These also have the base and general look of the Chapel Hill plants. Spores rough, elliptic, 5-5.7 x 9.5-11.5μ.

West Park.  Earle.  (N. Y. Bot. Gard. Herb.).  Spores rough, broadly elliptic, 4.4-5.9 x 8.2-10μ.

Horicon.  Peck.  (Albany Herb.).

Alcove.  Shear.  (N. Y. Bot. Gard. Herb., as *C. densa,* No. 118 of N. Y. Fungi).  Spores 3.5-4.4 x 8-9μ.

Connecticut:  Redding.  Coker.  (U. N. C. Herb.).

Canada:  Ontario.  Dearness.  (U. N. C. Herb.).  Spores rough, 4-5.3 x 9.3-12.2μ.  Basidia 8-9.3μ thick, 2-4-spored.

## Clavaria conjunctipes n. sp.

### PLATES 43 AND 91

Cespitose in gregarious clusters and arising in crowded clumps and rows from deep in the mold; up to 7 cm. high, their bases very slender, string-like, crowded and attached to ropy white strands which have branched to form them and which diffuse into the mold; bases of each clump touching but not fused, white where protected, branched several times upward, mostly dichotomously, with acute angles, into rather few branches which when young and very fresh are a beautiful saffron (yellow-salmon), the tips rather abruptly a delicate lemon yellow; after maturity the color fading to cinnamon-buff throughout except for the white base; surface smooth and even or varying to pitted and rugose (as in No. 5768).  Flesh concolorous, flexible and firm, cracking only when bent on self; tasteless and odorless.

Spores short-elliptic, smooth (to very minutely rough?), pale yellow in a light print and under the microscope, 4-4.5 x 7.4-8.5μ.

A remarkable plant, with its crowded, slender stems arising from deeply seated bases.  The stems are only 1.5-2.5 mm. thick at the surface, not at all or scarcely thicker than the branches, and taper downward to slender strands.  They may or may not branch below ground as well as above it.

The species is one of the most beautiful of all Clavarias, the colors approaching very near to those of the most perfect plants of *C. formosa.*  It is easily different from anything else we have seen, being separated from *C. formosa* by the quite different spores, much more slender and usually more numerous stems of a cluster, toughish texture, and very different behavior in drying, the plants then becoming shrunken and wrinkled with the flesh not at all chalky or friable.  The slender, crowded, deeply rooting stems separate the species from all colored Clavarias.    The form and habit is most like that of *C. cineroides* and *C. subcaespitosa.*

North Carolina: Linville Falls. Coker and party, No. 5732. On rich ground in deciduous woods, August 24, 1922. (Type). No. 5734. Same locality and date as above. Plants fully mature; color cinnamon-buff. Spores somewhat flattened on one side, wall rather thick, 4.2-4.8 x 6.8-8.6$\mu$. No. 5768. Same locality and date as above. Surface wrinkled and pitted. Spores oblong, 4-4.8 x 6.5-8$\mu$.

Tennessee: Murrill. (N. Y. Bot. Gard. Herb., as *C. tetragona*, and U. N. C. Herb.). Spores smooth, elliptic, 4.8-5 x 7-8$\mu$.

Connecticut: Redding. Coker, No. 36. Hemlock and frondose woods. September 7, 1919. Spores 3.8-5 x 7.4-10$\mu$.

## Clavaria conjunctipes var. odora n. var.

### PLATES 53 AND 86

Plants 6-7 cm. high in this case with distinct long stalks 2.5-4 cm. long, with tapering bases, main branches few, smooth, branching two or three times and ending in several small cusps; color light pinkish cream in the central region, the tips a light clear yellow in young plants, the stem pure white or nearly so. Flesh only moderately brittle, watery white with pale pinkish tint except in stem; taste mild, not bitter, slightly fungoid; odor faintly fragrant, medicinal, something like an old mowing machine (rancid oil?) but more aromatic (lost in drying).

Spores pale under a microscope (too few to make a print), smooth, short-ovate with an eccentric or lateral mucro at the larger end, 4.4-4.8 x 5.5-6.3$\mu$.

In this collection (No. 2595) there were two distinct plants which were grown together in the middle region. The plant is remarkable in its clear color, pure light yellow above, clear creamy pink in middle region, pure white below. The flesh is colored like the surface except at the tips where it is not so yellow as the surface. In drying the plant shrinks greatly and becomes cartilaginous-looking and not friable or very brittle. The variety differs from the type in the thicker and less crowded stems and in the odor.

North Carolina: Chapel Hill. No. 2595. Earth in mixed woods, Battle's Park, July 5, 1917. (Type).

**Clavaria subspinulosa** n. sp.

PLATES 44, 45, AND 86

Plants 6-10.5 cm. high, 3.5-7 cm. broad, stem distinct, usually not smooth but roughly felted, rather stout, about 2 cm. long and 1-2 cm. thick in middle, more or less grooved by descending ridges from the main branches, tapering downward, the base rounded or moderately pointed, scarcely or shallowly inserted, connected to the humus with fibrous strands like small rootlets; main branches few and short, their angles open and rounded, or rather closely or even densely packed, several times rebranched and finally terminating in a cluster of slender, delicate tips; often longitudinally rugose-wrinkled in the upper half; frequently several plants are partly fused at the base as in *C. formosa*, but never in the dense clumps often found in the latter; color when young a pale, lavender-pink above, shading downward through light cinnamon to the cinnamon-brown to sayal brown stem; or the stem may be at times a paler cinnamon-buff, not pure white at base even in the paler forms; at maturity the upper part of the plant darkens to pinkish cinnamon, a brownish pink-cinnamon (between ochraceous salmon and light ochraceous buff of Ridgway), the angles deeper colored from the spores (the lavender-pink color is quite obvious at the tips in youth but is scarcely noticeable at maturity); in age the color becomes a darker fleshy brown. Flesh opaque, colored like the surface when fresh and damp, whitish when less damp, moderately brittle, taste decidedly acid-bitterish, odor faintly musty like rotten wood; when dried the flesh is chalky and friable as in *C. formosa*; hyphae of flesh not parallel, much branched, 4-8μ thick.

Spores (of No. 2664) elliptic, nearly smooth, 4-5 x 9-10.5μ. Basidia 7-8.3μ with 4 sterigmata; hymenium about 90μ thick, multiple, containing many embedded spores.

Not rare in pine or mixed or deciduous woods in July and August.

This species is nearest *C. formosa* from which it is easily distinguished by the lavender-pink tips in youth, the scurfy-felted, cinnamon colored and less pointed stem and by the smoother and somewhat shorter spores. In youth the color above the base is much lighter than in *C. formosa*, which is a clear pink with the tips often yellowish, the white base contrasting strongly, while in

*C. subspinulosa* the upper part in youth is whitish pink, with a tint of lavender or heliotrope with concolorous tips, the deeper colored cinnamon base contrasting strongly.

A plant at the New York Botanical Garden from Italy determined by Bresadola as *C. spinulosa* Pers. (Obs. Myc. **2**: 59, pl. 3, fig. 1. 1796) is somewhat like our plants and has similar spores. There is also a collection from Blowing Rock, N. C., at Ithaca, determined by Bresadola as *C. spinulosa* which is like our plants and has spores which are identical, 4.8-5 x 9.3-11μ. Another plant from Ithaca, N. Y., (Kauffman) in the Bresadola Herbarium, determined by the latter as *C. spinulosa,* is the same; spores short-elliptic, with bent mucro, rough, 4.2-5 x 8.5-11.2μ. Two other collections from Italy in his herbarium so determined have similar spores, and from the looks of the plants may easily be the same. Bresadola is not consistent, however, in his determinations, as he has quite a different plant so labelled which looks very like our *C. secunda* or *C. obtusissima.* Another collection in his herbarium from Ithaca, N. Y., (Fitzpatrick) labelled *C. spinulosa* with a question is a slender form of *C. stricta.* Bresadola has kindly reported on a typical plant of our species sent by us and says, "according to the dried specimen and spores seems indeed *C. spinulosa,* but the diagnosis does not agree." We do not see how our plants can be the real *C. spinulosa* of Persoon, as the stem is not at all like Persoon's figure, nor have the tips the peculiar inequality he emphasizes in his species. The species is not represented in his herbarium. It is possible that *C. spinulosa* is really *C. fennica.* A fragmentary collection in the Curtis Herbarium from Schweinitz labelled *C. spinulosa* has hard flesh and is not this. The plant referred to *C. pallida* by Maire (Bull. Soc. Myc. Fr. **27**: 451. 1911) has lilac tips in youth, similar spores, apparently, and grows in pine woods, but the figures referred to by Maire as representing it are very unlike our plant.

North Carolina: Chapel Hill. No. 2390. On earth among pine needles, July 18, 1916. Spores light ochraceous, elliptic with a bent end. 4.5-5 x 9-10.5μ. No. 2631. Mixed upland woods, July 10, 1917. No. 2635. Upland woods, July 10, 1917. Spores 3.8-5 x 7.4-10μ. No. 2649. Low damp woods, July 11, 1917. Spores 3.8-4.8 x 7.5-11μ. No. 2653. Mixed pine and oak woods, July 12, 1917. Taste mildly bitterish; stem usually rather long, often several more or less fused together or the stems nearly separate. Spores 4.6-5.6 x 7.5-10.8μ, mostly about

4.8 x 9.3$\mu$.    No. 2664.    Mixed pine and oak woods by Battle's Branch, July 13, 1917. (Type).    No. 2689.    Mixed upland woods, July 17, 1917.    Spores slightly roughened 3.7-4.8 x 8.9-12.2$\mu$.    No. 2722.    Mixed upland woods, July 18, 1917.    No. 2724.    Low mixed woods, July 13, 1917.    Largest plant with lavender very conspicuous in upper part of stem.    Spores 4.4-5.4 x 8-9.5$\mu$, nearly smooth.    No. 2727.    Mixed upland woods, July 20, 1917.    Spores deep ochraceous.    No. 2856.    Growing from under a rotting oak log south of campus, October 2, 1917. Compared fresh with *C. formosa*.    The difference in color was marked, especially in the cinnamon stem.    Spores 4.4-4.9 x 8.5-9.5$\mu$.    No. 3151. Mixed deciduous and pine woods near Meeting of the Waters, August 9, 1918.    No. 3444.    In deciduous woods (no conifers near), August 17, 1919.    No. 3470.    In mixed pine and deciduous woods, August 16, 1919.    Tips of plants nearly mature still retain a little lilac.    No. 4635. In mixed woods near Meeting of the Waters, August 6, 1920.

Blowing Rock.    Atkinson.    (Cornell Herb., as *C. spinulosa*).

Linville Falls.    Coker and party, No. 5752.    (U. N. C. Herb.).

South Carolina:    Society Hill.    (Curtis Herb., unnamed but in the *C. aurea* fascicle).

Virginia:    Mountain Lake.    Murrill, No. 421.    (N. Y. Bot. Gard. Herb.). Spores nearly smooth, 4.8-5.5 x 9.5-11$\mu$, rarely up to 6.4 x 12.5$\mu$.

**Clavaria fennica** Karst.    Nat. Sällsk Faun. et Flora Fenn. **9**: 372. 1868.    (Not *C. fennica* Karst.    Bidr. Finl. Nat. Folk **48**: 47. 1889.=*C. decolorans* Karst.    Symbolae ad Myc. Fenn. **32**: 10. 1893).

?*C. rufo-violacea* Barla.    Champ. Nice, p. 87, pl. 41, figs. **3-13**. 1859.

*C. fumigata* Pk.    Rept. N. Y. St. Mus. **31**: 38. 1879.

*Ramaria versatilis* Quél. in Assoc. Fr. Av. Sci.    Compte Rendu **22**, pt. 2: 489. [1893] 1894.

*C. versatilis* (Quél.) Bourd. and Galzin.    Bull. Soc. Myc. Fr. **26**: 214. 1910.

*Clavariella versatilis* (Quél.) Maire.    Bull. Soc. Myc. Fr. **30**: 218, pl. 9, figs. 1, 1b, 1s. 1914.

### Plates 46, 47, and 86

Plants from 5 to 10 cm. high; main branches few, not channelled, branching repeatedly into many small, strongly ascending branchlets which end in several cusps.    Flesh toughish, not fragile, chalky white or watery (but see No. 921 below); taste slightly acrid at first, then mild.    Stem usually obvious and rather massive, often bulbous, from 2.5-5 cm. in diameter, pale or clear lilac, except at base, turning whitish on drying, rounded below and rooting only by fibers; branches usually a pretty, rather light lilac when young, soon becoming a smoky gray or smoky cinnamon, the lilac tinge slowly disappearing except on the stem.

Spores (of No. 486) cinnamon-buff, slightly rough, oblong with lateral mucro at one end, one oil drop, 3.7-4.4 x 9.8-11μ. Basidia (of No. 620) 7-8.4μ thick, 4-spored; hymenium 90-100μ thick; hyphae 3-8μ thick, much intertwined, with a few septa and no visible clamp connections.

Our plants agree well with *C. fennica* as described by Karsten and as understood by Bresadola (Fungi Tridentini, p. 24, pl. 28) except that the tips of the branches in our plant are not yellow and the spores are narrower.   The main distinguishing features of the species are the distinct lilac colored stem and the smoky body.   We find it rather plentiful in upland deciduous woods.   We have examined Peck's plants of *C. fumigata* and find them the same. The spores of the type are elliptic, finely rough, 3.7-4.4 x 7.7-9.3μ.

We can see no difference of consequence between the present species and *Clavaria versatilis*.   Maire gives the spores of the latter as yellowish, rough, 3-4 x 9-10.5μ.   *Clavaria Bataillei* Maire (Ann. Myc. **11**: 351, pl. 18. 1913) is evidently related but the differences are sufficient to separate it.   It should be looked for in coniferous woods in our mountains.   Compare also *C. cedretorum* Maire (Bull. Soc. Myc. Fr. **30**: 217, pl. 9, figs. 2, 3. 1914) which may not be different.

Illustrations: Burt.   Ann. Mo. Bot. Gard. **9**: pl. 2, fig. 10 (as *C. fumigata*).   1922.

Maire.   As cited above.

North Carolina: Chapel Hill.   No. 486.   Woods east of school house, October 3, 1912.   No. 619.   On side of hill near a rotting log, October 24, 1912.   No. 620.   Woods near Judge Brockwell's house, October 24, 1912.   No. 779.   In woods by path, September 17, 1913.   In this beautiful specimen not only was the base a clear and strong lilac, but the upper part was also tinted clearly with smoke-gray lilac.   Spores cinnamon-buff (Ridgway), long, elliptic, 3.7 x 8.3-9.2μ.   No. 806.   Battle's Park, September, 1913.   Spores 3.7-5.5 x 8.3-11.1μ.   No. 921.   In thick woods, October 15, 1913.   Color of plant when young a pretty lilac all over except the very base, which is white.   This plant showed the remarkable peculiarity of the flesh turning flesh color when firmly mashed and then, after some time, becoming rosy red.   Spores 4-4.8 x 10-11μ.   No. 1282.   On rocky hillside, mixed woods in pasture, September 29, 1914.  Plant clear uniform lilac all over, except white at very base.  Spores 4.2-5.5 x 7.6-11.9µ.  No. 2857.  In rocky upland frondose woods, October 1, 1917.

Blowing Rock.  Coker and party, Nos. 5511, 5524, 5550.  (U. N. C. Herb.).

New York: Ticonderoga, Selkirk, Sand Lake, etc.  Peck.  (Albany Herb., as *C. fumigata*).  There are several other collections in paper folders at Albany.  Peck gave some of these the provisional name of *C. lilacinipes*, but never published it.

Lake George.  Coker, No. 21.  September 3, 1917.  (U. N. C. Herb.).  Spores elliptic, rough, 3.7-4.4 x 9.3-11µ.

Ithaca.  Atkinson.  (Cornell Herb.).

Connecticut: Redding.  Earle.  (N. Y. Bot. Gard. Herb.).

Massachusetts: Newtonsville.  Miss Allen.  (Albany Herb.).  This is typical, the lilac-purple color can still be easily seen in the lower branches and stem.

## Clavaria gelatinosa  sp. nov.

### PLATES 48-50, AND 86

A strongly tufted, spreading and heavy plant with much the habit of *C. botrytis,* but not rooting and more massive at the base and far less fragile; clusters about 7-12 cm. high and 5-14 cm. broad, no distinct stem, the numerous crowded and conjoined branches arising from an amorphous, pallid (creamy white) base, which soon loses itself in the fibrous mycelium and is not rooting: branches very numerous and crowded, forming a dense mass and repeatedly rebranching to end finally in several pointed cusps. The massive base is nearly always furnished with small, undeveloped branches which remain whitish.  Color when very young pale creamy white, passing through creamy to creamy flesh then deep flesh color (a brownish cinnamon-flesh color, about buff-pink of Ridgway) and then darker, fleshy brown in age; the tips as light as or lighter than the branches at all ages.   The flesh colors appear first in the middle region, the base remaining creamy white. Flesh remarkable, gelatinous, transparent, toughish, elastic; taste distinctly acid, then bitterish and like tobacco; odor very slight when fresh but somewhat fruity when dry and to us distinctly like tobacco.

Spores (of No. 2413) 4.4-5 x 7.5-9µ, most about 4.6 x 8µ, elliptic, marked with numerous small warts under high power, a large, blunt, eccentric mucro, buff-yellow (Ridgw.) when seen at an angle across the paper, ochraceous buff (Ridgw.) in face view, almost exactly the color of those of *C. botrytis*; they are of a different color from the hymenium, a fact that can be easily seen where the spores gather in the angle of the branches. Basidia 4-spored, 8-11µ thick, projecting about 13µ beyond the surface; sterigmata about 7µ long, straight.

The structure of the flesh is the most peculiar character of the plant. With the exception of a thin surface layer it is from base to very top, and at all ages (except extreme youth), a clear, transparent, but cohesive and toughish jelly, with almost exactly the appearance and texture of table gelatine. It is composed of slender, little branched threads about 2-4.5µ thick, which run openly through the transparent jelly (fig. 10). This peculiar quality of the flesh can be detected without cutting by the soft but elastic feel of the plant. The color of the flesh is the same as the surface at all points. In very dry weather the flesh loses its peculiar appearance in part but a longitudinal section of the base will always show some transparency. As a result of its texture the plant dries out very slowly, taking several times as long as any other species.

There seems to be no reference to gelatinous flesh in the description of any *Clavaria,* but we have noticed a slight tendency in this direction in *C. botrytis,* as indicated by a mottled transparency in the flesh of the stem and larger branches.

This species seems nearest *C. formosa,* and in dry weather, when the flesh has largely lost its peculiar transparency, certain forms of the two might easily be confused from the somewhat similar color and form; but the spores, while of about the same surface and width, are distinctly shorter than those of *C. formosa.* In the dry state *C. gelatinosa* is darker and much harder than *C. formosa* and there is at times present in the flesh, especially towards the base, a central core or plate of very hard, black tissue like horn. This tissue is formed from the gelatinous flesh and its formation is probably dependent on the rapidity of drying. It is usually seen in the stem as thin plates here and there. Mature plants of *C. subspinulosa* are about the same color, but that species is very different in other ways.

This is the plant that Schweinitz referred to *C. grisea* Pers. as is shown by a collection in his herbarium with identical appearance and spores and with the horny, black internal tissue unusually developed.   There is also a bit of this from Schweinitz in the Curtis Herbarium which shows the same spores.   In the same herbarium is a good plant from Hillsboro, N. C., without specific name, but pinned on the same sheet with *C. aurea*.   It looks much like *C. gelatinosa* with the same dark, rather olive tint.   The spores are a little larger and hardly so rough as in our plants, 3.7-4.8 x 8-11μ.   Cotton has shown (confirmed by us) that Persoon's type plants of *C. grisea* are *C. cinerea* (Trans. Brit. Myc. Soc. **3**: 184. 1909) as Persoon himself stated in 1822.   It is possible that our plant exists in Europe and is the one that Fries erroneously interpreted as *C. grisea*.

North Carolina: Chapel Hill.   No.   2413.   Upland deciduous woods, July 22, 1916.   (Type).   No. 2677.   Low damp woods, July 16, 1917. No. 2700.   Low damp woods, July 16, 1917.   A young plant; tips pale, flesh just becoming gelatinous.   No. 2715.   Mixed upland woods, July 19, 1917.   No. 2744.   Mixed upland woods, July 21, 1917.   No. 2807. On hillside in woods, July 29, 1917.   No. 2861.   Mixed pine and frondose woods, October 4, 1917.   Spores distinctly rough, 4.4-4.8 x 8-9.8μ. No. 2880.   Pine and dogwood back of athletic field, October 6, 1917. Spores 4.4-4.8 x 7.7-9.2μ.   No. 2915.   Mixed woods south of athletic field, October 18, 1917.   No. 3436.   Deciduous woods, August 16, 1919. No. 3477.   Mixed woods near Meeting of the Waters, August 22, 1919. No. 4397.   Damp woods by north branch of Meeting of the Waters, July 14, 1920.

**Clavaria rufescens** Schaeff.   Fung. Bavar., pl. 288. 1770.
   *C. holorubella* Atk.   Ann. Myc. **6**: 57. 1908.

### PLATES 51 AND 86

Plants of medium to large size, up to 15 cm. high and 12 cm. broad, usually about 8-10.5 cm. high and same breadth; stem distinct, usually stout, short, glabrous, whitish, then tan or leather color, and often stained with deep, dull vinaceous rose color; branches delicate, very numerous and loosely crowded, spreading on the sides, terete or channelled, quite rugose, or at times not at all so, branching irregularly and ending in short, bluntish cusps; color light tan when fresh, the tips concolorous when very young but soon becoming pale rosy vinaceous then darker vinaceous and finally deep dull brick-brown.   Flesh white or often stained vinaceous rose below when the surface is so stained; when quite fresh moderately brittle, but soon pliable; taste bitterish or slightly acid or at times scarcely any, not krauty; odor none, or very slight.

Spores (of No. 2845) about cinnamon-buff (Ridgway), rod-elliptic, with a curved tip, characteristically marked with longitudinal striations, 3.3-3.8 x 11-13µ. Basidia (of No. 2862) 7.4-8µ. thick, 4-spored; hymenium 55-65µ thick; hyphae 3-8µ thick, clamp connections present.

Common in upland woods. Easily distinguished from *C. botrytis* by the wine colored instead of rose-pink tips, which grow deeper in age instead of lighter as in the latter species; also by the different taste, less firm and brittle flesh, and different spores. The striate spores separate it from all other species. *Clavaria obtusissima* has spores of like shape, but without the striations, and the plant has stouter branches without wine colored tips. A peculiarity of the plant is the spotted appearance that almost always results from the gnawing of grubs as maturity is passed. Another is the open way in which the branches dry. The species has been much confused with *C. botrytis,* which see for discussion. Migula's figure referred to below shows by the striate spores that he confused this species with *C. formosa.* Compare also *C. pallida* as interpreted by Maire (Bull. Soc. Myc. Fr. **27**: 451. 1911). The variety *frondosarum* Bres. of *C. rufescens* (in Schulzer, Hedwigia **24**: 148. 1885) is said to differ from the species in the tips not being red and in the white stem. It may not belong to this species. Quélet's interpretation of the species seems to be the same as ours. He speaks of the purplish tips, and the spores also agree. *Clavaria holorubella* is not to be distinguished from this species by the description and the spores are identical. We find them (in the type at Ithaca) striate, 3.7-5 x 10.5-13.3µ.

Illustrations: Britzelmayr. Hymen. Südb., Clavariei, fig. 16. Probably true, but not good.

Burt. Ann. Mo. Bot. Gard. **9**: pl. 2, fig. 6 (as *C. holorubella*). 1922.

Istvanffi. Icon. Fung., pl. 63, fig. 3. 1900.

Migula in Thomé. Krypt.-Fl. Deutsch. **3**, 2, 1: pl. 24 (as *C. formosa*). 1912.

Saccardo. Mycol. Venetae, pl. 8, figs. 9-10. 1873.

Schaeffer. As cited above.

Sterbeeck. Theatr. Fung., pl. 11, figs. A-B. 1675.

North Carolina: Chapel Hill. No. 531. Woods northeast of school house, October 8, 1912. Spores yellow-ochraceous, long, rod-shaped, smooth, 3-3.7 x 10.2-12µ. No. 563. By path to Meeting of the Waters, October 15, 1912. Spores 3-4.3 x 11-13µ, most about 3.5 x 11.5µ. No.

2845. In rocky, upland, frondose woods, October 1, 1917. No. 2862. Pine and frondose woods (mixed), October 4, 1917. Spores 3.7-4.4 x 11-13.5μ. No. 2868. Mixed woods, October 5, 1917. Just as in No. 2845 except base not so thick and tapering downward. No. 2877. In mixed woods, October 6, 1917. Tips a pretty light wine color. No. 2884. Pine, oaks and a little underbrush, quite rocky, October 6, 1917. Tips light wine color even though the plant was very fresh; quite rugose upward. Spores cinnamon-buff (exactly color of those of *C. formosa*), quite smooth, 3.7-4 x 11-12.2μ. No. 2887. Oaks, pines, cedars and much underbrush, October 6, 1917. Very large plants. No. 2901. Pines, oaks and some underbrush, October 8, 1917.

Linville Falls. Coker and party, No. 5722. (U. N. C. Herb.). Taste quite bitter. Spores 4-4.8 x 9.3-12μ.

## Clavaria xanthosperma Pk.    Bull. N. Y. St. Mus. **94**: 21. 1905.

### PLATE 86

We have not seen this in the fresh state, but from the description and the dried plants we take it to be a good species. The type consists of two plants, clear, pale ochraceous, 3.2-5 cm. high, and 3.8-4.4 cm. broad, bases pointed abruptly below, tips numerous; brittle, not friable; a few distinct red stains on the short stems. Spores nearly smooth, 3.8-4.8 x 12.2-15.5μ. The original description follows:

"Stem very short, firm, solid, divided into numerous branches, white, sometimes becoming red where wounded, ultimate branches short, blunt or obtusely dentate at the apex, the axils rounded, the whole plant white, becoming yellowish or cream-colored with age; spores pale yellow, oblong, 12.7-15.2 x 4-5μ, slightly and obliquely pointed at one end.

"It forms tufts about 2 inches high."

Illustration:  Burt.  Ann. Mo. Bot. Gard. **9**: pl. 3, fig. 15.  1922.

New York:  Smithtown.  Woods, August.  (Albany Herb., type).

## Clavaria verna n. sp.

### PLATES 52 AND 86

Plant up to 10 cm. high and 9 cm. wide, base distinct and plump, pointed below, white, all above base a pale fleshy tan, the tips concolorous. Branches open and lax, the angles broad and rounded, surface a little rugose towards the tips. Flesh lax and soft, but not very brittle, not crisp and not snapping, but tearing; nearly odorless and tasteless, mostly white, old bruised places are ochraceous at any point of plant.    Stem not very spongy, and tips not wine color.

Spores (of No. 3039) light fleshy tan, elliptic, nearly smooth, small, 3-3.3 x 6.6-7.4µ.  Basidia 4.8-6.6µ thick, 4-spored; hymenium 50-60µ thick; hyphae about 4.4µ thick.

This was the first *Clavaria* to appear in the spring of 1918.

It seems nearest *C. rufescens*.  It is not in the *botrytis* group, nor is it like *C. obtusissima, C. cacao,* etc.  The pale, uniform color, lax and open growth, soft but not brittle or crisp flesh, lack of taste and odor and the distinctly small, nearly smooth spores separate this species from all others.

North Carolina: Chapel Hill.  No. 3039.  Upland woods, with mostly deciduous trees, May 18, 1918. (Type).  No. 3053.  Strowd's lowground deciduous woods, May 22, 1918.  When young very pale whitish tan, the distinct rounded stem pure white, except for distinct or faint tints of rose that may appear on stem or larger branches, mostly where the two meet.  This is not due to rubbing and may fade out in large measure after a few hours.  Bruised or gnawed places do not turn reddish or rosy.  This seems near pale forms of *C. rufescens,* and is like it in the soft flesh that causes the plant to dry very open and with surface much gnawed by snails, also in distinct stem, etc.  No odor or taste when fresh, no odor of ham in drying, only a faintly aromatic odor of ferment.  Spores 3.7-4 x 7.4-8µ.  No. 3067.  Strowd's lowground deciduous woods, May 22, 1918.  Spores as in No. 3039, elliptic, minutely rough, 3.7 x 7-7.7µ.  No. 3068.  Strowd's lowground deciduous woods, May 22, 1918.  Stem very distinct and rounded, and with pretty, light rosy tints here and there, these not from bruises.  Color of plant pale tan or buff except the white stem; some of the apices soon turning brick color as in *C. rufescens*, but no wine color in tips.  Flesh very soft and delicate, but not snapping or crisp, tasteless and odorless.  Spores maize yellow, minutely rough, 3.3-3.7 x 7.5-9.5µ, most about 3.5 x 8-8.5µ, a very few up to 10.5µ.

**Clavaria aurea**  Schaeff.  Fung. Bavar., p. 121, pl. 287. 1770.

PLATE 86

There is no species that has been more confused than this. One can find almost all the large Clavarias so determined in American and European herbaria.  As there is no type in existence, it seemed to us for a time that it would be best to drop this name altogether.  It now appears, however, that there is a plant that has been determined as *C. aurea* by Bresadola, Romell, Peck, Atkinson and Burnham and this may be considered sufficient excuse for taking this plant as entitled to the name.   It is true that most or all of these students have also determined other species as *C. aurea* and more or less consistently confused these species, but in most cases all of their *C. aurea* except the plant we have in mind can be referred to other known species.   As we have notes by Mr. Burnham on color in the fresh state of his plants, and as they agree well in the dried state with plants from the other authors mentioned, we will take our description of the species from his collections.   The spores of these New York plants are slightly narrower than the European ones, but this difference does not seem important in consideration of the close resemblance of the spores in other respects.   We have not found in the living state a plant that we can believe identical with Burnham's, but we have in Chapel Hill a form which is apparently very near, differing only in the less withered and cartilaginous look of the dried plant and in the reddish stains when rubbed.   We are calling this var. *australis*.   From Mr. Burnham's plants and notes we draw the following description (Burnham, No. 102):

Plant large, repeatedly and densely branched from a rather small, pointed root, reaching a weight of almost a pound.   Color a uniform, beautiful orange except the basal parts which are white where hidden by leaves and humus.   Texture tender and rather brittle.   The dried plants are dull brown to reddish brown, shrunken, the base and young tips hard and cartilaginous-looking, taste rather strong and a little acid.

Spores yellowish under a lens, subelliptic, with a bent tip, minutely but distinctly rough, 4-4.8 x 11-13μ.

We have compared our plant with two collections of *C. aurea* from Bresadola's herbarium, one marked "genuina," the other "typica."   They look exactly like Burnham's plants in the dried state and the spores are the same except a little broader.   One lot (Sopramento, in woods, 1901) has spores 4-6 x 10-15μ, the other (Mendola, August, 1901) has spores 4-5.5 x 11-13.5μ.   The spores of both have the minutely rough surface and bent tip of those of the American plant.   Bresadola gives an inadequate description of a plant he took to be *C. aurea* (Fung. Mang., p. 110, pl. 102), but there is no reason to think that it is not the plant so labelled in his herbarium.   We have two good collections from Romell labelled *C. aurea,* one of which we take to be correct and like the above (spores rough, 4.5-5 x 11-14μ).   The other is *C. flava.*

Persoon did not recognize *C. aurea,* nor did Fries in his earlier works, but in his Epicrisis and in Hym. Europ. the latter includes it and refers to plates which agree very well with the plant described above.   Particularly good is Bulliard's plate 222 (as *C. coralloides*) and only a little less good is the lower figure in Schaeffer's plate 287.   A plant from Fries (Upsala) in the Curtis Herbarium labelled *C. aurea* is not unlike our plants and has spores slightly rough, 4.5-6.5 x 9.3-11μ, just like those of the Bresadola specimens referred to above.   In addition to the above, one of the few plates that really look like the American species is that of Venturi (Studi Micol., pl. 12, fig. 112, as *C. aurea*).

The species has not been recognized in the south except as our Chapel Hill variety, but seems to be common in the northern states.

Juel (cited under *C. cristata*) finds the basidium of a plant he determines as *C. aurea* to contain four nuclei, resulting from two apical transverse spindles, the number of chromosomes probably four.   The spores are larger and rougher than in *C. flava,* and contain one nucleus (pl. 3, figs. 56-66).

Illustrations: See above.

New York: Albany.   Peck.   (Albany Herb.).   The spores are slightly rough, 4.2-4.6 x 9.5-11μ.   A colored drawing shows the color a pale brownish yellow and the plants quite upright.

Vaughns.   Burnham, Nos. 51 and 102.   (U. N. C. Herb.).

Ithaca.   Atkinson.   (Cornell Herb.).   Spores rough, 4-5.5 x 9-13μ.

## Clavaria aurea var. australis n. var.

### PLATES 53-55, AND 87

Plants up to 11 cm. high and broad, compound from a small pointed base, and at times cespitose; delicate and soft, more or less rugose, branching quickly in an irregular way into a dense mass, the tips ending in bluntish cusps; color a rich buffy orange (between capucine-orange and orange-buff of Ridgway) all over except the base, which is at first nearly white, but is easily stained with vinaceous brown when handled.  Flesh delicate, not so firm as *C. botrytis* or *C. flava* and not snapping at a slight bend, but more easily breaking than in most species, white, mildly bitter, odor musty, faintly medicinal.

Spores (of No. 2912) buffy ochraceous, minutely rough, 3.9-4.4 x 11-13μ.  Basidia 7.4-9.3μ thick, 4-spored; hymenium 75-110μ thick; hyphae 3-9μ, set with small crystals, often swollen at septa but without clamp connections.

This all-orange plant varies into other color forms: one, represented by No. 2882a, in which only the tips are orange, the remainder when young, creamy flesh, then creamy tan; another (No. 2597) in which the plant is brownish tan with a dull pink tint, the base stained with deeper brown when rubbed.

Distinguished by the quick branching from a short, pointed, slightly rooting base, by the stains on basal region, by the fine rich color, by great delicacy, by absence of krauty odor or taste, and by the long, narrow spores.  It is evidently a close relative of *C. rufescens*.  It may be this species that is interpreted as *C. flava* by Bresadola, one of the foremost living mycologists.  In his Fung. Mang., p. 108, he describes the species in a way that seems to exclude all others.  He mentions the uniform yellow ("sulfur yellow") color, the wine-red stains on the stem and the elongated cylindrical spores, 4-5 x 10-14μ long.  At the New York Botanical Garden is a plant from him labelled *C. flava* which looks like our *C. aurea* var. *australis* and with spores faintly rough, 4-4.5 x 9-10.5μ.  That this is really the *C. flava* of Schaeffer seems highly improbable as such an interpretation is at variance with the opinion of most European and American students of the group.  See under *C. flava* for further discussion.

North Carolina: Chapel Hill.  No. 2597.  In woods mold, oak and pine upland woods, July 5, 1917.  Spores ochraceous, elliptic with a large eccentric mucro, minutely rough or smooth, 3.7-5 x 7.5-11μ, average about 9.3-10μ long.  No. 2882a.  Mixed woods south of athletic field, October 6, 1917.  Spores ochraceous, long and narrow, distinctly rough, 4-4.5 x 11-13μ, most about 4 x 12μ, exactly like those of No. 2912.  Tips dull brick-brown when bruised or on withering, base white, but turning dull wine-brown when rubbed (more purplish and not so red as in *C. rufescens*).  Flesh firm and brittle, light flesh color.  No. 2912.  Woods south of athletic field, pines, oaks and underbrush, October 18, 1917.  (Type).  No. 2913.  Same locality as No. 2912, October 18, 1917.

New York: Bolton. Peck. (Albany Herb.).
  Albany and Lebanon Springs. Peck and Clinton. (Albany Herb.).
  Spores 4.5 x 11μ.

## Clavaria testaceoflava var. testaceoviridis Atk. Ann. Myc. 6: 58. 1908.

This plant is known only from Blowing Rock. We have not been able to find the type. The original description by Atkinson is as follows:

"Plants clustered, extreme bases slightly joined; tufts 4-5 cm. high, 3-4 cm. broad; trunks short, 1-2 cm. high, 4-6 mm. stout, above abruptly branched, terminal branches somewhat enlarged and pluridentate; trunks and branches pale drab, tips olive green when fresh; spores oblong, roughened, 10-12 x 4μ."

*Clavaria testaceoflava* Bres. (Fungi Trid. **1**: 61, pl. 69. 1884) is like the above except that the tips are yellow, the rest cinnamon brown. Spores yellow, elongated, 4-5 x 10-14μ, roughness not mentioned or shown, but we find from authentic plants in the Bresadola Herbarium that the spores are slightly rough (3.8-5 x 11-14.8μ). Occurs in Alpine fir woods. The rather small size, enlarged or expanded pluridentate or somewhat crested yellowish tips (greenish in Atkinson's variety) mark the species.

Illustration: Burt. Ann. Mo. Bot. Gard. **9**: pl. 3, fig. 17. 1922.

North Carolina: Blowing Rock. On ground in woods, August 19-September 22, 1901. A. B. Troyer. (Cornell Herb., type, No. 10593. Not seen by us.)

## Clavaria obtusissima Pk. Bull. N. Y. St. Mus. **167**: 39. 1913.

  *C. albida* Pk. Rept. N. Y. St. Mus. **41**: 79. 1887. (Not *C. albida* Schaeff.)
  *C. obtusissima* var. *minor* Pk. Bull. N. Y. St. Mus. **167**: 34. 1913.
  *C. spinulosa* Pers. Obs. Myc. **2**: 59, pl. 3, fig. 1. 1799. (Sense of Schw.).

### PLATES 56 AND 87

Plants large, often 13 cm. high and of equal width, base massive, tapering downward to a rather deep root, the stout main branches quickly divided into a heavy mass of branchlets which finally terminate in blunt tips; surface even, not rugose, sometimes channelled; color pale cream when young, then creamy tan, the tips concolorous until maturity, then fading to reddish brown, the base whitish or nearly concolorous; flesh rather brittle, but not so much so as in *C. formosa,* not rigid, white, soft, taste distinctly bitterish, odor mildly rancid, becoming somewhat like old ham in drying.    A pink form of this seems to occur in the north, as we have a collection from Vaughns, N. Y. (Burnham, No. 96), that has the same spores and appearance, but that was flesh colored when fresh.

Spores (of No. 2866) ochraceous, long rod-elliptic, often bent or swaybacked, smooth, 3.7-4.4 x 11-13.8μ.    Basidia 7.4-9.3μ thick, 4-spored; hymenium 90-100μ thick; hyphae roughly parallel, 3-8μ in diameter, clamp connections frequent but inconspicuous.

This is much like *C. rufescens* in shape, taste and spores, but is without the wine colored tips and stains of this color on the stem, and the spores are without the striations seen in those of *C. rufescens.*

We have examined the type of *C. obtusissima* and find it the same as our plants, with spores 4-5 x 11-14.8μ.    From examination of the type of *C. albida* at Albany, we find it to all appearances the same.    The spores are indistinguishable, except for slightly larger size, smooth, 3.8-5 x 14-15μ.    The variety *minor* is a small form.    We have examined also the plant in the Schweinitz Herbarium labelled *C. spinulosa* which is referred to by Berkeley in establishing *C. secunda,* and find it to be not that but the present species.    The spores as well as other appearances in the dried state are the same.    There is also a bit in the Curtis Herbarium from Schweinitz with similar spores (4.5-5.3 x 14-16.5μ).

Illustrations: Burt.    Ann. Mo. Bot. Gard. **9**: pl. 4, fig. 18; pl. 3, fig. 16 (as *C. albida*).    1922.

North Carolina: Chapel Hill.    No. 577.    Woods near Dr. Pratt's home, October 7, 1912.    Spores smooth, 3.3-4 x 10.5-13μ.    No. 2860.    Mixed woods, October 4, 1917.    Spores 3.7-4 x 11-14μ.    No. 2866.    Pine, oak and cedar woods, October 4, 1917.    No. 2867.    Pine and frondose woods, October 4, 1917.    Spores 3.7-4.4 x 10-12.2μ.    No. 2870.    Mixed woods, October 5, 1917.    Spores 3.7-4 x 11-14μ.    No. 2896.    Mixed woods south of athletic field, October 8, 1917.    Odor in drying distinctly like old ham. Spores smooth, 3-4 x 11-14.5$\mu$. No. 2909. Pine and frondose woods, October 18, 1917. Odorless when quite fresh, taste mild, slightly sweetish-acid; color light yellowish buff (about pale orange yellow of Ridgw.), flesh pure white, firm and rather rigid, but not very brittle; tips fading late to dull then darker brown. Spores 3.2-3.7 x 8.7-12$\mu$. No. 2919. Mixed woods south of athletic field, October 18, 1917. Spores 3.2-3.5 x 9.3-11.3$\mu$, very regular in size. No. 3200. In pine and oak leaves, mixed woods, October 7, 1918. Base stout and distinct, usually with many little aborted branches on side. Texture pliable, taste faintly bitterish sweet, odor slightly meaty in drying, not strong of ham. Spores elliptic, nearly smooth, 3.8-5 x 10.5-13.5$\mu$.

Alabama: Auburn. Earle. (N. Y. Bot. Gard. Herb., as *C. secunda*). Spores smooth, oblong-elliptic, 3.3-4 x 9.3-11.1$\mu$.

New York: Bolton. Peck. (Albany Herb., as type of *C. obtusissima* var. *minor*).

Monands and West Port. Peck. (Albany Herb., as types of *C. albida*).

Vaughns. Burnham, No. 96a. Under hemlocks, August 19, 1917. (U. N. C. Herb.). "Flesh colored when fresh." Spores smooth, 4-5 x 12-15$\mu$.

Massachusetts: West Roxbury. Miss Hibbard. (Albany Herb., as type of *C. obtusissima*).

Stockbridge. Murrill and Thompson. (N. Y. Bot. Gard. Herb., as *C. secunda*). Spores smooth, 12-13$\mu$ long.

Stow. Davis. (Albany Herb., as *C. obtusissima*).

Missouri: St. Louis. Glatfelter. (Albany Herb., as *C. secunda*). Plant "6-8 in. broad, 4-6 in. high." Spores 3.5-4.5 x 11-15$\mu$.

*Clavaria obtusissima. Form with rough spores.*

We have one collection that would pass for *C. obtusissima* except for distinct roughness of spores. It may be distinct, but without more specimens we prefer to consider it a rough-spored form of this species.

Plant 9 cm. tall to the pointed base, 3-6 cm. broad. Stem thick, spongy, glabrous, white; branches rather open, pale creamy tan, then creamy ochraceous; tips concolorous; texture moderately brittle; odor none, taste faintly sweetish.

Spores ochraceous yellow, distinctly rough, subelliptic, 3.7-5.5 x 9.5-14.8$\mu$, most about 4.5 x 12$\mu$.

North Carolina: Chapel Hill. No. 3792. Close to Strowd's spring, mixed woods, November 22, 1919.

**Clavaria Strasseri** Bres. in Strass. Pilzflora Sontagberg **2**: 3. 1900.

PLATE 87

Plant 7-10 cm. high, 4-8 cm. broad, stem stout, distinct, more or less rooting, white or stained with tan; branches rather upright and open, angles spreading or at times acute, twigs ending in rather acute tips, color light creamy tan, the tips concolorous, deeper cinnamon-tan in age, the tips dull brown in withering. Flesh white, soft, fibrous, not very brittle; taste bitterish, odor faintly of old ham.

Spores (of No. 2897) yellowish buff, oblong-amygdaliform (approaching peach kernel shape), smooth, 4.8-6.7 x 14-18.5μ. Basidia 7.4-9.3μ thick, 4-spored; hymenium 90-110μ thick; hyphae 4-10μ thick, wavy, clamp connections present.

Closely related to *C. obtusissima, C. secunda,* and *C. rufescens,* but separated from all of them by the very large spores, and from the last by absence of wine colored stains. The odor is different from that of *C. secunda,* but like that of the other two. We have called this *C. Strasseri* because in appearance it is just like a plant so named from Bresadola in the New York Botanical Garden, and principally because the peculiar large spores are identical in both. Bresadola gives the spores as 4-6 x12-16μ. In the above specimens from him we find them to be 5-6.6 x 11.8-15.5μ. Others in his herbarium (Sontagberg, Strasser) have spores 3.8-5 x 13-15μ.

Except for the spores the relationship of this to *C. obtusissima* is so close that it might be best to consider the former a large-spored variety of the latter. The plant has been recognized so far in this country only in Chapel Hill.

*Clavaria incurvata* Morg. (Journ. Cin. Soc. Nat. Hist. **11**: 88, pl. 2, fig. 2. 1888) must remain doubtful as Prof. T. H. Mac-Bride writes us that the type is not represented in the Morgan Herbarium at the University of Iowa, and no authentic specimen is known. The figure somewhat resembles *C. Strasseri.* From its spores, *Ramaria Rieli* would seem to fall here. It is evidently an abnormal, dropsical form in any case.

North Carolina: Chapel Hill. No. 2897. In pine and frondose woods, south of athletic field, October 8, 1917. No. 2927. Same woods as No. 2897, October 18, 1917. Spores smooth, 5.5-6.3 x 14-17μ.

**Clavaria secunda** Berk.   Grevillea **2** : 7. 1873.

 *C. crassipes* Pk.   Bull. N. Y. St. Mus. **67** : 27. 1903.

 *C. pallida* Schaeff.   Fung. Bavar., pl. 286. 1770.   (Sense of Bres.   Not *C. pallida* B. & C.).

PLATES 57 AND 85

 Plants medium to large, stem distinct, usually short (about 2-3.5 cm. long), stout to very stout, up to 4 cm. thick, soft, white, glabrous, and usually very smooth and terete, main branches numerous, rather small, arising in an open fashion from the top of the broad stem, smooth (not rugose), branching a few times and ending in blunt or rather sharp tips.   Color pale creamy tan, with a faint flesh tint, except the white stem, which may be more or less stained with this color; tips concolorous, in fading becoming soaked reddish ochraceous.   Flesh pure white, fibrous and soft, spongy, not brittle, taste quite mild, distinctly sweetish; odor sweetish medicinal and a little rancid, rather pleasant and fainty like old ham.

 Spores (of No. 2876) ochraceous buff, elliptic, smooth, 4-4.4 x 8.5-11.4μ, most about 4.3 x 9.3μ.

 This is most like *C. obtusissima* in color and general appearance, but is distinctly different in the thicker, more discrete, more glabrous and very soft stem, which does not taper much downward but is rounded below and not much rooted; in the sweetish, mild taste, and in the shorter spores, which are never swaybacked.   The stem is nearly always set with a good many short, projecting points, representing very much reduced branches, as shown in the photos.

 The co-type in the Curtis Herbarium (Hillsboro, N. C., No. 534) has spores of the same characteristic shape and size, 4.5-5.5 x 10-12.2μ.   The collection at Kew (Ravenel, No. 991, Santee River, S. C.), also referred to in the original description, shows few spores but these seem to be like those of our No. 2876.

 Our plants are like Peck's types of *C. crassipes* and the spores are identical, smooth or nearly so, 4-5.5 x 10-12μ.   In a later collection by Peck (1916) they are smooth, 4-4.5 x 8.6-11μ;

in still another collection made in the same place in 1917 they are 5-5.5 x 11.5-12.5μ.  From two good plants in Bresadola's herbarium we think he has referred this species to *C. pallida* Schaeff. Both are from coniferous woods and were collected by him.  Of one he says "in growth pale flesh color, soon becoming whitish-alutaceous."  The spores are smooth or nearly so, 4-5.5 x 8.5-11μ. If the type of *C. extensa* Herfell (Hedwigia **52**: 391. 1912) exists it should be compared with the present species.

Farlow's figure of *C. aurea* (see below) is much more like this species than it is like our *C. aurea*.

Illustrations:  Bel.  Champ. Tarn, pl. 8.  1889 (as *C. flava* but not). May be *C. secunda*.

Burt.  Ann. Mo. Bot. Gard. **9**: pl. 1, fig. 4; pl. 7, fig. 51 (as *C. crassipes*). 1922.

Farlow.  Garden and Forest **7**: fig. 15 (as *C. aurea*; fig. 8 of separate). 1894.

Gillet.  Champ. Fr., pl. 100 (as *C. aurea*).  1874-78.

Krombholz.  Abbild., pl. 53, figs. 5 and 6 (as *C. formosa*).  1841.

Richon and Roze.  Atl. Champ., pl. 66, figs. 3 and 4 (as *C. aurea*). 1885-7.  Good.

North Carolina: Chapel Hill.  No. 2876.  Mixed pine and frondose woods south of athletic field, October 6, 1917.  No. 2918.  Among oaks and pines with much dogwood underbrush, October 18, 1917.  No. 2931. Mixed woods south of athletic field, October 18, 1917.
Hillsboro.  Curtis.  (Curtis Herb., as co-type).

New York:  Sand Lake.  Peck.  (Albany Herb., as *C. crassipes*).
Vaughns.  Burnham, No. 112.  (U. N. C. Herb.).  Spores slightly rough or smooth, 3.8-5.3 x 8-11.1μ.

## Clavaria cacao n. sp.

### PLATES 58 AND 87

Two plants, 7-8 cm. high, 5-6 cm. wide, rather upright; stem short, moderately thick, somewhat tapering, terete or channelled, glabrous, firm; branching in a rather open fashion into crooked branches, which terminate in short, stout, rather pointed and cusp-like tips; inconspicuously rugose in upper half at least; color when young a pale lavender-pink upward and to some extent throughout; this soon changing towards maturity from the base upward to pale tan, through buffy tan to buff, the upper part and tips retaining some of the lavender-pink until maturity, then darkening at the very points to brown when fading; base and stem whitish, but easily changing to wine color when handled, and bruised flesh changing to this color at any point, as around grub channels.   Flesh firm and rigid-elastic when quite fresh, soon pliable in fading, not brittle, pure white or with a faint tint of surface color; taste mild, faint, not bitter or krauty; odor none when quite fresh, but as soon as fading begins becoming very distinctly medicinal fragrant—much like cocoa butter of the pharmacist (not like edible chocolate), and not like that of *C. secunda* (No. 2876).   The odor is moreover very persistent, and even stronger in completely dry than in fading plants, and thus quite different from the disappearing odor of *C. secunda* and other species.   After six years the fragrance is still quite obvious.

Spores (of No. 2926) ochraceous, smooth, long and narrow, some sway-backed, $3.4 \times 12.7\text{-}16.6\mu$.   Basidia 4-spored, $5.9\text{-}9.3\mu$ thick; hymenium $65\text{-}95\mu$ thick, with medium sized crystals; threads of flesh very irregular, not parallel in longitudinal section, $3\text{-}7.7\mu$ thick, clamp connections present.

This species is much like *C. rufescens* in shape, texture, and in the vinaceous stains, but the color is otherwise not the same, as the whole upper part is a faint lavender-pink, not the vinaceous color of *C. rufescens,* which moreover is confined to the tips and is much more vivid and contrasting; also the upper part of *C. cacao* does not darken much in fading, only the very tips becoming dull brown, and the spores are without striations.   The very noticeable fragrance is the most distinctive character and separates it from all others near, the odor of *C. secunda* being different and the plant very different.   *Clavaria flava* has like stains on the stem, but is not otherwise similar.

North Carolina: Chapel Hill.   No. 2926.   On ground in woods (pine, oak and dogwood), October 18, 1917.

**Clavaria byssiseda** Pers.   Obs. Myc. **1**: 32. 1796.
   *C. pinophila* Pk.   Rept. N. Y. St. Mus. **35**: 136. 1884.
   ?*Clavaria epiphylla* Schw. (herb. name. Not *C. epiphylla* Quél.).

### Plates 28, 59, 60, and 87

Plants 1.5-5.6 cm. high, 0.5-4.5 cm. broad; stalk distinct, 3-4 mm. thick, 1-1.4 cm. long, distinctly rough or scurfy, nearly white, irregularly branched and rebranched 3 or 4 times, the ultimate tips fine, short and a little divaricating; rather dense; color of main body when quite fresh a delicate, very pale rosy pink or fleshy tan, becoming brownish when bruised; the tips shading gradually to whitish cream; after maturity darkening to about leather color (avellaneous to wood-brown) in main region, the tips unchanging or becoming very faintly tinted with green; no sterile plush-like areas among the branches, except in some of the angles (or such sterile lines present in some of the New York plants). Flesh quite tough and pliable, easily bending on self without breaking; taste slight, faintly woody; odor slight, reminding one of a sewing machine. (No odor to be noticed in plants from Vaughns, N. Y.)

Spores long, narrow, sway-backed, cream or faintly brown in a good print, narrowed toward the proximal end, (of No. 4395) 3.7 x 12-13.7$\mu$. Basidia clavate, 4-spored, 7.4$\mu$ thick; hymenium 40-50$\mu$ thick, deep yellow in section; hyphae of flesh loosely packed, septate, with clamp connections, 4-5$\mu$ thick.

Growing on twigs and leaves or fragments of rotting wood of beech or less often of maple, and probably under oak also; sometimes on these and white pine leaves mixed; often appearing in a row on twigs and bound together by rhizomorphic strands.

When quite fresh the bruised surface and cut flesh turn brown rather quickly. After standing in dry air a little while some of the minute tips turn deep reddish brown for about 1 mm. or less. When growing on leaves the plants spring immediately from a dense, flat, white pad about 5-13 mm. wide on top of the leaf. This pad is connected beneath to the byssoid strands between the leaves, which are characteristic of the species. In older plants even the tips may become tinted with leather color. At times several stems may be compounded and fused to make a denser mass.

Since Fries's time this species has not been well understood. It has often been confused with *C. crispula* and is very rarely met with in herbaria. What may be considered the type is represented in Persoon's herbarium by some mycelium and a few, minute prongs, the larger parts having been broken away. There is nothing in its appearance to exclude our *C. byssiseda,* but no spores were found. Except for the tips being frequently greenish our plants agree perfectly with Persoon's description and figure;

and they are certainly the species so interpreted by Bresadola, who has recently put the species on a sure basis (Ann. Myc. **1**: 112. 1903), although he is wrong in his list of synonyms (see note under *C. stricta*). His was the first correct description of the spores and it is in exact accordance with our own except that in our plants the spores are not quite so thick. There are no other spores at all like them among related species. (He says "Spores hyaline, elongate-sinuate, as if subsigmoid, 13-18×4-6μ.") Plants from Atkinson (U. S. A.) in the Bresadola Herbarium, determined by Bresadola as *C. byssiseda,* are just like ours, the spores the same shape but a little shorter, 3-4 x 8-10μ. Schweinitz distributed plants as *C. epiphylla,* a herbarium name, that he refers to under *C. crispula* in Syn. Fung. Am. Bor., p. 181, saying, "formerly called *C. epiphylla* by us." In the Curtis Herbarium there are two fragments from Schweinitz labelled *C. epiphylla* on the sheet with *C. crispula.* There is also a plant at Kew from him under the first name. We think these plants from appearance and the name are *C. byssiseda,* although we have not been able to find spores on any of them. They are not what we are calling *C. decurrens.* Patouillard's idea of the species is not the same—the very small spore excluding it (Tab. Analyt. Fung., p. 28, fig. 567). The colored figures by Pettersson made under the direction of Fries, now at Stockholm in the Riks Museum are exactly like the plants collected by us on twigs at Lake George, but Fries's idea of the species is certainly in part different. At Kew there are two collections from him (Upsala) so determined, one on spruce and one on pine cones. Both have the appearance of *C. apiculata,* but no spores could be found. Two collections from Romell (Upsala and Stockholm) labelled *C. elastica* v. Post (a herbarium name) are *C. byssiseda.* Notes by Romell on *C. byssiseda* agree very well with ours. He gives the spores as 10-14 x 4.5-5.5μ. Basidia 4-spored. Collections by Schweinitz labelled *C. byssiseda* (Bethlehem, Pa.), in both the Schweinitz and Curtis Herbaria are apparently *C. Patouillardii.* Peck's reference is probably correct (Rept. N. Y. St. Mus. **39**: 44. 1886). We have seen his Adirondack plants and they seem the same as ours. Quélet's conception of this species as given in Bull. Soc. Bot. de France **26**: 232, 1879, seems not to be this but our *C. stricta.*

Peck's *C. pinophila* is this species. The type collection represents a more compacted form than usual, but all important characters are the same. The spores of the type (East Berne, N. Y.) are
hyaline, smooth, 3.5-4 x 12.5-14.5μ, curved as usual. Peck described his *C. pinophila* as growing under pine, but later wrote
Morgan that it grew under deciduous trees as well (note by Morgan at New York Botanical Garden). For discussion of *Lachnocladium Micheneri* see under *C. stricta.*

In size and habit this is most like *C. apiculata* (which looks
very like it in the dried state) and *C. gracilis,* but these have quite
different spores. There is nothing in Fries's descriptions to clearly
exclude *C. epichnoa* from this as the spores are much nearer white
than in *C. botrytis* which Fries also places among the white-spored
species.

Illustration: Burt. Ann. Mo. Bot. Gard. **9**: pl. 7, fig. 50 (as *C. pinophila*). 1922.

North Carolina: Chapel Hill. No. 4395. On a thick layer of beech leaves
near Meeting of the Waters, July 12, 1920. No. 4460. Mixed woods,
beech and oak with some pine, near branch southwest of Pritchard's,
arising from the leaves and twigs, July 20, 1920. Spores faintly brownish in a good print. No. 4639. From same spot as No. 4395, August
6, 1920. No. 5302. On deciduous and pine leaves mixed, July 6, 1922.
Spores distinctly cream in a good print, crooked, 3.4-3.7 x 11-16.6μ.

Cranberry. Thaxter. (Thaxter Herb.).

Blowing Rock. Coker and party, No. 5589. (U. N. C. Herb.). Spores
typical.

Winston-Salem. Schallert. (U. N. C. Herb.). Spores long, crooked,
smooth, 3.4-4.4 x 12-15μ.

Also reported by Schweinitz (Syn. Fung. Car. Sup., p. 85) who says:
"Radiculis distincta. Rara inter folia putrescentia."

Pennsylvania: Bethlehem. Schweinitz. (Schweinitz Herb., Curtis Herb.
and Kew Herb. All as *C. epiphylla*).

New York: Adirondacks. Peck. (Albany Herb.).

Lake George. Coker. Two colls. Under beech on twigs, and on leaves of
maple and pine mixed, September 3, 1917. (U. N. C. Herb.).

Vaughns. Coker and Burnham. Several colls. on leaves under beech,
August 2, 1917; August 16, 1917; September 2, 1917. (U. N. C.
Herb.). Spores exactly as in the Chapel Hill plants and all other
essential points agreeing. Spores (of B. No. 90) 2.9-3.7 x 10-14μ.
Tips often compressed and palmate in appearance, faintly greenish on
drying; taste mildly bitterish, no odor.

Ithaca. Kauffman. (Bresadola Herb.).

East Berne.  Peck.  (Albany Herb., type of *C. pinophila*).
Jamesville.  Underwood.  (N. Y. Bot. Gard. Herb., as *C. pinophila*).
    Spores typical, 3.5-4 x 12-16.6μ.
Connecticut:  Redding, September 7, 1919.  Coker.  (U. N. C. Herb.).
    Plants up to 6 cm. high.  Spores curved, 3.8 x 13-15μ.

## Clavaria Patouillardii Bres.    Fungi Trid. **2**: 39; pl. 146, fig. 1. 1892.

### PLATES 60 AND 88

Gregarious, often crowded, broom-like, slender and delicate throughout, much and closely branched from the base or with a short stalk, 2-6 cm. high, about 2-4 cm. broad, tips slender and sharp, numerous, open but scarcely divaricating; surface smooth, not pubescent below except for the mycelium in protected places; color a pale leather-tan, the base darker leather color, the tips nearly white; when dry becoming a very even and distinctive umber brown (about drab or buffy drab), and often with an olive tint, particularly upward.  Flesh not brittle, but bending on self without breaking, odorless and tasteless, not changing color when bruised; when dry very brittle and delicate.  Mycelium white, farinose-flocculent, delicate and abundant, scarcely stringy, conspicuous in the leaves or humus.

Spores (of B. No. 781) very hyaline (white?), narrow, subelliptic, sigmoid, smooth, 2.2 x 7.4-7.7μ; basidia about 5μ thick, 4-spored.  Hymenium (of C. & B. No. 101a) simple, without embedded spores and very few on the surface, 48-55μ thick.

This interesting species is evidently rare.  We have it only from Pennsylvania and from Vaughns, N. Y., where it has been found by Mr. Burnham in two old groves of deciduous trees where it occurs from year to year, and by us in pure hemlock leaves under hemlock.  Mr. Burnham says, "The plants usually spring from the old humus of decaying leaves of several years, with more or less decaying twigs mixed with the vegetable mold: some of the plants (of No. 78) were found growing on rotten wood; so that the plants are not wholly dependent on decaying leaves for habitat."

From *C. flaccida* and *C. subdecurrens* which are nearest in size and habit and with which it may be associated the species is separated by the lighter color when fresh, the quite different color when dried, and by the different spores. From the latter it may also be separated by the white tips and mild taste. The color when dried is somewhat like that of *C. gracilis* at times, but that has more open and divaricated branching and very different spores. That our plant is *C. Patouillardii* is shown by comparison with that species in the Bresadola Herbarium (Stockholm), which is alike in all details, with the same peculiar farinose-flocculent mycelium. The spores are narrow, pointed-elliptic, smooth, 2.5 x 6.3-8μ. This was growing on frondose trash, but a collection by Patouillard in the herbarium of the University of Paris was taken from coniferous leaves and twigs. The description and figures agree in every detail. A plant from Bresadola at the New York Botanical Garden labelled *C. Patouillardii* var. *minor* has exactly the same spores (hyaline, smooth, 2.3 x 7μ) and the same mycelium. *Clavaria decurrens* var. *australis* is most like the present species in appearance when dry.

Pennsylvania: Bethlehem. Schweinitz. (Schweinitz Herb., as *C. byssiseda*). The plants seem like this species in the dry state and the peculiar spores are identical, hyaline, smooth, 2.3 x 7.7μ.

New York: Vaughns. Burnham. Several collections in rotting leaves or in humus near decaying deciduous wood, July, 1916, and July, 1917. Spores alike in all. Also C. & B. No. 101a. In Burnham's hemlocks growing near *C. flaccida* and *C. subdecurrens,* Sept. 2, 1917. Spores as above, 2.3 x 7-7.7μ. (U. N. C. Herb.).

**Clavaria apiculata** Fr.   Syst. Myc. **1**: 470. 1821.

?*C. virgata* Fr.   Syst. Myc. **1**: 472. 1821.

*C. Tsugina* Pk.   Bull. N. Y. St. Mus. **67**: 27. 1903.

### Plates 39 and 88

Plants of small or medium size, up to about 7 cm. high, crowded or single, branched from or near the base, the slender stems springing from abundant fibrillose mycelium or when on bark often fusing into an amorphous, white, flattened, tomentose tissue which extends between the layers. Main stems about 3-4 mm. thick, branching quickly into curving, somewhat flattened, elongated branches, the angles rounded, the ultimate branches ending in two or three long, sharp tips, which are straight or divaricating and whitish in youth; surface white-tomentose at the protected base, smooth elsewhere except scurfy tomentose areas which occupy the angles and often run up and down the branches for some distance; young plants and upper parts of older ones a light pinkish ochraceous color; base at maturity, and in age the entire plant, becoming a deeper ochraceous brown or reddish leather color. Flesh solid and dense, toughish, nearly odorless, and slightly bitter (a bitter taste is noted also by Bresadola). Threads of flesh about 3-7$\mu$ thick, with thick walls (1.5-2.5$\mu$) which in many places leave little or no lumen, running longitudinally and parallel under the hymenium, irregularly woven and often knotty in center. Dried plants are hard, rigid and brittle, and often blackish and metallic-looking at the tips. Immature tips when dried retain their whitish color.

Spores dull ochraceous, minutely warted, elliptic, 3.7-4.6 x 7.4-9.2$\mu$. Basidia 4-spored, long-clavate, about 7.4$\mu$ thick; hymenium 50-75$\mu$ thick, brown in section, composed of 2-4 more or less obvious layers and including a vast number of spores as in C. stricta. Subhymenial layer not so distinctly set off in color or density as is usual in C. stricta.

Common on dead coniferous wood, or from bark at the base of living conifers, often forming dense rows between slabs of bark, and not rarely on mats of decaying coniferous leaves. From C. suecica, which grows on coniferous leaves and has somewhat similar but smaller spores, C. apiculata is easily distinguished by the darker color, both when fresh and when dry, by the less bitter taste, and by the harder and tougher texture when dry. It is very closely related to C. stricta, and a careful study has brought out little difference in microscopical detail (the spores of C. apiculata average a trifle longer). As it stands at present, C. apiculata can be distinguished from C. stricta by its growth on coniferous wood or leaves, by its average smaller size, and by its denser and tougher flesh. The dried plants when soaked are tougher to cut and much stronger. Material in Bresadola's herbarium of what we are calling C. apiculata he has determined in part as C. apiculata and in part as C. stricta. He also includes under C. stricta the plant on frondose wood that we have so named. Of a plant on spruce labelled C. stricta he says, "tips rufescent or greenish." Good C. apiculata on hemlock from Ithaca (Atkinson) he determines as C. stricta, and so in other cases also.

That this is *C. apiculata* Fr. does not seem open to doubt. Fries's description does not disagree in any point (except that he describes the tip color as sometimes greenish.) We have three collections of *C. apiculata* from Stockholm sent us by Romell and so determined by him. They occur on coniferous wood and agree in every respect with the American plants. For example, the spores in one case are 4-5 x 7.5-9.3μ, faintly rough; hymenium complex, containing embedded spores. The threads of the flesh in many cases have very thick walls, in places closing the lumen. One collection is noted as having the tips green, and this occasional variation to green tips is the only difference that is to be made out in the European plant. At Kew is a collection in poor condition of *C. apiculata* from E. P. Fries (Upsala, October, 1856), which has the same dark tips well shown; spores 3.8-4.5 x 6-9.7μ. This is also the plant called *C. apiculata* by Schweinitz, as evidenced by a collection in his herbarium which is similar in appearance and spores (4-5 x 8-9.2μ). There is also a specimen from Schweinitz in the Curtis Herbarium (no locality given) labelled *C. apiculata* which is the same. Its spores are minutely rough, elliptic, 3.7-4.4 x 6.7-8.1μ. From a collection labelled *C. abietina* from Schweinitz in the Curtis Herbarium, it appears that his conception of that species was incorrect. The spores, which are short-elliptic, minutely rough, 4.8-5.5 x 7.5-9.3μ, show the plant to be *C. apiculata*. It is to be noted further that the plants early referred by Peck to *C. apiculata* (Rept. N. Y. St. Mus. **24**: 82. 1872) are the same as his *C. Tsugina*. After examining carefully the type of *C. Tsugina* as well as numerous other collections determined by Peck at Albany, we find no difference between it and our plants described above. In a good plant of *C. Tsugina* from Piseco determined by Peck, spores are minutely rough, 4 x 8.5-9.5μ. In Albany there are several collections of small plants on coniferous wood that were determined by Peck as *C. byssiseda*. They are almost certainly young plants of *C. apiculata,* and look just like our No. 2962. No spores could be found on them.

*Clavaria virgata* Fr. may also be this species. A fragment so labelled by Schweinitz from New York State now in the Curtis Herbarium looks much like *C. apiculata,* but we could find no spores on it. Fries gives it as growing on rotten pine wood, and

Karsten says it grows on mossy pine wood. Bresadola determines a plant from Rick (Holland) as *C. virgata* which is really a form of *C. cristata* ("Plant cinereous, stem cinereo-ochraceous. Spores 9-10 x 7-8μ").

Fries (Hymen. Europ., p. 673) gives *C. ochraceo-virens* Junghuhn (Linnaea **5**: 407, pl. 7, fig. 3. 1830) as a form (?) of *C. apiculata*. It is very green except the ochraceous base, and looks to us more like *C. abietina*.

Bresadola thinks (Ann. Myc. **1**: 112. 1903) that *C. leucotephra* (see p. 162) is the same as *C. byssiseda, L. Micheneri* and *C. fragrans,* and plants sent him from America which are like our *C. apiculata* have been given these names by him. We think he is right in his conception of *C. byssiseda* but wrong in thinking the others the same. From the appearance in the dried state and from the spores, *C. dendroidea* R. Fries seems most nearly related to *C. apiculata*. The abruptly pale tips and the quite smooth, slightly larger spores distinguish the former (pl. 91, fig. 21). *Clavaria Karstenii* Sacc. (Syll. **14**: 238, changed from *Clavariella divaricata* Karst.) should be compared with this and *C. stricta*.

Illustrations: Burt. Ann. Mo. Bot Gard. **9**: pl. 5, fig. 31 (as *C. Tsugina*). 1922.
  Junghuhn. Linnaea **5**: pl. 7, fig. 3.    1830.

North Carolina: Chapel Hill. No. 338. From outer bark at base of pine tree in Battle's Park, October 1, 1908. No. 804. Through the rotting bark at base of small cedar stump, September 21, 1913. No. 2802. On base of rotten pine stump and buried wood, July 28, 1919. Hymenium multiple and retaining embedded spores. No. 2962. On pine wood near Strowd's pasture, December 5, 1917. A very small specimen with spreading tips. Spores 3.7-4.2 x 6.6-9.4μ. No. 2939. On a pine stump, October 18, 1917. Spores 3.8-4.5 x 7.5-9.3μ. Many other collections with same appearance and spores.
  Pink Bed Valley. Murrill. (N. Y. Bot. Gard. Herb., July, 1908, as *C. pinophila*).
  Black Mountain, Yancey Co. Altitude 5700 ft., on rotten sap wood of spruce, August 2, 1918. J. S. Holmes. (U. N. C. Herb.). Spores 3.7-4.3 x 6.5-7.5μ.
Alabama: Baker. (N. Y. Bot. Gard. Herb.). No notes, but evidently growing on rotting leaves under pines. Spores 3.7-4.2 x 7.6-9.8μ.
  Auburn. Earle. (N. Y. Bot. Gard. Herb., 1900; also Earle and Baker, 1897).
Tennessee: Unaka Springs. Murrill. (N. Y. Bot. Gard. Herb.).

Kentucky: Bowling Green. Price. (N. Y. Bot. Gard. Herb.). Spores roughish, 4-4.6 x 7.3-8.3μ.

New Jersey: Schweinitz. (Schw. Herb.).

New York: Botanical Garden, New York City. On hemlock leaves and a hemlock stump, September 6, 1919. Coker. (U. N. C. Herb.). Plants exactly like those from Chapel Hill, reddish leather color downwards, pale leather tan above, in age darkening upwards. Taste only slightly bitter; odor none. Hymenium 3 or 4 layers thick, with many embedded spores.

Ithaca. Atkinson. (Albany Herb.). Spores about 4 x 7.5μ.

Sand Lake. (Albany Herb.).

Farmington. Ellis. (N. Y. Bot. Gard. Herb.). Spores roughish. 4.8-5.3 x 7.5-8μ.

Vaughns. Burnham, No. 114. On an old pine stump pile, August 20, 1919. Bitter taste. Spores minutely rough, 3.7-4 x 7.4-9.3μ.

Numerous other collections in Albany Herb. from various places in New York State.

Washington: North Bend. (N. Y. Bot. Gard. Herb.). In damp coniferous woods. Spores elliptic, minutely roughened, 3.5 x 7-8.5μ.

## Clavaria pinicola Burt. Ann. Mo. Bot. Gard. 9: 25, pl. 5, fig. 32. 1922.

### PLATE 91

We have studied material from the type collection (No. 16946) kindly sent us by Dr. Weir, and find the spores as described, smooth, short-elliptic, 4.2-5.5 x 7.5-10μ. Hymenium about 50-60μ thick, containing many embedded spores and therefore deep brown. Basidia 7.5-8μ thick, with 4 straight sterigmata. Flesh tough; threads of flesh 3.5-6.5μ thick, in places having rather thick walls; no clamp connections seen. It is a western form of *C. apiculata,* (which often has smooth spores among the roughened ones,) and is hardly of varietal rank. Another collection from the same place (Weir, No. 16955) determined by Burt as *C. apiculata* has the same appearance and similar spores, smooth or nearly so, 4.2-5.5 x 7.8-11μ. Hymenium obscurely 2-layered, containing embedded spores.

Burt's description of *C. pinicola* follows:

"Fructifications rarely solitary, usually in clusters of 2-6 from a common white mycelium, slender, of rather uniform diameter

throughout, sometimes simple but usually once to thrice dichotomously forked, the branches cylindric, spreading, drying everywhere buffy brown, the apices acute; spores slightly colored under
the microscope, even, 7.5-9 x 4.5-5μ."

Idaho: Priest River. On bark of log of *Pinus contorta*, October 10, 1920.
     Weir, No. 16946. Type. (Mo. Bot. Gard. Herb., Weir Herb., and
     U. N. C. Herb.).

**Clavaria acris** Pk.    Rept. N. Y. St. Mus. **54**: 155, pl. H, figs.
     37-39. 1901.

PLATE 89

The following description is from Peck:

"Stem short, branching from near the base, the branches repeatedly and subpalmately branched, sometimes compressed, tough,
solid, reddish incarnate, whitish within, tips acute, whitish or concolorous, the axils often rounded; taste acrid; mycelium white;
spores broadly elliptic, pale ochraceous, 4-5 x 6-7.6μ [original in
inches].

"Much decayed wood of coniferous trees. . . . It forms tufts
1.5-3 inches high and nearly as broad."

This seems most like *C. apiculata,* but the spores are distinctly
shorter (averaging about 7μ long), and the former is not acrid.
We have examined the type and find the spores to be minutely
warted, 3.8-4.8 x 6-7.4μ, darker under the microscope than those
of *C. apiculata* or *C. suecica.* It is quite different from the very
acrid *C. pyxidata.* Plants received from Weir (Priest River,
Idaho) determined as this species by Burt have much longer
spores, 3.8-5 x 7.4-10μ, which are paler under the microscope.

Illustrations: Burt. Ann. Mo. Bot. Gard. **9**: pl. 5, fig. 30. 1922.
    Peck. As cited above.
New York: Floodwood. August. Peck. (Albany Herb. and Burt Herb.).

**Clavaria stricta** Pers.    Comm., p. 45 (177). 1797.
     ?*Lachnocladium Atkinsonii* Bres. Journ. Myc. **8**: 119. 1902.
     *C. leucotephra* B. & C.   Grevillea **2**: 7. 1873.
     *C. condensata* Fr.   Epicr., p. 575. 1838. (Sense of Bresa-
     dola and Romell).

*C. syringarum* Pers.    Myc. Europ. **1**: 164. 1822.
*C. Kewensis* Mass.    Journ. Bot. (Britten's) **34**: 153. 1896.
*Lachnocladium odoratum* Atk.    Ann. Myc. **6**: 58. 1908.

PLATES 61, 62, AND 88

Plants growing in colonies on dead wood of deciduous trees; height 4-8.5 cm. above the more or less amorphous mass at the base, which may extend several centimeters between the flakes of bark and in most cases is attached below to a single large rhizomorph; branching usually at once, on emerging from the wood, into several flattish and channelled divisions which rebranch several times in a very irregular way into rather strictly upright and crowded branches; the ultimate branches terminating in several small pointed teeth; color where exposed a very light fleshy tan at first, turning a little darker at maturity, and deeper brown where bruised.    The hidden base, the rhizomorph, and the mycelium are pure white and covered with a conspicuous fibrous pubescence which extends upon the branches when these are hidden in the bark.    Texture very tough and elastic, not at all brittle, the branches not breaking even when bent back on themselves; taste bitterish; odor of radish, at least at times.    Sterile areas of a different appearance, showing a roughish, plush-like surface under a lens, are commonly found running more or less extensively throughout the plant.

Spores (of No. 1228) about cinnamon-buff, almost imperceptibly rough, elliptic with a large oblique mucro on one end. 3.8-4.4 x 7.5-9$\mu$.    The spores are peculiar in that a small proportion of them have the contents collapsed away on one side near the mucro.    This gives the impression except under high power of a very long and abrupt mucro.    Basidia 6.2-9$\mu$ thick, with 4 sterigmata about 4.5-5$\mu$ long; young hymenium 35-40$\mu$ thick, growing and becoming multiple, 3 to 4 layers thick, in age; otherwise remarkable in containing a vast number of embedded spores which are often arranged in more or less clearly defined layers and indicating periods of growth.    Subhymenial layer typically well marked off by yellowish color and much denser structure, the threads closely packed and parallel.    The remainder of the flesh much less dense and composed of irregularly woven threads which are about 3-7.5$\mu$ thick with thick walls, in places closing the lumen.

The species is occasional on oak, birch, maple and other deciduous wood throughout a large territory, but seems rare at

Chapel Hill as we have found it here only a few times.    See under *C. apiculata* for comparison with that species.

Unfortunately there is nothing in Persoon's herbarium that can be taken as the type of *C. stricta*.    There are two sheets, each of which is labelled with a question.    One is from North America ("Am. Bor."), and is the same as our *C. stricta*.    The other is from Europe ( ?), grew on earth, and is very doubtful. *Clavaria syringarum* is well represented by what may be considered as the types.    There are three plants collected under *Syringa*, apparently by Persoon himself.    They look exactly like *C. stricta* and have the same spores, minutely rough, 3.5-4.8 x 6.3-9µ.    He says the species is like *C. stricta* but "differs in growth on earth under *Syringa* and in the spongy tuberous base," adding that it has a taste of bitter almonds.    The species is not mentioned by Fries.

*Clavaria leucotephra* is represented in the Curtis Herbarium by the co-type from Hillsboro, N. C. (No. 6362).    It is in very bad condition, but the spores are exactly like those of *C. stricta*, 3.7-4.4 x 7.4-8.9µ, ochraceous.    There is also a plant at Kew under the same type number and with the same appearance and spores, 3.8-5 x 7.5-9.3µ.    As the description is not at variance we are considering them the same.    For some reason we have been unable to find at Albany the type of *C. densissima* Pk. (Bull. Torr. Bot. Club **30**: 98. 1903), but from the description and from the photo of the type given by Burt (l. c., pl. 1, fig. 5) we see no reason to think that it is anything but *C. stricta*.

After a careful study of the co-type and authentic specimens of *Lachnocladium Micheneri* B. & C. (Grevillea **1**: 161. 1873), it is impossible for us to say with certainty what the species really is. Slides made by us by scraping the co-type (Curtis Herbarium; Curtis No. 3534, Michener No. 479) show no spores ( ?), but a slide of this made by Farlow and now with it shows a large number of spores which are like those of *C. stricta*, slightly rough, about 3-4 x 8-9µ.    From slides of No. 3534 sent us by Dr. Farlow and recently by Dr. Dodge we find that the hymenium is 38-50µ thick, deep yellow in section; basidia about 5.5µ thick; threads of flesh 3-5.5µ thick and almost parallel in longitudinal sections.    We have not been able to find any spores like those of *C. byssiseda* either on the co-type or on an authentic specimen from Dr. Michener in the Farlow Herbarium or on a plant sent from Kew by Massee (in New York Botanical Garden) which was probably taken from Berkeley's part of the type.  Both of those last mentioned have the exact appearance of the Curtis specimen.  The species resembles *C. byssiseda* in the dry state except that it is larger and apparently emerges *through* rotting leaves instead of being seated upon them.  It is about the size of small *C. stricta,* but the spores are certainly extremely scarce in comparison with the universally abundant spores on dried plants of *C. stricta,* and the hymenium is distinctly thinner.  That it was growing among leaves instead of on wood is probably of small consequence.  In American herbaria most plants under the name *Lachnocladium Micheneri* are *C. stricta* or *C. apiculata* and Bresadola has determined plants of the latter species as *L. Micheneri,* and in his discussion of *C. byssiseda* (Ann. Myc. **1**: 112. 1903) he considers *C. leucotephra, C. fragrans, C. pinophila,* and *L. Micheneri* as the same and equal to *C. byssiseda.*  The spores of the first two are much shorter than of *C. byssiseda* and of different form.  We find at the New York Botanical Garden a plant from Newfield, N. J., labelled *C. leucotephra* by Ellis which was examined by Dr. Farlow and determined by him as *L. Micheneri.*  The plant is in reality what we are calling *C. gracilis,* the spores agreeing exactly with that species in size and appearance, smooth, 3-3.5 x 5-5.5µ.

*Lachnocladium Atkinsonii* Bres. is very likely the present species or *C. apiculata.*  There is nothing in the description to exclude it from either.  We cannot find the type at Ithaca, and the species is not represented in the Bresadola Herbarium at Stockholm.  There seems to be no doubt that Atkinson's *L. odoratum* is also the same.  We have not been able to find the type at Ithaca, but there are no discrepancies in the description and the distinctive characters are brought out, the tomentose, sterile lines being characteristic of *C. stricta.*  The spore measurements given by Atkinson (3.5-4.5 x 7-10µ) agree.  The sweet odor (*suaveolens*) noted by Atkinson may mean the same thing as the anise odor found in Beardslee's Asheville plant.

From the description of *C. Berkeleyi* Mont. (Syll. Crypt., p. 180. 1856), it may be the same as this.  Saccardo says that the

dried plants of the former are blackish.    Its spores are not known.
A collection from Sweden sent us by Romell and determined by
Brèsadola as *C. condensata* is almost certainly our *C. stricta,* as is
also another European collection in Bresadola's own herbarium.
Romell's plant grew on wood, has the same appearance and the
same spores, which are about 4 x 8.5μ., nearly smooth.    Bresadola
gives the habitat of *C. condensata* as both fir and frondose woods,
and his plate (Fungi Tridentini, pl. 101) shows it on coniferous
leaves and does not look much like anything we have seen.    But
Bresadola has also determined as *C. condensata* a quite different
plant like our *C. abietina* of pine woods.    Three other collections
sent us by Romell and determined as *C. condensata* by von Post,
Romell, and Massee are either *C. stricta* or *C. apiculata.*    This is
also true of the collection in Rabenhorst, Pazschke Fung. Europ.
No. 4144, labelled *C. condensata,* collected by Hennings at Marchia
under bushes in twigs and pieces of wood, September, 1896.    The
appearance of the latter in the dry state is identical, the flocculent
mycelium, color and form the same; spores  3.7-4.5 x 7.5-10μ.
Fries gives *C. rubella* Schaeff. as a synonym of *C. condensata,*
and Bresadola has a plant on wood under the former name which
is like *C. stricta.*    It is possible that the real *C. condensata* of
Fries is not this species, but *C. decurrens* var. *australis,* which see.
Plants of *C. stricta* from Cotton (on rotting wood, Kew Gardens,
England) are just like ours.    We agree with Cotton that *C. Kewensis* is this species.    The type at Kew looks the same and has the
same spores, nearly smooth, 3.6-4.4 x 6-7.5μ.    *Clavaria pruinella*
Cesati in Rabenhorst's Fungi Europ. Exs. Cent. 5, No. 14, 1861,
is probably a form of *C. stricta,* but is said to grow on earth, not
wood.

Peck describes a var. *fumida* which differs only in having a
dingy, smoky brownish hue (Rept. N. Y. St. Mus. **41**: 86. 1888).

Illustrations: Berkeley.   Outlines, pl. 18, fig. 5.   1860.
   Britzelmayr.   Hymen. Südb., Clavariei, figs. 25 and 83.
   Burt.   Ann. Mo. Bot. Gard. **9**: pl. 4, fig. 21 (as *C. leucotephra*).   1922.
   Clements.   Minnesota Mushrooms, fig. 74.   1910.
   Dufour.   Atlas Champ., pl. 69, fig. 154.   1891.
   Flora Danica, pl. 1302, fig. 1.   1806.

Gibson.   Edible Toadstools and Mushrooms, pl. 31.   1895.

Gillet.   Champ. Fr., pl. 109 (115).   1874-78.

Hard.   Mushrooms, fig. 388.   1908.

Krombholz.   Abbild., pl. 54, fig. 23.   1836.

Lloyd.   Photographs Am. Fungi, pl. 16, fig. 1.   1895.

Michael.   Führer f. Pilzfreunde, Vol. 3, No. 21.   1905.

Persoon.   Comm., pl. 4, fig. 1.   1797.   Copied in Ann. Mo. Bot. Gard. 9: pl. 4, fig. 23.   1922.

North Carolina: Chapel Hill.   No. 1228.   On rotting oak bark shed from a fallen trunk, September 9, 1914.   No. 4587.   On rotting oak log, July 30, 1920.   Color cinnamon to sayal brown, shading upward to the creamy tips when fresh; tips wilting to deep brown and all parts turning a dull reddish brown when rubbed; odor of radish, taste slightly bitter.   Spores nearly smooth, 3.7-4.5 x 7-9µ.   No. 4591.   On rotting oak bark, July 30, 1920.   Branches crowded, rather few.   Spores 3.6-4.2 x 7-9µ.   No. 7020. On very rotten wood from oak log, August 2, 1923.   Hymenium multiple and retaining spores as usual.

Hillsboro.   Curtis.   (Curtis Herb., as co-type of *C. leucotephra*).

Asheville.   Beardslee, No. 15089.   (U. N. C. Herb.).   Spores minutely tuberculate, 4-4.5 x 7.5-8.2µ.   Hymenium up to 4 layers thick and including many embedded spores.   This is a typical specimen of the species, but Beardslee says: "a strong odor of anise on drying."   We can find no record of an anise odor in this plant, but a sweet odor is noted for *L. odoratum*.

Blowing Rock.   Coker and party, No. 5826.   (U. N. C. Herb.).   Spores 3.6-4.2 x 7-8.5µ.

New York: Arkville.   Murrill.   (U. N. C. Herb.).   Spores 4-4.5 x 8-8.8µ.

Vaughns.   Burnham, No. 63.   (U. N. C. Herb.).   Spores 3.7-4.2 x 7.4-9.3µ.

West Fort Ann.   Burnham.   (U. N. C. Herb.).

Lake Placid.   On birch.   Murrill.   (N. Y. Bot. Gard. Herb.).

New Jersey: Newfield.   (N. Y. Bot. Gard. Herb., as *C. leucotephra*).

Connecticut: Redding.   Coker.   (U. N. C. Herb.).   Hymenium multiple and containing embedded spores as usual.

White.   (Cornell Herb., as type of *L. odoratum*).

Vermont: Newfane.   Miss Hibbard, No. 9.   (U. N. C. Herb.).   Spores short-elliptic, rough, 3.6-4.2 x 6-8µ.

New Hampshire: Wilson.   (U. N. C. Herb.).

Chocorua.   Farlow.   (U. N. C. Herb. from Farlow Herb. as *C. pyxidata*). Spores nearly smooth, 3.6-4 x 7.5-9.6µ.

Maine: (Curtis Herb.).

Indiana: Putnam County.   Underwood.   (N. Y. Bot. Gard. Herb.).

Idaho: Rust, No. 944.   (N. Y. Bot. Gard. Herb., as *C. leucotephra*). Spores nearly smooth, 4-5 x 8-10µ.

Canada: Ontario.   Mrs. Gardner.   (U. N. C. Herb.).   Spores smooth to minutely rough, 3.7-4.5 x 8.2-10.5µ.

**Clavaria suecica** Fr.    Obs. Myc. **1** : 156. 1815.

  *C. circinans* Pk.    Rept. N. Y. St. Mus. **39** : 43, pl. 1, figs. 21, 22. 1886.

  *C. flavula* Atk.    Ann. Myc. **6** : 56. 1908.

  *C. Invalii* Cotton and Wakefield.    Trans. Brit. Myc. Soc. **6** : 176. 1919.

PLATES 63, 85, AND 89

Plants about 2-6 cm. high and 0.4-4 cm. broad, distinctly stalked, the few main branches upright and usually rather long, rebranching from one to three times into more or less numerous rather closely pressed branches of about the same height, which form a very brush-like mass, with pointed tips.  Stem smooth, the base somewhat incrassated by and expanding into the fibrous white mycelium; color of stem pale whitish flesh-color when young, the color deepening upward to deeper flesh, the very tips concolorous or often whitish; in age becoming tan or pale cinnamon-buff, especially below; flesh pliable, toughish, nearly white or pinkish, odorless, bitterish; in drying becoming very soft, brittle and chalky, and remaining light colored and quite bitter (by these characters when dry easily separated from *C. apiculata*).

Spores (of Burnham, No. 57) rather light buffy ochraceous, elliptic with an eccentric mucro, covered with very minute warts, 3-4 x 7.8-8μ.  Basidia (of No. 19) 6-7.4μ thick, with 4 slender sterigmata; hymenium 50-70μ thick, not layered and not so dark as in *C. apiculata;* threads of flesh loosely woven, much branched, 3-6μ thick, irregular, walls thin, clamp connections conspicuous.

In troops and often in lines under conifers in the northern states.

A plant at Kew from E. P. Fries (Upsala, 1850) determined as *C. suecica* is like our plants and has similar spores, slightly rough, 3.8-4.2 x 7-9μ.

*Clavaria circinans* Pk. is certainly the same as *C. suecica,* as shown by spores and appearance of the type plants.  There are in Albany plants of this species labelled by Peck *C. pinea,* but we cannot find that he ever published this name.  *Clavaria flavula* is also the same, as shown by the type at Ithaca.  Atkinson gives the spores as 9-12 x 3-3.5μ, but we find the spores, which are abundant on the type, to be 3.4-4 x 7-9.3μ, in every respect like those of *C. suecica,* and Atkinson's description does not disagree in any particular, granting that his plants had reached the buffy yellow color of full maturity. *Clavaria Invalii* from type locality determined by Cotton is *C. suecica.* The plants are alike and so are the spores, minutely rough, often pointed toward mucro end, 3.5-4.2 x 6-8μ. Cotton and Wakefield do not include *C. suecica,* a species which is to be expected in England in a similar habitat.

Illustrations: Britzelmayr. Hymen. Südb., Clavariei, fig. 23.
  Burt.  Ann. Mo. Bot. Gard. **9**: pl. 5, fig. 33 (as *C. circinans*).  1922.
  McIlvaine.  Am. Fungi., pl. 142 (as *C. circinans*).  1900.
  Peck.  As cited above (as *C. circinans*).
  Schaeffer.  Fung. Bavar., pl. 177 (as *C. rubella*).  1763.  Fries refers to this (Syst. Myc. **1**: 469), but it is not good.

New York: Adirondacks.  Peck.  (Albany Herb., as type of *C. circinans*).
  Hudson Falls.  Burnham, No. 57.  (U. N. C. Herb.).  Under hemlock, July 22, 1917.
  Lake George.  Coker, No. 19.  (U. N. C. Herb.).  In clumps or in rows on white pine needles, by path to Prospect Mountain, September 3, 1917.  Spores as in B. No. 57, 3.7-4.2 x 7.5-8.2μ.
  Syracuse.  Underwood.  (N. Y. Bot. Gard. Herb., as *C. pinea*).
  Vaughns.  C. & B. No. 118.  In hemlock woods.  B. No. 94.  Under white pines, August 19, 1917.  (U. N. C. Herb.).
  Ithaca.  Atkinson.  (Cornell Herb., as type of *C. flavula*).

New Hampshire: Chocorua.  Farlow.  (U. N. C. Herb., from Farlow Herb., as *Lachnocladium Micheneri*).  Taste quite bitter.  Spores 3.5-4 x 6.7-8.2μ.

**Clavaria gracilis** Pers.  Comm., p. 50 (182). 1797.
  *C. alutacea* Lasch in Rabenhorst.  Klotzschii herbarium vivum mycologicum, Cent. 16, No. 1519.  1851.
  *C. fragrans* E. & E.  N. Am. Fungi, 2nd. Ser., No. 2023. 1888.
  *C. fragrantissima* Atk.  Ann. Myc. **6**: 57. 1908.
  *C. flavuloides* Burt.  Ann. Mo. Bot. Gard. **9**: 28, pl. 5, fig. 34. 1922.

PLATES 64 AND 88

Plants small, gregarious, often crowded, slender and delicate, or varying to densely branched and compact, about 2-5 cm. high and 1-4 cm. broad, stem 1-2 mm. thick, short or long, smooth, the base attached to the stringy white mycelium; branches and twigs rather numerous and crowded, the numerous tips pointed and upright, or at times open and spreading; color when young whitish, then delicate flesh color towards maturity with the tips remaining white, the base shading to pale ochraceous; in drying becoming pallid buff. Flesh delicate, but not very brittle, not changing color when bruised; odor distinct, a rather medicinal fragrance, lost on drying; taste none.

Spores (of C. & B. No. 107) rather light yellowish ochraceous, much lighter than in *C. abietina,* varying from smooth to very minutely rough, 3-3.3 x 4.8-6μ. Basidia 4.4-5.5μ thick, 4-spored; hymenium 40-55μ thick; threads of flesh very variable in diameter, up to 8μ thick. Just under the hymenium the threads are parallel and fairly regular, but in the center of the plant they are very irregular and much intertwined. The walls of the hyphae vary from thin to thicker than the diameter of the space inside them, the hymenium arising from the thin-walled threads; clamp connections present.

Not rare among rotting leaves and twigs under pine in the northern states and in the mountains of North Carolina and collected several times in Chapel Hill; also found in Dismal Swamp, Va., under junipers (*Chamaecyparis*). Easily distinguished from all others by the combined characters of color, odor, spores, and place of growth.

The determination of this species is fortunately made certain by the presence of a good plant of the type in Persoon's herbarium. The appearance and the characteristic spores which are very minutely rough, oval, 3-3.6 x 5-6μ, are conclusive. Persoon's original description also agrees perfectly, and our plants are evidently the same as those interpreted as *C. gracilis* by Karsten who says they are slightly fragrant, with elliptic, ochraceous spores 3 x 5-6μ (Bidr. Finl. Nat. Folk **37**: 188. 1882). Fries says that the plant has a slight anise odor, and our plants from Chapel Hill had this fragrance to a distinct though faint degree.

A plant from Bresadola in the New York Botanical Garden Herbarium, labelled *C. gracilis,* looks in the dried state like the plant we are calling *C. Kunzei,* and has the same minute spores; other collections in the Bresadola Herbarium at Stockholm labelled *C. gracilis* are also *C. Kunzei,* as one from Atkinson with asperulate spores 3 x 4μ. However, there is one collection in his herbarium from Eichler on leaves of *Pinus* determined as *C. gracilis* that is the same as ours with spores 3-4 x 5.5-6.5μ. We have received from Juel (Upsala) a good specimen of *C. gracilis* with spores oblong-oval, barely rough, 3-3.6 x 4.2-5.5μ, rarely 6.5μ. In Bresadola's herbarium we find three species determined by him as *C. palmata*. One is *C. suecica,* one the *flaccida* form of *C. abietina,* and a third *C. gracilis*. Another plant from Bresadola (in N. Y. Bot. Gard. Herb.), labelled *C. palmata* Pers. with a question mark, is also *C. gracilis* and has spores which are distinctly yellowish, 3.5 x 6.5μ. There are also plants of this species in the Cornell Herbarium determined as *C. palmata,* with spores smooth or minutely roughened, 3.3-4 x 5-6.6μ. In spite of these determinations, we think it quite unsafe to consider *C. palmata* a synonym of *C. gracilis,* as one is white and grows in beech woods and the other is distinctly colored and grows characteristically in coniferous woods. These reasons are equally against considering *C. palmata* a synonym of *C. alutacea.* (See note under *C. cristata*). An authentic specimen of *C. alutacea* at Kew collected by Lasch himself (Rabenhorst's Exsiccati, No. 1519) is certainly *C. gracilis,* with the same block-like spores, 3.4-3.8 x 5-6.5μ. Another collection by him in the Rehm Herbarium, Stockholm, is the same. That Peck's idea of *C. gracilis* was the same as we have adopted is indicated by several collections at Albany, although not all of his were correctly determined.

*Clavaria fragrans* is this species, as is shown by two collections from Newfield, N. J., (Ellis) at the New York Botanical Garden, which agree in all respects; spores 3-3.7 x 5.5-6.5μ. A bit of the co-type (No. 2023) at Kew has similar appearance but we could find no spores. *Clavaria fragrantissima* also has the same appearance and spores.

Illustrations: Burt. Ann. Mo. Bot. Gard. **9**: pl. 5, fig. 34 (as *C. flavuloides*) and fig. 35 (as *C. fragrantissima*). 1922.

North Carolina: Chapel Hill. No. 7069. On leaves, mostly pine, August 10, 1923. Odor of anise. Spores minutely warted, 3-3.5 x 5-6.5μ.

  Asheville. Beardslee, No. 18183. (U. N. C. Herb.). "Spores ochraceous or deep cream, 6-7μ long."

Blowing Rock. Atkinson. (Cornell Herb., as *C. corrugata* Karst.).
Appearance and spores exactly like those of *C. gracilis*. Also several
typical collections by us with spores as usual. (U. N. C. Herb.).

?Salem. Schweinitz. "On shaded banks" (Syn. Fung. Car. Sup. No.
1085. 1822). We can find no collection in either the Schweinitz or
Curtis Herbarium to support this.

Pink Bed Valley. Murrill and House. (N. Y. Bot. Gard. Herb., as *C.
fragrans*, No. 364). Spores nearly smooth, 3-3.4 x 4.8-7$\mu$.

Virginia: Dismal Swamp. J. S. Holmes. (U. N. C. Herb.). Spores
nearly smooth, 2.8-3.5 x 4.5-6.6$\mu$.

New Jersey: Newfield. Ellis. (N. Y. Bot. Gard. Herb., as *C. fragrans*)
Spores minutely rough, oblong, 3-3.7 x 5.5-6.5$\mu$.

New York: Vaughns. Burnham, No. 30. Spores apparently smooth,
3 x 5$\mu$. B. No. 31. Under white pines, September 12, 1915. Spores
nearly smooth, 3 x 5.2$\mu$. B. No. 80. Near Tripoli, July, 1919. Spores
as usual. C. & B. No. 107. Under white pines, September 2, 1917.
Spores minutely rough, 3-3.3 x 4.8-6$\mu$. C. & B. No. 109. Spores as
usual, about 3 x 5.5$\mu$. (All in U. N. C. Herb.).

Hudson Falls. Burnham, No. 56. (U. N. C. Herb.). Spores elliptic,
rough, 2.5-3.9 x 4.8-7$\mu$.

Farmington. Ellis. (N. Y. Bot. Gard. Herb., No. 57). Spores smooth,
3 x 4.8-6.3$\mu$.

Lake George. Under white pine. Coker, No. 6. Spores 3-3.6 x 5-6$\mu$. No.
18. Typical, fragrant. Spores minutely rough, 2.8-3.4 x 4.3-6.5$\mu$. (U.
N. C. Herb.).

Connecticut: West Goshen. In pine woods. Underwood. (N. Y. Bot.
Gard. Herb.). Spores minutely warted, 3-3.3 x 5.2-7$\mu$.

Vermont: Newfane. Miss Hibbard. (U. N. C. Herb.). "Fragrant of
anise." Spores as usual.

Michigan: Distributed by E. & E. as *C. leucotephra*. Spores nearly smooth,
3 x 5.2$\mu$.

## Clavaria subdecurrens n. sp.

### PLATES 65 AND 89

Size and shape and habitat as in *C. flaccida* (treated by us as
a form of *C. abietina*), 2-3.3 cm. high and 1-2.5 cm. broad. Com-
pactly branched at or near the ground, terete or more or less flattened and angled, tips small, pointed, numerous, often crested as
in *C. cristata*; color when young pale creamy ochraceous except
the tips, which are abruptly lavender, varying from deep lavender
to very pale lavender or fleshy lavender; at maturity the body
color somewhat deeper, but still pale ochraceous, the tips not chang-

ing.  Flesh pliable, tender; taste distinctly acid or acid-bitter; odor none.

Spores (of No. 111) deep ochraceous (color as in *C. decurrens*), narrow, the tapering tip bent, minutely tuberculate, 2.5-3 x 5.9-7μ.  Basidia 4.4-5.1μ thick, 4-spored; hymenium about 50-55μ thick, the surface densely packed with spores and a large number of spores also embedded in the hymenium and in places arranged in a row about half way down, thus showing the hymenium to be doubled by periodic growth.

Nearest *C. decurrens* and *C. flaccida*, from the first of which it differs in lavender tips, sour taste, absence of color change when bruised, and different spores.

This beautiful and delicate plant was found twice in hemlock leaves in two different groves.   In each case it was growing near but not mixed with *C. flaccida,* which was of the same size, habit and not very different in color, except at the tips.   This tip color varies from very strong, almost purplish, lavender to very pale whitish lavender.   The crested tips, which were conspicuous in several of the plants in one collection, were not seen in any case in *C. flaccida,* which was much more abundant.   The spores also are distinctly narrower and of a different shape from those of *C. flaccida.*

At first glance one might suspect this to be the same as *C. Holmskjoldi* Oudemans (Nederlandsch Kruidkundig Archief, series 3, **2**: 672, pl. 3, fig. 2), which is of the same shape and about the same color, with purplish tips at maturity; but in the latter the spores are said to be round (4.2μ in diameter) and there is a strong odor of anise.   *Clavaria afflata* Lagger (Flora **19**: 231. 1836) has points in common with our plants but the body color is said to be white, then grayish smoky.   The spores are not known.

New York: Oneida.  House, No. 1447.  August, 1914.  (U. N. C. Herb.).
Spores as in type, minutely rough to apparently smooth, 2.5-3 x 5.5-6.3μ.
Vaughns.  Burnham, No. 81.  Grassy woods margin, July 27, 1917.
Spores minutely rough, 3-3.3 x 6.6-7.7μ.  C. & B. No. 101.  Under hemlocks, Burnham's grove, September 2, 1917.  (Type).  C. & B. No. 111.  Golden's hemlocks, September 2, 1917.  (All these in U. N. C. Herb.).

**Clavaria decurrens** Pers.   Myc. Europ. **1** : 164. 1822.

?*C. muscigena* Pers.   Myc. Europ. **1** : 169.  1822.

?*C. crispula* Fr.   Syst. Myc. **1** : 470. 1832.

*C. curta* Fr.   Monog. Hymen. Suec. **2** : 281. 1857.

*C. pusilla* Pk.   Buf. Soc. Nat. Sci. **1** : 62. 1873.   (Also in Rept. N. Y. St. Mus. **25** : 83. 1873).   (Not *C. pusilla* Pers., which is a *Pistillaria;* or *C. pusilla* Quél, which is *Nyctalis*).

PLATES 66, 88, AND 92

Plants small and delicate, about 1.5-3 cm. high and 1.2-3 cm. broad; stem distinct, 5-15 mm. long, 1.5-7 mm. thick, terete or grooved or flattened, glabrous, toughish, not rooting, but soon disappearing into the fibrous mycelium; branches rather few and open, spreading, mostly flattened and angular, tips small, subulate, acute, spreading; color when fresh a dull creamy white all over except for pinkish stains that are apt to be present on the stem; in age and in drying becoming olivaceous-yellow or about drab.   Flesh pliable, tasteless and odorless, turning deep purplish pink when bruised; threads of flesh 1.6-8µ thick, average about 4µ thick, loosely packed and much intertwined, clamp connections present.

Spores (of C. and B. No. 120) deep buffy yellow (about chamois of Ridgway), pip-shaped, minutely tuberculate, 2.3-3 x 4.5-6µ.   Basidia 4-spored, 4-4.8µ thick, hymenium 35-40µ thick, containing very many included spores which show that the hymenium has increased in thickness by proliferation.   There are also a great number of spores encrusting the surface.

This small plant which we are taking as typical is known with certainty in America only from New York, in damp, shady places under hemlock and pine.   For the southern variety see page 177.

A well marked species, easily recognized by its small size and habitat, by change to pink when bruised, peculiar color when dry, flattened and angular branches and tips, and by the spores.   By the authentic plants of *C. decurrens* in the Persoon Herbarium, the American plants are shown to be the same.   His plants are about 5 cm. high, and the spores are minutely rough, about pip-shaped, 2.5-3.5 x 4.5-6µ.   Our collections are certainly the same as *C. pusilla,* as the dried plants look exactly like the type and like another better collection from Westport, N. Y. (determined by

Peck), and as the spores are identical with those of the type and different from any others, being distinctly smaller than in *C. flaccida* or *C. abietina*.  Peck says *C. pusilla* differs from *C. tetragona* by the terete stem and irregular ramification, but Peck's collections labelled *C. tetragona* are apparently *C. crocea*.  From *C. gracilis* the present species may be distinguished by the quick change to purple-pink when bruised and by the different spores, which are not only minutely warted but collapse more easily than those of *C. gracilis* and lack the very distinct oil drop of the latter. As to *C. curta* we have seen an authentic specimen of this at Kew Gardens determined by Fries.  The plants are like *C. pusilla* and so are the spores, minutely rough, 2.8-3.5 x 4.2-5μ.  A collection in the Bresadola Herbarium determined by the latter as *C. curta* is also the same, with spores 2.5-3.5 x 3.8-5μ.  There has been much confusion in regard to the identity of *C. crispula*.  In his first publication of the species (see above) Fries evidently had a vague idea of his plant, as he refers to both the white and colored figures of Bulliard (pl. 358, figs. A-C) as representing it.  Later (Epicr., p. 576) he refers only to the colored figures and gives *C. decurrens* as a synonym.  Confusion in Fries's mind in regard to the species is still further indicated by plants labelled *C. crispula* in his herbarium.  There are two plants not on wood that have the appearance and spores of *C. Kunzei*, while one other specimen on wood is exactly like a plant sent us by Romell and determined by him as *C. epichnoa* and has spores smooth, elliptic, 2.5-3 x 5-7μ. Juel (cited under *C. cristata*) finds that in a plant considered by him to be *C. epichnoa* (pl. 3, figs. 84-86) the microscopic characters are the same as in the plant he considers *C. crispula* (pl. 3, figs. 91 and 92).  Neither of his plants is *C. decurrens*.  However, we have received from him a collection labelled *C. crispula* with a question which is exactly like the present species in the dry state and has the same spores, nearly pip-shaped, minutely rough, 2-3 x 3.5-5μ.  Specimens in Persoon's herbarium collected near Paris and determined by him as *C. crispula* are in good condition and are indistinguishable from our collections.  The spores are the same, 2.5-4 x 4.4-6.6μ.  *Clavaria muscigena* Pers., which was also regarded by Fries as a synonym, is not represented in the herbarium of Persoon.  In the Bresadola Herbarium at Stockholm are three collections determined as *C. crispula*. One is on rotten wood and looks exactly like our plants and has the same spores ("yellow, asperulate, 4-5 x 2.5-3µ"); another on spruce leaves and moss also looks like our No. 120, open and crisped, and has same spores ("asperulate, cremeo-ochraceous, 4.5-5 x 3-3.5µ. Basidia 16-20 x 4-5µ; hyphae 2-3 (-6)µ"); the third, apparently on rotten wood or trash, is 3.5-5 cm. high and looks more like our southern variety *australis*. At Kew Gardens under the name *C. crispula* are a variety of species, as *C. stricta, C. cristata,* and *C. pyxidata*. In the opinion of Fries *C. canaliculata* Ehrenb. (Nova Acta Acad. Caes. Leop. Nat. Cur. **2**: 213, pl. 14, figs. 1-9. 1821) is also a synonym of the present species. We have received several collections from Romell labelled *C. abietina,* one of which is the present species, with spores minutely rough, 3 x 4-5µ. Another labelled "*C. abietina* or probably *C. cyanescens* v. Post" (Stockholm) is also this species.

*Clavaria crispula* has been reported from a number of states, as South Carolina, New England, Maine, Ohio, Illinois, Pennsylvania, but it is not at all certain that any of these reports are based on the plant that we have described. For example, a collection in the Albany Herbarium from Greig, N. Y., is not this but *C. stricta,* as is one in the New York Botanical Garden Herbarium from Fern, Ind. (Underwood). In the Schweinitz Herbarium is a plant with spine-like points that is labelled *C. crispula* but is not this. In the Curtis Herbarium are several collections labelled *C. crispula,* one of which is on fir or spruce leaves from Europe and looks like *C. flaccida*. Another collection from New England (Sprague) has the appearance of a tall slender *C. Kunzei* and has spores like that species. This last is labelled "crispulae affinis sed differt."

Illustrations: Bischoff. Kryptogamenkunde, fig. 3472 (as *C. crispula*). 1860.

Britzelmayr. Hymen. Südb., Clavariei, fig. 52 (as *C. crispula*).

Burt. Ann. Mo. Bot. Gard. **9**: pl. 4, fig. 27 (as *C. pusilla*). 1922.

Ehrenburg. As cited above (as *C. canaliculata*). We have not seen this.

Flora Danica, pl. 2272, fig. 1 (as *C. crispula*). 1839.

Payer. Botan. Cryptog., p. 3, fig. 2, and p. 57, figs. 238-239 (as *C. crispula*). 1868.

New York: North Elba. Peck. (Albany Herb., as type of *C. pusilla*). Identical with our collections from Vaughns. Spores roughish, oval, 2.5-3 x 4.5-5.5µ.

Westport. Peck. (Albany Herb., as *C. pusilla*).

Vaughns. Coker and Burnham. (U. N. C. Herb.). No. 120. Among hemlock leaves in a damp place by a brook. C. & B. No. 106. Under white pines. Both collections made September 2, 1917. Color (of No. 106) peculiar, light olive drab throughout, except the pinkish purple stem; not very brittle; flesh turning deep pinkish purple when cut or bruised; yellowish olivaceous when dry. Spores as above.

Canada: Ottawa. Macoun. (Albany Herb., as *C. crispula*). Dried plants look like ours and the spores are the same, rough, 3-3.5 x 4.1-5.5µ.

## Clavaria decurrens var. australis n. var.

### PLATES 50, 67, AND 88

Plants of medium to small size, but of slender, delicate habit, gregarious and single or clustered and often partly fused; about 4-10 cm. high and 2-8.5 cm. broad; stalk distinct, 1-2 cm. long, 3-12 mm. thick, smooth, not rooting but deliquescing soon into the white, membranous and fibrous mycelium; main branches spreading, their subdivisions turning upward and ascending in a crowded manner, the ultimate branches very numerous and slender and simple or toothed, the tips all pointed; all parts smooth and terete; color when young a light buffy yellow, between chamois and buff-yellow of Ridgway, the tips remaining this color until maturity, lower parts soon becoming a darker honey-yellow or isabella color and finally the whole thus colored, the base white where protected by leaves, but becoming flesh color then brown when bruised. Flesh rather toughish and not brittle, pale with a tint of the surface color, becoming distinctly *flesh-pink when cut;* taste distinctly bitter, odor none. In drying the plant becomes a deep brown, about Dresden brown of Ridgway, and nearly the color of dried *C. abietina.* There is a distinct contrast in color when dry between the hymenium and the sterile areas in the angles, which are darker.

Spores (of No. 2769) about pip-shaped, minutely but distinctly spinulose-warted, deep buffy yellow (about chamois color of Ridgway), 2.5-3 x 5-6.5µ. Basidia 4.8 x 22µ, with 4 curved sterigmata.

Among rotting leaves in deciduous woods. Known at present with certainty only from Chapel Hill and from Vaughns, N. Y.

It differs from all others at all like it except the species in the quick change of flesh to deep pink and in the spores.    It is like *C. decurrens* in almost identical spores, change of color when bruised and in the color of the dried plants.    The latter differs in growth under conifers, much smaller size and different color when fresh.

As interpreted by Bresadola, Romell, and several other European botanists, *C. condensata* is *C. stricta,* as shown by their specimens, but it is doubtful if the real *C. condensata* is that species. The present species agrees well with Fries's description of *C. condensata,* the crowded bases and fibrillose mycelium in leaves of frondose trees being particularly convincing.    Sowerby's plate 157 (as *C. muscoides*), to which Fries refers, is also very like our plant.    That Sowerby's plate does represent our plant is rendered more probable by the occurrence of the same species in the Kew Herbarium (Massee, November, 1903, under lilacs, Kew Gardens), labelled "*C. rubella* Schaeff. (*C. condensata* Fr.)"    This has exactly the appearance of our Chapel Hill plants, with spores also the same but averaging a little shorter, 2.5-3.5 x 4-5μ.

North Carolina: Chapel Hill.    No. 2769.    In a thick layer of rotting leaves of deciduous trees just outside of center gate of Arboretum, July 25, 1917.    A large number of fine plants. (Type).    No. 3116.    Same spot as No. 2769 and exactly like it, June 8, 1918.    No. 3144.    Same spot as above, August 4, 1918.    No. 3279.    Among rotting leaves in same spot as above, June 2, 1919.    No. 3304.    In rotting leaves under privet in northeast corner of Arboretum, June 6, 1919.    No. 4385. Same spot as No. 2769, July 10, 1920.

New York: Vaughns.    Burnham, No. 4.    (U. N. C. Herb.).    In frondose woods, July 29-30, 1915.    Spores roughish, 3-3.5 x 6-6.5μ.    These plants have the same reddish stains on the surface in dry state that the Chapel Hill plants do, and in all other ways are exactly alike.    No notes on fresh state.

**Clavaria myceliosa** Pk.    Bull. Torr. Bot. Club **31**: 182. 1904.

### PLATE 88

This seems to be the western representative of *C. decurrens,* with smaller spores.    The types at Albany are very delicate little plants, the spores pip-shaped, minutely papillate, about 2-2.2 x 3.5-4μ.    Peck's description follows:

"Stem slender, solid, irregularly branched above, tawny, with an abundant mycelium which forms whitish, branching strands among decaying leaves and twigs; branches short, divergent or wide spreading with few branchlets, colored like the stem, the ultimate branchlets mostly acute, whitish; spores subglobose, 4μ long. Scattered or gregarious, 1-2.5 cm. tall, stems about 0.5 mm. thick.

"The abundant rhizomorphoid mycelium is a marked feature of this species. The plant is inodorous but has a slight peppery taste. It is allied to our eastern *C. pusilla,* but it is a smaller, more slender plant with the slender stem branched above only, and with the few short branches more widely spreading."

Illustration: Burt. Ann. Mo. Bot. Gard. **9**: pl. 6, fig. 37. 1922.

California: E. B. Copeland. In mountains near Stanford University, among fallen leaves and twigs under redwood trees, December. (Type. Albany Herb.).

## Clavaria abietina Pers. Neues Mag. Bot. **1**: 117. 1794.

### PLATES 68 AND 89

The following description is made from plants taken by us at Vaughns, N. Y. (No. 132):

Plants small, about 2-4 cm. high and 1-3 cm. broad, branched at or near the base, the branches numerous and crowded, the tips not so numerous and fine as in the *flaccida* form, color dull ochraceous above, brownish ochraceous below when very fresh, but soon with tints of olive green at any point or all over, deep olive green when bruised. Flesh pliable, hardly breaking when bent on self, tips not whitish at any age. Color a little darker than in the *flaccida* form when quite fresh, then much darker with the olive-brown tints of age. Taste hardly bitter, rather mouldy, odor none.

Spores (of C. & B. No. 110) deep yellowish ochraceous, pipshaped, papillate-warted, $3-3.7 \times 6.2-8.5\mu$. Hymenium $35-45\mu$ thick, containing very many embedded spores which are not arranged in layers.

In hemlock woods on decaying hemlock needles in the northern states, and rarely in the South.

On account of its change to green, we have taken the above to represent the typical *C. abietina,* although the usual difficulties are met with in comparing our plants with European descriptions. In his original description Persoon says that *C. abietina* grows in pine woods, is at first sordid yellow to alutaceous, becoming greenish; base white-tomentose; spores saffron, etc. In his Commentatio, p. 47 (178), he has a fuller description of *C. abietina* giving the stalk as 4 lines thick, form obconic, always in pines, color sordid yellow to alutaceous then greenish. The species is represented in Persoon's herbarium by two plants in good condition which may be considered as the types. The plants are about 2-4 cm. high, the spores 3.5-4.5 x 5-8μ. There is no tint of green on the dried plants. In size they more closely resemble our large plant of pines which in America has no tint of green. Two other sheets from France (Chaillet, coll.) so determined are apparently the same.

Fries describes *C. abietina* as having the trunk white-tomentose and growing in fir woods, while *C. flaccida,* he says, grows in pine woods and is much more delicate than the former. This is the opposite of our observations on the American plants, the larger plant with a distinct stalk growing among pine needles, the smaller, more delicate plant occurring under hemlock and spruce. The carelessness of Fries's study of Clavarias is shown in many cases. At Kew are three collections from him determined as *C. abietina* which represent three different species. One is apparently correctly determined, another is *C. apiculata,* and another *C. cristata.* Greville's plate 117 referred to by Fries (Epicr., p. 574) does not look like our green plant of hemlock, but is big and more stalked like our form of pines; a slight greenish tint is shown on one side of his figure. The Flora Danica figure, also referred to by Fries, is likewise a large plant with a good stalk. Gillet's figure is smaller than the others but shows a stalk.

In the Curtis Herbarium is a collection labelled *C. abietina* from Fries (through Berkeley). The plant is like ours as described above, about 4 cm. high and 3 cm. wide, well branched from the ground. The spores also are exactly the same, minutely warted, elliptic to pip-shaped, 3.7-4.4 x 6.6-8.5μ. The species is not represented in the Fries Herbarium at Upsala.

Spores of *C. abietina* from Bresadola (N. Y. Bot. Gard.) are pip-shaped, 3.5-3.8 x 6.5-7μ, minutely papillate, ochraceous. The plants are small, not over an inch high. Others in his own herbarium are similar. Other European specimens under this name in the New York Botanical Garden Herbarium vary much in delicacy and some cannot be distinguished from the *flaccida* form, which is supposed to be more delicate. A good collection from Upsala sent us by Romell and determined by him as *C. abietina* with *C. ochracea* von Post (not published) as a synonym looks just like our plant of pines, and has the same spores, which are dark colored, distinctly warted, 4 x 7-8.2μ. In regard to this Romell writes: *"Clavaria abietina* which von Post called *'ochracea'* is to my eyes distinct from the 'forma minor, contrita virens' which von Post called *'cyanescens'* and which must be very like to and perhaps is sometimes considered as *'flaccida'* ere the color is changed." Plants received from Romell labelled "*C. cyanescens* v. Post=*C. abietina* forma Fries, Stockholm, autumno, 1889" are indistinguishable from *C. flaccida* in the dried state, with spores, 3.6-4.2 x 6-7.4μ. We have received from Juel (Upsala) as *C. abietina* typical plants which are distinctly green in the dried state; spores pip-shaped, often narrowly so, distinctly rough, 3.4-4.2 x 7-9μ. Another collection from him looks more like our form of pines. *Clavaria testaceoflava* Bres. may be distinguished by larger spores, yellow tips and vinaceous color of flesh when bruised. It is 3-5 cm. high and grows in fir woods in mountains. Still another plant of the same size and habit as *C. flaccida* and *C. abietina* and with stringy mycelium is *C. Patouillardii* Bres., which see.

Juel (cited under *C. cristata*) studied this species and finds the basidia filled with yellow granules, short, the nuclear spindles apical and transverse, the four spores elongated and spiny and figured with one nucleus (pl. 3, figs. 67-69).

The plant from Utah, entered below, is strongly olivaceous in places, with densely crowded, thick, short branches, the spores as in *C. abietina* except that they are larger. It may prove to be a distinct variety.

Illustrations: Cooke. Handb. Brit. Fungi 1: fig. 88.
  Gillet. Champ. Fr. 5: pl. 98. 1897. Good.
  Greville. Scott. Crypt. Flora 2: pl. 117. 1824.
  Hard. Mushrooms, fig. 390. 1908.
  Patouillard. Tab. Fung., fig. 566. 1887.
  Swanton. Fungi and How to Know Them, pl. 29, fig. 4. 1909.

North Carolina: Salem. "Ad terram lignosam non frequens." Schweinitz.
  (Curtis Herb.). The small fragments show little except the spores,
  which are 4-4.5 x 7.4-8.5μ.

Tennessee: Unaka Springs. "Mixed woods, evergreens predominating."
  Murrill. (N. Y. Bot. Gard. Herb., as *C. flaccida*). Spores 3.4-3.7 x 5-7.4μ.

New York: Vaughns. Coker and Burnham, No. 110. Under hemlocks,
  September 2, 1917. Olive yellow, deep olive green when bruised; about
  2-3.5 cm. high and 1.5-3 cm. broad. C. & B. No. 132. Under hemlocks, same date as No. 110. (U. N. C. Herb.).
  Adirondacks. Murrill. (N. Y. Bot. Gard. Herb.). Dried plants show
  olive tints.

Missouri: St. Louis. "Wooded hills, not common." Glatfelter. (Albany
  Herb.). Dusky and olivaceous stains.

Colorado: Jack Brook. Clements. (Path. and Myc. Herb., as *C. abietina
  minor*). Plants small, about 1-1.5 cm. high. Spores 3.7-4.1 x 7.4-7.8μ.

Utah: Brighton, in Big Cottonwood Canyon. Miss Barrows, 1920. (U.
  N. C. Herb. and N. Y. Bot. Gard. Herb.). Dried plants greenish; spores
  dark, papillate, 3.8-5.3 x 8-10.6μ.

Washington: Seattle. (N. Y. Bot. Gard. Herb. from Young Naturalists'
  Soc. Herb., No. 195).

Canada: Macoun. (N. Y. Bot. Gard. Herb.). Spores 3.5-4 x 7-7.5μ.


*Clavaria abietina. Non-virescent form of pines.*
  ?*C. corrugata* Karst. Nat. Fauna et Flora Fenn., p. 371. 1868.

### PLATES 69 AND 89

Plants 2.5-8 cm. high, gregarious in large numbers, cespitose
with the stems more or less fused, single individuals about 1.5-2
cm. broad above, usually in clumps of 2-4; stem distinct, about
1.5-2 cm. long, 3-5 mm. thick, the base enlarged and incrassated
by the creamy, flocculent mycelium which may ascend the
stem more or less and which binds together a mass of pine needles
as well as adjacent plants; main branches rather few, dividing
irregularly about twice into compacted divisions which end in
several rather sharply pointed teeth; color yellowish cinnamon, the
stem a darker brownish cinnamon or in youth nearly concolorous,

all parts darker in age, but not turning greenish in age or when bruised; flesh rather tender and brittle, white or nearly so; taste musty-woody; odor slight.

Spores yellowish ochraceous (color of the hymenium), elliptic-pip-shaped, distinctly short-spinulose, variable in size in the same collection, 3.4-4 x 6.3-9$\mu$ (a few up to 10$\mu$ long). Basidia (of B. No. 91) about 5.5$\mu$ thick, 4-spored; hymenium about 75$\mu$ thick, with very many embedded spores as is usual in this group; threads of flesh very irregular and variable in thickness, clamp connections present and variable in size.

Gregarious in clumps among rotting leaves of pine. Easily distinguished, except from its own group, by the small size, yellowish color, cespitose habit, occurrence under pine, and characteristic spores. In the numerous plants we have seen there was no green tint nor did bruises turn greenish. There seem to be all variations between this and the more delicate plant with olive tints found in hemlock woods that we refer to typical *C. abietina* and its non-virescent form (*C. flaccida*). Only extremes can be separated with certainty in the dried state.

Our plants are the same as a collection from West Albany by Peck labelled *C. corrugata* Karst., but we are in some doubt as to whether the latter species is the same as ours. Karsten's description fits only moderately well, as he says the stem is glabrous and the tips acute. His plant was found in pine woods among alders and is said by Saccardo to be intermediate between *C. abietina* and *C. flaccida*. For a good illustration reputed to be *C. corrugata* see Britzelmayr, Hymen. Südb., Clavariei, figs. 17 and 80-81.

Illustrations: Flora Danica, pl. 2030, fig. 2 (as *C. abietina*). 1830. Photographic copy in Ann. Mo. Bot. Gard. **9**: pl. 5, fig. 28. 1922.

North Carolina: Blowing Rock. Coker, No. 5784. Under white pines by Lake Chetola, August 25, 1922. (U. N. C. Herb.). Spores warted, pip-shaped, 3.4-3.8 x 6-8$\mu$.

New York: Hudson Falls. Burnham, No. 91. Among rotting needles under white pines, August 16, 1917. (U. N. C. Herb.).

Delmar. (Albany Herb.). Exactly like B. No. 91.

Albany. House. (Albany Herb.). Like B. No. 91, but running smaller.

West Albany. Peck. (Albany Herb., as *C. corrugata*). Spores 4 x 7.6$\mu$.

*Clavaria abietina.   Small, non-virescent form.*
   *C. flaccida* Fr.   Syst. Myc. **1** : 471. 1821.

PLATES 70 AND 88

We do not find it possible to make any satisfactory distinction between *C. abietina* and *C. flaccida* as understood by Fries and other mycologists.   Small delicate plants of the *C. flaccida* form may turn green and large, much stouter plants may not.   As mentioned earlier, our largest American form occurs in pines, the only habitat given for *C. abietina* by Persoon, and does not turn green so far as we have met with it.   Mixed with these are smaller forms which connect directly with the typical *C. flaccida*.   Any delicate form of *C. abietina* that is not green would be referred to *C. flaccida,* and it certainly has not been shown that the green change has any specific value in this little group.   We are therefore considering the delicate, non-virescent plant called *C. flaccida* by Fries, as the *flaccida* form of *C. abietina*.   Typical plants of this nature found by us at Vaughns, N. Y., may be described as follows:

Plants small, about 1.5-3 cm. high and 0.6-2.7 cm. broad, branched at or near the ground, branches smooth, terete or more or less flattened, dense or rather open, the tips very numerous, delicate, pointed and concolorous; color light creamy ochraceous all over, or at times dull flesh color in youth; towards or after maturity the basal half a deeper dull ochraceous; in drying becoming deep ochraceous all over.   Flesh pliable, tender, not changing when bruised; taste slightly mouldy and at times a little peppery in plants from deciduous woods; odor faintly similar; mycelium white, stringy, conspicuous.

Spores deep ochraceous, pip-shaped, minutely warted, 3-3.7 x 5-7.7μ.   Basidia 4.4-5.5μ thick; hymenium 45-60μ thick, in most places with a distinct row of embedded spores in the center, indicating a renewal by proliferation; threads of flesh variable in thickness, most about 3.7μ thick, parallel and closely packed just under the hymenium, irregular and loosely packed in the center of plant, clamp connections present.

Abundant under hemlock and more rarely in frondose woods in the northern states, and to be expected in our higher southern mountains.   See *C. abietina* for other notes.

In the Fries Herbarium (Upsala) are two collections labelled *C. flaccida,* which have been kindly sent us by Dr. Juel. One of these is true *C. flaccida* (Christian Blyth, coll.) with the usual appearance and spores minutely rough, 3-3.7 x 5.5-7μ; the other, labelled in Fries's own hand, is not this species but typical *C. Kunzei* except that the spores which are spherical (3.7-4.5μ thick) are apparently quite smooth, a character found also in the spores of some American plants of *C. Kunzei.* As this collection could not possibly be *C. flaccida* as described by Fries, it must be ignored as evidence and added to the long list of Fries's mistakes in this genus.

In the Curtis Herbarium is a specimen from Fries (Upsala) labelled *C. flaccida,* a small plant about 2 cm. high that looks like ours and has the same spores, which are minutely warted, 2.8-3.7 x 5-6μ. Another collection from Fries (Upsala) in the Kew Herbarium is the same thing with spores pip-shaped, minutely rough, 3.4-3.7 x 5-7μ. Plants from Finland at the New York Botanical Garden determined as *C. flaccida* by Karsten are ochraceous in the dried state and look like our plants described above, except that they are a little taller. The spores are the same, being pip-shaped, minutely tuberculate, 2.6-3.3 x 5.5-6.6μ.

Illustrations: Britzelmayr. Hymen. Südb., Clavariei, figs. 21 and 82 (as *C. flaccida*).

Burt. Ann. Mo. Bot. Gard. **9**: pl. 4, fig. 26 (as *C. flaccida*). 1922.

Fries. Icon. Hymen., pl. 199, fig. 4. 1884. Photographic copy in Ann. Mo. Bot. Gard. **9**: pl. 4, fig. 25 (as *C. flaccida*). 1922.

Patouillard. Tab. Fung., fig. 39 (as *C. flaccida*). 1883.

New York: Catskills. (N. Y. Bot. Gard. Herb., as *C. cinerea*). "Common upon leaf mold; spores ochraceous." Spores pip-shaped, rough, about 3.5 x 7μ.

Jamesville. Underwood. (N. Y. Bot. Gard. Herb., as *C. flaccida*). Spores 3.7 x 5.5μ.

Hudson Falls. Burnham, No. 56. Golden's hemlocks, east of Tripoli, July 22, 1917. Spores covered with very fine warts, 2.5-3.9 x 4.8-7μ. B. No. 58. Golden's hemlocks, July 23, 1917. Spores 2.5-2.9 x 5-5.5μ. (U. N. C. Herb.).

Vaughns. Burnham, No. 52. Deciduous woods, July 16, 1917. Taste distinctly but mildly bitterish-peppery. No. 55a. On beech stump in woods, July 20. 1917. In drying it became a deep ochraceous brown. Spores 3-3.7 x 5-6.6μ. No. 84. Burnham's hemlocks, August 2, 1917. Spores 3-3.5 x 6-7.3μ. No. 86. Deciduous woods, August 9, 1917. "Flesh colored, tinged with yellow." Spores deep ochraceous,

3-3.5 x 6.3-7$\mu$.    No. 87.   Under white pines.   Plants small and apparently not different from the form under hemlock.   Spores 3.3 x 5.7-6.8$\mu$. No. 88.   Under hemlocks.   Spores 3.3 x 5.7-7.6$\mu$.   Burnham and Coker, No. 102.   Hemlock woods, September 2, 1917.   Typical form from which the description was mostly drawn.   Spores 3-3.7 x 5-6.3$\mu$.   No. 108.   In pines, and intermediate between the *flaccida* form of hemlock and the larger one of pines, September 2, 1917.   Tips pale yellowish ochraceous, shading downward to ochraceous; no green.   No. 117.   Maple woods (no hemlocks), September 2, 1917.   Exactly like the form under hemlocks.   Spores 3.2-3.7 x 6.3-7.7$\mu$.   Burnham, No. 119b.   Same deciduous woods as No. 52, August 13, 1918.   Taste mildly bitterish-peppery; no change in cut flesh.   (Above colls. in U. N. C. Herb.).

Vermont: Newfane.   Miss Hibbard.   (U. N. C. Herb.).

Michigan: Agricultural College.   On rotten wood.   Hicks.   (N. Y. Bot. Gard. Herb., as *Lachnocladium Micheneri*).   Spores pip-shaped, minutely warted, 2.5 x 5.2$\mu$.

Canada: On earth in woods, September 9, 1908.   Macoun.   (Ellis Collection, N. Y. Bot. Gard. Herb., as *C. flaccida*).   Spores typical, 3 x 7-7.4$\mu$.


**Clavaria Broomei** Cotton and Wakefield.   Trans. Brit. Myc. Soc. **6**: 170. 1919.
   ?*C. oblectanea* Britz.   Hymen. Südb. **10**: 179, Clavariei, fig. 87. 1894.

PLATES 71 AND 89

Plants 3-7 cm. high, solitary or gregarious, with a distinct and usually long stalk, which varies from 2-5 cm. long and 2-4 mm. thick below; usually thicker upwards and there crested with a cluster of short, thickish, blunt or acute branches, or at times dividing further down into two or three long upright branches which are similarly crowned with short branches; color ochraceous brown when fresh, in age a darker reddish brown and often blackish in part on drying, the tips lighter when young, the base whitish or pinkish where covered with leaves.   Flesh not very brittle, watery white, not changing color when bruised, tasteless and odorless; hyphae about 3.7$\mu$ thick, regular, parallel, closely packed, clamp connections present.

   Spores deep reddish ochraceous, elliptic with a bent end, distinctly papillate, 4.4-6 x 12.5-18.4$\mu$.   Basidia (of B. No. 74) 9-10$\mu$ thick, 4-spored; hymenium 55-75$\mu$ thick, yellow in section.

In woods mold or leaves in frondose or mixed frondose and hemlock woods.   Known in America at present only from Vaughns, N. Y.

Plants of this species first sent to Peck were considered by him as a form of *C. grandis,* as is shown by a collection from Mr. Burnham, so labelled by him at Albany.    Since then the plant has been found a number of times by Mr. Burnham near the same spot, and Mr. Burnham and the author succeeded in finding a few small specimens in the same place in September, 1917.    The species is in the *grandis* group, and is nearest *C. longicaulis,* which is easily separated by the spores of quite different shape.    The stem of *C. Broomei* may extend a little way into the leaves but has no rhizomorph and is soon dissipated into the white, rather scanty mycelium.    That our plants are *C. Broomei* is shown by the types at Kew, which in the dried state have the same brownish, velvety-looking surface, about the same shape, and the same long, spiny spores, 5-7 x 12.5-19.5μ.

*Clavaria oblectanea* is probably the same, but the spore size is not given and we have seen no authentic specimen.    In the Bresadola Herbarium there is a collection from Westphalia marked *C. nigrescens* Brinkmann, but we can find no record of the publication of this species.    The plants are the same as ours with the characteristic spores, spiny, 5.5-7 x 14-19.5μ.    We have received from Romell (Archipelago of Stockholm) good examples of *C. Broomei.*    The spores are spiny, 5-6.5 x 11-16μ.

The fresh plants shown in the photograph are immature, with the branches scarcely more than teeth as yet.    The dried plants shown are of mature form.

New York: Vaughns.    Collections below all in leaf mold in frondose or mixed woods—maple, beech and hemlock, R. C. Burnham's farm.    B. No. 74.    August 13, 1915.    Spores 4.8-5.6 x 13.5-15.8μ.    B. No. 98.    September 3, 1917.    Spores 4.8-6 x 12.5-18.4μ.    C. & B. No. 141.    September 1, 1917.    Spores 4.4-5.5 x 13.6-16μ.    (All in U. N. C. Herb.).    There is also one of Mr. Burnham's collections in the Albany Herbarium (as *C. grandis*).

## Clavaria longicaulis Pk.    Bull. Torr. Bot. Club. **25**: 371. 1898.

### PLATES 72-74, 89, AND 90

Plants of small to moderate size, strict, narrow, distinctly stalked, 2.5-9 cm. high, 1.3-4 cm. broad; stem about 1.3-4 cm. long and 1.5-7 mm. thick, irregularly branched above into a tuft of upright, closely pressed, terete and even or somewhat rugosely wrinkled branches, which after several subdivisions end in several small cusps; whitened below and soon fading into the mycelium which extends in all directions in many threadlike strands which are white when undisturbed, but turn pink when exposed as do also the whiter parts of the stem base (a form occurs with a long, tough, pinkish rhizomorph, as No. 2730, which see); color above cinnamon-tawny (about tawny olive of Ridgway), darkening downwards to about that of *C. grandis* (antique brown or buckthorn brown of Ridgway), the tips somewhat lighter, but not abruptly whitish. Flesh whitish or cinnamon, not very brittle, bitter, odor slight. When dry becoming a deep reddish brown, from Sudan brown to Brussels brown of Ridgway; with the hymenium of a more or less velvety appearance.

Spores (of No. 2287) ovate to pip-shaped, with a stout eccentric mucro, the surface set with prominent, irregular, warty spines, color deep rusty ochraceous in front view of a good print, about orange ochraceous of Ridgway in side view, 4.8-5.3 x 8-11μ, most about 5 x 8μ. Basidia 4-spored, 5.5-7μ thick; hymenium 60-75μ thick; hyphae about 3.7μ thick, regular, parallel and very closely packed, small clamp connections present.

Gregarious or loosely cespitose in leaf mold or moss in low frondose woods; rather rare.

Peck's type plants from Alabama are like ours and the spores are indistinguishable. In the type they are strongly warted, 4.4-5 x 7.5-8.5μ. On the label with the type Earle says, "On moist earth, dark brown throughout, end of branches blunt, spores ochraceous, ovate, sharply echinulate, 6 x 4μ." Peck's character of "wrinkled" stem and branches is evidently based only on the dried plant and without significance.

The rhizomorphic form above mentioned is very striking. However, in the absence of any other discernible difference, we are considering it only a form. No. 4416, a typical example, shows the spores 4.8-5.9 x 5.9-8μ, rarely 10μ; basidia 7.4μ thick, 4-spored; hymenium 65-75μ thick; threads of flesh as in the typical form. The presence of the rhizomorph is probably due to some character in the substratum, plants in decaying leaves or pure humus lacking the rhizomorph, those in earth usually possessing one.

The species is in the *C. grandis* group and is distinguished from its nearest relatives as follows: from *C. grandis* by the smaller size, the much smaller spores, and the absence of the abruptly white tips, and from *C. Broomei* by the much more branching habit and different spores. On the label of the type of *C. longicaulis* Earle has noted "near *C. compressa* Schroet.", but that is described as yellow and only 1.5-2.5 cm. high.

From the description this might possibly be *C. megalorhiza* B. and Br. from Ceylon (Journ. Linn. Soc. **14**: 75. 1875) but that is said to grow on wood and the spores are smaller and otherwise different. The type at Kew shows two good plants, branched from the base, dark ochraceous, dense, about 2.5 cm. high and 2-3.5 cm. broad. We find the spores to be nearly pip-shaped, 3.5-3.8 x 5-7μ, warted but distinctly less so than in *C. longicaulis*. On the same page is described *C. echinospora* B. & Br. (see under *C. cyanocephala*) which is said to be nearly allied to *C. megalorhiza*, but to turn black on drying and to have larger spores. In the Cornell Herbarium are several collections labelled *C. megalorhiza* that are not different from *C. abietina*.

Illustration: Burt. Ann. Mo. Bot. Gard. **9**: pl. 2, fig. 8. 1922.

North Carolina: Chapel Hill. No. 866. On ground by path to Meeting of Waters, October 2, 1913. Rhizomorphic. No. 2287. On ground in leaf mold by Battle's Branch. No. 2648. By path in low damp woods, July 11, 1917. Rhizomorphic. No. 2659. In moss in path, July 13, 1917. No. 2713. By path in low mixed woods, July 19, 1917. Rhizomorphic, 11 cm. high and 6 cm. broad. No. 2730. By path in Battle's Park, July 21, 1917. Rhizomorphic. No. 2762. In decaying oak leaves, thick, damp woods, July 24, 1917. Spores 5.5-7 x 7.4-7.7μ. No. 2803. Among fallen leaves, mixed woods, July 28, 1917. No. 2814. Same spot as No. 2659, July 30, 1917. No. 3465. In damp sandy soil in path near stream, August 16, 1919. No. 3469. In humus, deciduous woods, a few pines 30 or 40 feet away, August 17, 1919. A fine lot of plants, characters as usual. No. 3479. Mixed woods, August 22, 1919. No. 4416. Deciduous woods by Meeting of the Waters branch, July 16, 1920. Flesh turns dull vinaceous pink when bruised. Taste sour-bitter; odor faintly medicinal. Texture fleshy above, much more tough in the stem. Spores 4.8-5.6 x 7.5-8.5μ. No. 4523. Mixed woods, July 26, 1920.

Asheville. Beardslee. This is just like our Chapel Hill plants. Spores identical, 4.8-6.7 x 8.2-10.4μ. (U. N. C. Herb.).

Alabama: Auburn. On moist earth. Earle. (Albany Herb., type).

District of Columbia: Braendle. (Albany Herb., as a small form of *C. grandis*). Spores as in the type, about 5 x 7.5μ.

Massachusetts: Davis. (Albany Herb., as a small form of *C. grandis*). Spores as in the type, about 5.3 x 7.5μ.

## Clavaria Murrilli n. sp.

### PLATES 77 AND 91

Plants single, gregarious, 1.5-5.5 cm. high (in the dried state), slender and with a long, pale, tough stalk less than 1 mm. thick (when dry) which is loosely covered through most of its length with long, pale, flexuous, cottony threads; branches few, elongated, ascending, once or twice rebranched, the tips subacute. Color of the stem when fresh, dull carneous, of the branches ferruginous, the tips brownish; when dry the stem is grayish white, shading gradually into the Dresden brown to Brussels brown branches which are flattened and wrinkled, as is the stem, as though shrinking much in drying.

Spores brown under the microscope, long-pip-shaped, 3-3.7 x 8.5-9.3$\mu$, strongly asperulate with slender, sharp spines. Basidia clavate, 4.8-5.5$\mu$ thick, 4-spored. Hymenium 50-60$\mu$ thick; threads of flesh parallel, closely packed, 3.3-5.5$\mu$ thick, with clamp connections at the nodes.

This species we take pleasure in naming for Dr. W. A. Murrill, who found it in 1904. The color in the fresh state was noted by Dr. Murrill. Except for this the description is drawn from the dried plants, which now number nine or ten, with some fragments. It seems evident that the plant is in the *grandis* group and is nearest *C. longicaulis,* as indicated by the long, incarnate stem, dark brown branches and large, brown, asperulate spores. The spines on the spores are more like those of *C. grandis* than any other member of the group. The species is clearly marked by its slender form, pale, cottony stem and long, narrow, sharply spiny spores. The dried plants are now attached to a mixture of pine, hemlock and oak leaves.

Tennessee: Unaka Springs. In leaves, mixed woods, altitude 1700 feet. Murrill, No. 907. (U. N. C. Herb., type, and N. Y. Bot. Gard. Herb., co-type).

**Clavaria cyanocephala** B. & C.   Journ. Linn. Soc. **10**: 338. 1869.
  *C. Zippellii* Lév.   Ann. Sci. Nat., 3rd. ser., **11**: 215. 1844.
  *C. echinospora* B. & Br.   Journ. Linn. Soc. **14**: 75. 1875.
    (Not *C. echinospora* Boud. & Pat. or *C. echinospora* P.
    Henn.).
  *C. aeruginosa* Pat.   Bull. Soc. Myc. Fr. **14**: 189. 1898.

PLATE 90

As this striking species of the *C. grandis* group occurs in Cuba
Porto Rico, and Trinidad, as well as in the Orient, we are including it for its interest.   It is not at all improbable that a number
of West Indian species may some day be found in Florida.

In the New York Botanical Garden are specimens from Porto
Rico without a name.   We find that in appearance as well as in
spores they agree with the present species.   The spores are
strongly echinulate, 6-7.5 x 9-15µ.   According to von Höhnel
(Sitzungsb. d. Kaiserl. Akad. d. Wiss. Wien **118**: 15. 1909), who
is probably right, *C. cyanocephala* and *C. aeruginosa* (from Java)
are the same as *C. Zippellii* (from Java).   See note on *C. Zippellii* by Bresadola in Ann. Myc. **5**: 239. 1907.   He gives the
spores as obovate, aculeate, 12 x 15-18µ, including the spines, the
basidia two-spored, 10-13 x 60-65µ; the entire fungus from gray
to chestnut-brown.   The type of *C. echinospora* (from Ceylon) is
not represented at Kew, but plants from Borneo (H. Winkler,
coll.) determined as the latter by Bresadola and now in his
herbarium are to all appearances the same and have identical
spores, which are strongly asperulate, 6-7.5 x 9-12.5.

At Kew are plants from Trinidad (J. H. Hart, coll.) which
are labelled *Lachnocladium tubulosum* Fr.   They are not the
latter, which is quite different, but the present species.

The type of *C. cyanocephala* at Kew (Wright, No. 458, Cuba)
is dark brown and looks in every way like the Porto Rican plants
mentioned above.   The spores are large, elliptic, spiny,
5.5-7.4 x 11-14µ.   The types are 5-6 cm. high, and up to 3.5 cm.
broad, the main branches few and long, the terminals rather
crowded.   The original description is (trans.):

"Stem subdivided, branches and branchlets furcate, intensely cerulean above, apices short, bifid, obtuse, subfastigiate. Among leaves in thick woods. June. Hab. Bonin Isles. About 3 inches high."

It will be noted that the word "cerulean" is usually interpreted as "blue," but it may also mean greenish as is probably the case here (see note under Jamaica entry below). The co-type in the Curtis Herbarium agrees in every respect with the Kew specimens. The spores are elliptic, strongly spiny, about 7.4 x 13μ. (In both herbaria preparations from the plant show an abundance of smooth, subspherical spores in addition to the authentic ones). There is also a good specimen (Wright, No. 458) in the Farlow Herbarium.

This species differs from *C. grandis* in the more slender form, different color in the dried state, and the shorter and blunter spines of the spores, not to mention color in the fresh state. From *C. longicaulis* it differs in the larger spores and different color in the fresh state.

Illustration: Burt. Ann. Mo. Bot. Gard. **9**: pl. 3, fig. 14. 1922.
Cuba. Wright. (Kew Herb., Curtis Herb., and Farlow Herb., as *C. cyanocephala*).
Porto Rico. Johnson, No. 997. (N. Y. Bot. Gard. Herb.).
Jamaica. Castleton Gardens. On ground under bamboo. (N. Y. Bot. Gard. Herb. and U. N. C. Herb.). Spores 7.4-8.1 x 11.8-16μ, omitting spines; basidia 2-spored. Notes on fresh state mention a greenish tint.
Trinidad. Hart. (Kew Herb., as *L. tubulosum*).
Borneo. Winkler. (Bresadola Herb., as *C. echinospora*).

**Clavaria grandis** Pk.   Bull. Torr. Bot. Club. **29**: 73. 1902.
  *C. spiculospora* Atk.   Ann. Myc. **7**: 368. 1909.

PLATES 75, 76, AND 90

Plants single, gregarious, 6-15 cm. high, 2-12 cm. broad, usually with a distinct, stout, rather deeply rooted stem 1-6 cm. long and 1-2 cm. thick, divided into few or numerous upright, crowded branches, these dividing once or twice more and ending in stout abruptly rounded cusps; the angles rounded; surface glabrous; color of the upper part of the stem and all the branches, except the very tips, which are abruptly white, a uniform deep brick brown (antique brown of Ridgway), almost the color of dead leaves and thus very hard to find.    In drying the plant remains this color or turns a somewhat lighter color (Buckthorn brown), the same color as dried plants of *C. abietina*.    The stem surface below the hymenium is closely white-tomentose where protected in angles, etc., but where rubbed by soil or fingers the color is dull brownish lavender or purple.    Flesh firm, but very tender, pure white at first, but immediately turning to lavender-brown when cut; taste mildly acid-bitterish and after a few minutes astringent; hyphae 4-7.4μ thick, roughly parallel, very closely packed and having anastomosing connections between adjacent ones.

Spores (of No. 1186) antique brown, obovate, 6.3 x 12μ, exclusive of the spines, covered except at the curved point with long sharp spicules about 1.5μ long.    Basidia 2-spored, about 10μ thick; sterigmata stout, 7μ long; hymenium (of No. 4407) about 60μ thick, multiple and up to 4 layers thick.

Common in frondose woods near upland branches, etc.    This remarkably fine species, the darkest colored of our large Chapel Hill Clavarias, and one of the most handsome and striking, was first described by Peck from plants sent him from Maryland. *Clavaria spiculospora,* which is the same thing, was described by Professor Atkinson from plants collected by us in Chapel Hill. While common this plant is often overlooked as the color is very like that of the dead leaves in which it grows.    It often happens that only the tips are exposed above the leaves.    It usually grows in cool damp woods among decaying leaves, but we have also found it at the base of an oak stump in a lawn.    We have not tested the edible qualities of this species, but Mr. Braendle, who first collected it in Maryland, reported it as edible when pickled.

*Lachnocladium giganteum* Pat. (Journ. de Bot. **3**: 34, pl. 1, fig. 1. 1889) is certainly very near, and the spores and basidia are indistinguishable; but fine authentic specimens in the Paris Museum from French Guiana while large are distinctly more slender, as is also shown in the figure, and in the dry state they are more brittle and have a different taste from *C. grandis*.    The spores are 7.4-9 x 11-14.8μ, strongly spinulose; basidia 7.4μ thick, 2-spored; hymenium covering the surface, 130-150μ thick, in our sections *three layers deep*.    Patouillard places the species under his sub-genus *Dendrocladium,* which he defines (l. c., p. 33) as having the hymenium unilateral.   This, however, is not the case in our sections of his plant.

The present species is not to be confused with *C. dendroidea.* Fries's colored figures of the latter (Icon. Hymen., p. 200, fig. 1) strongly recall our plant in structure and color, the yellowish tips abruptly contrasting, but that is very distinct and belongs to a different group.   The spores from authentic specimens determined by Robert Fries are smooth, elliptic, 4-4.8 x 8-10μ (pl. 91, fig. 21).

Illustrations: Burt:   Ann. Mo. Bot. Gard. **9**: pl. 2, fig. 11 (as *C. spicu-lospora*); pl. 3, fig. 13 (as *C. grandis*).   1922.

North Carolina: Chapel Hill.   No. 1186.   Near branch, by a dead pine tree, July 22, 1914.   No. 1236.   In rich, damp, shaded soil by path by branch, September 23, 1914.   No. 1252.   Battle's Park, September 23, 1914.   No. 1785.   Pushing up under dead leaves, only the tips showing, side of Lone Pine Hill, September 14, 1915.   No. 2125.   At base of an oak stump in a lawn, June 16, 1916.   No. 2398.   By path along branch in mixed woods, July 20, 1916.   No. 2414.   Low woods, Battle's Park, July 22, 1916.   No. 2706.   Mixed woods by branch, July 5, 1917.   No. 2734.   Low mixed woods, July 21, 1917.   No. 2799.   Low damp woods near a spring, Battle's Park, July 28, 1917.   Plants up to 18.5 cm. high.   No. 3489.   Mixed woods, Battle's Park, August 22, 1919.   No. 4407.   Deciduous woods, July 14, 1920.

Black Mountain.   Coker, No. 953.   (U. N. C. Herb.).   On ground in deep woods in North Fork Valley, elevation about 3500 feet, August, 1913.   Spores in this collection were just as in the Chapel Hill plant, deep brown, long-obovate and curved at the small end, 6.3-7 x 11-13μ, not counting the spicules.   Spicules sharp, 1.5μ long, larger than in any other *Clavaria.*

Winston-Salem.   Schallert, No. 38.   (U. N. C. Herb.).   Spores pip-shaped, strongly spiny, about 7 x 13.5μ.

Maryland:   Braendle.   (Albany Herb., type.)

## LACHNOCLADIUM

If the usage of modern mycologists is to be accepted, the genus *Lachnocladium* is in a state of chaos.   It would have been much better if Persoon's original genus *Merisma* had been retained and modified as occasion demanded by the addition of new genera, as was done in fact by Léveillé in the establishment of his genus *Lachnocladium* (Ann. Sci. Nat., 3rd. ser., **5**: 158, 1846, as *Erio-cladus,* later changed to *Lachnocladium*).   In redefining the genus *Merisma* (l. c., p. 157) Léveillé made little change in Persoon's definition in Syn. Met. Fung., p. 582, except to omit any reference to the pilose tips.  He says: "Receptacle coriaceous, branched; branches compressed dilated or rather terete, glabrous everywhere, covered with 4-spored basidia.  Fungi growing on earth or wood, related to Thelephoras and Clavarias."  He confined *Lachnocladium* to tough plants in which even the branches (hymenium) were tomentose; no reference to spores.  His description is: "Receptacle leathery, branched, branches compressed or terete, tomentose over the entire fruiting surface.  Coralloid fungi growing on wood or earth."  *Merisma* as defined by Persoon would include plants which we now know to be Tremellodendrons, and which if removed would leave his genus in a form to greatly clarify the present *Lachnocladium* confusion.  This would then place in *Merisma* our only species from the United States which, it seems to us, cannot be accommodated in *Clavaria*.  There is a great difference between the leathery (coriaceous) texture of *Lachnocladium semivestitum* and the pliable, toughish flesh of many Clavarias that have been placed in *Lachnocladium*.  Moreover, this last group of Clavarias intergrades imperceptibly through the more fleshy-pliable ones into the more tender and fragile species.  *Merisma* on the other hand is as tough as a *Stereum* and like species of that genus, together with *Thelephora* and *Tremellodendron,* has pilose tips when in active growth.  The genus *Merisma* would then be defined as coriaceous (very tough), pliable, tips pilose in the growing state, always branched in a shrub-like manner; the hymenium glabrous and covering the plant completely except for the tomentose tips and sterile base; spores smooth, white; basidia simple, 2-4-spored.  Separated from *Clavaria* by really leathery texture and pilose tips in growth.  Examples: *L. semivestitum, L. cartilagineum.*

Patouillard's redefinition of the genus *Lachnocladium* (Essai tax. s. l. fam., etc.) is as follows:

"Receptacle erect, hard, almost woody, formed of a trunk branched into fastigiate divisions, cylindric, rarely simple; branches compressed at the forks, often channelled on one side, sharp or enlarged at the tips; hymenium powdered by the spores, exposed over all the surface or limited to the furrowed portion, which is smooth or tomentose; basidia with 2-4 sterigmata, cystidia none or delicate and scarcely projecting; spores brown, ovoid or tear-shaped, smooth or echinulate. The flesh is homogeneous or with a hardened central axis."

This is considerably more inclusive than Léviellé's genus in regard to the tomentum, which may be present or absent, but more restricted on the other hand by emphasis on the hard, almost woody texture and brown spores. This definition would exclude all species of *Clavaria* from the United States and Canada now placed in *Lachnocladium* by various authors. In a somewhat earlier treatment of the genus (Journ. de Bot. **3**: 23, 33. 1889) he divides it into three sections, as *Lachnocladium* Lév., *Coniocladium* Pat. and *Dendrocladium* Pat., stating that the last two sections should be placed in the *Thelephoraceae*. In his Essai taxonomique he reduced the sections to two, as (A) *Dendrocladium* (spores verrucose, asperulate or aculeate) and (B) *Coniocladium* (spores smooth). As we are treating here only one species of *Lachnocladium* (*Merisma*) we do not think it an appropriate time to reorganize the genus. Numerous new species have been recently described.

## Lachnocladium semivestitum B. & C.   Grevillea **1**: 161. 1873.

### PLATES 78-80 AND 90

Plants tree-like, 2.7-6.3 cm. high, the distinct terete stem about 2 cm. long and 1.3-3.2 mm. thick, branched at top into several more or less compressed leaders which diverge above and rebranch in a somewhat palmate way into several more terete secondaries which may or may not again branch sparingly, the tips when growing blunt, whitish and finely pubescent, after maturity shrinking to a point and becoming darker; color all over pale buffy straw (pale avellaneous) except the tips which after maturity soon wither and become blackish brown. Surface glabrous except the growing tips and somewhat incrassated base, no plush-like sterile areas, the line between the hymenium and the stem not distinct. Texture tough throughout, the stem almost unbreakable by the fingers. In drying the entire plant becomes dull drab except for the dark, cartilaginous-looking tips (as in Nos. 4620, 4626, 4631), or the entire plant may become reddish cartilaginous (as in Nos. 2789, 5270, 5304).

Spores (of No. 4514) white, smooth, subelliptic to amygdaliform, 6-6.8 x 15-18μ, the mucro end curved. Basidia 4-spored (a few 2-spored in other collections and in No. 2789 nearly all were 2-spored), 11-14μ thick, with long sterigmata. Cells of the flesh long, filamentous, very little branched, about 3μ thick, no clamp connections.

This is, we think, the true *L. semivestitum* as shown by the co-type in the Curtis Herbarium from Pennsylvania (Michener, No. 1184; Curtis, No. 4260). The collection consists of two plants, one 4 cm. high; the branches slender, upright; apices reddish cartilaginous, remainder grayish brown; one plant branched into two parts a little above the ground, the other with more stalk; surface without tomentum at any place, appearing, with the exception of the reddish tips, as if dusted superficially with a most minute grayish or yellowish pulverulence. We could find no spores on these plants, but microscopic examination of the co-type at Kew shows it to be in full agreement with ours. Forms of this species (as No. 4631) look in passing much like slender forms of *Tremellodendron,* but are easily distinguished by the absence of viscidity. Burt has seen our No. 2789 and referred it to this species. We have received from Juel (Upsala) as *Thelephora contorta* a collection that seems to be the present species. The spores are long-elliptic with oblique mucro, 6-7.4 x 17-22μ.

It is not easy to believe that all our numbers referred here are the same species. No. 2789 and No. 4514 may be considered extremes of size and of appearance in the dried state. The former when dry is dull drab and opaque except for the tips, the latter is dark cartilaginous throughout except for clay colored stripes. Microscopic characters fail, however, to show any differences that can be associated with those above mentioned, and we are therefore treating them all as the same.

*Lachnocladium cartilagineum* B. & C. (Journ. Linn. Soc. **10:** 330. [1869] 1868) is closely related to the present species, but is easily separated by the spores. From the type at Kew we find them to be subspherical to oval, drop-shaped, smooth, hyaline,

5.5-7.4 x 6.2-8.5μ, with a distinct apical mucro; basidia 2-spored in the several seen (pl. 91, fig. 15). Another difference between that and the present species is the unilateral hymenium, which is plainly shown in our sections of the Kew plant. This is also noted by Patouillard (Journ. de Bot. **3**: 26). *Lachnocladium cartilagineum* is also represented in the Farlow Herbarium by No. 388 of Fungi Cubensis Wrightiani which looks just like the type specimens.

Under the name *L. Micheneri* B. & C. at Cornell are two collections from Ithaca which are *L. semivestitum*. Notes by Atkinson on one of these collections (13354) are as follows: "Trunk and branches dull drab, tips whitish, branches compressed, tips cristate. Basidia clavate, 4-spored. Spores 15-20 x 5-7μ." The dried plants are about 2-3 cm. high, abruptly branched into rather numerous tips which are long and slender. Color when dry buffy tan, not so dark as *C. apiculata* nor so cartilaginous-looking, brittle when dry. One collection is on moss and one on mossy soil. *Clavaria brunneola* B. & C. (Journ. Linn. Soc. **10**: 338 [1869] 1868) is a *Lachnocladium* related to the present species, as shown by the co-type in the Curtis Herbarium. It is, however, not the same, as the spores are subspherical, 7.4-9.5 x 11.5-12.5μ.

We have studied the type of *C. gigaspora* Cotton (The Naturalist, p. 97. 1907; also published in Trans. Brit. Myc. Soc. **3**: 33. 1908) from Kew and find that in all important respects except the thickness of the spores it agrees with the present species, as in size, color and texture in the dry state, and in microscopic details. The spores are large, ovate-elliptic, smooth, 6.5-8.5 x 13.5-18μ; basidia 11-16μ thick, with 4 (rarely 2) large, long, curved sterigmata; hymenium about 150μ thick, packed with crystals; threads of flesh very closely packed, about 3μ thick (pl. 91, figs. 16, 17. That Cotton's species is the same as *Merisma tuberosum* Grev. (Scott. Crypt. Fl. **3**: 178, pl. 178. 1825; *Thelephora tuberosa* Fr. Elench. Fung., p. 167. 1828) in the sense of Bresadola is shown by good specimens in his herbarium from Sweden (R. Fries, coll.). The plants are just like the English ones (and like ours) in appearance and have spores of practically the same shape, which are, according to Bresadola, 6-7 x 16-24μ. It is evident that our plants are the American form of the European plant and the slight spore difference is hardly enough to establish a varietal distinction. *Clavaria tenuipes* B. & Br. (Ann. and Mag. Nat. Hist. II, **2**: 266. 1848) looks much like the present species. The type at Kew is small and simple, with very slender stems expanding into thick clubs which are a little lobed and have the surface appearance of this group. Cotton has a note on the type saying spores "a few, 7 x 3μ," but the spores are doubtful. A related species is *C. dendroides* Jungh. (Fl. Crypt. Java, p. 33, pl. 6, fig. 20, 1838), later changed to *Pterula* (Nova Acta Soc. Sci. Upsala III, **1**: 117. 1855), and also to *Thelephora* by Léveillé (Ann. Sci. Nat. Bot., 3rd. ser., **2**: 209. 1844). If specimens from Java in Persoon's herbarium are correctly determined, which seems probable, it is a *Lachnocladium* in the same group with *L. cartilagineum* and *L. semivestitum*. The basidia are 2-spored, 4-6μ thick; the spores smooth, oval, about 7.4 x 11μ. A collection of plants in the herbarium of the University of Paris labelled *Clavaria compressa* Boud. (herbarium name?) also belongs to the same group. *Lachnocladium chartaceum* Pat. (Ann. Myc. **5**: 365. 1907) from Brazil in the same herbarium has a similar appearance, and so does *L. clavarioideum* Pat. (Journ. de Bot. **3**: 27. 1889), but these last have smaller spores, "6 x 4μ" in the first and "4-5 x 3μ" in the second. In the Kew Herbarium is a plant from Schweinitz (Salem, N. C.) determined by him as *C. palmata* Pers. which is probably the present species, but we could find no spores on it.

Illustration: Burt. Ann. Mo. Bot. Gard. **6**: 272, fig. 10. 1919.
  Greville. As cited above. European form; stout examples.

North Carolina: Chapel Hill. No. 2789. In moss and thin grass under elms, July 26, 1917. A small form 1.5-2.7 cm. high. Spores 4.8-6 x 15-20.2μ; basidia long-clavate, 11-14μ thick, mostly 2-spored, a few 4-spored, the sterigmata stout and curved. No. 4514. By branch, July 25, 1920. No. 4620. Arising from bits of rotting wood on damp, rich soil, July 29, 1920. Spores 6.6 x 15μ; basidia 4-spored, large. No. 4626. By Battle's Branch, August 3, 1920. Spores fusiform, 5.2-6 x 14-15.2μ; basidia 10.6-12.5 x 50-60μ, mostly 4-spored but often only three sterigmata visible. No. 4631. In very damp, sandy soil, August 6, 1920. Spores pure white, 5.5-7 x 17-22μ; basidia about 11 x 30μ. No. 5270. In swampy, deciduous woods, July 2, 1922. Spores 4-6.6 x 13-16.7μ; basidia 4-spored, about 11μ thick. No. 5304. On mossy bank by branch, July 7, 1922. Spores 4-5.5 x 11-19μ; basidia 4-spored.

Pennsylvania: Michener. (Curtis Herb., co-type).

New York: Ithaca. Atkinson. (Cornell Herb., No. 13354, etc., as *L. Micheneri*).

## TYPHULA

Plants small, simple or slightly branched; stalk filiform, flaccid, very distinct [exceptions] from the slender, cylindrical to sub-clavate club which is fleshy or waxy or toughish.   Basidia clavate, 2-4-spored; spores white, smooth.   Growing on dead leaves, twigs or wood or on dead herbaceous stems, in some species springing from a distinct sclerotium.

This genus, like *Clavaria,* is poorly defined and several of the definitive characters are of very slight or no systematic value. The discrete stem is shared by a number of accepted Clavarias and the same species of *Clavaria* may have forms with discrete stems and others without.   Size is a character of difficult application, and growth on vegetable detritus is of questionable importance and cannot be sharply defined.   The result is that a number of species of *Clavaria* are excluded from *Typhula* by only one char-acter, as *C. mucida,* by the stalk not being distinctly marked off; *C. filipes* by growth on soil; *C. subfalcata* by growth on soil and slightly too large size of some specimens; *C. luteo-ochracea* by growth on soil and the gradual fading of the stem into the club; *C. appalachiensis* by too great thickness.   On the other hand, *Typhula phacorrhiza* has been placed in *Typhula* although it has no sharply distinct stem.   *Clavaria juncea* is so like the last species that we are following Karsten in placing them together under *Typhula*.   As we are not undertaking to treat in full other genera than *Clavaria* in this book, we include only these two last men-tioned species of *Typhula*.   We have not seen either of them in the living state.

**Typhula juncea** (Fr.) Karst.   Bidr. Finl. Nat. Folk **37**: 181. 1882.

   *Clavaria juncea* (Alb. & Schw.) Fr.   Syst. Myc. **1**: 479. 1821.
   *Clavaria triunciales juncea* Alb. & Schw.   Consp. Fung., p. 289. 1805.
   *Clavaria hirta.*   Fl. Danica, pl. 1257. 1799.
   *Clavaria juncea* var. *vivipara* Fr.   Epicr., p. 579. 1838.
   *Clavaria virgultorum* Pers.   Myc. Europ. **1**: 186. 1822.

### PLATE 84

Plants single but gregarious in large colonies, very slender and threadlike, about 2-8 cm. high (8-12.5 cm., Cotton), obtuse or acute, equal throughout the club, pale yellowish to leather color, even or crumpled, glabrous or at times finely pubescent all over, with a small clean-cut hollow, the base attenuated, attached by fibrous mycelium and strigose-hairy where protected; texture delicate and soon withering but not fragile or brittle even when dry. Flesh of densely compacted, parallel cells of parenchyma-like appearance in cross section.

Spores of plants from Vaughns, N. Y., white, smooth, oblong to pip-shaped, with a large mucro, 3.8-4.8 x 6-9.3μ (a few up to 10.5μ). Basidia 4-spored, about 6.5μ thick.

Growing among leaves of deciduous trees during very wet weather in northern latitudes. The tomentose form occurs with the smooth and is what is called var. *vivipara* by Fries. Bulliard's figure shows both forms on the same leaves. Harper (Mycologia **10**: 56. 1918) gives the spores of his Michigan plants as 4-5 x 9-12μ, while Schroeter says they are 4-5 x 8-9μ. *Clavaria juncea* is well represented in the Persoon Herbarium by plants of the usual appearance. The type specimens of *C. virgultorum* in the same herbarium show clearly that it is the same as *C. juncea,* but we could get no spores from them. *Clavaria filata* Pers., which is considered a synonym of *Typhula incarnata* Lasch ex Fries by Fries and others, looks in the dry state exactly like this species, but we could find no spores other than small spherical ones that appeared to be those of a mold. A tuber is not mentioned by Persoon. Others have noted the close kinship of this group, and Gillot and Lucand (Cat. Rais. Champ. Sup., p. 439. 1891) treat *T. phacorrhiza* as a variety of *Clavaria juncea.*

Illustrations: Boudier. Icon. Myc. **1**: pl. 176. Photographic copy in Ann. Mo. Bot. Gard. **9**: pl. 10, fig. 98. 1922.
  Britzelmayr. Hymen. Südb., Clavariei, fig. 59.
  Bulliard. Champ. Fr., pl. 463, fig. 2 (as *C. fistulosa*). 1789.
  Cooke. Engl. Fung., pl. 695. 1874.
  Gillet. Champ. Fr. **5**: pl. 105 (111). 1878.
  Harper. Mycologia **10**: pl. 5. 1918.
  Patouillard. Tab. Fung., fig. 469. 1886.
  Sicard. Hist. Nat. Champ., pl. 63, fig. 326. 1883.
West Virginia: Fayette County. Nuttall. (N. Y. Bot. Gard. Herb.).
New York: Fort Edward. (Albany Herb.).
  Vaughns. Burnham. (U. N. C. Herb.).

New Hampshire: Chocorua. Farlow. (U. N. C. Herb. from Farlow Herb.).

California: Pasadena. McClatchie. (N. Y. Bot. Gard. Herb.).

## Typhula phacorrhiza (Reich.) Fr.    Obs. Myc. **2**: 298. 1818.

In form and appearance in the dried state this is scarcely distinguishable from *T. juncea* except for the base, which springs from a flattened disc-shaped, shining brown tuber or sclerotium, the base of the stem just above the tuber being clothed with a rather dense tuft of hair in specimens we have seen.

The clubs are variously described as white or pallid or pale fuscous. The microscopic structure except for the spores is almost identical with that of *T. juncea,* the flesh delicate and flexible and composed of densely compacted, parallel cells, surrounding a small, clean-cut hollow.

Spores (in plants from Portville, N. Y.) elliptic, smooth, hyaline, 4.4-5 x 9-14$\mu$; basidia 4-spored, about 55$\mu$ thick. A good collection from Seattle, Wash., by Murrill has exactly the same appearance and structure; spores 4-5.9 x 9.3-14.8$\mu$; basidia 4-spored, 5.5$\mu$ thick. Of this last Murrill has the following note on the fresh condition: "On leaf mold, gregarious, abundant, about 12 cm. high and 0.5 mm. thick, pale fulvous, shining [arising] from a flattened, double, seed-like sclerotium." This reference to a "double" sclerotium refers to the fact that some (or most) of the plants arise from the margins of two sclerotia, one on each side, and connect them, looking like a shoot between two flat cotyledons. The plants from New York show only one sclerotium to a plant, but this is the only difference we can find except that the Seattle plants are twice the height. We do not know if *T. incarnata* Fr. is really different from the present species. Descriptions lack the detail necessary for a decision. Our plants seem to be just like those shown by Greville in his plate 93 (as *Phacorrhiza filiformis*). Sowerby's plate 233 (as *Clavaria phacorrhiza*) may or may not be the same.

### PTERULA

Slender and filiform throughout, small, in our species much branched from a distinct stalk; texture elastic, toughish, not fragile. Hymenium glabrous, covering the branches. Basidia 2-4-spored; spores white, smooth. Growing on wood or fallen leaves and twigs.

The genus is the same as *Merisma* Lév. (Ann. Sci. Nat. Bot., 3rd. ser., **5**: 157. 1846). See the Genus *Pterula* (C. G. Lloyd. Myc. Notes No. 60: 863. 1919).

This genus is mostly tropical, and only two or three species are known from the United States and Canada. Our Chapel Hill plant can hardly be different from the Schweinitz and Peck species, as the divaricating habit is well shown in some of our specimens and we are very near the place where Schweinitz found his plants. We have not studied the types. *Pterula densissima* B. & C. from New England (Grevillea **2**: 17. 1873) is a much denser plant and is apparently distinct (see Lloyd, l. c., fig. 1469). Lloyd treats as distinct another plant that he calls *C. penicellata* (from a mss. name of Berkeley). *Pterula setosa* Pk. (Rept. N. Y. St. Mus. **27**: 105. 1875) is a minute plant growing on dead *Polyporus elegans*. Patouillard transfers it to *Hirsutella* (see p. 7). We have not seen it. *Pterula multifida* E. P. Fries of Europe has much the same appearance as the present species but is said to grow only on coniferous substrata. *Pterula merismatoides* (Schw.) Sacc. and *P. tenax* (Schw.) Sacc. are both *Tremellodendron* (see Burt, Ann. Mo. Bot. Gard. **2**: 740. 1915 and **9**: 67. 1922).

**Pterula plumosa** (Schw.) Fr.    Linnaea **5**: 532. 1830.
   *Pterula divaricata* Pk.    Rept. N. Y. St. Mus. **32**: 36. 1879.

### PLATE 77

Plants small, slender, brush-like, 2.5-4 cm. high, the slender main stalks about 0.5-1 mm. thick and springing from a distinct, hair-like, grayish brown mycelium; several or many stems arising close together, main branches dichotomously divided about four times into long slender twigs which end in simple sharp points; color of main stems a soaked wood-brown, the remainder of the plant a lighter gray-brown which dries to a light gray or brownish gray; texture not fragile, but elastic and toughish, with a taste like musty wood. As the branches dry they shrink to mere hairs in diameter.

Spores white, elliptic, 3-3.7 x 6.5-7.4μ.

843. On twigs and rotting leaves, by Howell's branch, September 26, 1913.

# THE PLATES

The eight full-color plates (Numbers 1, 9, 19, 23, 28, 39, 50 and 62) are reproduced in a special section following Plate 20.

PLATE 2

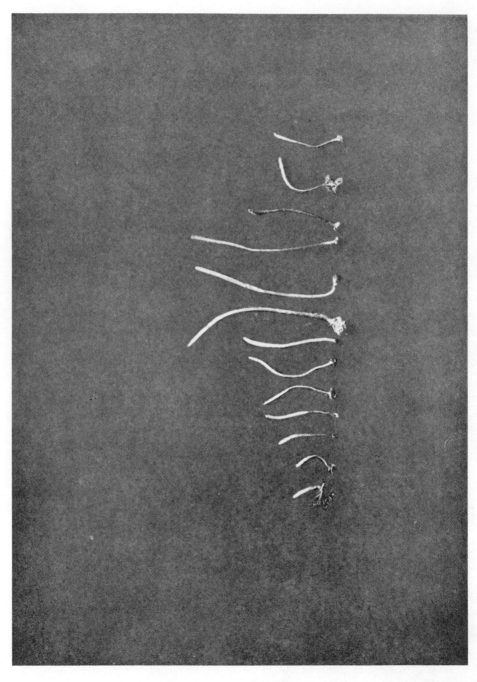

CLAVARIA SUBFALCATA. Blowing Rock. No. 5630.

PLATE 3

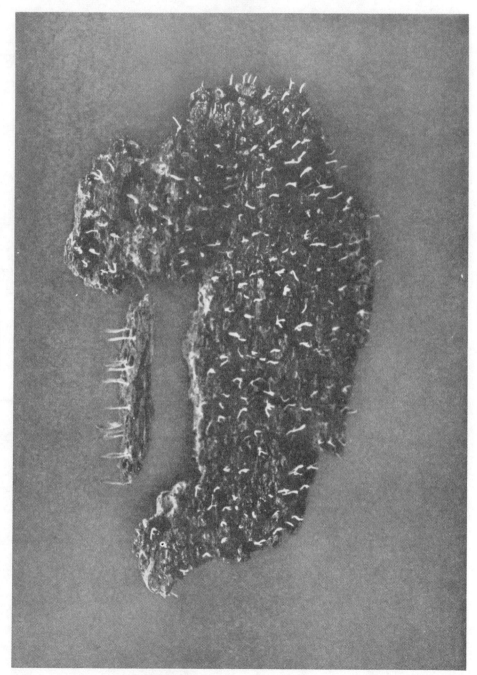

PLATE 4

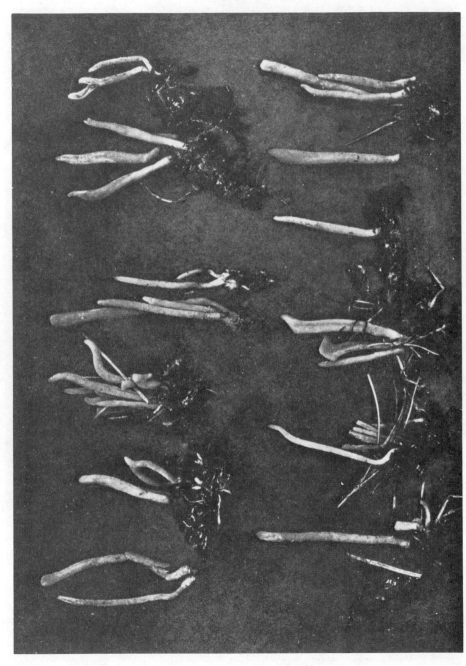

PLATE 5

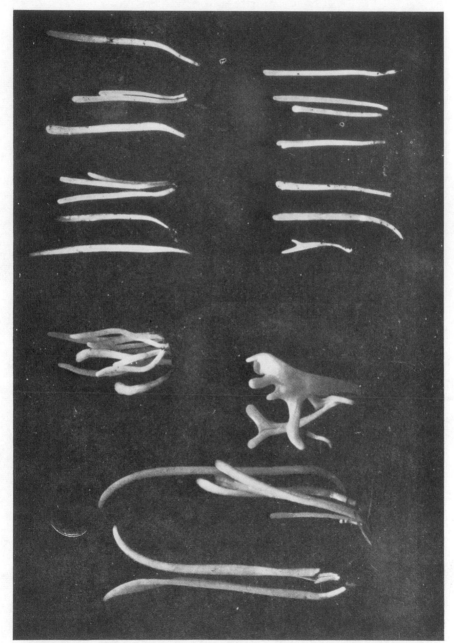

CLAVARIA VERMICULATA. No. 2787 [left]; No. 2751 [right].

PLATE 6

CLAVARIA VERMICULATA. C. & B. No. 130 [above].
CLAVARIA PULCHRA. No. 3149 [below].

PLATE 7

CLAVARIA FUMOSA. No. 2402.

PLATE 8

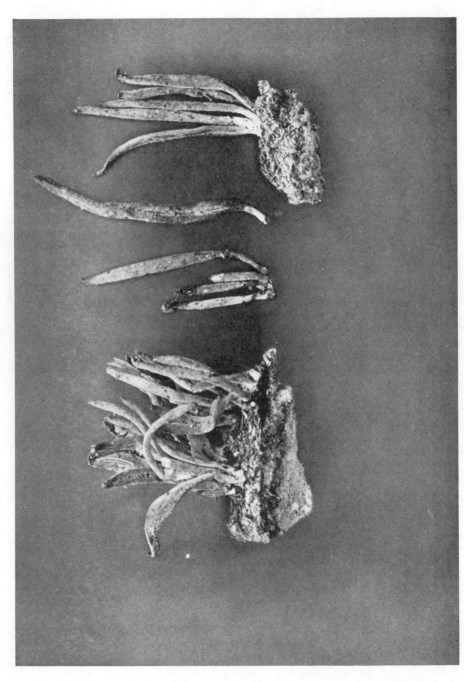

CLAVARIA PURPUREA.   No. 4860.

PLATE 10

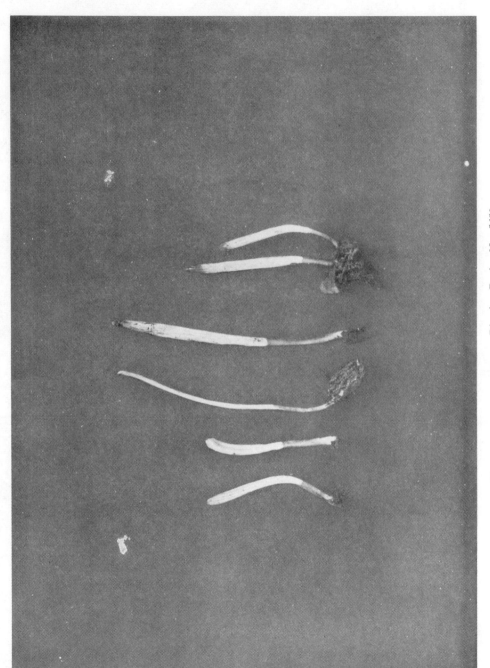

CLAVARIA APPALACHIENSIS. Blowing Rock. No. 5650.

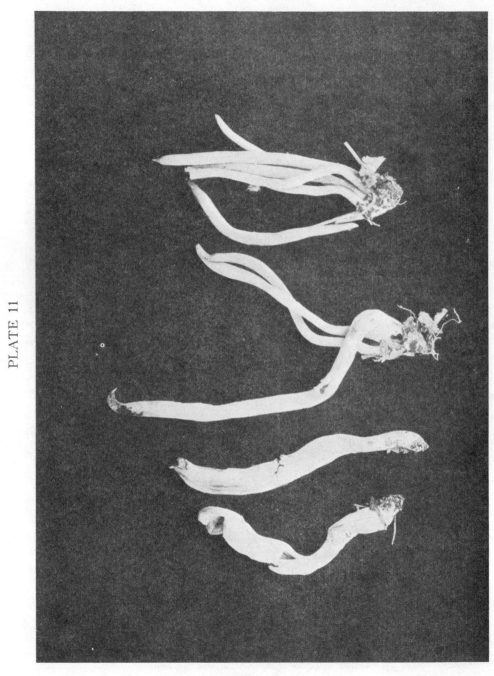

PLATE 11

CLAVARIA FUSIFORMIS. Hartsville, S. C. No. 26.

PLATE 12

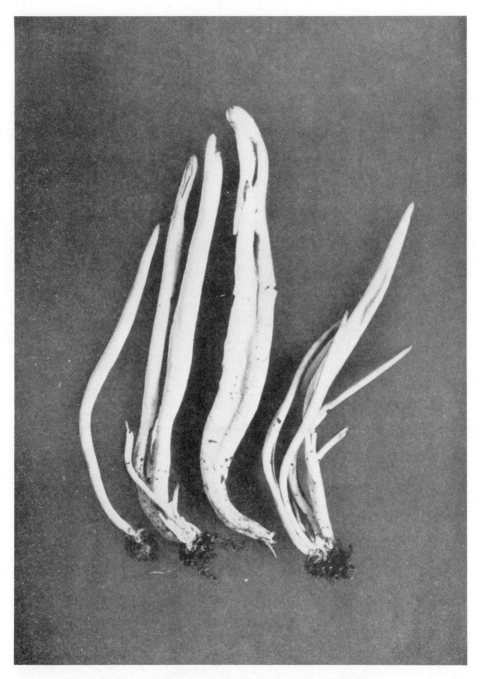

CLAVARIA FUSIFORMIS.   Blowing Rock.   No. 5790.

PLATE 13

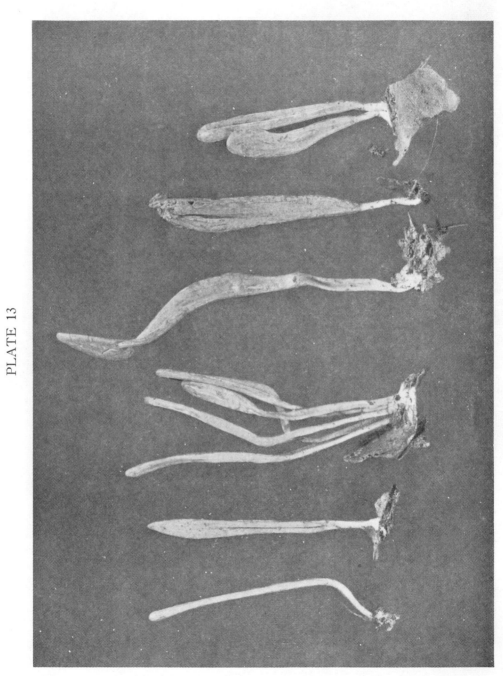

PLATE 14

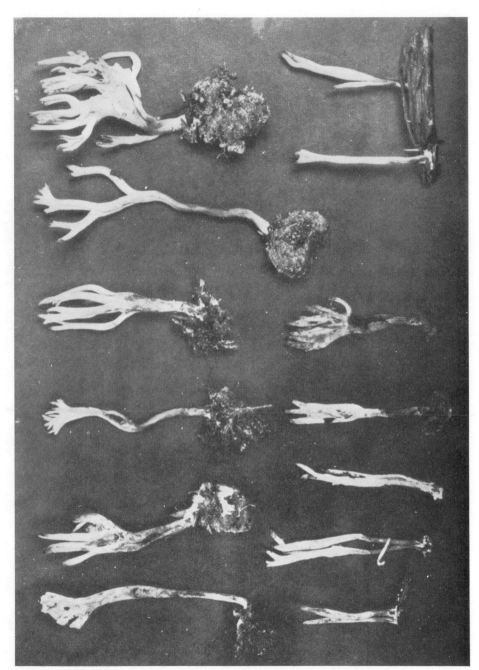

PLATE 15

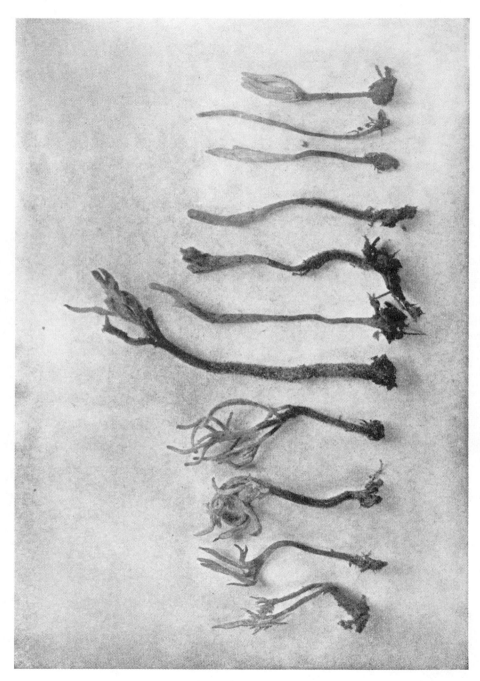

CLAVARIA ORNATIPES. Blowing Rock. No. 5671.

PLATE 16

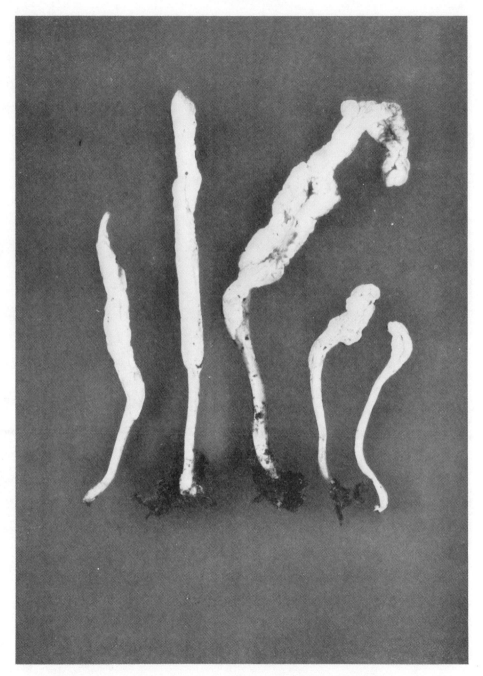

CLAVARIA RUGOSA. Blowing Rock. No. 5812.

PLATE 17

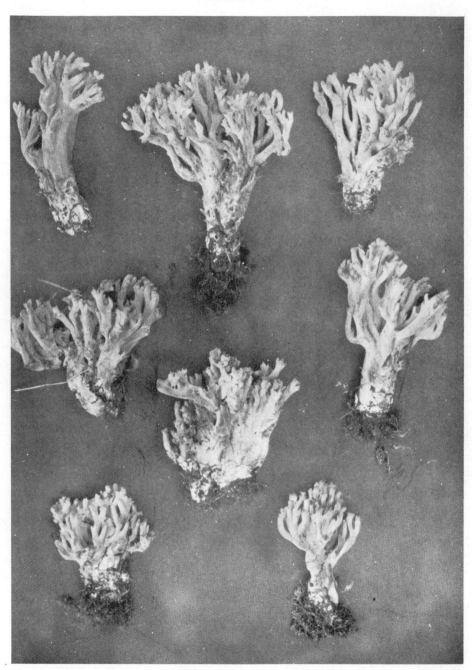

CLAVARIA CRISTATA. No. 2251.

PLATE 18

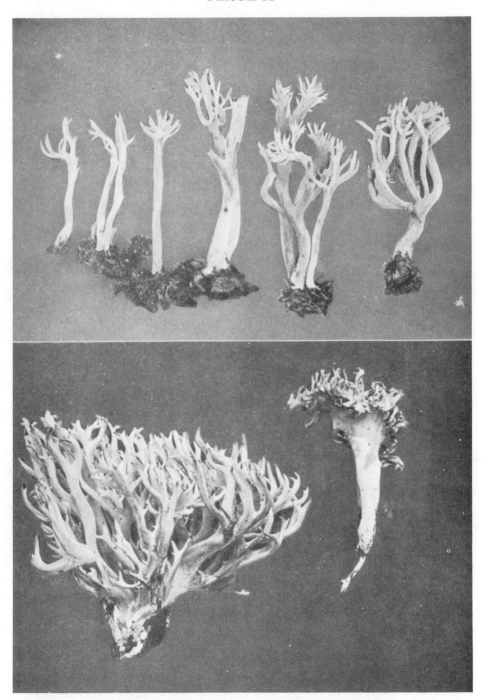

CLAVARIA CRISTATA. No. 2387 [above] ; No. 2660 [below].

PLATE 20

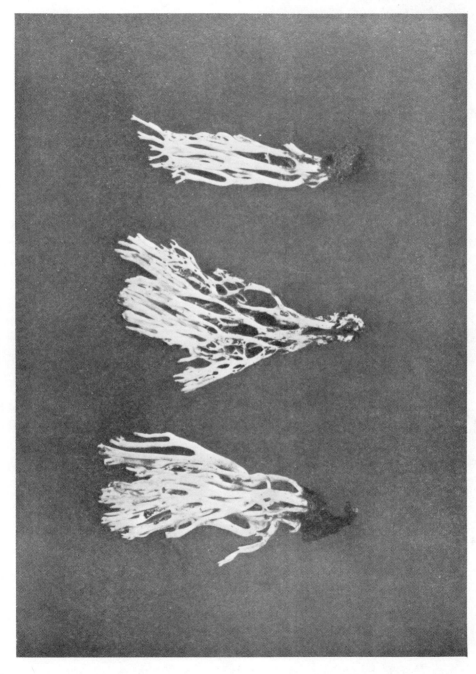

CLAVARIA CINEROIDES. Linville Falls. No. 5751.
Middle figure damaged in development of plate.

PLATE 1

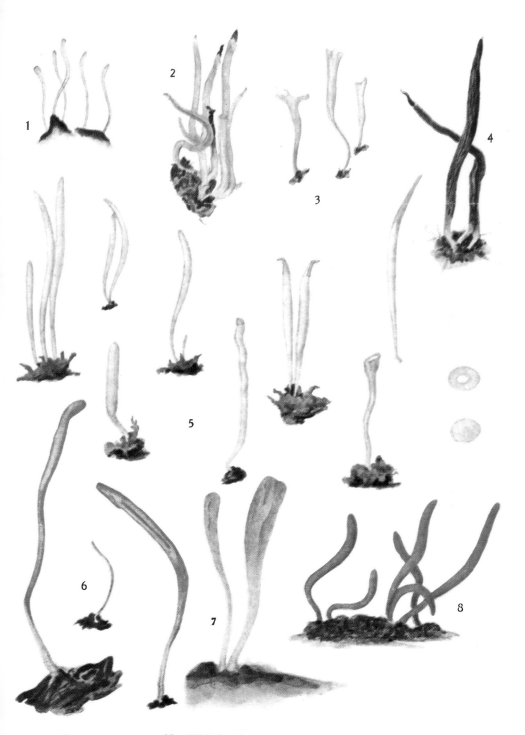

CLAVARIA FILIPES. No. 2804, fig. 1.
CLAVARIA HELVEOLA. No. 4368, fig. 2. (The tip of one plant is too red).
CLAVARIA LUTEO-OCHRACEA. No. 16a, fig. 3.
CLAVARIA NIGRITA. No. 2794, fig. 4.
CLAVARIA CITRICEPS. Redding, Conn., fig. 5.
CLAVARIA PULCHRA. Redding, Conn. (No. 17), fig. 6; Newfane, Vt., fig. 7.
CLAVARIA AURANTIO-CINNABARINA. No. 2801, fig. 8.

PLATE 9

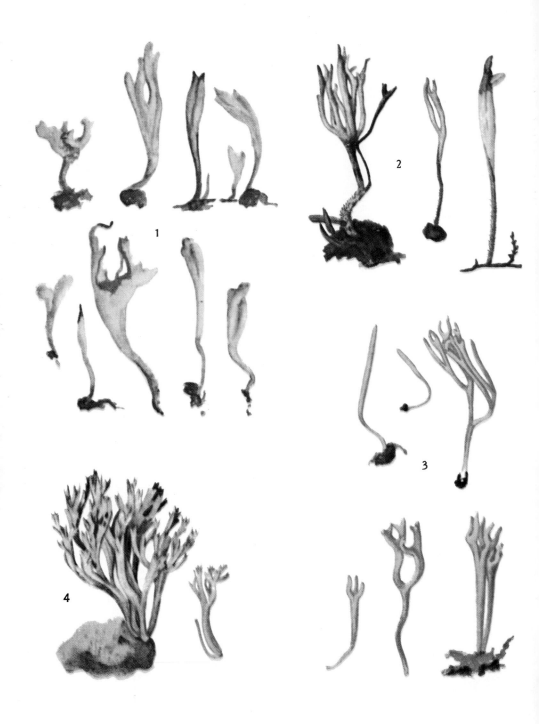

CLAVARIA AMETHYSTINOIDES. Hartsville, S. C. (No. 42), fig. 1.
CLAVARIA ORNATIPES. Redding, Conn. (No. 29), fig. 2.
CLAVARIA MUSCOIDES. Redding, Conn. (No. 20), fig. 3.
CLAVARIA CRISTATA. New York (Murrill), fig. 4.

PLATE 19

CLAVARIA CRISTATA. Newfane, Vt., fig. 1; No. 3293 (*cinerea* form), fig. 2; New York (Murrill), fig. 3; Redding, Conn., (No. 25), fig. 4.

PLATE 39

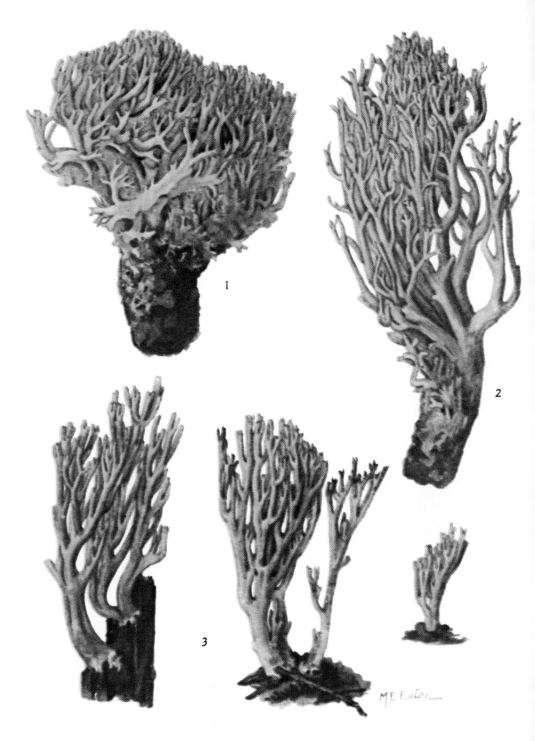

CLAVARIA FLAVA.  Redding, Conn. (No. 26), figs. 1 and 2
CLAVARIA APICULATA.  New York Botanical Garden, fig. 3.

PLATE 50

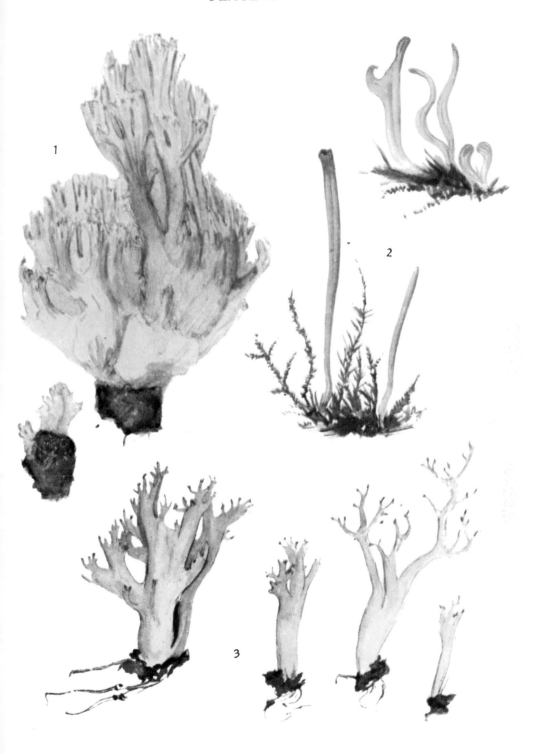

CLAVARIA GELATINOSA. No. 2677, fig. 1.
CLAVARIA SIMILIS Boud. and Pat., from Holland, fig. 2.
CLAVARIA DECURRENS VAR AUSTRALIS. No. 3279, fig. 3.

PLATE 62

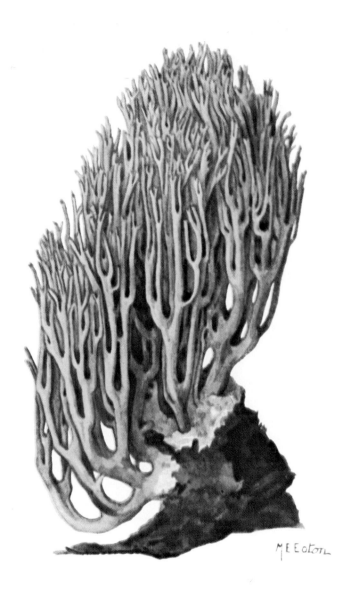

CLAVARIA STRICTA. Redding, Conn.

PLATE 21

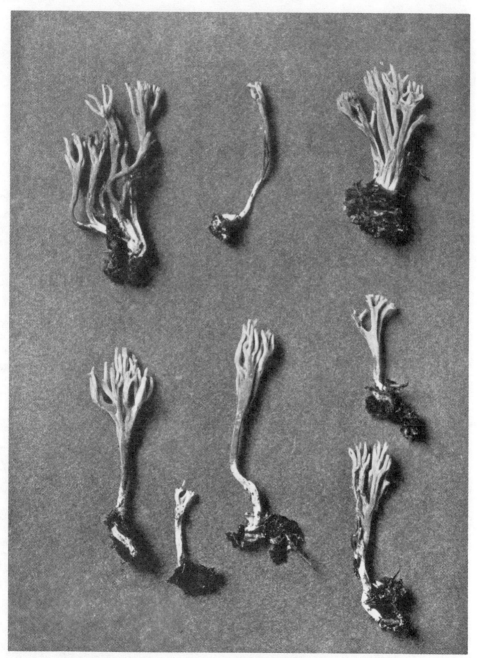

CLAVARIA MUSCOIDES. Lake George, No. 7.

PLATE 22

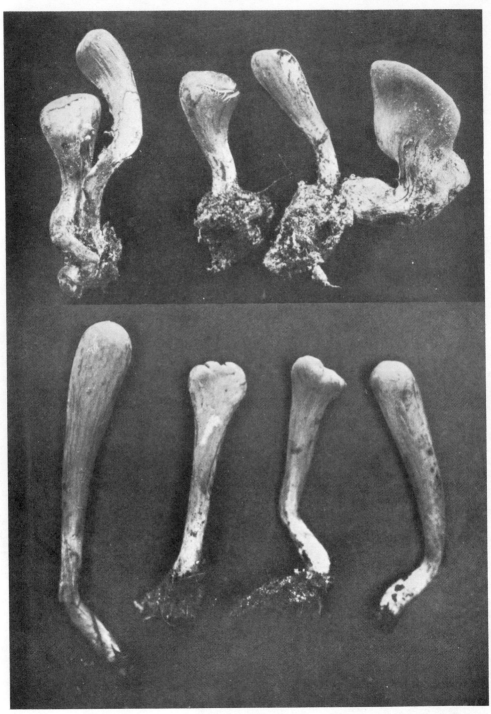

CLAVARIA PISTILLARIS.   No. 1994 [above] ;   No. 1913 [below].

PLATE 24

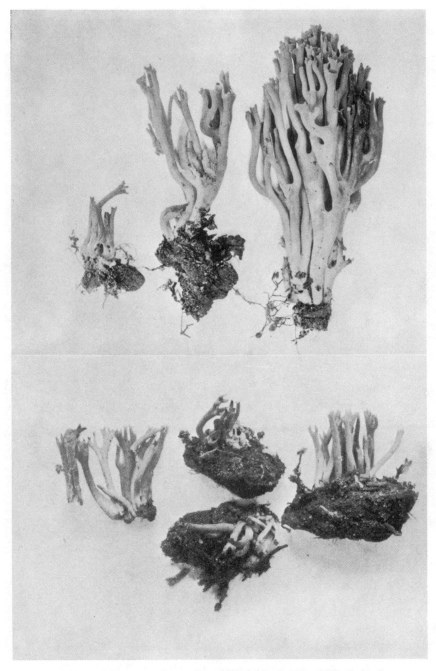

CLAVARIA AMETHYSTINA.  No. 2622 [above]; No. 2282 [below].

PLATE 25

CLAVARIA AMETHYSTINA. No. 4363.

PLATE 26

CLAVARIA PYXIDATA. No. 3103.

PLATE 27

CLAVARIA PYXIDATA. No. 1611.

PLATE 29

CLAVARIA KUNZEL. No. 1704.

PLATE 30

CLAVARIA ANGULISPORA. No. 844.

PLATE 31

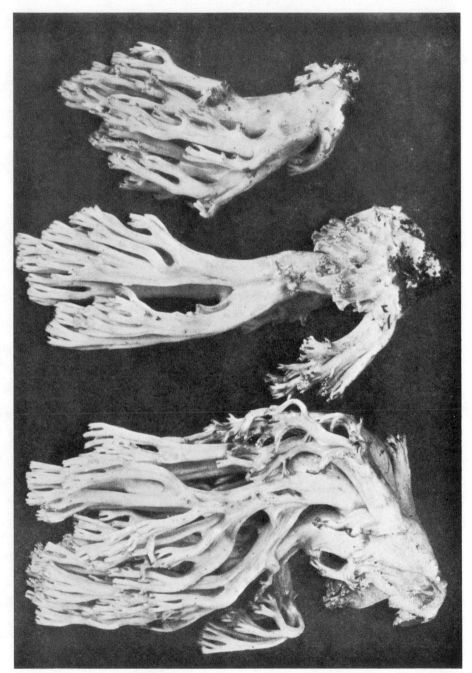

CLAVARIA BOTRYTIS. No. 2395.

PLATE 32

CLAVARIA BOTRYTIS.  No. 2899.

PLATE 33

CLAVARIA SUBBOTRYTIS.  No. 2621.

PLATE 34

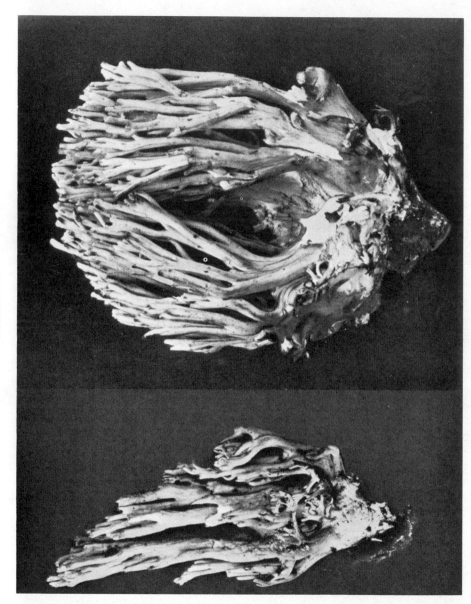

CLAVARIA SUBBOTRYTIS VAR. INTERMEDIA
No. 2847 [right]; No. 2825 [left].

PLATE 35

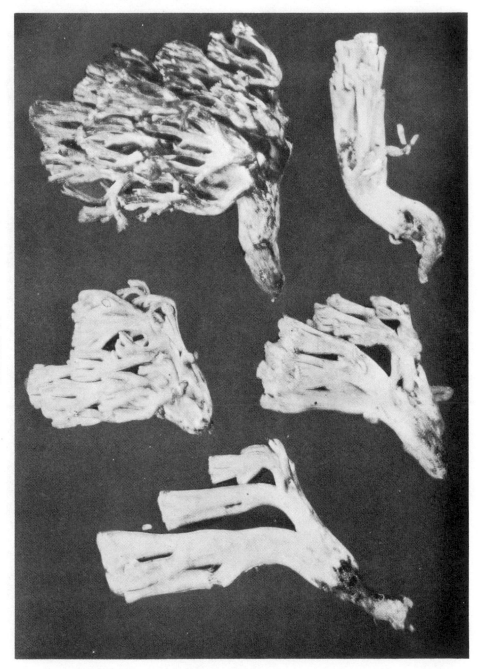

CLAVARIA SANGUINEA. No. 2656.

PLATE 36

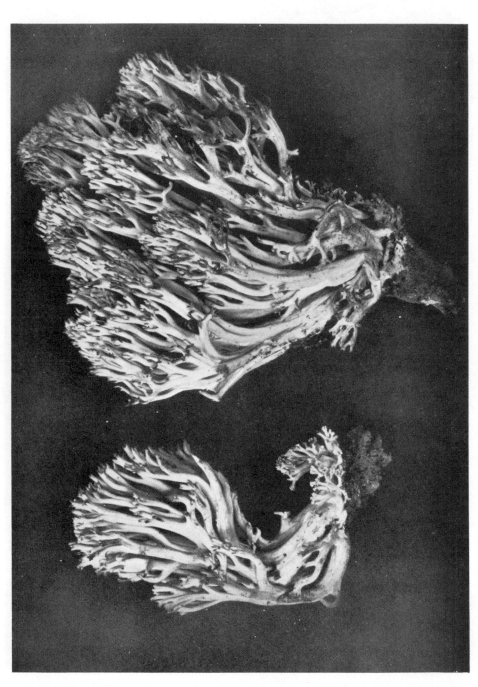

PLATE 37

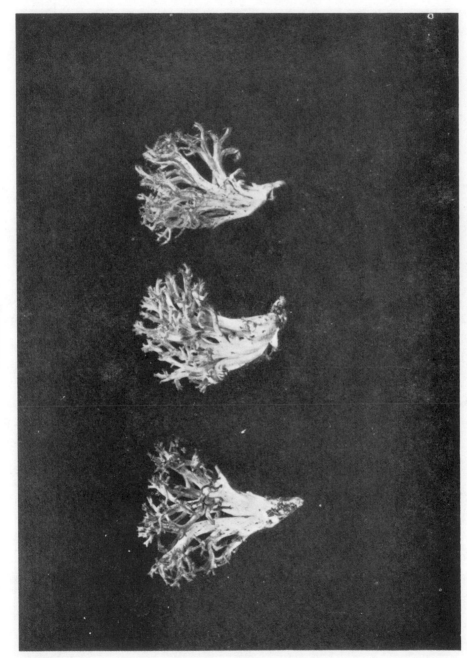

CLAVARIA FLAVA. No. 3150.
[Small pale form].

PLATE 38

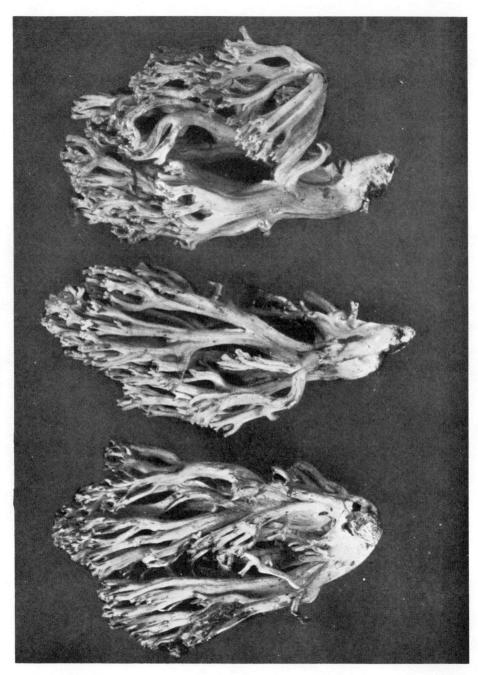

CLAVARIA FLAVA VAR. AUREA.  No. 2851.

PLATE 40

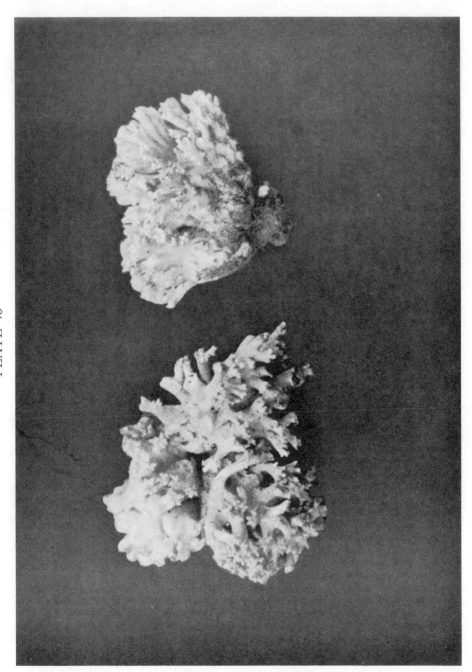

CLAVARIA DIVARICATA. No. 1250.

PLATE 41

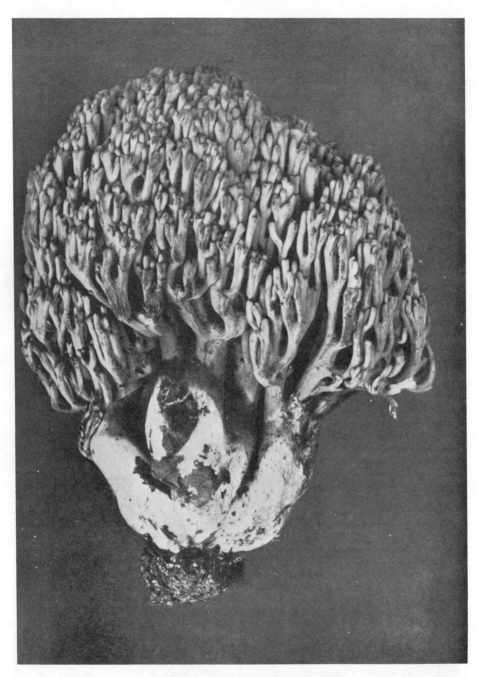

CLAVARIA FORMOSA.  No. 2844.

PLATE 42

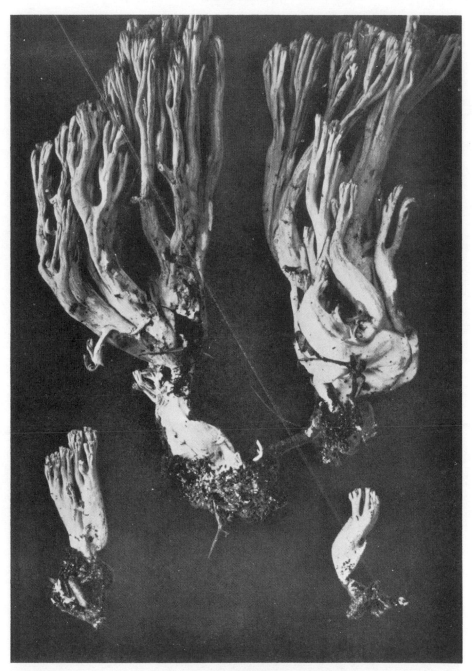

Clavaria formosa.  No. 2826.

PLATE 43

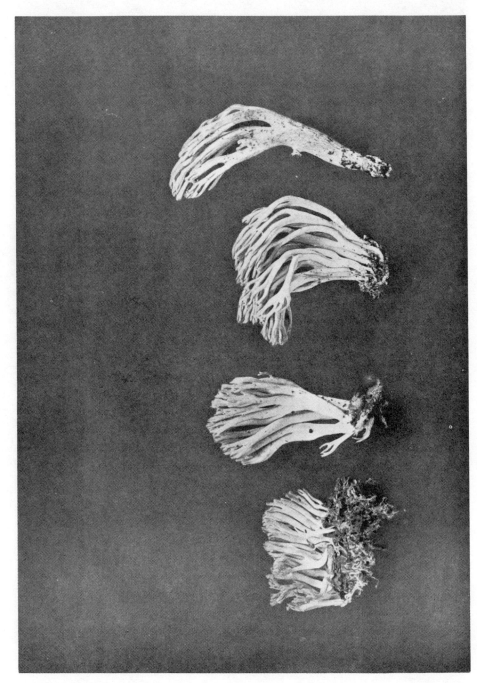

CLAVARIA CONJUNCTIPES. Linville Falls. No. 5732.

PLATE 44

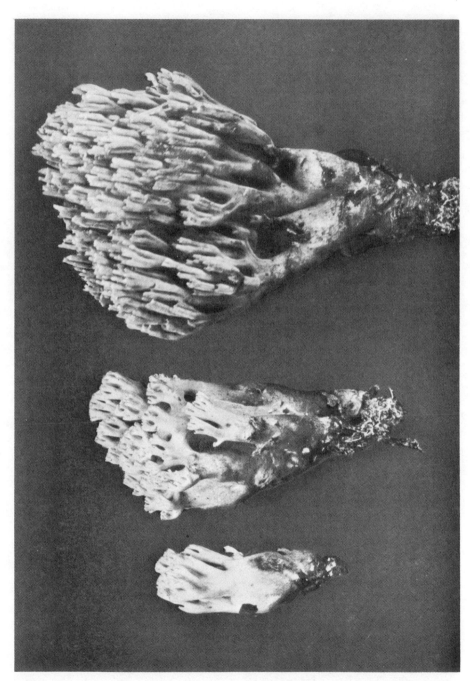

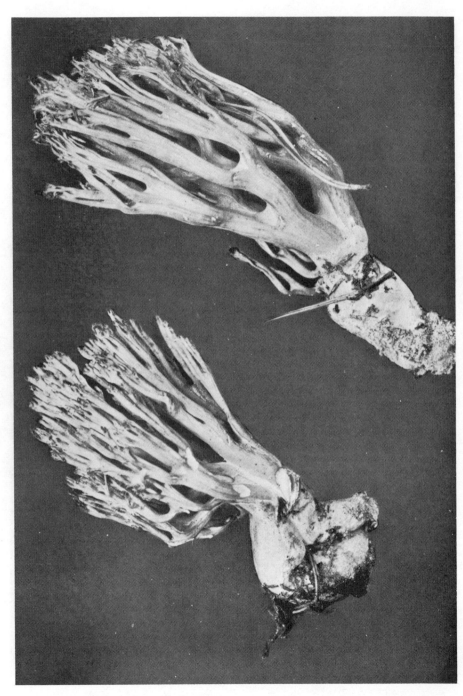

PLATE 45

CLAVARIA SUBSPINULOSA. No. 2653.

PLATE 46

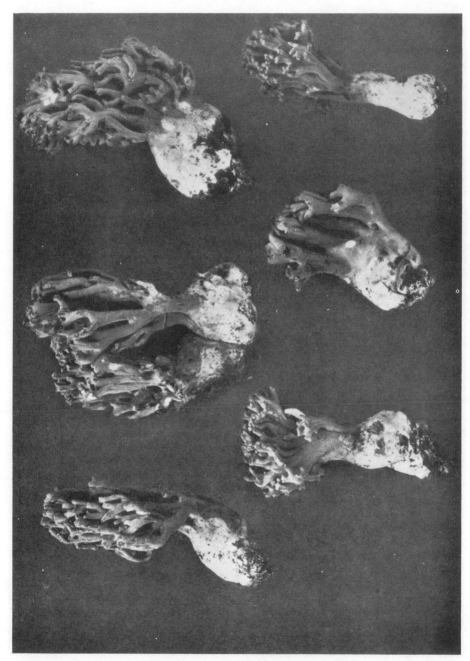

CLAVARIA FENNICA. No. 2857

PLATE 47

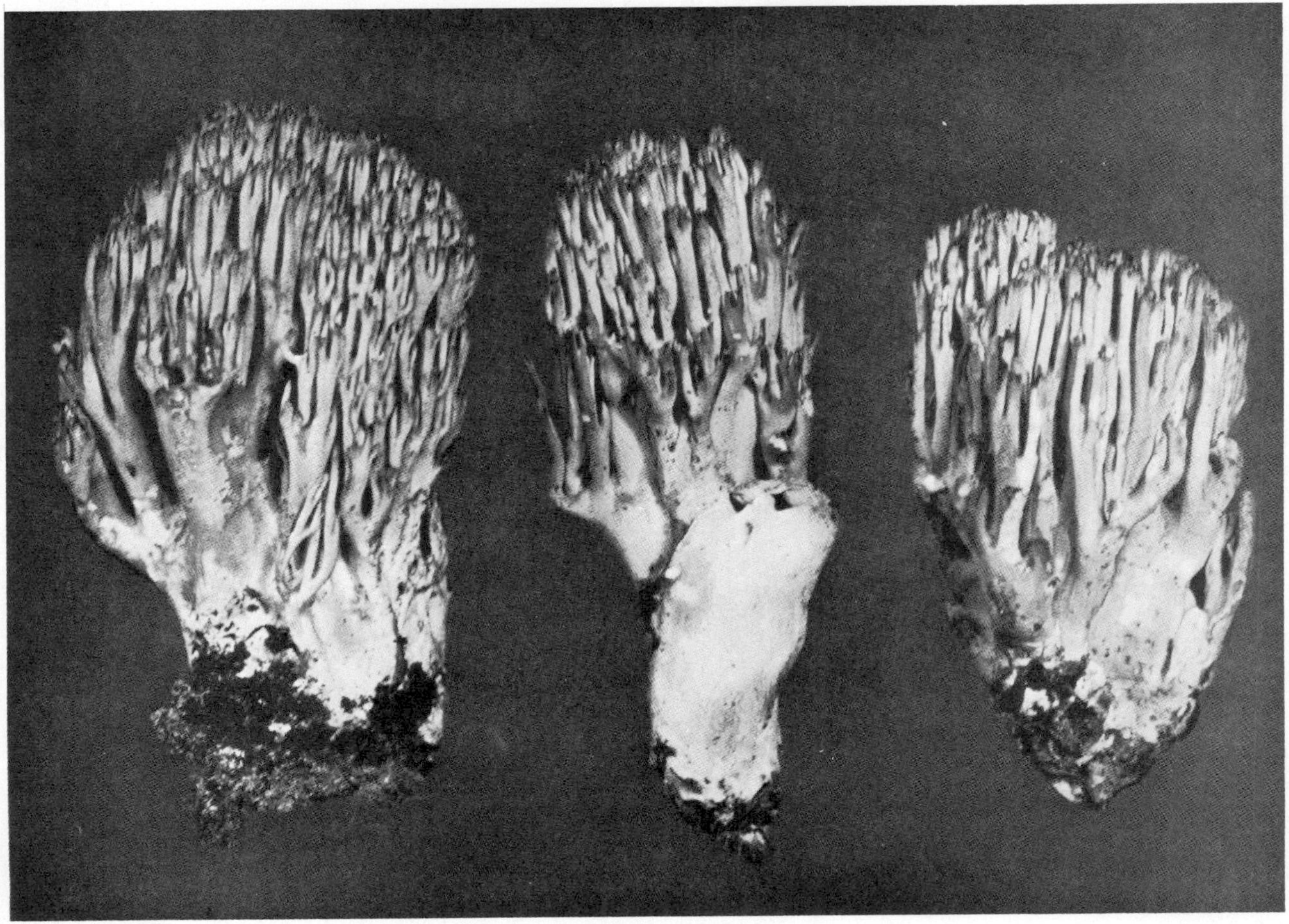

PLATE 48

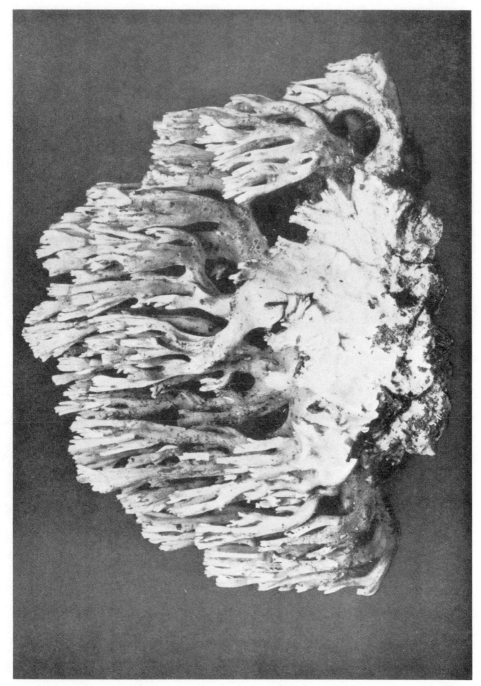

PLATE 49

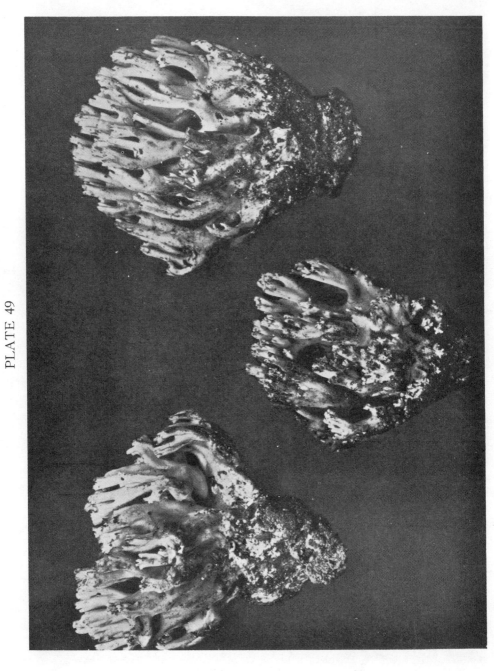

CLAVARIA GELATINOSA. No. 2744.

PLATE 51

CLAVARIA RUFESCENS. No. 2845.

PLATE 52

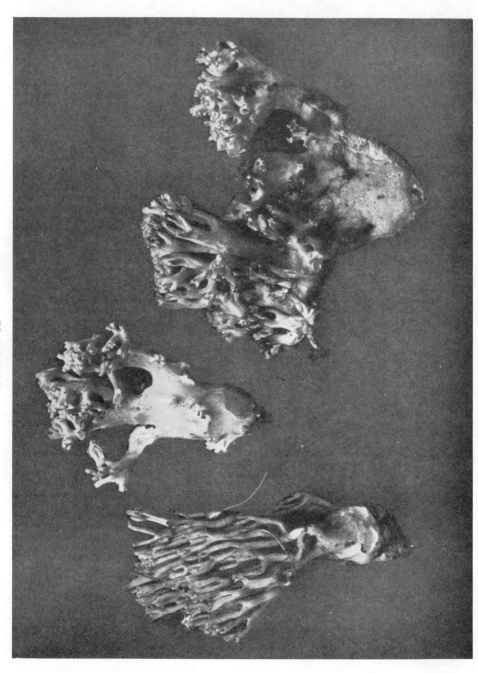

CLAVARIA VERNA. No. 3053 [largest and smallest] ; No. 3068 [medium plant].

PLATE 53

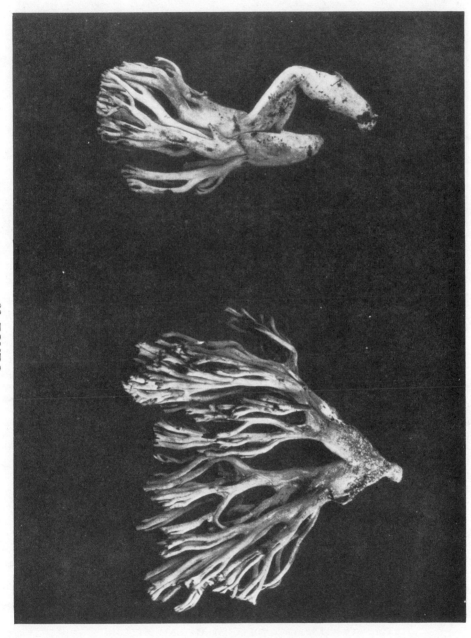

Clavaria aurea var. australis. No. 2913 [left].
Clavaria conjunctipes var. odora. No. 2595 [right].

PLATE 54

CLAVARIA AUREA VAR. AUSTRALIS.  No. 2912.

PLATE 55

Clavaria aurea var. australis. No. 2597.

PLATE 56

CLAVARIA OBTUSISSIMA. No. 2866.

PLATE 57

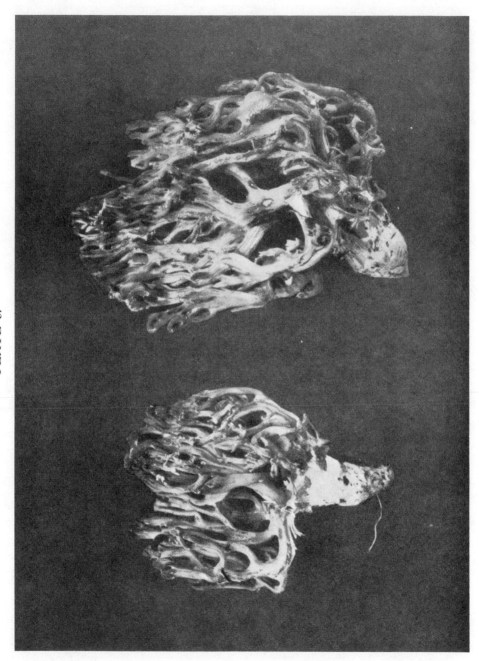

CLAVARIA SECUNDA. No. 2918.

PLATE 58

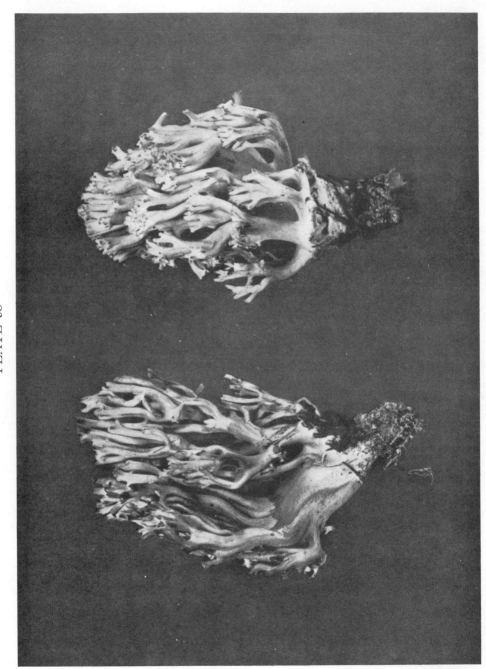

PLATE 59

CLAVARIA BYSSISEDA. No. 4460.

PLATE 60

Clavaria Patouillardii.  C. & B. No. 101a [lower left fig.]
Clavaria byssiseda.  C. & B. No. 113 [all other figs.].

PLATE 61

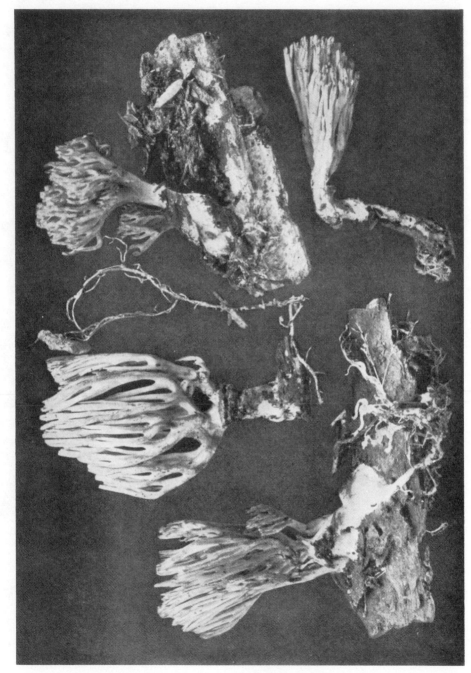

Clavaria stricta.  No. 1228.

PLATE 63

CLAVARIA SUECICA.  C. & B. No. 118 [above]; B. No. 19 [below].

PLATE 64

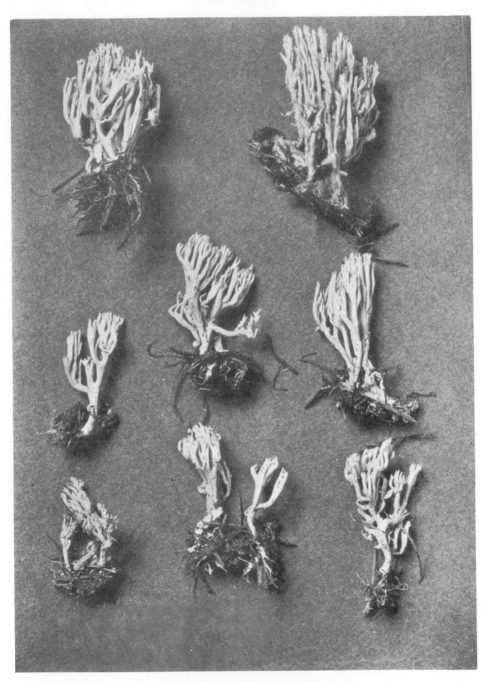

CLAVARIA GRACILIS. No. 6.

PLATE 65

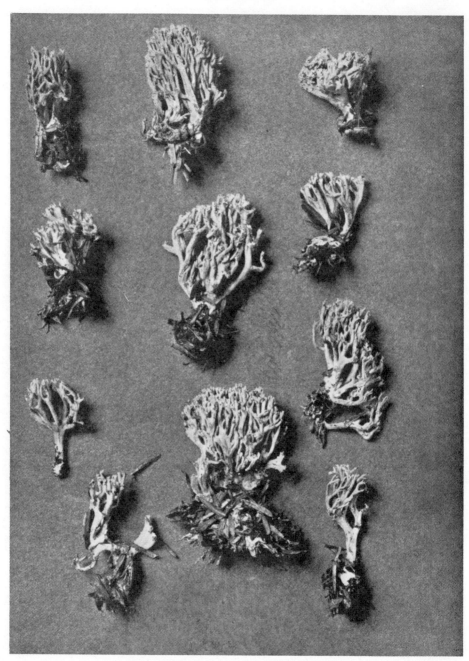

CLAVARIA SUBDECURRENS. C. & B. No. 101.

PLATE 66

CLAVARIA DECURRENS. C. & B. No. 120.

PLATE 67

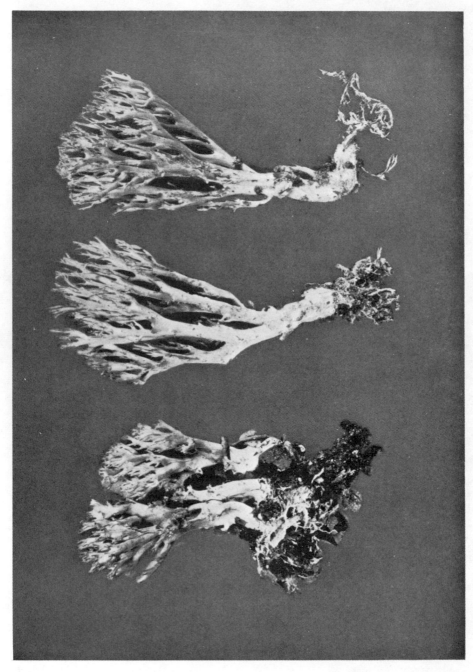

CLAVARIA DECURRENS VAR. AUSTRALIS. No. 3116.

PLATE 68

CLAVARIA ABIETINA. C. & B. No. 132.

PLATE 69

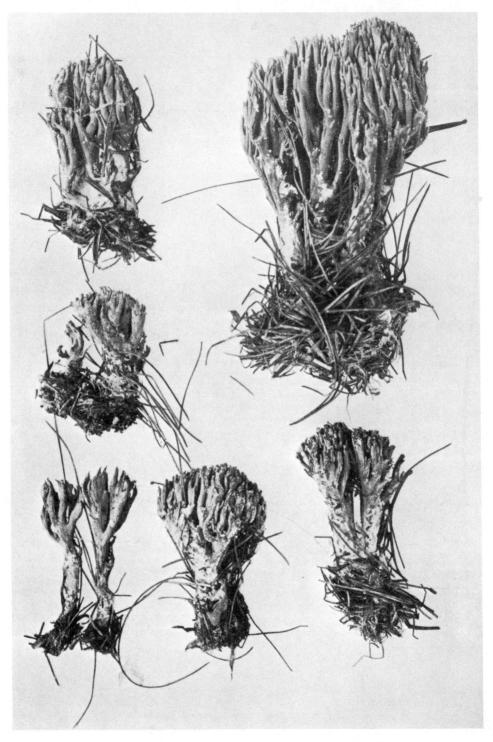

CLAVARIA ABIETINA. Large form of pines. B. No. 91.

PLATE 70

CLAVARIA ABIETINA, FLACCIDA FORM.   C. & B. No. 102.

PLATE 71

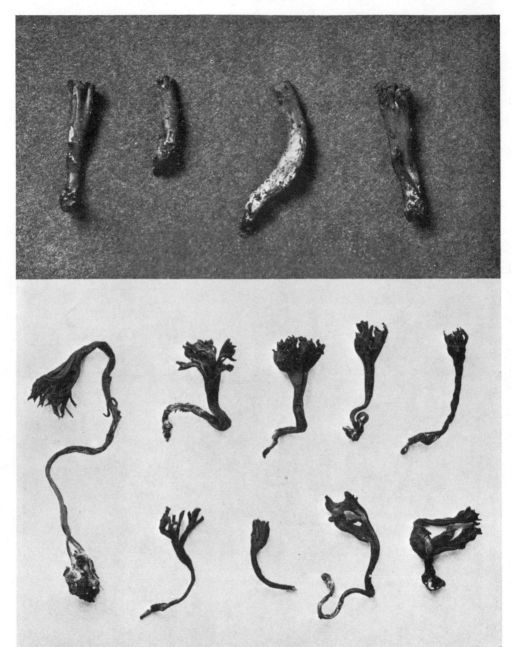

CLAVARIA BROOMEI. C. & B. No. 141 [above]; B. No. 74 [below, photographed when nearly dry].

PLATE 72

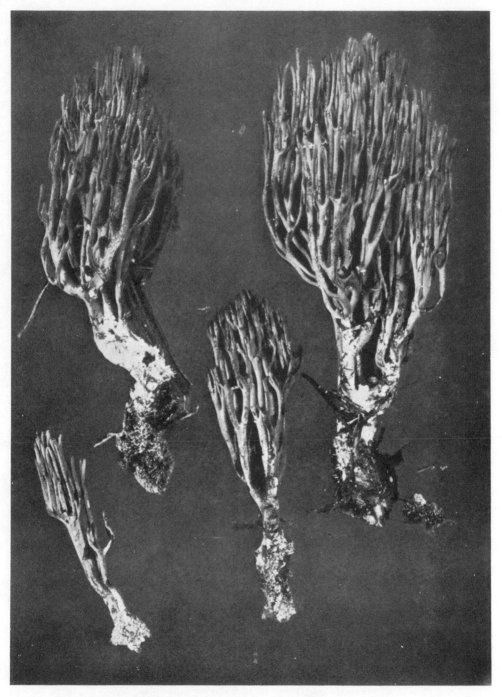

CLAVARIA LONGICAULIS.   No. 2814.

PLATE 73

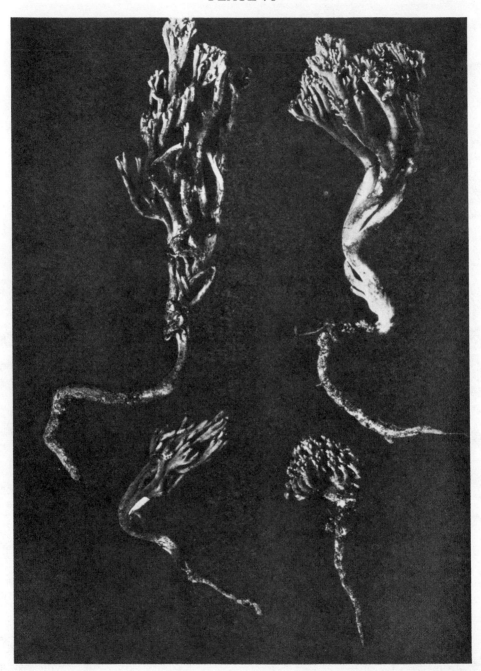

CLAVARIA LONGICAULIS, FORM WITH RHIZOID.   No. 2730.

PLATE 74

CLAVARIA LONGICAULIS, FORM WITH RHIZOID. No. 2648.

PLATE 75

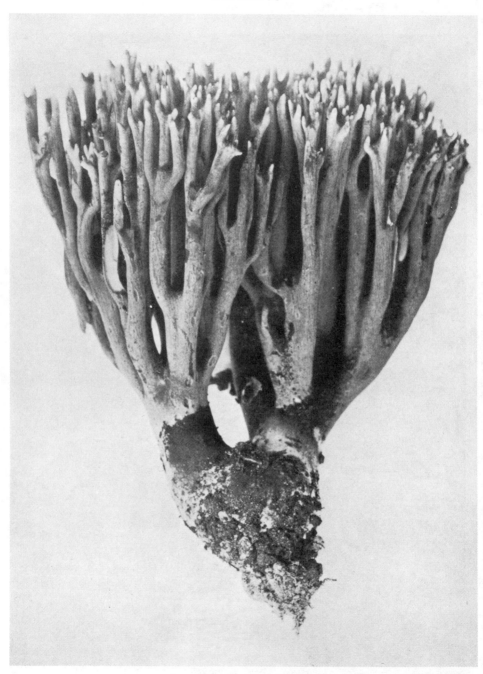

CLAVARIA CRANDIS.   No. 2734.

PLATE 76

CLAVARIA GRANDIS. No. 2398.

PLATE 77

PTERULA PLUMOSA. No. 843 [above].
CLAVARIA MURRILLI. Unaka Springs, Tenn., No. 907 [below].

PLATE 78

LACHNOCLADIUM SEMIVESTITUM. No. 2789.

PLATE 79

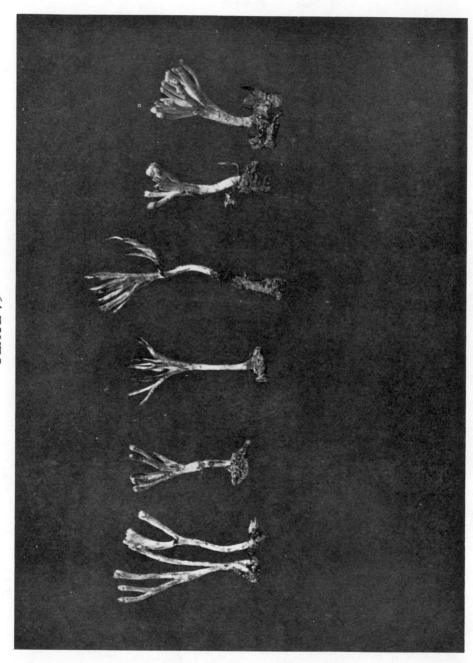

PLATE 80

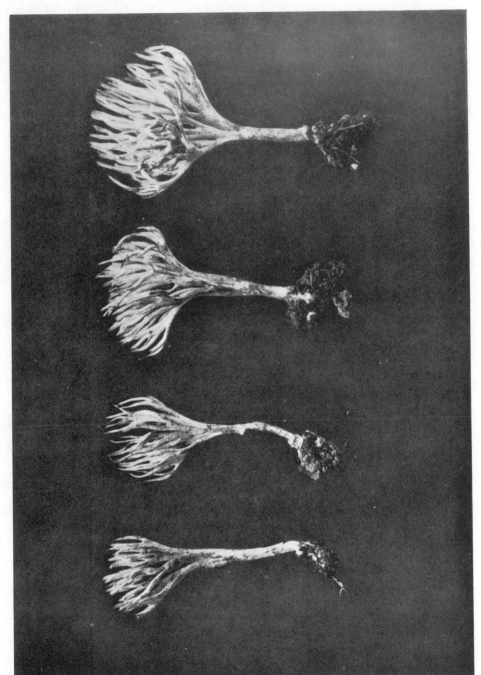

LACHNOCLADIUM SEMIVESTITUM. No. 4514.

## PLATE 81

C. filipes. No. 2806, figs. 1 and 2; type, fig. 3.

C. subfalcata. Blowing Rock, N. C. (Atkinson, co-type, No. 10689), fig. 5.

C. fuscata. No. 3459, fig. 4; Amsterdam (type locality, Miss Cool), figs. 6 and 7.

C. acuta. England (Cotton), fig. 8.

C. argillacea. Darbyshire, England, fig. 9; Savigné, France (Herb. Univ. Paris, as *C. obtusata*), fig. 11.

C. pallescens. Type, fig. 10.

C. helveola. No. 2818, fig. 12; No. 4368, figs. 13 and 14.

C. luteo-alba. Dolgelly, England (Cotton, Kew Herb.), fig. 15.

C. rosea. Nice (Bresadola), figs. 16 and 17; Persoon Herb. (no data), fig. 18; New York (Burnham, No. 44), fig. 19.

C. asperulospora. Type fig. 20.

C. inaequalis. Epping Forest, England (Cotton), figs. 21 and 22.

C. mucida. No. 3579, figs. 23 and 24; Stockholm, Sweden (Rommell), fig. 25.

Fig. 2 x 502; figs. 14 and 24 x 810; figs. 7 and 16 x 1012; fig. 21 x 562; others x 1620.

PLATE 81

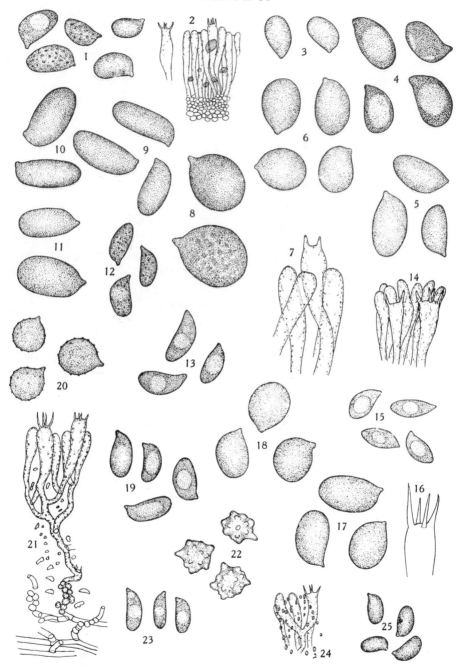

## PLATE 82

C. vernalis.  Lake Pleasant, N. Y., fig. 1.

C. nigrita.  No. 2794, figs. 2 and 3.

C. citriceps.  Redding, Conn. (No. 3428), fig. 4.

C. vermiculata.  No. 2773, fig. 5; Vaughns, N. Y. (C. & B. No. 130), fig. 6.

C. fumosa.  No. 2402, fig. 7; No. 2815, fig. 8.

C. purpurea.  No. 4860, figs. 9 and 10; Sweden (Romell), fig. 11.

C. nebulosa.  Newfoundland (co-type), figs. 12 and 13.

C. fusiformis.  No. 1362, fig. 14.

C. persimilis.  South Wales (Cotton), fig. 15.

C. pulchra.  Lake George, N. Y. (No. 22), fig. 16; type, fig. 17; No. 1717,
fig. 18.

C. aurantio-cinnabarina.  Bethlehem, Pa. (Schweinitz), fig. 19; No. 2801,
figs. 20 and 21; Cold Spring Harbor, L. I., fig. 22.

C. amethystinoides.  No. 4532, figs. 23 and 24; Hartsville, S. C. (No. 42),
fig. 25.

Figs. 2, 6, 16, 21, 23, 24 x 810; fig. 8 x 562; fig. 10 x 487; fig. 13 x 1012;
fig. 22 x 502; others x 1620.

PLATE 82

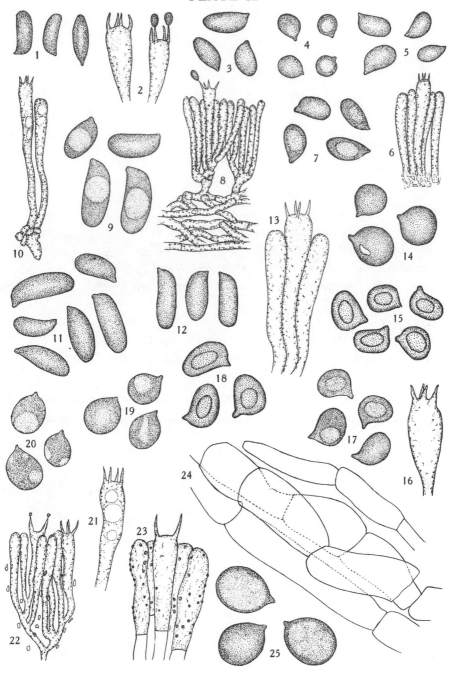

## PLATE 83

C. ornatipes.   Redding, Conn. (No. 29), figs. 1 and 2.

C. amethystinoides.   Type, fig. 3.

C. cristata.   No. 2387, fig. 4; No. 4561, figs. 6 and 7.

C. compressa.   Schweinitz Herb. (now in Curtis Herb.), fig. 5 (showing only 2-spored basidia).

C. cineroides.   Type, figs. 8 and 11; Tripoli, N. Y. (No. 99), figs. 9 and 10.

C. muscoides.   Lake George, N. Y. (No. 7), fig. 12; Tripoli, N. Y., fig. 13.

C. pistillaris.   No. 1913, fig. 14; No. 3793, fig. 15; Redding, Conn. (No. 27), fig. 16; No. 3885, fig. 17.

Fig. 2 x 502; figs. 5-7, 13, 17 x 810; figs. 10 and 11 x 1012; others x 1620.

PLATE 83

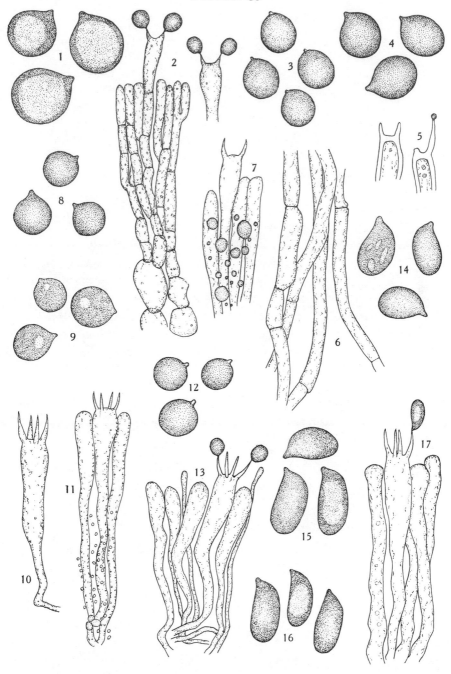

PLATE 84

C. ligula.  Adirondacks, N. Y. (Murrill), figs. 1 and 2.

C. fistulosa.  Europe (Bresadola, as *C. contorta*), fig. 3.

Typhula juncea.  Vaughns, N. Y. (Burnham), fig. 4.

C. amethystina.  No. 2622, fig. 5.

C. pyxidata.  No. 1875, fig. 6; No. 3593, fig. 7 ( hymenium, basidia and a cystidium).

C. asperula.  Ithaca, N. Y. (Atkinson), fig. 8.

C. Kunzei.  Vaughns, N. Y. (Burnham, No. 111), fig. 9; No. 1704, fig. 10; Vaughns (Burnham, in Albany Herb.), fig. 11; Vaughns (Burnham, No. 59a), fig. 12 (hymenium apparently 2-layered by proliferation); Monengo Creek, N. Y. (Schweinitz Herb., as *C. subcorticalis*), fig. 13; Newfield, N. J. (E. & E., Cornell Herb., as *C. velutina*), fig. 14; Swansea, England (Cotton), fig. 15; Vaughns (Burnham, No. 40), fig. 16; Pink Bed Valley, N. C. (Murrill and House), fig. 17; Upsala, Sweden, (Th. M. Fries), fig. 18.

C. subcaespitosa.  Type, fig. 19.

C. angulispora.  No. 844, fig. 20; No. 3442, fig. 21.

Lachnocladium dubiosum.  Type, fig. 22.

C. lentofragilis.  Type, figs. 23 and 24.

C. asterella.  Type, fig. 25.

C. crocea.  Redding, Conn. (No. 21), fig. 26; No. 4843, fig. 27; No. 4660, fig. 28.

C. tenuissima.  Type, fig. 29.

C. bicolor.  Type, fig. 30.

Figs. 2, 7, 12 x 502; figs. 16, 17, 27 x 1012; figs. 21, 28 x 810; others x 1620.

PLATE 84

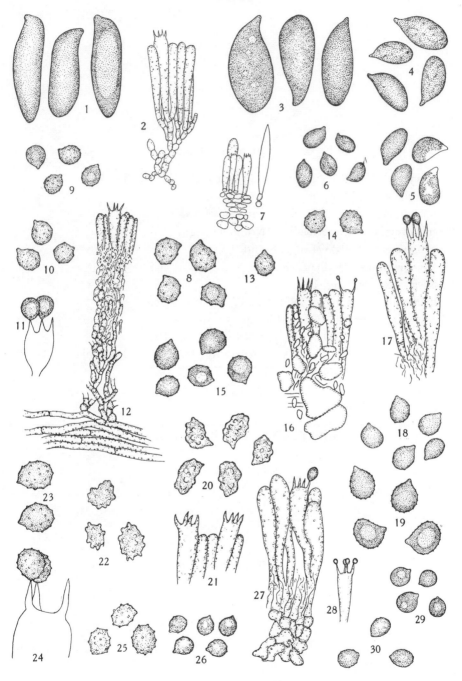

PLATE 85

C. botrytis.   No. 661, fig. 1; No. 2395, fig. 2; No. 74, fig. 3.
C. botrytoides.   Type, fig. 4.
C. subbotrytis.   No. 2621, figs. 5 and 6.
C. subbotrytis var. intermedia.   No. 2847, fig. 7.
C. sanguinea.   No. 4394, figs. 8 and 9.
C. flavobrunescens.   Type, fig. 10.
C. flava.   No. 560, fig. 11.
C. flava var. aurea.   No. 2851, fig. 12.
C. flava var. subtilis.   No. 2843, figs. 13 and 14.
C. divaricata.   No. 3037, fig. 15; No. 3063, fig. 16.
C. secunda.   Co-type, fig. 17; No. 2876, fig. 18; Italy (Bresadola, N. Y. Bot.
      Gard. Herb., as *C. pallida* Schaeff.), fig. 19.
C. flavula.   Type, fig. 20.
C. crassipes.   Type, fig. 21.

Figs. 9 and 14 x 810; figs. 3, 5, 16 x 1012; others x 1620.

PLATE 85

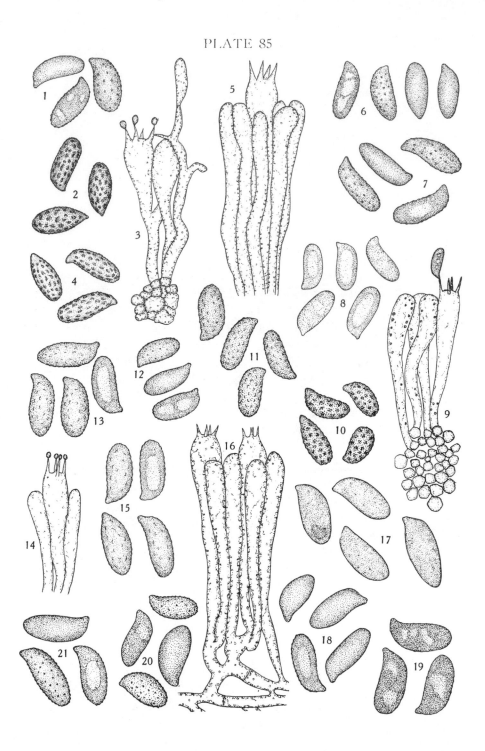

## PLATE 86

C. formosa.   No. 543, fig. 1; No. 4636, fig. 2.

C. conjunctipes var. odora.   No. 2595, fig. 3.

C. subspinulosa.   No. 2664, fig. 4; No. 4635, fig. 5; Italy (Bresadola, N. Y. Bot. Gard. Herb., as *C. spinulosa*), fig. 6.

C. fennica.   No. 620, fig. 7; No. 486, fig. 8.

C. gelatinosa.   No. 2413, fig. 9; No. 4397 (threads of flesh), fig. 10.

C. verna.   No. 3039, fig. 11; No. 3053, fig. 12.

C. xanthosperma.   Type, fig. 13.

C. rufescens.   No. 2862, fig. 14; No. 2877, fig. 15.

C. holorubella.   Type, fig. 16.

C. aurea.   Sopramento (Bresadola Herb.), fig. 17.

Fig. 10 x 502; fig. 5 x 810; figs. 2, 7, 11, 14 x 1012; others x 1620.

PLATE 86

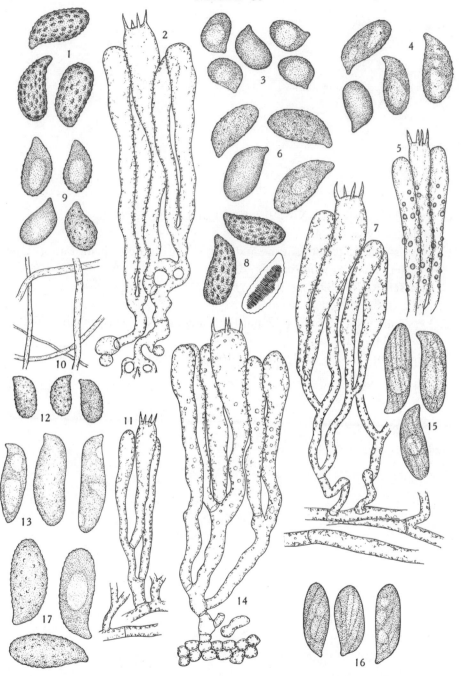

## PLATE 87

C. aurea var. australis.   No. 2912, figs. 1 and 2; No. 2597, fig. 3.

C. albida.   Type, fig. 4.

C. obtusissima.   No. 2866, figs. 5 and 6; type, fig. 7; Bethlehem, Pa.   (Schw. Herb., as *C. spinulosa*), fig. 8.

C. Strasseri.   No. 2897, fig. 9.

C. cacao.   No. 2926, figs. 10 and 11.

C. byssiseda.   No. 4395, figs. 12 and 13; Vaughns, N. Y. (Burnham, No. 90). fig. 14.

   Figs. 1, 6, 11, 12 x 1012; others x 1620.

PLATE 87

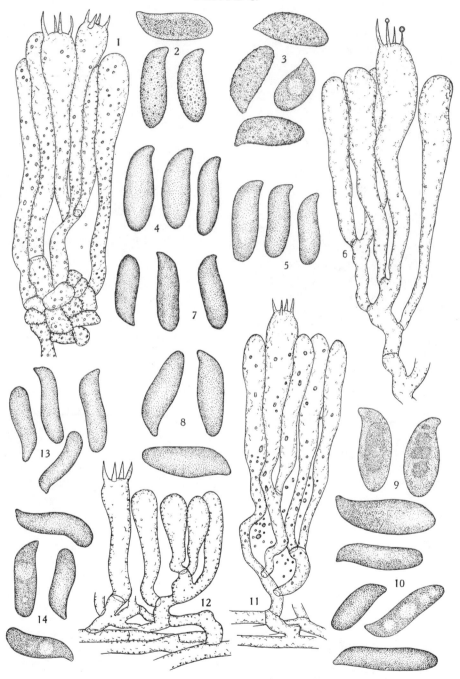

PLATE 88

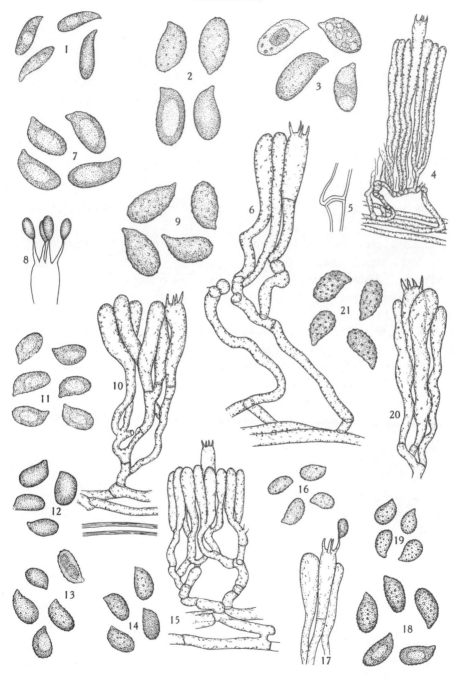

PLATE 89

C. subdecurrens.  Vaughns, N. Y. (C. & B. No. 111), figs. 1 and 2.
C. abietina.  Type, fig. 3; Upsala, Sweden (Fries in Curtis Herb.), fig. 4;
    Vaughns, N. Y. (C. & B. No. 110), fig. 5.
C. abietina, non-virescent form of pines.  Vaughns, N. Y. (Burnham, No.
    91), figs. 6 and 7.
C. suecica.  Lake George, N. Y. (No. 19), figs. 8 and 9.
C. circinans.  Type, fig. 10.
C. acris.  Type, fig. 11.
C. longicaulis, form with rhizomorph.  No. 4416, fig. 12; No. 866, fig. 13.
C. megalorhiza.  Type (No. 197), fig. 14.
C. Broomei.  Vaughns, N. Y. (Burnham, No. 98), fig. 15; same locality
    (B. No. 74), fig. 16; Bath, England (type), fig. 17; Westphalia, Ger-
    many (Bresadola Herb., as *C. nigrescens*, Brinkmann), fig. 18.

Fig. 12 x 810; figs. 1, 7, 8, 16 x 1012; others x 1620.

PLATE 89

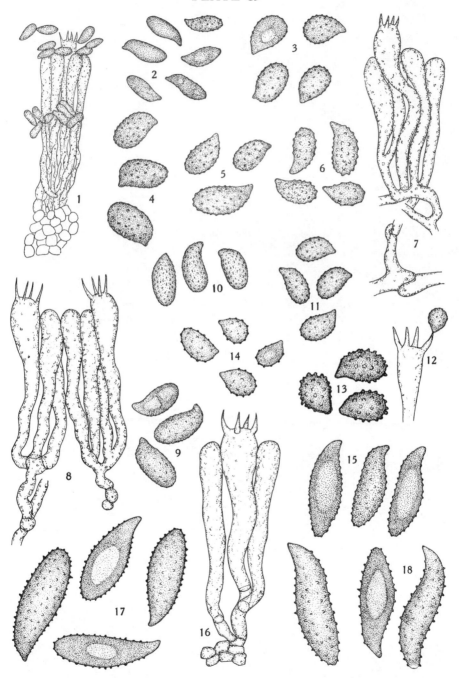

## PLATE 90

C. grandis. No. 3489, fig. 1 (hymenium 3-layered) ; No. 1186, fig. 6.

C. longicaulis. No. 2287, fig. 2.

C. echinospora. Borneo (Bresadola), fig. 3.

C. cyanocephala. Porto Rico (Johnson, No. 997), fig. 4; Trinidad (Kew Herb., as *Lachnocladium tubulosum,*) fig. 5.

Lachnocladium semivestitum. No. 2789, figs. 7 and 8; co-type, figs. 9 and 10; No. 4514, fig. 11.

Figs. 1, 9 x 1012; figs. 8, 11 x 810: others x 1620.

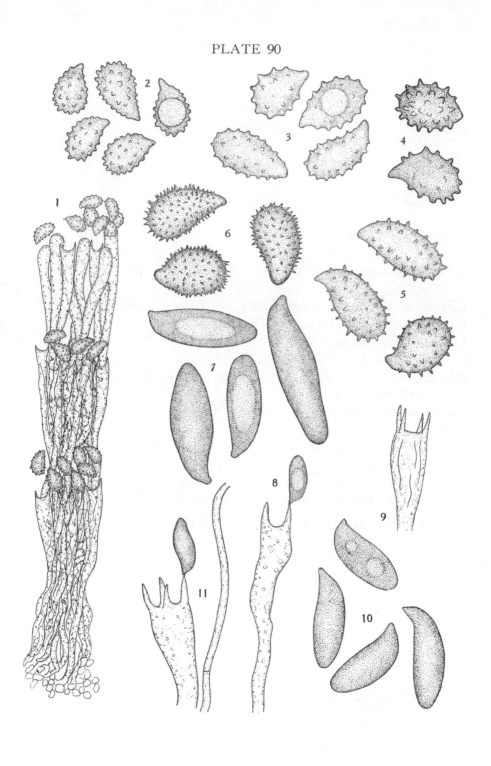

PLATE 90

## PLATE 91

C. gracillima.   Type, figs. 1 and 2.

C. biformis.   Co-type (No. 10699), fig. 3.

C. luteo-ochracea.   Type distribution (No. 64), fig. 4; New York (No. 16a), fig. 5.

C. rufipes.   Blowing Rock (No. 5501), figs. 6 and 7; type, fig. 8.

C. delicata.   Upsala (Fries, Kew Herb.), fig. 9.

C. dealbata.   Type, fig. 10.

C. pinicola.   Co-type (No. 16946), fig. 11.

C. conjunctipes.   Linville Falls (No. 5768), fig. 12.

C. appalachiensis.   Type, figs. 13 and 14.

Lachnocladium cartilagineum.   Type, fig. 15.

C. gigaspora.   Type, figs. 16 and 17.

C. Murrilli.   Type, figs. 18 and 19.

C. Macouni.   Type, fig. 20.

C. dendroidea.   Upsala (Romell, det. by Robert Fries), fig. 21.

C. subfalcata.   Blowing Rock (No. 5630), fig. 22.

Fig. 1 x 810; figs. 14, 17, 18 x 1012; others x 1620.

PLATE 91

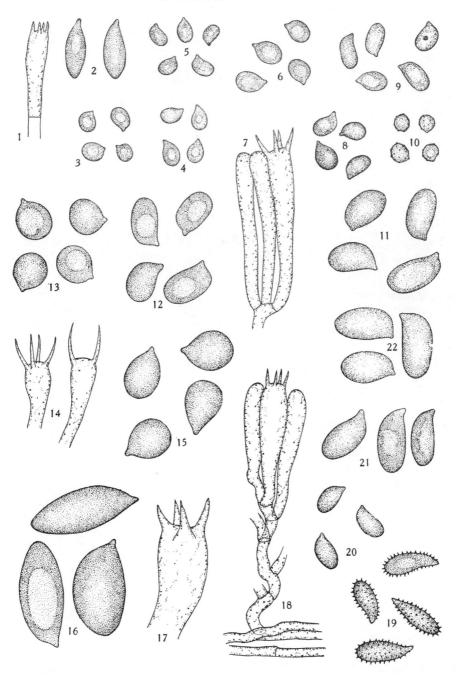

## PLATE 92

C. acuta.  New York Botanical Garden (U. N. C. Herb., No. 3189a), figs. 1
and 2.

C. vernalis.  No. 6071, figs. 3-7.  Figs. 5-7 show the fungal threads running
over and around the algal cells.

C. crispula.  Portugal (Bresadola.  N. Y. Bot. Gard. Herb.), fig. 8.

C. umbrinella.  Type, figs. 9 and 10.

C. Macouni.  Type, fig. 11 (basidium).

Figs. 1, 7, 11 x 810; figs. 4-6, 9 x 1012; others x 1620.

PLATE 92

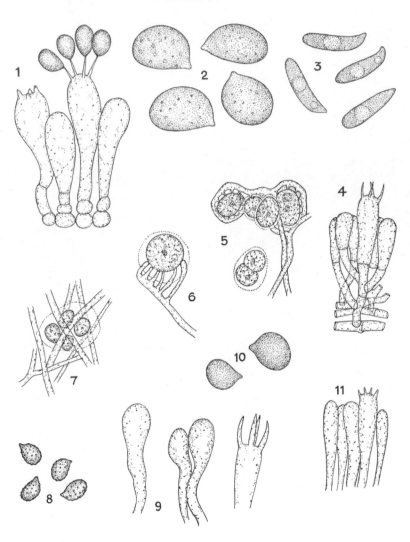

# INDEX

# A CATALOGUE OF SELECTED DOVER BOOKS
## IN ALL FIELDS OF INTEREST

# A CATALOGUE OF SELECTED DOVER BOOKS
## IN ALL FIELDS OF INTEREST

AMERICA'S OLD MASTERS, James T. Flexner. Four men emerged unexpectedly from provincial 18th century America to leadership in European art: Benjamin West, J. S. Copley, C. R. Peale, Gilbert Stuart. Brilliant coverage of lives and contributions. Revised, 1967 edition. 69 plates. 365pp. of text.

21806-6 Paperbound $3.00

FIRST FLOWERS OF OUR WILDERNESS: AMERICAN PAINTING, THE COLONIAL PERIOD, James T. Flexner. Painters, and regional painting traditions from earliest Colonial times up to the emergence of Copley, West and Peale Sr., Foster, Gustavus Hesselius, Feke, John Smibert and many anonymous painters in the primitive manner. Engaging presentation, with 162 illustrations. xxii + 368pp.

22180-6 Paperbound $3.50

THE LIGHT OF DISTANT SKIES: AMERICAN PAINTING, 1760-1835, James T. Flexner. The great generation of early American painters goes to Europe to learn and to teach: West, Copley, Gilbert Stuart and others. Allston, Trumbull, Morse; also contemporary American painters—primitives, derivatives, academics—who remained in America. 102 illustrations. xiii + 306pp. 22179-2 Paperbound $3.00

A HISTORY OF THE RISE AND PROGRESS OF THE ARTS OF DESIGN IN THE UNITED STATES, William Dunlap. Much the richest mine of information on early American painters, sculptors, architects, engravers, miniaturists, etc. The only source of information for scores of artists, the major primary source for many others. Unabridged reprint of rare original 1834 edition, with new introduction by James T. Flexner, and 394 new illustrations. Edited by Rita Weiss. 6⅝ x 9⅝.

21695-0, 21696-9, 21697-7 Three volumes, Paperbound $13.50

EPOCHS OF CHINESE AND JAPANESE ART, Ernest F. Fenollosa. From primitive Chinese art to the 20th century, thorough history, explanation of every important art period and form, including Japanese woodcuts; main stress on China and Japan, but Tibet, Korea also included. Still unexcelled for its detailed, rich coverage of cultural background, aesthetic elements, diffusion studies, particularly of the historical period. 2nd, 1913 edition. 242 illustrations. lii + 439pp. of text.

20364-6, 20365-4 Two volumes, Paperbound $6.00

THE GENTLE ART OF MAKING ENEMIES, James A. M. Whistler. Greatest wit of his day deflates Oscar Wilde, Ruskin, Swinburne; strikes back at inane critics, exhibitions, art journalism; aesthetics of impressionist revolution in most striking form. Highly readable classic by great painter. Reproduction of edition designed by Whistler. Introduction by Alfred Werner. xxxvi + 334pp.

21875-9 Paperbound $2.50

ALPHABETS AND ORNAMENTS, Ernst Lehner. Well-known pictorial source for decorative alphabets, script examples, cartouches, frames, decorative title pages, calligraphic initials, borders, similar material. 14th to 19th century, mostly European. Useful in almost any graphic arts designing, varied styles. 750 illustrations. 256pp. 7 x 10.                                                           21905-4 Paperbound $4.00

PAINTING: A CREATIVE APPROACH, Norman Colquhoun. For the beginner simple guide provides an instructive approach to painting: major stumbling blocks for beginner; overcoming them, technical points; paints and pigments; oil painting; watercolor and other media and color. New section on "plastic" paints. Glossary. Formerly *Paint Your Own Pictures.* 221pp.                22000-1 Paperbound $1.75

THE ENJOYMENT AND USE OF COLOR, Walter Sargent. Explanation of the relations between colors themselves and between colors in nature and art, including hundreds of little-known facts about color values, intensities, effects of high and low illumination, complementary colors. Many practical hints for painters, references to great masters. 7 color plates, 29 illustrations. x + 274pp.
20944-X Paperbound $2.75

THE NOTEBOOKS OF LEONARDO DA VINCI, compiled and edited by Jean Paul Richter. 1566 extracts from original manuscripts reveal the full range of Leonardo's versatile genius: all his writings on painting, sculpture, architecture, anatomy, astronomy, geography, topography, physiology, mining, music, etc., in both Italian and English, with 186 plates of manuscript pages and more than 500 additional drawings. Includes studies for the Last Supper, the lost Sforza monument, and other works. Total of xlvii + 866pp. 7⅞ x 10¾.
22572-0, 22573-9 Two volumes, Paperbound $10.00

MONTGOMERY WARD CATALOGUE OF 1895. Tea gowns, yards of flannel and pillow-case lace, stereoscopes, books of gospel hymns, the New Improved Singer Sewing Machine, side saddles, milk skimmers, straight-edged razors, high-button shoes, spittoons, and on and on . . . listing some 25,000 items, practically all illustrated. Essential to the shoppers of the 1890's, it is our truest record of the spirit of the period. Unaltered reprint of Issue No. 57, Spring and Summer 1895. Introduction by Boris Emmet. Innumerable illustrations. xiii + 624pp. 8½ x 11⅝.
22377-9 Paperbound $6.95

THE CRYSTAL PALACE EXHIBITION ILLUSTRATED CATALOGUE (LONDON, 1851). One of the wonders of the modern world—the Crystal Palace Exhibition in which all the nations of the civilized world exhibited their achievements in the arts and sciences—presented in an equally important illustrated catalogue. More than 1700 items pictured with accompanying text—ceramics, textiles, cast-iron work, carpets, pianos, sleds, razors, wall-papers, billiard tables, beehives, silverware and hundreds of other artifacts—represent the focal point of Victorian culture in the Western World. Probably the largest collection of Victorian decorative art ever assembled— indispensable for antiquarians and designers. Unabridged republication of the Art-Journal Catalogue of the Great Exhibition of 1851, with all terminal essays. New introduction by John Gloag, F.S.A. xxxiv + 426pp. 9 x 12.
22503-8 Paperbound $4.50

## "ESSENTIAL GRAMMAR" SERIES

All you really need to know about modern, colloquial grammar. Many educational shortcuts help you learn faster, understand better. Detailed cognate lists teach you to recognize similarities between English and foreign words and roots—make learning vocabulary easy and interesting. Excellent for independent study or as a supplement to record courses.

ESSENTIAL FRENCH GRAMMAR, Seymour Resnick. 2500-item cognate list. 159pp.
(EBE) 20419-7 Paperbound $1.25

ESSENTIAL GERMAN GRAMMAR, Guy Stern and Everett F. Bleiler. Unusual shortcuts on noun declension, word order, compound verbs. 124pp.
(EBE) 20422-7 Paperbound $1.25

ESSENTIAL ITALIAN GRAMMAR, Olga Ragusa. 111pp.
(EBE) 20779-X Paperbound $1.25

ESSENTIAL JAPANESE GRAMMAR, Everett F. Bleiler. In Romaji transcription; no characters needed. Japanese grammar is regular and simple. 156pp.
21027-8 Paperbound $1.25

ESSENTIAL PORTUGUESE GRAMMAR, Alexander da R. Prista. vi + 114pp.
21650-0 Paperbound $1.35

ESSENTIAL SPANISH GRAMMAR, Seymour Resnick. 2500 word cognate list. 115pp.
(EBE) 20780-3 Paperbound $1.25

ESSENTIAL ENGLISH GRAMMAR, Philip Gucker. Combines best features of modern, functional and traditional approaches. For refresher, class use, home study. x + 177pp.
21649-7 Paperbound $1.35

A PHRASE AND SENTENCE DICTIONARY OF SPOKEN SPANISH. Prepared for U. S. War Department by U. S. linguists. As above, unit is idiom, phrase or sentence rather than word. English-Spanish and Spanish-English sections contain modern equivalents of over 18,000 sentences. Introduction and appendix as above. iv + 513pp.
20495-2 Paperbound $2.75

A PHRASE AND SENTENCE DICTIONARY OF SPOKEN RUSSIAN. Dictionary prepared for U. S. War Department by U. S. linguists. Basic unit is not the word, but the idiom, phrase or sentence. English-Russian and Russian-English sections contain modern equivalents for over 30,000 phrases. Grammatical introduction covers phonetics, writing, syntax. Appendix of word lists for food, numbers, geographical names, etc. vi + 573 pp. 6⅛ x 9¼.
20496-0 Paperbound $4.00

CONVERSATIONAL CHINESE FOR BEGINNERS, Morris Swadesh. Phonetic system, beginner's course in Pai Hua Mandarin Chinese covering most important, most useful speech patterns. Emphasis on modern colloquial usage. Formerly *Chinese in Your Pocket*. xvi + 158pp.
21123-1 Paperbound $1.75

EAST O' THE SUN AND WEST O' THE MOON, George W. Dasent. Considered the best of all translations of these Norwegian folk tales, this collection has been enjoyed by generations of children (and folklorists too). Includes True and Untrue, Why the Sea is Salt, East O' the Sun and West O' the Moon, Why the Bear is Stumpy-Tailed, Boots and the Troll, The Cock and the Hen, Rich Peter the Pedlar, and 52 more. The only edition with all 59 tales. 77 illustrations by Erik Werenskiold and Theodor Kittelsen. xv + 418pp. 22521-6 Paperbound $3.50

GOOPS AND HOW TO BE THEM, Gelett Burgess. Classic of tongue-in-cheek humor, masquerading as etiquette book. 87 verses, twice as many cartoons, show mischievous Goops as they demonstrate to children virtues of table manners, neatness, courtesy, etc. Favorite for generations. viii + 88pp. $6\frac{1}{2}$ x $9\frac{1}{4}$.
22233-0 Paperbound $1.25

ALICE'S ADVENTURES UNDER GROUND, Lewis Carroll. The first version, quite different from the final Alice in Wonderland, printed out by Carroll himself with his own illustrations. Complete facsimile of the "million dollar" manuscript Carroll gave to Alice Liddell in 1864. Introduction by Martin Gardner. viii + 96pp. Title and dedication pages in color. 21482-6 Paperbound $1.25

THE BROWNIES, THEIR BOOK, Palmer Cox. Small as mice, cunning as foxes, exuberant and full of mischief, the Brownies go to the zoo, toy shop, seashore, circus, etc., in 24 verse adventures and 266 illustrations. Long a favorite, since their first appearance in St. Nicholas Magazine. xi + 144pp. $6\frac{5}{8}$ x $9\frac{1}{4}$.
21265-3 Paperbound $1.75

SONGS OF CHILDHOOD, Walter De La Mare. Published (under the pseudonym Walter Ramal) when De La Mare was only 29, this charming collection has long been a favorite children's book. A facsimile of the first edition in paper, the 47 poems capture the simplicity of the nursery rhyme and the ballad, including such lyrics as I Met Eve, Tartary, The Silver Penny. vii + 106pp. 21972-0 Paperbound $1.25

THE COMPLETE NONSENSE OF EDWARD LEAR, Edward Lear. The finest 19th-century humorist-cartoonist in full: all nonsense limericks, zany alphabets, Owl and Pussycat, songs, nonsense botany, and more than 500 illustrations by Lear himself. Edited by Holbrook Jackson. xxix + 287pp. (USO) 20167-8 Paperbound $2.00

BILLY WHISKERS: THE AUTOBIOGRAPHY OF A GOAT, Frances Trego Montgomery. A favorite of children since the early 20th century, here are the escapades of that rambunctious, irresistible and mischievous goat—Billy Whiskers. Much in the spirit of Peck's Bad Boy, this is a book that children never tire of reading or hearing. All the original familiar illustrations by W. H. Fry are included: 6 color plates, 18 black and white drawings. 159pp. 22345-0 Paperbound $2.00

MOTHER GOOSE MELODIES. Faithful republication of the fabulously rare Munroe and Francis "copyright 1833" Boston edition—the most important Mother Goose collection, usually referred to as the "original." Familiar rhymes plus many rare ones, with wonderful old woodcut illustrations. Edited by E. F. Bleiler. 128pp. $4\frac{1}{2}$ x $6\frac{3}{8}$. 22577-1 Paperbound $1.25

ADVENTURES OF AN AFRICAN SLAVER, Theodore Canot. Edited by Brantz Mayer. A detailed portrayal of slavery and the slave trade, 1820-1840. Canot, an established trader along the African coast, describes the slave economy of the African kingdoms, the treatment of captured negroes, the extensive journeys in the interior to gather slaves, slave revolts and their suppression, harems, bribes, and much more. Full and unabridged republication of 1854 edition. Introduction by Malcom Cowley. 16 illustrations. xvii + 448pp. 22456-2 Paperbound $3.50

MY BONDAGE AND MY FREEDOM, Frederick Douglass. Born and brought up in slavery, Douglass witnessed its horrors and experienced its cruelties, but went on to become one of the most outspoken forces in the American anti-slavery movement. Considered the best of his autobiographies, this book graphically describes the inhuman treatment of slaves, its effects on slave owners and slave families, and how Douglass's determination led him to a new life. Unaltered reprint of 1st (1855) edition. xxxii + 464pp. 22457-0 Paperbound $2.50

THE INDIANS' BOOK, recorded and edited by Natalie Curtis. Lore, music, narratives, dozens of drawings by Indians themselves from an authoritative and important survey of native culture among Plains, Southwestern, Lake and Pueblo Indians. Standard work in popular ethnomusicology. 149 songs in full notation. 23 drawings, 23 photos. xxxi + 584pp. 6⅝ x 9⅜. 21939-9 Paperbound $4.50

DICTIONARY OF AMERICAN PORTRAITS, edited by Hayward and Blanche Cirker. 4024 portraits of 4000 most important Americans, colonial days to 1905 (with a few important categories, like Presidents, to present). Pioneers, explorers, colonial figures, U. S. officials, politicians, writers, military and naval men, scientists, inventors, manufacturers, jurists, actors, historians, educators, notorious figures, Indian chiefs, etc. All authentic contemporary likenesses. The only work of its kind in existence; supplements all biographical sources for libraries. Indispensable to anyone working with American history. 8,000-item classified index, finding lists, other aids. xiv + 756pp. 9¼ x 12¾. 21823-6 Clothbound $30.00

TRITTON'S GUIDE TO BETTER WINE AND BEER MAKING FOR BEGINNERS, S. M. Tritton. All you need to know to make family-sized quantities of over 100 types of grape, fruit, herb and vegetable wines; as well as beers, mead, cider, etc. Complete recipes, advice as to equipment, procedures such as fermenting, bottling, and storing wines. Recipes given in British, U. S., and metric measures. Accompanying booklet lists sources in U. S. A. where ingredients may be bought, and additional information. 11 illustrations. 157pp. 5⅝ x 8⅛. (USO) 22090-7 Clothbound $3.50

GARDENING WITH HERBS FOR FLAVOR AND FRAGRANCE, Helen M. Fox. How to grow herbs in your own garden, how to use them in your cooking (over 55 recipes included), legends and myths associated with each species, uses in medicine, perfumes, etc.—these are elements of one of the few books written especially for American herb fanciers. Guides you step-by-step from soil preparation to harvesting and storage for each type of herb. 12 drawings by Louise Mansfield. xiv + 334pp. 22540-2 Paperbound $2.50

INCIDENTS OF TRAVEL IN YUCATAN, John L. Stephens. Classic (1843) exploration of jungles of Yucatan, looking for evidences of Maya civilization. Stephens found many ruins; comments on travel adventures, Mexican and Indian culture. 127 striking illustrations by F. Catherwood. Total of 669 pp.
20926-1, 20927-X Two volumes, Paperbound $5.00

INCIDENTS OF TRAVEL IN CENTRAL AMERICA, CHIAPAS, AND YUCATAN, John L. Stephens. An exciting travel journal and an important classic of archeology. Narrative relates his almost single-handed discovery of the Mayan culture, and exploration of the ruined cities of Copan, Palenque, Utatlan and others; the monuments they dug from the earth, the temples buried in the jungle, the customs of poverty-stricken Indians living a stone's throw from the ruined palaces. 115 drawings by F. Catherwood. Portrait of Stephens. xii + 812pp.
22404-X, 22405-8 Two volumes, Paperbound $6.00

A NEW VOYAGE ROUND THE WORLD, William Dampier. Late 17-century naturalist joined the pirates of the Spanish Main to gather information; remarkably vivid account of buccaneers, pirates; detailed, accurate account of botany, zoology, ethnography of lands visited. Probably the most important early English voyage, enormous implications for British exploration, trade, colonial policy. Also most interesting reading. Argonaut edition, introduction by Sir Albert Gray. New introduction by Percy Adams. 6 plates, 7 illustrations. xlvii + 376pp. 6½ x 9¼.
21900-3 Paperbound $3.00

INTERNATIONAL AIRLINE PHRASE BOOK IN SIX LANGUAGES, Joseph W. Bátor. Important phrases and sentences in English paralleled with French, German, Portuguese, Italian, Spanish equivalents, covering all possible airport-travel situations; created for airline personnel as well as tourist by Language Chief, Pan American Airlines. xiv + 204pp.
22017-6 Paperbound $2.00

STAGE COACH AND TAVERN DAYS, Alice Morse Earle. Detailed, lively account of the early days of taverns; their uses and importance in the social, political and military life; furnishings and decorations; locations; food and drink; tavern signs, etc. Second half covers every aspect of early travel; the roads, coaches, drivers, etc. Nostalgic, charming, packed with fascinating material. 157 illustrations, mostly photographs. xiv + 449pp.
22518-6 Paperbound $4.00

NORSE DISCOVERIES AND EXPLORATIONS IN NORTH AMERICA, Hjalmar R. Holand. The perplexing Kensington Stone, found in Minnesota at the end of the 19th century. Is it a record of a Scandinavian expedition to North America in the 14th century? Or is it one of the most successful hoaxes in history. A scientific detective investigation. Formerly *Westward from Vinland*. 31 photographs, 17 figures. x + 354pp.
22014-1 Paperbound $2.75

A BOOK OF OLD MAPS, compiled and edited by Emerson D. Fite and Archibald Freeman. 74 old maps offer an unusual survey of the discovery, settlement and growth of America down to the close of the Revolutionary war: maps showing Norse settlements in Greenland, the explorations of Columbus, Verrazano, Cabot, Champlain, Joliet, Drake, Hudson, etc., campaigns of Revolutionary war battles, and much more. Each map is accompanied by a brief historical essay. xvi + 299pp.
11 x 13¾. 22084-2 Paperbound $6.00

TWO LITTLE SAVAGES; BEING THE ADVENTURES OF TWO BOYS WHO LIVED AS INDIANS AND WHAT THEY LEARNED, Ernest Thompson Seton. Great classic of nature and boyhood provides a vast range of woodlore in most palatable form, a genuinely entertaining story. Two farm boys build a teepee in woods and live in it for a month, working out Indian solutions to living problems, star lore, birds and animals, plants, etc. 293 illustrations. vii + 286pp.

20985-7 Paperbound $2.50

PETER PIPER'S PRACTICAL PRINCIPLES OF PLAIN & PERFECT PRONUNCIATION. Alliterative jingles and tongue-twisters of surprising charm, that made their first appearance in America about 1830. Republished in full with the spirited woodcut illustrations from this earliest American edition. 32pp. 4½ x 6⅜.

22560-7 Paperbound $1.00

SCIENCE EXPERIMENTS AND AMUSEMENTS FOR CHILDREN, Charles Vivian. 73 easy experiments, requiring only materials found at home or easily available, such as candles, coins, steel wool, etc.; illustrate basic phenomena like vacuum, simple chemical reaction, etc. All safe. Modern, well-planned. Formerly *Science Games for Children.* 102 photos, numerous drawings. 96pp. 6⅛ x 9¼.

21856-2 Paperbound $1.25

AN INTRODUCTION TO CHESS MOVES AND TACTICS SIMPLY EXPLAINED, Leonard Barden. Informal intermediate introduction, quite strong in explaining reasons for moves. Covers basic material, tactics, important openings, traps, positional play in middle game, end game. Attempts to isolate patterns and recurrent configurations. Formerly *Chess.* 58 figures. 102pp. (USO) 21210-6 Paperbound $1.25

LASKER'S MANUAL OF CHESS, Dr. Emanuel Lasker. Lasker was not only one of the five great World Champions, he was also one of the ablest expositors, theorists, and analysts. In many ways, his Manual, permeated with his philosophy of battle, filled with keen insights, is one of the greatest works ever written on chess. Filled with analyzed games by the great players. A single-volume library that will profit almost any chess player, beginner or master. 308 diagrams. xli X 349pp.

20640-8 Paperbound $2.75

THE MASTER BOOK OF MATHEMATICAL RECREATIONS, Fred Schuh. In opinion of many the finest work ever prepared on mathematical puzzles, stunts, recreations; exhaustively thorough explanations of mathematics involved, analysis of effects, citation of puzzles and games. Mathematics involved is elementary. Translated by F. Göbel. 194 figures. xxiv + 430pp. 22134-2 Paperbound $3.00

MATHEMATICS, MAGIC AND MYSTERY, Martin Gardner. Puzzle editor for Scientific American explains mathematics behind various mystifying tricks: card tricks, stage "mind reading," coin and match tricks, counting out games, geometric dissections, etc. Probability sets, theory of numbers clearly explained. Also provides more than 400 tricks, guaranteed to work, that you can do. 135 illustrations. xii + 176pp.

20338-2 Paperbound $1.50

MATHEMATICAL PUZZLES FOR BEGINNERS AND ENTHUSIASTS, Geoffrey Mott-Smith. 189 puzzles from easy to difficult—involving arithmetic, logic, algebra, properties of digits, probability, etc.—for enjoyment and mental stimulus. Explanation of mathematical principles behind the puzzles. 135 illustrations. viii + 248pp.
20198-8 Paperbound $1.75

PAPER FOLDING FOR BEGINNERS, William D. Murray and Francis J. Rigney. Easiest book on the market, clearest instructions on making interesting, beautiful origami. Sail boats, cups, roosters, frogs that move legs, bonbon boxes, standing birds, etc. 40 projects; more than 275 diagrams and photographs. 94pp.
20713-7 Paperbound $1.00

TRICKS AND GAMES ON THE POOL TABLE, Fred Herrmann. 79 tricks and games—some solitaires, some for two or more players, some competitive games—to entertain you between formal games. Mystifying shots and throws, unusual caroms, tricks involving such props as cork, coins, a hat, etc. Formerly *Fun on the Pool Table*. 77 figures. 95pp.
21814-7 Paperbound $1.00

HAND SHADOWS TO BE THROWN UPON THE WALL: A SERIES OF NOVEL AND AMUSING FIGURES FORMED BY THE HAND, Henry Bursill. Delightful picturebook from great-grandfather's day shows how to make 18 different hand shadows: a bird that flies, duck that quacks, dog that wags his tail, camel, goose, deer, boy, turtle, etc. Only book of its sort. vi + 33pp. 6½ x 9¼.   21779-5 Paperbound $1.00

WHITTLING AND WOODCARVING, E. J. Tangerman. 18th printing of best book on market. "If you can cut a potato you can carve" toys and puzzles, chains, chessmen, caricatures, masks, frames, woodcut blocks, surface patterns, much more. Information on tools, woods, techniques. Also goes into serious wood sculpture from Middle Ages to present, East and West. 464 photos, figures. x + 293pp.
20965-2 Paperbound $2.00

HISTORY OF PHILOSOPHY, Julián Marías. Possibly the clearest, most easily followed, best planned, most useful one-volume history of philosophy on the market; neither skimpy nor overfull. Full details on system of every major philosopher and dozens of less important thinkers from pre-Socratics up to Existentialism and later. Strong on many European figures usually omitted. Has gone through dozens of editions in Europe. 1966 edition, translated by Stanley Appelbaum and Clarence Strowbridge. xviii + 505pp.
21739-6 Paperbound $3.00

YOGA: A SCIENTIFIC EVALUATION, Kovoor T. Behanan. Scientific but non-technical study of physiological results of yoga exercises; done under auspices of Yale U. Relations to Indian thought, to psychoanalysis, etc. 16 photos. xxiii + 270pp.
20505-3 Paperbound $2.50